so by Paul Kix

The Saboteur

YOU HAVE TO BE PREPARED TO DIE BEFORE YOU CAN BEGIN TO LIVE

*Ten Weeks in Birmingham
That Changed America*

PAUL KIX

CELADON
BOOKS
NEW YORK

www.celadonbooks.com

Library of Congress Cataloging-in-Publication Data

Names: Kix, Paul, author.
Title: You have to be prepared to die before you can begin to live : ten weeks
  in Birmingham that changed America / Paul Kix.
Description: First edition. | New York : Celadon Books, 2023. | Includes
  bibliographical references and index.
Identifiers: LCCN 2022055913 | ISBN 9781250807694 (hardcover) |
  ISBN 9781250807700 (ebook)
Subjects: LCSH: Birmingham (Ala.)—Race relations—History—20th century. |
  Civil rights movements—Alabama—Birmingham—History—20th century. |
  Protest movements—Alabama—Birmingham—History—20th century. | King,
  Martin Luther, Jr., 1929–1968. | Abernathy, Ralph, 1926–1990. | Shuttlesworth,
  Fred L., 1922–2011. | Southern Christian Leadership Conference. | Alabama
  Christian Movement for Human Rights. | Nineteen sixty-three, A.D.
Classification: LCC F334.B69 B53 2023 | DDC 976.1/781063—dc23/eng/
  20230104
LC record available at https://lccn.loc.gov/2022055913

First Edition: 2023

10 9 8 7 6 5 4 3 2 1

CONTENTS

PART III: THE GOOD FRIDAY TEST

PART IV: THE WRITING ON SCRAPS OF NEWSPRINT

PART V: "... AND A CHILD SHALL LEAD THEM"

PART VI: D-DAY AND BEYOND

PART VII: "BUT FOR BIRMINGHAM . . ."

PHOTOGRAPH BY BILL HUDSON © ASSOCIATED PRESS

PROLOGUE

A decade ago, when my three kids were toddlers, I started obsessing over a photograph. It was taken in the spring of 1963 in Birmingham, Alabama. The picture showed a German shepherd closing his snarled jaws around the midsection of a Black teenaged boy. The dog was leashed and held by a white police officer, but there was slack in the line, as if the cop were unable or, more likely, unwilling to stop the attack. In every viewing, my eyes settled on the boy. He was somehow tranquil. Despite the ferocity of the assault, his body was relaxed and erect. His arms remained at his side. He was not fighting the dog or protecting himself. It was as if he were *giving* himself to the German shepherd—and to posterity. As if he had a premonition that his almost casual bravery would be studied long after this day, even by a thirtysomething white man in the suburbs of Connecticut fifty years later.

The photo was taken on May 3, 1963, otherwise known as Double D-Day by Martin Luther King Jr. and his fellow civil rights activists, the culmination of weeks of protests in Birmingham. The photo was so stark and unrelenting that it ran across three columns of the front page of the following day's *New York Times*. When he saw it there, President Kennedy said the image made him "sick."

I studied it more closely. In the background, distressed Black men and women distanced themselves from the snarling dog, their backs turned, seemingly about to run. Some people, curious, craned their necks to see how bad the boy was about to get it. Even the cop holding the leash grimaced. Everyone seemed on the verge of panic except the boy, a fifteen-year-old named Walter Gadsden. What gave Gadsden this serenity? This courage? Answering these questions was suddenly pertinent fifty years after the fact because of the circumstances of my life.

I grew up on a farm in Iowa and, after college and a move to Dallas, fell in love with Sonya Castex, a Black woman from inner-city Houston. We married in 2007 and by 2013, the time of my obsession with the Gadsden photo, Sonya and I had three kids in diapers: our daughter, Harper, and our twin boys, Marshall and Walker. When the kids were old enough to understand themselves, there was no question that they would identify as Black. "Because America will see them as Black," Sonya said, a sentiment echoed by her mother, Connie, who, with time, moved into our home in Connecticut as well. This was the reason I returned day after day to the photo from Birmingham in 1963. The Black family was my family. The Black experience was intertwined with my own. Even though I'm not Black, my life was bound forever, thankfully, with Black lives. It was my job to understand my children's heritage as a way to understand what might lie in store for their future.

There was something appalling about the Gadsden photo, much as Jack Kennedy said. There was also something magnetic about it. In its luridness you saw the whole story of America. The violence and terror that white people visited upon Blacks. The dignity with which Black people responded. How this photo could have been taken in the Jim Crow South in 1913 and nothing about it would be different. How this photo in 2013 marked lasting progress, because Sonya and I personified King's famous dream. And yet dreams are not fairy tales and talking about this photo and then comparing it to the other images that filled our screens—of Trayvon Martin's murder; of Chicago cops killing Laquan McDonald—led my mother-in-law, Connie, one night to turn from the television and, with memories of a childhood in that Jim Crow South, to say to Sonya and me: "Same old shit."

There was something damning and hopeful and, because of that contradiction, something eternal about the Gadsden photo.

For years I studied it.

Then, in 2020, another image preoccupied me and the rest of America: Officer Derek Chauvin suffocating George Floyd.

For Sonya and Connie and me, the murder felt personal. George had grown up in Houston, in Third Ward. Sonya had spent her weekday afternoons at her grandma's, in the adjacent and equally hard-up Fifth Ward. George was Sonya's age, forty-six, and he'd gone to Yates High. Sonya's cousins had gone to Yates. Her cousin Derrick knew George back then, watched him as a tight end on the Yates football team that made the state championship game.

In part because of the overlap between Sonya's history and George's, we didn't shield our kids from the coverage of his death like we had the others, all the unarmed Black men whom police had killed and whose murders had also been recorded by security footage or cellphones.

No, with George Floyd, we sat on the couch and watched him die on CNN.

"That could have been Derrick," Sonya said as we saw officer Chauvin absentmindedly, almost playfully, grind his knee into the back of George's neck.

We looked at each other and couldn't say what we both thought.

That could be one of our boys.

The twins were nine by then, and Harper ten, old enough to see the outline of the story that lay just beyond the images on TV, the truth that would define their lives: This was the Black experience as well. We allowed them to watch George die, and the boys in particular had questions about it. *Why did those cops do that?* And when Sonya and I explained, they asked: *Are all cops racist?* And when we explained that: *How many people are like those bad cops?* Every answer only led to harder questions: *Will people not like me?* And the hardest one: *Am I inferior?*

We could see it, the perceptions the boys were forming, the steps leading down to self-hatred. We tried to stave it off: "We love you boys, and you can do whatever, go wherever you want in this life."

"We'll just have to be careful?" Walker asked.

I hesitated, and Sonya did, too, because George had been careful. Unarmed, handcuffed, he'd begged Officer Chauvin to listen to him. Breonna Taylor had been careful. She was asleep in her bedroom, behind a locked door, when Louisville cops barged in and shot her eight times for a crime she did not commit. Ahmaud Arbery had been careful. He'd gone for a run in a coastal Georgia town and three white men in a pickup truck killed him where he ran. No amount of vigilance has ever kept children like ours safe. In our hesitation responding to Walker's question, the boys' faces hardened.

It was another reason George Floyd's murder felt personal: The twins lost their innocence that day.

They eventually lost more than that. Two months later, Jacob Blake walked away from cops in Kenosha, Wisconsin, and those cops shot him seven times in the back while Blake's three children screamed from his car.

Our kids saw that footage, too.

"Why do they keep trying to *kill us*?" Walker yelled, running from the room in tears with Marshall following him. It was a tough time, the latter half of 2020. The fear our kids felt hardened eventually into a cynicism, which wizened and callused them to a certain extent, even protected them, but also enclosed them in a prison of their own rage. We saw it. We *heard* it. How everything about their country was awful and bloody and how they would move away from here just as soon as they could. The footage on the news they saw, the images *they* studied, portrayed a pessimism about America that approached hopelessness.

I thought of the Gadsden photo again, and all it contained, all that was eternal and perhaps even transcendent about it. A plan formed in my mind, and when I shared it with Sonya she said I had to do it—*we* had to do it. It would be a family project of sorts, a means of inspiring our children and ourselves, a chronicle of our answers to troubling questions.

The truth was I had done much more than study the iconic Gadsden photo. In the intervening years I had read books about it and the broader protests of the 1960s. Now, I contacted archives and learned that newly recorded interviews and oral histories showed even more than these books did: ten weeks in 1963 that not only defined the civil rights movement but shaped the next sixty years of America. Ten weeks in Birmingham that, because of all they set in motion, still shaped *my* life every day, and my wife's and children's, too.

So much of the American experience in the twenty-first century was birthed in Birmingham, Alabama, in the spring of 1963.

I had to write about it. I had to show that the despair Martin Luther King Jr. and his deputies felt was not dissimilar from my children's. How King responded to that despair could uplift Harper and Marshall and Walker now.

I would write this book for them. I would write this book for anyone who was ever blinkered by cynicism, crippled into tweeting bitchfests of inaction, sneering at the idea that America had ever stood for anything good and could again. Because reading the oral histories and declassified FBI memos and transcripts from the Kennedy White House, one thing became clear: Those guys in the movement had hope long after they should have.

Then they acted on their optimism. That was the other thing. They acted on it until they shaped America to their liking. Pulled it into the multicolored reality of King's dream. This was something else I hoped my kids would understand from that spring in Birmingham: how the only way to lead a life was to claim it for yourself, unshackle your aspirations not only from oppression but also from the bounds of victimhood.

The book I had in mind went far beyond the grainy images of fire-hosed protesters that my kids saw in school when their history classes studied Birmingham in 1963. My book would not be a history at all but a *story*.

A story that, first off, focused only on those pivotal weeks in Birmingham, which no book, to the best of my knowledge, had done before. This story would feature King, of course, but he would share equal billing with his deputies, the ones who shaped Birmingham and the next sixty years of America but who are largely forgotten to that nation now: the brilliant and even immoral Wyatt Walker, the executive director of King's Southern Christian Leadership Conference; the righteous and frightening James Bevel, the SCLC's director of direct action; and Fred Shuttlesworth, the Birmingham pastor whose fearlessness remains unlike any American's I've encountered.

There would be others in this story. Jack and Bobby Kennedy, governing a resistant nation. Harry Belafonte, far more an activist than an actor. Bull Connor, a villain so terrifying that no national organization dared to stage a civil rights protest in Birmingham until King, desperate, thought he had to. The story would show, above all, what it felt like to live through those ten weeks from every character's vantage point, each chapter rooted in the perspective of a protagonist or an antagonist, because to see Birmingham through these leaders' eyes was to see ourselves today, too. In that way, the book would mirror the ultimate aim of King and those deputies: empathy for the other, a message as relevant to 1963 as 2023.

The more time I spent researching Birmingham, the more I realized it was the most dramatic of all American stories. Overmatched heroes who fought not just brutal men but an evil system, and who turned to a plan of action in Birmingham that other men of faith saw as sinful. It was effective, though. It accomplished what Abraham Lincoln had not been able to a hundred years earlier. It forged our lives to this very moment.

It was quite a story indeed. Harper, Marshall, and Walker: I hope you are guided in your own lives by it.

This book is for you.

Part I

GENESIS

1

A POINT THAT EVERYONE SHOULD CONSIDER CAREFULLY

They met in secret. They met outside the presence of the executive board and without even Martin Luther King Sr.'s knowledge. This was how King's own son, Martin Luther King Jr., wanted it. Only a few people, the absolutely necessary ones, were to be invited to the two-day retreat outside Savannah where the most dangerous idea of the civil rights movement would be discussed.

It's unclear how many showed. The number is somewhere between eleven and fifteen. Accounts vary due in part to the secrecy of the conference and the egos of those in the movement. The attendees were Southern Baptists, and Christians, like anyone else—and maybe more than anyone else—want to be among the chosen few, especially when posterity asks, *Were you there?* What we do know is that the majority of those anointed arrived in Savannah that January morning in 1963 by jet or train, coming from all over the country, and headed now, by various cars, through a piney coastal Georgia until they reached a clearing some thirty miles south, the Dorchester Academy, in Midway. The academy spread across 105 quiet and shaded acres, manicured and expansive, and on the estate rose eight simple buildings, the mark of the academy's history and its ongoing ambition. It began in 1871 as a one-room schoolhouse for freed slaves. It expanded to a larger school and then added a dormitory for all the Black people who ached to read. The academy built a credit union on the grounds in the 1930s to help Blacks buy homes and open businesses. By the 1960s Martin Luther King Jr.'s organization, the Southern Christian Leadership Conference (SCLC), used the estate to train hundreds of volunteers in King's preferred form of civil disobedience, the nonviolent protest.

The majority of secret-meeting attendees on that clear but cool January morning had been to Dorchester before. They parked their cars and walked to the white-pillared brick dormitory without a newcomer's sense of reverence. They had too much on their minds for awe. A grimness followed them and even matched their conservative suits. It lined their faces. They sensed what they were going to discuss.

They settled in one of the dormitory's meeting rooms, where the humidity in the summer had cracked and peeled the paint off the beige walls, and huddled near one another in seats that faced the front of the room. King directed the proceedings, but the one who stood before them now was Wyatt Walker, the SCLC's executive director. A tall northerner with a thin mustache and even thinner build—he looked at thirty-four like a malnourished, radicalized grad student—Walker commanded the room with his piercing gaze and flair for the dramatic. "The Madison Avenue streak in me," he later said. From behind his big black-rimmed glasses he took in those assembled around him and told them they were about to embark on a campaign unlike any other.

"I call it Project X," Walker said. Because X marked the spot of confrontation.

And *confrontation* because there had not been enough of it.

Walker discussed what he and so many of those present had just endured: the SCLC's sustained civil rights campaign in Albany, Georgia, the year prior, in 1962. It had failed completely. It had failed for numerous reasons, Walker said, but one of them was that the nonviolence the SCLC favored and had learned from Gandhi's success in India—assembling marchers and having them sit at the seat of white power, and then not move—needed to be met by violent white authority to work. When white authority in India or the American South used violence against peaceful protesters, their brutality called into question not only the acts of violence but also the authority figures' rule of law. To question unfair rules was the first step, Gandhi and King found, to changing them. In Albany, Georgia, though, the bigoted but clever police chief, Laurie Pritchett, had read up on King and then Gandhi and realized he could deter these Black leaders by accommodating them. He told his force to put away their billy clubs. He told his force to arrest the marchers with unctuous care, especially when the bulbs of any news camera popped—cameras that hoped for a bloody spectacle, had even been promised one by King and Walker, but instead got images of Pritchett removing his hat and bowing his head, as if in prayer himself, before gently handcuffing the kneeling Black pastors at his feet. The news media grew restless and then hostile at how long the Albany campaign continued, off and on for eight months. When King and the SCLC lost the support of local protesters, they left town, humiliated.

Albany was "a devastating loss of face" for the movement, the *New York Herald Tribune* wrote. Perhaps "the most stunning defeat" of King's career.

There had been many.

Failure followed the SCLC everywhere now. Walker and King knew it, and so did the rest of the SCLC's leadership huddled in that beige room. The movement's biggest success, the Montgomery bus boycott, had also been its first, and that was seven years ago. But thanks to the intransigence of the Alabama government and the fear of the Klan, Montgomery's bus lines in 1963 were as segregated as they'd been in 1933. "Most Negroes," one journalist noted, "have returned to the old custom of riding in the back of the bus." The younger Black organizations, like the zealous Student Nonviolent Coordinating Committee (SNCC), led by John Lewis, sensed the middle-aged King's ineffectiveness and mocked him these days almost as ruthlessly as the southern press did. In Albany, a campaign initially staged by SNCC but usurped by King, SNCC and other organizers took to calling King "De Lawd": the one who knew what was best for you. The mocking phrase played off King's pomposity in dress and speech and sneered at who his sermons attracted: older crowds who would *amen* alongside King from the pews but wouldn't take action on the streets. De Lawd didn't give people agency. De Lawd preached because De Lawd refused to lead people away from the pulpit. "You are a phony," one SNCC organizer telegrammed King.

The cynicism and infighting between the organizations of the civil rights movement reflected a broader frustration nearly all Black people in America felt. Nothing had improved. *Brown v. Board of Education* had become law in 1954, and yet in the nine intervening years virtually every school in the South remained segregated. Blacks everywhere earned 45 percent less than whites. In the South only 28 percent were registered to vote—and this after a giant registration drive by the Democratic Party in 1960. Even liberal President Kennedy had cooled on King and the civil rights movement. King wanted a second Emancipation Proclamation, a document that would update what Lincoln had written in 1863 and at last liberate Black people from Jim Crow. Kennedy had seemed enthused about the idea when King met with him at the White House in 1962. Kennedy had even asked King to write a draft of the document. King hoped that the president would deliver the speech on January 1, 1963, on the hundredth anniversary of the original Emancipation Proclamation. But after Kennedy received the draft prepared by King and the SCLC, the president and his administration stalled, returning the SCLC's urgent messages days or weeks later. The hundredth anniversary of the Emancipation Proclamation came and went, with segregation the law of the South and oppression felt everywhere else, too, and nary a word from Jack Kennedy about any of it.

So if America was going to change, Wyatt Walker said to the privileged few at Dorchester that January day, America had to be shocked into changing.

This was the point of Project X.

We need to go to Birmingham, Walker said.

Birmingham? Those assembled shifted uncomfortably in their seats. This was the bad news they'd feared. The people in that beige room had heard the joke about Birmingham:

One morning a Black man in Chicago wakes up and tells his wife that Jesus has come to him in his dream.

"Really?" she says.

"Yeah," the man says. "Jesus told me to go to Birmingham."

She's horrified. "Did Jesus say he'd go with you?"

"No," the man responds. "Jesus said he'd go as far as Memphis."

Birmingham, Alabama, was not so much a city in 1963 as a site of domestic terror. It was known, sometimes gleefully, and by public officials, as "Bombingham." More than fifty residences and Black-owned businesses had been bombed since the end of World War II. Bombings were so frequent in one Black neighborhood that it was now called Dynamite Hill. These bombings went unsolved for the same reason cops routinely exercised their "rights" to shoot any Black "suspects" who turned their backs and fled. The force was overseen by Eugene "Bull" Connor, a virulent racist and public safety commissioner with barely cloaked ties to the Ku Klux Klan. The point of Bull's Birmingham—and make no mistake, Bull ran Birmingham—was fear. The police raped Black women. The Klan castrated Black men. The cops and klavern tapped the phones and, no doubt, bombed the houses of anyone who tried to improve the lives of the oppressed. Not long after President Kennedy's inauguration, CBS's Edward R. Murrow reported from Birmingham. The city had the reputation as the most segregated, most racist, most violent place in America. Murrow came to agree. Just before he left town, he told his producer he hadn't seen anything like it since Nazi Germany.

That was Birmingham. And the city's violence, its hatred, was also its appeal. Walker told the crowd at Dorchester that the SCLC needed to go to the very site of white terror and anger every terrible person there.

In order for its nonviolence to work, the SCLC needed to subject itself to the full wrath of Birmingham, in the hope that white people outside the city might at last see, through the SCLC's suffering, the plight of all Blacks in America. The SCLC needed, Walker said—and you can almost see him pacing the room at this point, part preacher, part professor, and all stringbean showman, those black-rimmed glasses accentuating his gauntness and erudition like some mystic from the Georgia pines—the SCLC needed to go to Birmingham to turn the city into a metaphor of the Black experience.

How to do that? How to show white America and the Kennedy brothers who governed it what it meant to be Black in America?

You have to escalate the situation, Walker said.

"Project X will have four stages," he said, and here Walker handed out a blueprint among the assembled, eight typed pages that revealed his organizational prowess as executive director of King's SCLC. The first stage, Walker said, involved mass meetings at night whose purpose would be to draw recruits to the sit-ins the SCLC would carry out by day. These sit-ins would be at the lunch counters of segregated restaurants in Birmingham and infuriate Bull Connor.

The second stage would call for a boycott of Birmingham's downtown business district. Black people spent about $4 million a week downtown. They accounted for roughly 25 percent of the money spent in the city. The profit margins of those stores were small enough, Walker said, that if Black people didn't spend there, white businesses couldn't survive there.

The third stage would escalate from a boycott of downtown merchants to a mass protest of Birmingham itself, its segregation and racism. White people, Bull Connor especially, would be irate by this third stage, and the sea of Blacks protesting throughout the city would lead to mass arrests. Mass arrests would fill the jails. Filling the jails would further escalate the situation because the optics of crammed cells were the optics of success. They would inspire more people to join the movement, Walker said. And when the SCLC kept marching in spite of the mass arrests, Bull Connor would be confronted with a choice: allow these Black people to protest in his city, which would humiliate him, or suppress these Black people and turn his terrible vengeance on them, which would give the waiting press corps all the gory copy they needed.

Walker thought Connor would choose the latter. This would lead to the fourth stage of Project X.

Seeing grotesque images on the nightly news and in the pages of newspapers and newsweeklies would cause a furor across the nation and a not insubstantial number of people to descend on Birmingham itself, to protest alongside the SCLC and its brave volunteers. These justice-seeking tens of thousands, hundreds of thousands, millions, would march the streets and boycott the stores, Blacks and whites alike, and together they all would force Bull Connor and Birmingham City Hall—without options, without jail cells to put the marchers in or excuses to hide behind—to broker a fairer and more equitable future for Birmingham. Together they all would help the people of Birmingham in ways no one had before. Together they all would end segregation in the most racist of American cities.

And by ending segregation there—by X marking the spot—together they all would show they could end segregation anywhere.

That, Walker said, was why they had to go to Birmingham.

King loved it. Positioned among the dozen or so at Dorchester, King thought Project X showed why Walker had "one of the keenest minds" in the movement. Project X escalated tension as it expanded its ambition. The plan was not unlike Walker himself. In the three years he'd been SCLC's executive director, Walker had made many staffers cry from his punctilious demands, but he had also transformed the SCLC from a fallow nonprofit with tax problems into a respected organization. King heard all the time from the ever-growing body of staffers how bossy and unbearable Walker was. Walker *was* bossy and unbearable. That ever-growing body also proved his worth. Walker breathed life into King's organization, gave it strength. The fastidious accounts he kept reflected the dream Walker and King shared, and had always shared, since they'd

met more than a decade earlier as grad students at an inter-seminary conference, both of them presidents of their respective seminary classes. They
had planned to use their education to serve God and Blacks in the segregated South. When King in 1960 asked Walker to quit his pastorship
in Virginia and join the SCLC, King knew he was getting more than a
bookkeeper. King was getting a publicist, one who'd been born in Massachusetts and understood the northern press—could even mimic the nasal
northern cynicism with which the reporters at national outlets talked.
In Walker, King was also getting a hard-ass, a Bobby Kennedy to King's
Jack, a man who by his own admission would "alter my morality for the
sake of getting a job done." Above all, King was getting an optimist in
Wyatt Walker, someone who, like King, saw beyond the gray and bleak
present into a southern future that no longer noticed color. Project X,
moments after the presentation, was already vintage Walker: a grand vision,
a precise and even ruthless means of achieving it, and the potential for a
lasting and epoch-defining victory.

There was little discussion of it. That was the shocking thing. It
seemed ingenious, and it was all there, on those eight meticulous pages.
The pages forced the assembled into contemplation and perhaps cowed
them into silence, but Walker's plan was so thorough, so epic in its implications, that many at Dorchester simply wanted to believe in it.

The group that day altered nothing of Walker's blueprint.

James Bevel was perhaps the lone person who saw that as a problem. As the
talks proceeded and then exhausted themselves, as the assembled prayed
about Walker's plan and then discussed it again, Bevel kept wondering
why no senior executive of the SCLC—not Stanley Levison, the most liberal member of the secret caucus; not Andrew Young, the most conservative; not Dorothy Cotton, the lone woman; not Fred Shuttlesworth, the
lone Birminghamian; not Ralph Abernathy, King's best friend; and not
King himself—would state what seemed obvious to Bevel: that Walker's
arrogance had infected his plan and corroded the SCLC.

Bevel was one of the youngest at Dorchester, a twentysomething who had the kind of reputation that took other men a lifetime to achieve. In 1960 Bevel had co-led massive sit-ins alongside SNCC at Nashville lunch counters. During one sit-in, the merchant had fled his store but locked the doors behind him, trapping the Black protesters inside and then gassing the place, literally fumigating it with insect repellent while the protesters gagged and choked on the poison. Just as people passed out, Nashville firefighters arrived, breaking windows and saving lives.

Bevel responded by continuing the protests.

That kind of militant fearlessness inspired John Lewis and the rest of SNCC. Bevel was a touch older than the college students of SNCC but as righteously committed to justice, and his alliance with Lewis eventually attracted Martin Luther King Jr. King saw in Bevel the revolutionary his own organization needed, and recruited him to the more middle-aged SCLC. If Bevel heard cries of betrayal from his SNCC friends, he ignored them. Bevel was his own man. A young preacher who wore overalls instead of pastoral robes because country bibs bore no airs in his native Mississippi. A student of God who placed a yarmulke on his shaved head each day because Old Testament prophets like Ezekiel inspired him. Their strength summoned his own. Bevel had a strange power: to be young and of this fraught moment in the 1960s and yet wizened and even, somehow, ancient. He pushed for a new dawn that many Black people were uncomfortable with while using the language of the Torah to do it: "Thus saith the Lord," said James Bevel. He was twenty-seven but seemed as if he'd always existed. Many in the movement called him "The Prophet."

By that January day at Dorchester in 1963, he carried a somewhat redundant title within the SCLC: the director of direct action. It meant Bevel was the operations man, the one who took the vision and manifested it. Looking at Birmingham through an operational lens, Bevel saw the classic flaws of the modern SCLC.

Walker's Birmingham plan assumed too much, he said. It assumed Black people in a city run by fear would subject themselves to the worst impulses of the white authority that oppressed them simply because Martin Luther King Jr. asked them to at nightly mass meetings. It assumed hundreds if not thousands of people would be inspired rather than frightened by a few jailed Black brethren, and would rush to be thrown into similar dank cells for the movement. It assumed, mostly, what the SCLC assumed in Albany and had always assumed: that a hierarchical top-down strategy would inspire people from the bottom up. This was the fault of King and staid vestigial thinking from the 1950s, Bevel said, but it was mostly the fault of Wyatt Walker. The executive director who loved his title. The one whose arrogance coursed through the organization until every staffer lost his own humility. The one whose grand plan in Birmingham patronized the very people it meant to serve.

Bevel snickered at the blueprint in his hands. He couldn't believe that *Wyatt Walker* really believed that Birminghamians had no notion of a less-suffocating life until Walker scrawled his X on their city. Did Walker think they hadn't fought to integrate? One year before, in 1962, the courts had at last ruled Blacks could stroll across the same parks and golf courses as whites in Birmingham. How had Bull Connor responded? He'd shut down all city parks. He'd shut down all municipal golf courses. That was Birmingham, Bevel said, the unrelenting totality of its suppression: Even if they kept to themselves, Blacks and whites could not share the same square mile of public space. And—what?—Wyatt Walker was going to change Bull's thinking by force, when a U.S. district court hadn't by decree? Or richer still: Wyatt Walker was going to change Black people's thinking by dint of a four-stage plan that escalated tension? Poor Black people of the Deep South, not unlike the sort Bevel had known in his hometown, Itta Bena, Mississippi: rustic, conservative, and proud of whatever they'd clawed from the white devil? And here came light-skinned Wyatt Walker with his graduate degree and club ties telling these Black Birminghamians, *No no! You've been fighting the wrong way; I know better.* And they were supposed to follow that man? That man who, even when he dressed down, as he did at Dorchester, ironed a crease into his blue jeans? That man whose own well-off preacher daddy had read every day in Hebrew and Greek while so many Black adults in Birmingham had parents who could not read at all?

That man?

That man, Bevel said to those assembled at Dorchester, was more a "boss" than a "brother." Bevel thought a campaign like the sort Walker proposed could not succeed by even the greatest feats of organizational ingenuity. The ingenuity showcased the plan's sanctimony. Too assured of its own infallibility. Too reliant on "getting hired hands to get something done," Bevel said.

Bevel thought you could not order a liberation on eight typed pages. Birmingham would only succeed organically, through a commitment from the community itself. To get that, Bevel felt, you had to understand that community, be of it, move with it. You had to relate to people, adjust to their needs, live among them if necessary, and only when they saw you giving everything *you* had to break the chains of oppression would they consider doing the same for themselves.

That was how Bevel lived. That was how he worked. He thought the best way for Birmingham to succeed would be when he and not Walker were in charge.

It's unclear if he said that last part aloud to the group or privately to King. In any case, the force of Bevel's argument highlighted the egos King had to manage. These men of faith who humbled themselves before God could still stand quite tall before each other. King had a way in encounters like this of letting each man say his piece, so even though there's no official record of what Bevel said to King—just later recollections—it's fair to assume King let Bevel say all of it. King had a tendency to hear his deputies out. He had a tendency to remain composed. These traits did not come naturally. Leading the SCLC had been as demanding an education for Martin Luther King Jr. as obtaining his PhD in the 1950s. Walker's and Bevel's competing views reinforced one of King's core findings. He had learned, he later wrote, "that we all want to be important, to surpass others, to achieve distinction." This was true of all his deputies in the SCLC, men and women who through gritted teeth had bettered themselves, received an education, or gained a dignity that so few southern Blacks could obtain. King's breakthrough as their leader—it was something he had to display at Dorchester, whether guiding public discussions or private meetings—was to take this capital-*I* individualism and never shame it or shout it down but *redirect* it toward the instinct all men and women of faith shared: love.

A love of God and, because of it, a love of the most oppressed of God's people. That's whom they were working for, he reminded his staff at Dorchester. They were to lift up the masses to the SCLC's heights. As King later wrote in a sermon that was as much a record of his managerial techniques as his faith: "I want you to be first in love. I want you to be first in moral excellence. I want you to be first in generosity." This idea of striving toward an excellence in love influenced how the SCLC acted in the world, and how its staffers acted among themselves. When was it best to assert one's views in a meeting and when was it best to listen?

It was the genius of King's managerial style. Many members of his executive team were too bullheaded to be led, so King taught them how to govern themselves. And *that* education, a very particular self-education, the deputies obtaining something like self-actualization, endeared the men and women of the SCLC to King all the more. It was how someone as egotistical as Wyatt Walker could call King "Mr. Leader" during the sessions at Dorchester. It was how someone as righteous as James Bevel could defer to King and not storm out of Dorchester when King said publicly that he liked Walker's plan.

But King also understood Bevel's points. The SCLC could not patronize Birminghamians. It could not assume their cooperation. Within the last few months, King had delivered a sermon to his own congregation at Ebenezer Baptist in Atlanta about the need to work *with* the underprivileged instead of sweeping in to do work *for* them. In that "with" was an ethos, a whole world. "The true neighbor is the man who will risk his position, his prestige, and even his life for the welfare of others," King had preached. That was what Bevel wanted in Birmingham and how King promised he would lead there.

Even though it's unknown how much King and Bevel discussed Walker at Dorchester, we do know a couple of things. We know King liked Walker as executive director because it brought him peace. "Whenever I give Wyatt an assignment," King once told Walker's wife, Theresa, "I never have to think about it a second time. I know it will be done." He'd asked Walker a week earlier to devise a plan for Birmingham for the Dorchester conference. Walker, as always, had delivered.

We also know King's trust in Walker did not diminish his faith in others. James Bevel fascinated and even frightened King. The originality of Bevel's presence, the clarity of his thinking, the strength of his convictions: No one had these qualities in the abundance that James Bevel did. His persona meant he lived in absolutes. King knew that if they got to Birmingham and confronted the totality of evil there, the time would come when the whole of the movement, even Wyatt Walker, would need to rely on James Bevel.

The time would come when Bevel would lead them.

The Dorchester conference lasted two days. Its secret sessions convinced the attendees to commit to their boldest public action yet. The SCLC would attempt to integrate a city when a U.S. district court hadn't been able to integrate its parks, when the U.S. Supreme Court hadn't been able to integrate its schools. Toward the end of the conference the attendees gave their closing thoughts. The Jewish lawyer Stanley Levison, the secret caucus's lone white man, said massive and well-run unions had failed to organize in Birmingham, too. Bull Connor had broken them up. In fact, every liberal movement or court order had failed in Bull's Birmingham and every single one of them had more strength than the SCLC did. King's organization was weak, thanks to Albany. It was nearly broke, thanks to Albany. Birmingham, then, wasn't just bold but quixotic. "A campaign in Birmingham would surely be the toughest fight in our civil rights careers," King later wrote.

But Wyatt Walker was right. Win there and you could win anywhere.

Break segregation in Birmingham and you "break the back of segregation all over the nation," King wrote. "A victory there might well set forces in motion to change the entire course of the drive for freedom and justice."

So they would proceed.

When the others at Dorchester had delivered their closing thoughts, King looked at each of the faces around him. He drew out the moment. King had, as Wordsworth would say, a faith that stared through death. His home had been bombed; on another occasion, its window had been blasted by shotgun shells. At a public reading in New York, a woman had stabbed King in the chest and the blade had missed his heart by a literal hair's breadth. He and his family received ongoing death threats by phone and mail and still King refused to travel with a security detail or carry a gun. Some of his aides said it was as if he believed the nonviolent lifestyle to which he was committed provided its own defense, God bestowing a supernatural shield on King.

But not even God could protect the SCLC in Birmingham.

"I want to make a point that I think everyone here should consider very carefully," King said at last to those around him at Dorchester. "I have to tell you that, in my judgment, some of the people sitting here today will not come back alive from this campaign."

2

"THIS IS NOT GETTING ANY BETTER"

The confidential memo reached the desk of Attorney General Robert F. Kennedy one week later, forwarded from FBI director J. Edgar Hoover.

Bobby Kennedy never knew what to expect from a Hoover memo. Hoover was dogged but bizarre. Bobby often received word from Hoover about Bobby's own actions. One time, Hoover sent an official report to Bobby that said the FBI director had sources confirming that Attorney General Kennedy and his brother Jack, the president, had met with a group of young women on the twelfth floor of the fashionable La Salle Hotel in Washington. Bobby didn't know how to interpret that. Was the report a threat? An attempt at sarcasm? A weird form of vicarious flattery? It could be all three, frankly. By his third year as attorney general, Bobby knew *Hoover* wanted it known he had moles everywhere.

The memo before Bobby now was dated January 16, 1963, and had been forwarded from Hoover without comment. Bobby breathed out and flipped to the first page.

FBI agents in the bureau's field office in Atlanta wrote that they'd surreptitiously snapped photos and filmed footage of the SCLC's bigwigs—Wyatt Walker, Martin Luther King Jr., Ralph Abernathy, and several others—greeting each other at the Savannah airport on the morning of

January 10. The agents wrote that they then trailed the bigwigs as they headed to Dorchester Academy, some thirty miles south of the city. The FBI did not secretly record what happened at Dorchester, and while the bureau's sources within the SCLC were "all familiar with some activities in the racial field," those same sources, the report noted, "had no information" on what exactly was discussed at Dorchester. The confidential memo did state that top leaders of King's organization had spent two days at Dorchester, which suggested a meeting of considerable consequence.

Bobby Kennedy scanned the names of people who'd waited for one another at the airport in Savannah before the group headed to Dorchester. On that list were the activist Jack O'Dell and the lawyer Stanley Levison. Both names exasperated Bobby. He believed them to be Communists. Bobby and his aides had warned King about O'Dell and Levison repeatedly over the last two years in private meetings, and had strongly suggested that King and the SCLC drop all association with the two men. Now, with this report, Bobby saw that King had flouted his recommendation.

Bobby Kennedy did not like Communists. He saw them as a threat to democracy. Bobby had worked in the 1950s for Senator Joe McCarthy, investigating claims of Communist infiltration in the United States and among its allies. Bobby thought McCarthy's now infamous Senate hearings had taken the witch hunt too far, but Bobby still felt his own investigative findings stood up. Communism *was* a threat, and anyone who thought otherwise was "badly informed," Bobby said.

This was the zealot in Bobby. He held firm to his convictions. Aides in the Kennedy administration said that between the brothers, Bobby was the Puritan and Jack the Brahmin. Jack carried himself with grace and an ironic disposition. Bobby was graceless, all intensity, all the time. The thing about which he was most zealous was his brother. Bobby not only loved but protected Jack. "He seemed to look at every aspect of a given situation, asking himself, 'Now, how can this affect Jack? How can it hurt Jack?'" noted General Maxwell D. Taylor, chairman of the Joint Chiefs of Staff, who knew the Kennedys well. It was why in every candid White

House photo with his brother, Bobby seemed to be forever slouched forward, brow furrowed, arms crossed, a handsome man turned ugly by his own seriousness. This was Bobby on high alert, ready to swat away John F. Kennedy's problems. To the outsider it seemed ludicrous that the scrawny, graceless younger brother could be the muscle, the sentry standing watch over the confident and athletic Jack Kennedy. But no less a source than the brothers' father, Joe Kennedy, said that for all of Jack's charm, and even his heroism—all that PT boat stuff in the Pacific, with a badly injured Jack swimming to a Solomon Islands shore in 1943 to save the lives of his shipmates—for all of that, "Bobby's the tough one." The family hard-ass. The one who saw in each of life's encounters some sort of moral test. Bobby chose football at Harvard *because* he was undersized and bad at it. He ended up lettering in the sport, which Jack never did, and in his senior year played on a broken leg against Yale, the whole thing in an enormous cast. *That* was Bobby. The gritted-teeth underdog who never, ever lost. Jack elevated Bobby to attorney general despite Bobby not really practicing law because Jack needed him in the administration: the moral, abrasive, resilient one. In the White House Jack leaned on Bobby, his most trusted advisor. The fact that Bobby was seven years younger than Jack made Bobby's responsibility all the graver. He had to somehow be wiser than his older brother.

That was the problem here. Like Hoover with his memos, Bobby Kennedy did not know how to interpret Martin Luther King Jr. King wanted what both Kennedys believed in—liberty—but the means by which King sought it inflamed Bobby. Consorting with Communists was bad enough. There was a larger problem, though. King sought to change America in ways that humiliated the people who governed it. How else was Bobby to understand King? The unrelenting speeches and media appearances and protests from the civil rights leader, always highlighting the inequities Blacks faced. Why did all his criticism of white America happen to occur in the America the Kennedys ruled? Why was King so determined, so impatient with the pace of change? What did King really want? "The stage had been set," one confidant of both men later wrote, "for a curious, long-running drama, in which Kennedy and King would test each other warily, again and again, wondering how much each could trust the other." That was just it: Bobby didn't trust King, not entirely. And because Bobby couldn't trust King entirely, he would not allow Jack to trust him at all. Which meant there was no way in hell the Kennedy administration would fully back Martin Luther King Jr. in any endeavor.

Bobby forwarded the confidential FBI memo, with its details of Communist infiltration and an SCLC meeting of considerable consequence, to Burke Marshall, his civil rights chief within the Department of Justice. Before Bobby sent it on, he scrawled a note on the memo: "Burke—This is not getting any better."

3

WHAT IT TAKES TO BEGIN TO LIVE

At thirty-four, King was a young man but in no way a naive one. He assumed the FBI monitored him. He assumed it tapped his phones, which is why when he discussed a fundraiser for the Birmingham protests with Harry Belafonte, the singer and Hollywood star who had also become a major donor for the SCLC, they used code words. Eventually, even those weren't secure enough, and Belafonte and King felt the only place they could be safe was Belafonte's New York apartment. They would just stage the fundraiser there. Belafonte would hand-select the guests. And so on March 31, two months after the SCLC's two-day conference at Dorchester and four days before the start of Project X, King traveled to New York with Ralph Abernathy, his dear friend, and Fred Shuttlesworth, the Birmingham pastor helping to oversee the upcoming protests. The three arrived at 300 West End Avenue, on the Upper West Side. The men looked at the brick building's stolid thirteen stories, where tonight they would carry out the biggest and most consequential fundraiser of their lives.

The SCLC had almost no operational cash. Maybe $500, according to Wyatt Walker's books. For the Birmingham protests to succeed, King and the others would need tens if not hundreds of thousands of dollars. The SCLC had only loose plans for obtaining it outside of tonight's fundraiser.

In other words, even before the SCLC's biggest gamble of a protest, there was the still larger gamble of how to finance it. They had traveled north on the blind faith that Belafonte could gather rich New Yorkers and that the preachers could part them from their money.

King and Abernathy and Shuttlesworth looked at each other, three Southern Baptists pastors, three sons of, respectively, a Black reverend and farmer and ne'er-do-well, and strode inside.

Belafonte owned the building. He'd purchased it two years prior, in 1961, when the landlord, the son of the Dominican Republic's dictator, Rafael Trujillo, refused to lease an apartment to Belafonte because he was Black. Harry got pissed and bought 300 West End outright. That showed up Trujillo. The purchase also created a fairly literal safe house for Black intellectuals and celebrities. Belafonte invited everyone over and turned the building into a co-op. Lena Horne rented the penthouse. She sometimes performed impromptu concerts with Belafonte in the building. It became known in Black New York as "Harry's Home."

King and his entourage moved to an elevator and hit the button for the fifth floor. They'd dressed formally, in suits, and if King was nervous about tonight's event, Ralph Abernathy was there to soothe him. That was his role, and perhaps always had been, going back to the days when King and Abernathy were seminary students and the stout-bodied Ralph, with rounded and almost cherubic country-boy features, was stood up for a date one night only to later see the woman on the arm of the thinner, more urbane, and far richer Martin Luther King Jr. That Ralph would not castigate the woman and instead turned the night into the seedling for the friendship that blossomed between Ralph and Martin showed why King adored him. Ralph was kind. Unlike everyone else in the SCLC, Ralph demanded nothing of Martin. He offered King what he had: companionship, time, reflection. Abernathy nurtured King, some said he "mothered" him, there to double-check an overbooked itinerary or flick the lint off one of the dark suits King favored before an appearance like this one.

The elevator doors opened. Sprawling before them was a twenty-one-room apartment, 7,200 square feet in all. Belafonte had knocked down the wall separating the A unit from the B and then dedicated one-half of his massive space to living and the other to entertaining. The place was a home and nightclub in one, with four functional fireplaces and paintings by Diego Rivera on the walls. But tonight, the apartment felt to King and his entourage a little cramped.

There were so many guests.

More than seventy-five people were here. They stopped sipping their drinks or chatting with friends to stare at the leaders who would be the night's headliners. Looking back at the pastors were the actors Ossie Davis and Sidney Poitier, the latter of whom was the first Black actor nominated for an Academy Award and arguably the only one present who was a bigger deal than Belafonte. There was James Wechsler, the editor in chief of the liberal *New York Post*. Hugh Morrow, Governor Nelson Rockefeller's top advisor. Tom Wicker and Anthony Lewis from the *New York Times*, the paper's most prominent and powerful writers. Above all, there were dozens of deep-pocketed New Yorkers who sized the preachers up, people who'd stopped by Harry's Home for what Belafonte had billed as a secret and very special evening.

Belafonte smiled and greeted the guests of honor and, moments later, gathered the whole crowd in his palatial living room.

As he thanked King and the entourage for coming and expressed other opening platitudes, Harry Belafonte no doubt encountered the problem he encountered everywhere: It was hard for people to focus on his words.

He was tall and broad and so very square-jawed handsome that he'd done the impossible: He'd broken through not only Hollywood's color line but the music industry's. A feat like that suggests otherworldly talent. Harry *was* talented, and ambitious, and determined, and everything else it took for a midcentury American Black man to succeed in two terribly discriminatory industries. But what Belafonte really was was beautiful. A walking Greek statue. A demigod. His *Harry Belafonte—Calypso* outsold

Elvis *and* Sinatra in 1957, and when the *New Yorker* later tried to figure out why, the best explanation the magazine got came from the Black folk singer Odetta: "Did you get a look at that man?"

Belafonte's appeal to America and even the liberal whites gathered that night in his New York home lay in part in his skin tone. "The thing is," the Black poet and critic Stanley Crouch later said, "Harry isn't *black* black." Harry's Jamaican grandmother was white. Harry's own complexion had yellow undertones—he was high yellow, as he learned as a kid in Harlem—and this made him less threatening to whites. "I think people perceive him as a nice person," Johnny Carson once said.

Harry hated that. He was not "nice." He was not "approachable." He was instead deeply aware of the broad discrimination against all Blacks—he had grown up in a New York more segregated than his forebears' colonial Jamaica—*and* the gradients of discrimination *between* Blacks of different skin tones. This obsession with complexion enraged Harry. "For Dad, it was about changing *all* of society," his daughter Adrienne said, and that change started with what Belafonte could do. "I wasn't an artist who'd become an activist," Belafonte later wrote. "I was an activist who'd become an artist." It was Harry's most admirable trait, even more alluring than his high cheekbones. He was never interested in the life his beauty afforded him. He was never interested in passing. In spite of his skin tone or perhaps because of it, Belafonte chose the hard road of true activism. That night in his living room, introducing the entourage from the SCLC, he had already given so much to the civil rights movement. He'd given his money to it: hundreds of thousands of dollars to date and eventually millions. He'd given his marriage to it: His first wife, Marguerite, divorced him after FBI agents stopped by one too many times with questions about Harry's involvement in protests. He'd given his reputation to it: Ed Sullivan thought he was a Communist and Hollywood producers thought he was "difficult." By 1963, Harry refused to star in any movie in which the Black character was kindhearted and even-tempered, the film's propped-up eunuch, which was in Harry's view every movie Hollywood made.

For the movement, he effectively abandoned his film career. *Harry* was now the man King turned to when the SCLC needed money. *Harry* was now the one Bobby Kennedy called when the AG wanted to "reason" with King. "Martin would say that one of his greatest strategic decisions was recruiting me to the movement," Harry once boasted.

That night at Harry's Home showed Belafonte's strengths. *He'd* gathered this crowd, and he'd done it by promising the moneyed New Yorkers a sneak peek of the SCLC's biggest action to date. That distinction—the chance to *invest* in an upcoming cause instead of *donating* to an ongoing one—was Harry's brainchild. The SCLC hadn't thought to do it before. An evening like tonight would flatter the guests when they learned the secret of Project X's locale. It was the reason the crowd was so large.

When he finished speaking, Harry turned to King to share the news.

King stepped forward and looked at the people around him.

We're going to Birmingham, King said. *We're going in four days, and we're going there to break segregation or be broken by it.*

Never before had the SCLC attempted what it was about to do, King told the crowd. The SCLC was a parent organization. It funded and then assisted other civil rights groups, which then led the protests: SNCC in Albany the previous year; CORE with the Freedom Rides in 1961; the NAACP, going way back, with its voter drives and lawsuits. Too many acronyms. Too many chefs.

No longer. King told the crowd the time had come for one group to stage one massive and era-defining protest. The SCLC would be that group. This privately excited King. He would at last assume full leadership of the civil rights movement. It also terrified him. The site he and the SCLC had chosen concentrated the hate and history of the United States into one locale. King shared with the New Yorkers some of what Wyatt Walker had told the much smaller crowd at Dorchester. King then told the people in Belafonte's apartment that Birmingham was much more than its terrible nickname of Bombingham. The city was a test of faith.

The SCLC planned to pour everything—its money, its personnel, and, after the disaster of Albany, its remaining reputation—into this protest. Birmingham would be the civil rights movement's D-Day. If King failed in Birmingham, the movement itself would fail and an already segregated South would drift backward in time.

It had begun to happen in Alabama. Former governor Jim Folsom, who had at least alluded to civil rights when he'd said, "All people are just alike," had been run out of office by George Wallace, a racist who talked about his "niggering" problem and had shouted at his inaugural address just three months ago, "Segregation now, segregation tomorrow, segregation forever!" If King failed in Wallace's Alabama and Bull Connor's Birmingham, politicians like them would be still more emboldened to spread their evil doctrine. The stifling Jim Crow South would regress to the suffocating antebellum South.

King said that was the test before the SCLC: pitting all it had against the numerical strength and historical advantage of white power in America. The test was even greater than that. If King failed in Birmingham, nonviolence failed. Faith failed. Love failed.

It was the biggest gamble of the protesters' lives, King told the crowd. And he wanted everyone in this room to put their money on it.

At least some donors remained uncertain about whether to give. That was fine. King had scheduled Fred Shuttlesworth to speak next. Shuttlesworth, the only Birmingham pastor involved with the planning of Project X, was in many ways the main event. He rose and stepped forward.

Suave, with a thin mustache and cutting gaze, Shuttlesworth looked as if Billy Dee Williams had committed his life to God. Fred had known the worst poverty in Alabama, in a childhood home without running water, without a pair of dress pants until he was twelve, but now stood ramrod straight in his well-tailored suit before these moneyed New Yorkers, with the ropy musculature of a lightweight boxer and that boxer's kinetic energy, too. Fred had a tendency wherever he was to pace, to claim the room through his presence and prowling. He was a man of *action* who, unlike King, spoke plainly—"Shit, do something, goddammit," he often said to people unsure about following him in a protest—and so he spoke plainly to these New Yorkers.

Though it's unclear how long he talked or how much he revealed, we do know he shared anecdotes from his time in Bull Connor's Birmingham. One anecdote, arguably Fred's best, began in the Christmas season of 1956.

Shuttlesworth had wanted to integrate the bus lines in Birmingham, as King and Abernathy had just done down in Montgomery. It had been a huge deal, that integration in Montgomery. It'd taken a year of protests and a Supreme Court order, but King had won. Now Fred wondered if he could do the same up in Birmingham.

Fred helmed a civil rights organization in the city: the Alabama Christian Movement for Human Rights (ACMHR). He'd assembled it in 1956 after the Alabama attorney general outlawed the NAACP in the state. "They can outlaw an organization," Fred had said, "but they can't outlaw the movement of a people determined to be free." The ACMHR met every Monday, sometimes at Fred's church, Bethel Baptist, on the north side of town. They called the meetings Movement Monday or Mass Monday, for the hundreds of people who showed. Christmas Eve in 1956 fell on a Monday and despite it being the most sacred of nights, Fred said they'd have their movement meeting. Fifteen hundred people came.

Now Birmingham, as everyone knew, was the most racist and segregated city in Alabama. It had plenty of laws and statutes saying Blacks and whites couldn't mingle in any real and human way, and certainly couldn't sit together on the city's buses. Fred took to the lectern on that Christmas Eve Movement Monday and said he didn't give a damn about Bull Connor's laws. The Supreme Court had just said that they could integrate. Fred Shuttlesworth would integrate.

He said he would lead a procession of ACMHR members and sit in the front of the bus in two days' time, on December 26. He'd already written a petition to do as much, requesting permission from the three City Hall commissioners to integrate the bus line.

This was a bold and perhaps careless move on Fred's part. Old Bull

Connor had just been reelected as one of those commissioners, the public safety commissioner, so for Fred to put his intention in writing and then *send* it to Bull? No one knew how the city would respond, Supreme Court order or no. What's more, Bull so despised Fred Shuttlesworth that he had cops sit in on Movement Monday meetings. Bull wanted Fred *watched*. And those cops weren't hard to spot. They were the white guys in the pews, taking notes, reporting back to Bull all they'd heard. They were there on that Christmas Eve. So for Fred to say at the movement meeting that he planned to integrate the bus lines December 26 was Fred in essence doubling down on his intention. It was Fred daring Bull to stop him.

The next morning, the twenty-fifth, Fred held the Christmas service at Bethel Baptist. A packed house, Fred looking dapper: Even the cops who surveilled him later admitted Fred always dressed well. Fred's sermon that day, though, wasn't just about Jesus's birth. From the pulpit Shuttlesworth sprinkled in allusions to Jim Crow. Even went so far as to say, "If it takes getting killed for integration, I'll do just that thing." This was the Alberta in him, his mother, who'd raised nine God-fearing kids and instilled in Fred, her oldest, the drive to fight for what was his. When Alberta watched boxing on television, she jabbed and ducked alongside the fighters, mimicking their movements. Fred learned to do the same.

After the Christmas service ended, the Shuttlesworths walked next door to their home, the church parsonage. Nothing fancy, but a comfortable place. Fred and his wife, Ruby, had four children and so after they opened presents, Fred tried to relax. Tomorrow was the big day.

He was in his pajamas that night, shorts and an undershirt, when one of Bethel's deacons knocked on the parsonage door. Charlie Roberson and his wife, Naomi. Good people. It'd become a tradition for the Robersons to pay a visit to Fred and Ruby on Christmas night. The Robersons came in and the women chatted in the den while two of the Shuttlesworths' daughters, Ricky and Carolyn, watched TV. Fred Jr. played in the dining room, still dressed in the red-and-white football uniform he'd gotten that day as a present. Charlie and Fred went to Fred's bedroom to discuss that most pressing of church business: the haul from the Christmas Day offering.

So they were in there talking church, Fred and Charlie, and Christmas Day could be a long one for any pastor, so eventually Fred just lay down on his bed. He was comfortable enough around Charlie to do it. Just lie down, head on the pillow, get cozy in what Fred called his skivvy pajamas, and keep chatting with Charlie, who stood across the room, leaning against the vanity.

About 9:40 p.m., Ricky Shuttlesworth, still in the den watching TV, heard what sounded like a newspaper slapping against the front porch. She turned toward it and—

The power from sixteen sticks of dynamite burst through the parsonage. A blast strong enough to knock the foundation out from under the home and send belongings within it flying through the air, landing in a vacant lot some four houses down the street. A blast strong enough to bring down the roof of the parsonage, to rip holes through the children's bedrooms, to dig a massive crater in the front yard.

Where the bomb exploded was right next to Fred and Ruby's bedroom—the bedroom where Fred and Charlie Roberson were talking. The force of the explosion demolished the wall and blew out the floor. Fred fell into the resulting gap, with the bed's mattress landing on him.

Everyone should have died.

In the bedroom, big shards of wood had flown like arrows and stuck to the wall. The mirror on the vanity had shattered into a million pieces. Charlie Roberson could claim no protection from any of this, but when it was over Charlie had only two or three cuts on him.

In the dining room and den, farther back from the site of the explosion, the kids and wives were shaken but unharmed.

Underneath that mattress and with the smell of fire and gunpowder in his nostrils, Fred Shuttlesworth realized what had happened, realized he was alive—and realized something else, too. He didn't so much hear as *feel* a voice express to him: "Underneath you are the everlasting arms" (Deuteronomy 33:27). As Fred gathered himself, he knew God had protected him.

He pushed the mattress off him.

The blast had been so loud it'd shattered windows a good mile from the parsonage, and in a few moments it was like the whole neighborhood had descended on the Shuttlesworth home. Bethel Baptist congregants called Fred's name and sifted through the flaming wreckage even before the firefighters and cops arrived. When they did, more Black people showed up, too, some of them armed with pistols and shotguns, angry and ready to protect themselves in a Bombingham where this happened far too often. The white cops didn't like the idea of armed Black citizens and hurled obscenities and slurs at the crowd. The crowd hurled them right back.

Guns were raised. The scene got tense.

Through all this, neighbors and cops kept calling out, *Reverend Shuttlesworth, Reverend Shuttlesworth, are you okay?* Deep in the ruins of the parsonage, Fred climbed out of the blast hole and stood in what remained of the bedroom. He took stock of the situation. His attire. He decided it was one thing to talk to Charlie Roberson in his skivvies, but he'd be damned if he was about to address all the people he heard out there looking like this. He shouted to everyone assembled on the front lawn: "I'm not coming out naked!"

This seemed to ease the tension outside.

Fred found a gabardine overcoat still on its hanger in the closet, and a wide gray fedora. He placed the hat on his head at the rakish angle he liked, buttoned up the coat, and walked carefully out of the bedroom.

When he got outside and faced the crowd, everyone gasped.

Fred raised his hand in the air.

"The Lord has protected me!" he proclaimed. "I am not injured."

For the assembled it seemed impossible, given the smoky ruins behind him, and yet there was Fred Shuttlesworth, on his front porch, not bleeding or limping or in pain, raising a biblical hand to the heavens and shouting that the Lord was with him.

A congregant yelled out: "Godsent!"

A big white cop bawled, overwhelmed by it all.

The cop then approached Shuttlesworth.

"I didn't think they would go this far. I know these people," the cop said of the members of the Klan who'd almost certainly thrown the dynamite on Fred's porch. "Reverend, if I were you, I'd get out of town as fast as I could. These people are vicious."

Now, Fred knew *these people* could be the Klan, or, shit, Birmingham cops who wore the white hoods at night. Both could be taking orders from Bull Connor, whom cops would see at Klan rallies, whom cops would hear bark orders back at police HQ not to investigate certain bombings and not to interview the Klan members suspected of carrying them out. For Fred, the whole thing—the Klan, the cops, Bull—was one thing. The same thing. And some blubbering cop telling him to leave because the cop knew these people may have solidified Fred's suspicion about white authority in Birmingham, but it wasn't about to change his mind.

"Officer, you're not me," Fred said. "Go back and tell your Klan brothers that if the Lord saved me from this, I'm here for the duration."

Fred then looked beyond the cop to the Black people on the lawn, the ones locked and loaded.

"Put those guns up," he said. "That's not what we're about. We are going to love our enemies.

"Go home."

The crowd dispersed, but the next day, the twenty-sixth, they reappeared at the ACMHR's rendezvous point for the planned bus protests. The meeting place they'd chosen was the A. G. Gaston Funeral Home. It seemed fitting. When Fred walked in it was like he'd risen from the dead. The two hundred or so waiting ACMHR members gave him a standing ovation. Word had spread of the bombing's destruction. "You couldn't find but pieces of the spring and pieces of the mattress or anything—and he was in the bed," one member recalled of hearing of the damage and seeing Fred that morning. "Couldn't nobody do that but God. There ain't no luck that will bring him through that."

Everyone came to see if Fred would actually stick to the plan. Would they still try to integrate the buses?

The white man had tried to kill Fred the previous night. The white commissioners had decreed just that morning that anyone who integrated the buses would be thrown in jail. Some of the ACMHR board members spoke up now to say, "We ought to stop and think this out."

For Fred, there was nothing to think out. He remembered the night before, walking out of his bedroom and seeing the Christmas tree somehow still standing. He remembered later that night, when his youngest, six-year-old Carolyn, had asked him if those white people would kill the Shuttlesworth family. "No, baby," he'd said. "They can't kill hope." He realized not only that God had protected him during the blast but that God always would, from this day forward, in any situation. God would be his everlasting defender. Fred understood that, strangely enough, even as the power of the dynamite rushed over him. *You can know something in a second*, Fred thought, *that you never read in a book nor ever will. You can feel something in a second that will be with you the rest of your life.*

Fred was sure the only reason God had saved him was to lead the fight for civil rights.

He quieted the board members around him who were debating whether to ride.

"Hell yeah we're gonna ride," Shuttlesworth told the crowd. "Find you any kind of crack you can to hide in if you're scared, but I'm walking downtown after this meeting and getting on the bus. I'm not going to look back to see who's following me."

So they left. Probably some two hundred people behind him, Black folk who'd never done anything like this and were scared. City Hall put fifty extra cops on patrol to stop the protests with brutal force, but Fred at the front of the procession didn't care. He just kept leading the way down the street. People parted to let him pass. From the looks of them, they'd heard what'd happened the previous night and were amazed Reverend Shuttlesworth was upright *and* carrying out his promise to protest. There were no cops around, either, which was its own miracle. Fred had the procession behind him split up and walk to other bus stops; the more they split up, the more buses they could ride. Fred and his own small entourage walked to 12th Street North and waited for the bus there.

When it came, Fred got on and took a seat about halfway back. Well within the white section. The three people with him did the same.

"This is all right," Fred said, as much to his companions as to God.

Two white ladies huffed as they rose from their seats and got off, but the bus pulled out of the stop and drove on. At the next bus stop, more Black people boarded. They saw Fred and it was the inspiration they needed. They sat down in the white section, too. Some Black people in the back of the bus couldn't believe it. They told Fred that he and the rest up front were about to risk the lives of everyone as soon as the cops came on. Those in the back pleaded with Fred to join them. What was he doing? Did he want *every* Black house bombed?

Fred ignored the pleas. He stayed in his seat.

The bus filled up. Just kept rolling along as if all this were normal, all these Blacks up front, all these whites baffled by Fred's effrontery or terrified of his courage but in either case having to take seats wherever they could find them. And no cops anywhere. When white people had to stand because there were no more seats, Fred felt he had made his point. He kindly turned to the white lady hovering above him: "Would you like my seat?"

She nodded and thanked him, and Fred got off the bus.

It went like that all day. Fred rode and rode and the cops never arrested him, couldn't track him. In some ways he and his other freedom fighters were staging a guerrilla-warfare campaign. Black people who, to white eyes, looked like any other Black Birminghamian—fearful and compliant—but who swooped in and filled the fronts of buses and then got off and disappeared back into Black neighborhoods.

And then got on somewhere else in the city and did it again.

By day's end, around two hundred people had ridden in the front of buses. Only twenty-one were arrested. No one was hurt. No one died. The Lord protected Fred and everyone brave enough to follow him.

As Fred later preached: "I shall be dead before I'll ever be a slave again."

The people in Harry Belafonte's New York apartment stared at Fred Shuttlesworth as he told his stories, transfixed, mouths agape, just as Birminghamians had when Fred rose from the wreckage of his home and told the press, "The fight is on." To some New Yorkers, Fred's very presence proved God's miracle or man's fortitude or both. Many in the movement had already drawn similar conclusions. Especially for poor and working-class Blacks in Birmingham and across Alabama—and to some extent through the whole of the South—Fred Shuttlesworth's courage translated to mass adoration. "They just loved the man," one Birmingham activist said. In the words of another: "I would follow Shuttlesworth quicker than I would Martin Luther King because, to me, he is a much stronger man. Now Martin knows how to say it; Fred knows how to do it."

There were many other stories of Fred doing it after the Christmas Day bombing. Stories of an almost mythical bravery. But Fred didn't need to say too much more to these New Yorkers. He had them. He had that preacher sense, the instinct to know how much storytelling and sermonizing was necessary to get people primed for what happened after the allegories: the offering. There would have to be a massive offering in Harry Belafonte's apartment to underwrite the largest action, the biggest story Fred Shuttlesworth would ever tell: the carrying out of Project X.

Fred was an extemporaneous pastor. He'd write one thing but say a whole lot more. So we don't know exactly what he said that night as he moved toward the close of his speech. We don't know if he mentioned how after the Christmas Day bombing he told white cops he wouldn't rebuild the parsonage because he wanted to "let the people see what America is." We don't know if he talked about how his very existence threatened Bull Connor: "I believe you the worst thing that ever happened to the Negro in this city," Bull had told Fred as Fred filed new petitions to protest after the bombing. We don't know if Fred shared with the New Yorkers that his courage threatened all of white Birmingham, too. Bombings of Black residential properties increased after the bombing of Fred's parsonage. By the mid-1960s, more than forty such bombings remained "unsolved" by the Birmingham PD. We don't know if Fred said how Bethel Baptist formed a security team, how congregants staffed the church at all hours, rifles and shotguns at the ready. We don't know if Fred shared that after his rides at the front of the bus he filed lawsuits against the city to mandate integration, and how the city and its lawyers ultimately got around Fred's suits by passing an ordinance that said bus drivers themselves could decide where people sat. Because those drivers were white, segregation remained the de facto law in Birmingham. "If the Klan don't get you, the police will; and if the police don't get you, the courts will," Fred said at the time.

We do know one thing. Fred Shuttlesworth talked about hope. On that night of anecdotes from his life, hope was Fred's ur-story. Hope had blossomed amid the ruins of his parsonage. Everything—Fred's faith, his love, his courage—stemmed from a hope that he could be the change he wanted to see in the world. It was a preposterous idea in Birmingham, Alabama, but Fred Shuttlesworth was a preposterous man. He believed in his hope so much, he would ultimately be arrested more than thirty times for his activism and be named in more cases that reached the Supreme Court than any other person in American history. The perseverance it took to continue to hope was girded by a belief, something that ran through Fred's head so often after that Christmas Day bombing it became a refrain for his life, and something he shared with the New Yorkers now.

"You have to be prepared to die before you can begin to live."

That line got to them. It hung in the air, stunning the moneyed whites and famous Blacks in Harry Belafonte's apartment. *You have to be prepared to die before you can begin to live?* Wow. Here was an American original, an American *radical*, fierce and untamed. And untam*able*. Even in those business suits he seemed to like, untamable. *You have to be prepared to die before you can begin to live?*

Of *course* you do. Of course *anyone* did in Birmingham, Alabama, which made this Project X all the more romantic for the New Yorkers. To go down there, knowing the chance of success was low, knowing the chance of death was high—it made the protests nobler. More alluring. Epic. These New Yorkers accrued their money in so many different ways—in selling newspapers or stocks or political causes or movies—but they all dealt by one means or another with narrative, and this was suddenly a story they wanted to be part of.

"What can we do to help?" one New Yorker asked.

King stepped forward and said they could invest in the cause.

How much do you need?

Whatever you can give, King said. The SCLC was effectively broke after Albany and would require a considerable amount of funds for something as ambitious as Project X.

How will you use it?

Bail bonds, King said. And because Birmingham was to be a sustained protest, money for motel rooms, food, office supplies, all the planned-for minutiae of mass protests and all the unexpected and perhaps terrible costs as well.

So anything they could give, King said.

In the end they gave $475,000. It was the biggest haul the SCLC had ever received.

4

WHAT WAS PROMISING AND IMPOSSIBLE

After the guests left and Fred Shuttlesworth begged off to sleep, Harry Belafonte toasted the night with King and Abernathy. Julie Robinson, Harry's second wife, brought out glasses and a bottle of Martin's favorite sherry, Harveys Bristol Cream. King loved it so much that each time he visited the Belafontes, he made a show of finding the sherry and inspecting the line he'd traced on the bottle to see if Harry or Julie had drunk it in his time away. Julie, a Russian Jew whose dark complexion and progressive politics had once attracted Marlon Brando, was familiar with bizarre behavior, so she laughed as Martin inspected the bottle. Now the drinks were poured, the glasses hoisted, and the four of them—the two Belafontes, King, and Abernathy—savored everything.

Harry had been right. Revealing to the donors the secret of Project X had flattered them, and they had in turn pumped new life into the SCLC. But Martin had been wise to use Shuttlesworth as he did. It meant the evening had a freshness and perspective that previous fundraisers at Harry's Home had lacked. If the movement leaders were honest, no one had thought tonight's gala would work. Wyatt Walker had stayed behind and snickered that the evening would be nothing more than "a little razzmatazz." But to witness the response to that thundering quote from Fred?

Jackpot.

Harry turned to Martin and said he had noticed something in that moment, too. Harry said that when Fred delivered the line, Martin had snapped his head back, as if he were flinching.

What was that about?

Martin met Harry's eyes.

There were two ways for King to respond: the full answer, and anything else.

The full answer was King's obsession with death. Years later, Martin's wife, Coretta, would talk about it: He thought about death constantly. He was convinced he'd be assassinated. An aide would later say: "Every time he made a commitment to something . . . he was committing his life. . . . He thought in everything he did it meant his death." Martin wished he had Fred Shuttlesworth's faith, which gave Fred an almost reckless bravery during dangerous encounters. King did not have that kind of faith. His God was a foreboding, forewarning one. "When I look up at the cross I recognize its meaning," he later wrote. "The cross is something that you bear, and ultimately that you die on." King's willingness to lead the SCLC but refuse the security details and offers of concealed weapons demanded a personal strength. If no less a source than God is telling you that you will die, you have to make your peace with it.

This was hard. The effort to face death showed itself these days in an anxious, head-yanking tic.

Martin didn't say this to Harry, though. To Harry, Martin just complained about his "nerves."

Harry didn't buy it. The tic kept surfacing. As Harry later wrote, "It was easy enough to see what had set that tic off. The prospects of violence in the weeks to come could hardly be greater."

And would facing death matter? Would anything ahead of them actually improve the lives of Birminghamians? Of Blacks across the nation?

Would the protests impress upon the Kennedy administration that most distant of dreams: real and impactful civil rights legislation?

Probably not.

King and Belafonte sipped their drinks and talked about how the Kennedys disappointed them constantly. From the start, the Kennedys had equivocated. Yes, Jack Kennedy had pledged at the 1960 Democratic National Convention an enforcement of voting rights laws, new legislation for fair-employment practices, and federal action that might end discrimination in housing and education. But Bobby Kennedy, who had not read that speech in advance, who was stunned by what it promised Blacks and worried how it might antagonize whites, had moved throughout the convention floor assuring southern delegates that Jack only endorsed protests if they were "peaceful and legal" by the standards of those southern states. It would later come out that Bobby had privately chastised Jack for the way his civil rights position alienated southern whites: "You might not get votes from them but there is no sense in turning on them at this moment." And so Jack had also said during the closing months of the campaign: "I am happy and proud to receive support from delegates from *any* part of the United States."

This was the angling politician Belafonte had met in New York, back in 1960—a Jack Kennedy who would promise what needed promising to gain support for his campaign. Harry saw right through it. "To him, I could tell, the Black vote was just a constituency you bought each election, if not with dollar bills and vague promises, then with star endorsements and public lip service," Harry said. He couldn't trust Kennedy. He phoned King to say Martin shouldn't, either. Kennedy was "cold, calculating," and "unschooled" in civil rights, Belafonte said. King nonetheless met with Kennedy, who asked for an endorsement. Martin weighed the request in call after long-distance call with Harry. Harry pleaded with him to back away from the Kennedys. "You can't afford to endorse him," Harry said. "If you anoint him and become his Black mouthpiece, you'll pay a huge political price if he lets us down."

In the end, King endorsed no one.

Within days of the inauguration, Kennedy walked back his commitment to civil rights. He placed white Virginians as liaisons to his civil rights strategy, Virginians who renamed a conference on civil rights the National Conference on *Constitutional* Rights in American Freedom. Kennedy watered down Congress's all-powerful Rules Committees, the groups in the House and Senate that passed so much meaningful legislation, by giving white southerners important seats. He then had the gall to complain to King, to whoever would listen, how civil rights legislation seemed impossible. Why "go to the wall on a lot of civil rights demands that can't pass anyway?" he asked.

It infuriated King. He wrote in the SCLC newsletter that the administration was "paralyzed" and "helpless," staffed by "vigorous young men" who showed a certain "élan" but "had waged an essentially cautious and defensive struggle," "aggressively driving only toward the limited goal of token integration." If Bobby Kennedy wanted to improve Blacks' lives as AG, where was his enforcement of voting rights laws? Even as the Belafontes and King and Abernathy downed their drinks that night, Alabama remained one of five states to place a poll tax on its Black voters. If Jack Kennedy was really so concerned about redlining, where was the end of housing discrimination that the president had promised with a "stroke of a pen"? That slogan had become such a sour joke that Black people now mailed the White House bottles of ink and ballpoints. In all of this were the Kennedys' half measures. "It does no good to apply Vaseline to a cancer," King said.

And yet those half measures were better than what the movement had received before. President Eisenhower thought *Brown v. Board of Education* set the South back. The Kennedy brothers may have been many terrible things, but they were also northern, and liberal, and on occasion showed they cared about Black people.

During the Freedom Rides in 1961, when white and Black students rode buses through the South to end segregation on interstate bus lines and those buses were firebombed outside Birmingham and the riders themselves beaten bloody within the city limits, Bobby Kennedy had deployed four hundred federal marshals to protect the Freedom Riders. He personally got on the phone with Greyhound to see which drivers could take the riders through the rest of the South, safely. "I am—the Government is—going to be very much upset if this group does not get to continue their trip," Bobby told a Greyhound representative. "Under the law they are entitled to transportation provided by Greyhound." Bobby then asked the governing body overseeing interstate travel, the Interstate Commerce Commission (ICC), to issue regulations that would end segregation at southern bus terminals, a move that bypassed a Congress reluctant to pass such legislation. The ICC did Bobby's bidding. "White" and "Black" signs came down at various southern bus depots. When southern politicians howled, Jack defended Bobby's move.

It was promising and also impossible to deal with the Kennedys. Nothing better illustrated this truth for the Belafontes and King and Abernathy than the SCLC's last campaign, the Albany campaign. When city leaders there had refused to negotiate with King and local Black activists on their handful of demands, Jack Kennedy had intervened from Washington. "I find it wholly inexplicable why the city council of Albany will not sit down with the citizens of Albany," the president said. "The United States government is involved in sitting down at Geneva with the Soviet Union. I can't understand why the . . . city council of Albany cannot do the same for American citizens." The position impressed King so much he wired the president to say he was "gratified by directness of your statement to Albany crisis."

And yet when King, liberal members of Congress, and the NAACP asked Bobby Kennedy's Department of Justice to bring lawsuits that would help the Albany cause—suits to desegregate local schools and to prevent local cops from arresting Black citizens who sought public services—Bobby refused. He didn't want to involve himself in Albany the way he had the year prior, during the Freedom Rides. The Kennedy administration had taken a political hit for Bobby's Freedom Rides intervention. By 1962, during the Albany campaign, there was already Jack's reelection bid for Bobby to consider. Jack needed the support of the South to win in '64.

So Bobby ignored King in Albany. If anything, Bobby helped the segregationists. When King had no choice but to leave the city, humiliated and with none of his demands met, Bobby called Albany's mayor to congratulate him for keeping the peace. Bobby had to have known what would happen next: The mayor told every member of the national press remaining in the city about Bobby's call. And *that*—the resulting newspaper headlines about Bobby's congratulatory conversation concerning "one of the most stunning defeats of King's career"—*that* was what haunted the SCLC and its reputation still, even as the Belafontes and King and Abernathy chatted in Harry's Home and sipped their Harveys Bristol Cream.

Bobby Kennedy had intentionally harmed the movement. And he'd done it to help his brother in a South that was turning against the Kennedys.

It was easy to assume this kind of brinkmanship, and maybe even correct. How else could anyone, really, understand Bobby Kennedy, Jack's shrewd protector?

Dawn neared. The weight of it all—how Bobby might respond in Birmingham, how Bull might—led the four people in Harry's apartment to sink deeper into their seats. King turned to Abernathy.

"Let me be sure this time," Martin said drolly, "to get arrested with people who don't snore."

Ralph saw the sudden playfulness in his best friend, and with a slight smirk said he had done no such thing in Albany.

King lit up with delight. "Oh you are torture!"

King explained to the Belafontes how in Albany they'd been jailed for demonstrating and thrown in a cell with an activist who, unlike King and Abernathy, had never been arrested before. That man went mad behind bars. He kept screeching how King was the messiah, waking King up at night with new visions that crossed before his eyes. King told the

Belafontes that between the madman and Ralph's snoring, King hadn't gotten a wink.

Ralph protested again that he didn't snore.

Now Martin roared with laughter. Which got the Belafontes chuckling. And then Ralph, too, though he did so warily. He sensed what was really happening here.

When Martin was at his most anxious, his humor was at its blackest. It's why at Dorchester, after saying some of the leaders would not come back alive from Birmingham, Martin had thought it appropriate to go around the room delivering mock eulogies. It was macabre. It almost certainly didn't help anyone else in attendance, but it helped Martin, a man who Ralph knew had "to laugh and joke at the grim business of leading a movement."

Martin laughed harder now, and his best friend laughed alongside him, seeming to understand everything the laughter drowned out. Martin's stress. Martin's fear. Martin's certainty that Birmingham would be worse by orders of magnitude than anything the two of them had experienced in their decade of activism.

"White folks ain't invented anything in the world that can get to me like you do!" Martin said to Ralph, howling.

"Anything they want me to admit to, I will!" Martin said, fairly screeching himself now. "If they'll just get me out of your cell!"

Martin laughed.

And laughed.

And laughed.

Part II

PROJECT CONFRONTATION

5

DEPARTURES

This was his life now, this endless travel. She had to accept it. Coretta Scott King told herself she did.

She waited for Martin to arrive at the hospital and take her and newborn Bernice home.

Bernice was Martin and Coretta's fourth child, and while Martin had not missed Bernice's birth, he had certainly done his part to hurry it along. Martin had been worried that the delivery of Bernice in Atlanta would overlap with the start of Project X in Birmingham and had asked Coretta's doctor in late March to induce labor. Coretta was at term and on bed rest, with Martin running up and down the staircase of their two-story home bringing her meals or a bedpan. It did little good. The baby stayed put. Physically uncomfortable and all too cognizant of Martin's travel itinerary, Coretta had decided she couldn't wait for even the scheduled inducement. She swallowed a spoonful of castor oil, something a girlfriend had recommended for mothers at term. Nothing happened. The next day Coretta took a larger spoonful. This time she went into labor, and on March 28, Bernice Albertine King was born, named after, respectively, the girl's maternal and paternal grandmothers. Martin kissed Coretta and the baby in the delivery room and then rushed to the airport for a flight, ultimately, to New York and Harry Belafonte's fundraiser.

Now it was the morning of April 2 and Martin had just flown back from New York to take Coretta and Bernice home from the hospital. Martin arrived there the way he arrived anywhere these days: with the understanding he had to be somewhere else soon. He would fly on to Birmingham later that day. From there Project X would begin.

He loaded Coretta and baby Bernice into his nine-year-old Pontiac, a car whose make and model shocked Atlanta's upper-class Blacks. Shouldn't King drive a Cadillac? He had the prestige for one. In the early years after the Montgomery bus boycotts and the cover of *Time* and the best-selling publication of Martin's book *Stride Toward Freedom*, the offers to speak domestically and internationally overwhelmed the Kings, and Coretta traveled with Martin: Paris, Geneva, Rome, and the best trip, the one to India where Martin met the leaders who knew King's idol in non-violence, Gandhi. But these days Coretta seldom traveled with Martin, in part because no one could keep pace with his schedule and in part because Coretta had to care for four children: Yolanda, seven; Martin III, five; Dexter, two; and five-day-old Bernice, riding home in the Pontiac.

"Did I feel abandoned or neglected . . . ?" Coretta later wrote. She told herself she didn't. "Martin and I shared values. I knew he loved his family, but we both had a higher calling and purpose that was much larger than the fulfillment of our own desires. As much as I loved Martin, I knew he belonged not just to me but to his calling." She knew, though, that he placed the movement above her and the children. "You know," he'd once said to her, "a man who dedicates himself to a cause doesn't need a family." She told herself she was fine with such abrasiveness, too. It was Martin balancing his spiritualism against the world's earthly bounties.

What pained her was something more personal. She'd begun the movement thinking she was an equal partner in it. The night before the Montgomery bus boycott started in 1955, it was she who'd stayed up late with Martin. Would Black people actually refuse to ride the buses the next day? Would they continue to refuse day after day, month after month, until the city was so damaged economically by Blacks withholding their fares that city leaders would be forced to negotiate with Martin for equal treatment on the bus lines? "We were both filled with doubt," Coretta wrote. "Attempted boycotts had failed in Montgomery and other cities." No one else was in the house that night but their fussy firstborn, baby Yolanda. It was Martin and Coretta, facing a very uncertain future but one they'd agreed to share. They went to bed around midnight and woke before 6:00 a.m. because at six the first bus would roll to a stop outside their home.

The job fell to Coretta to peer out the window at the appointed time; Martin was too anxious.

The bus came to a stop.

"Martin! Martin! Come quickly!" she'd said, and he'd rushed over.

No Blacks were on the bus. All these years later she still remembered how his face had lit up. Hers did, too. They stood together, the two of them, waiting for the next bus. When it came to a halt, no Black people were on that one, either. "We were so excited we could hardly speak coherently," Coretta wrote. It was not only thrilling but, for her, validating. She'd met Martin just three years earlier, in 1952, in Boston, where she was a scholarship student at the New England Conservatory of Music and he was working toward a PhD in theology at Boston University. He had talked of marriage on their first date, and she'd wanted none of it. Marrying Martin, or any man, would end her dream to be a classically trained singer and performer. She had not come from Alabama all the way to Boston just to get married and move back south. But Martin's mind fascinated her as one date became many: a young man who read Kant and Hegel and Nietzsche, who *despaired* over Nietzsche, even, over what his gruff *Will to Power* meant for any other person's hope to influence the world through collective action and love. She had never met anyone as voraciously intellectual as Martin, and really no one as fun, either. He liked parties. He liked to tease. To dance. He *loved* music. When Coretta felt herself falling for him, when she knew what falling for him represented, she prayed: "Oh Lord, help me to make the right decision."

She realized her voice, that beautiful soprano, could do more than sing to serve God's will. After all, Martin had told her, "I must have a wife who will be as dedicated as I am."

So she'd married him, and they'd moved to Montgomery, where Martin had accepted his first pastorship at Dexter Avenue Baptist. On that first morning of Martin's activism in Montgomery, the sort he'd been planning in some manner since Boston, Coretta and Coretta alone stood beside him. It was *their* activism. And together they stood before God. "I felt that my husband was being prepared—and I, too—for a special role about which we would learn later," Coretta wrote. "We felt a sense of destiny, of being propelled in a certain positive direction. We had the feeling that we were allowing ourselves to be the instruments of God's creative will."

Martin had watched the empty buses drive by that morning in Montgomery and told her he was taking the car to "see what's happening in other places in the city." He rushed out of the house and picked up Ralph Abernathy, who pastored at First Baptist, the largest Black church in the city, a reverend who believed the civil rights struggle was worth its cost. Ralph and Martin set out to see what their protest had wrought.

In some sense they were still out there, forever witnessing what they put in motion. The cause had become so much bigger by 1963 than the discussions they'd once had over dinner, when it was just her and Martin and Ralph and his wife, Juanita, talking about the future. The future was here and the movement everywhere, debated in Washington and discussed abroad. When Coretta and Martin visited Ghana, people kept coming up to him. Even in Ghana, Martin was known. God's creative will had imagined and set loose in the world a Martin Luther King Jr. who was much larger than his five-foot-seven frame. There were times it raised gooseflesh on Coretta's arms.

Where did it leave her, this new presence of Martin's that filled churches, filled banquet halls, filled arenas? There was somehow no longer room to stand beside him. She told herself she was fine with it. She was a preacher's wife now, and the wife of arguably the most important preacher. If serving the movement meant supporting Martin and caring for his children, well, as far back as the halcyon days of Montgomery she had also been Martin's secretary. In some sense for the whole eight years of their activism she had been his unseen bulwark. She had to accept that.

And yet she sometimes thought about that trip to India. It had been wonderful for her, too. She'd met Indira Gandhi (no relation to Mohandas), the daughter of India's first prime minister and a woman central to Indian politics. By the time of the Kings' trip, Indira served as president of the Indian National Congress and would later become the country's prime minister. Coretta was so taken by Indira: her grace, her intellect, and above all her ambition. She was going to change the world. "From that first meeting, Indira and I became friends," Coretta wrote. Indira's life was hard—"women can be condemned for doing exactly the same things for which their male predecessors are praised," Coretta wrote—but Indira's life was always her own. It was riveting to meet her. "The high point of my pilgrimage," Coretta wrote.

Now Martin parked the Pontiac before their home on Johnson Avenue, on Atlanta's east side, which was not as fashionable an area as Coretta would have preferred but was close to Ebenezer Baptist, where Martin pastored now. It was practical to live here, he'd argued. She'd relented. They got Bernice out of the car, a baby whom Coretta had delivered on a schedule that served Martin's needs. They brought Bernice inside, into a home they rented because the asceticism that Martin had read about in the Gospels and then in Gandhi's essays had become a guide to his own life, too, one where Martin renounced purchasing nearly anything for himself. The lease was in Coretta's name and their accommodations so modest Martin even wondered if he kept too many books. Martin asked for a $6,000-a-year salary from Ebenezer Baptist, a sum so meager it shocked M. L. King Sr., Martin's prosperity-preaching father and Ebenezer's co-pastor. Martin's fees for any lecture, anywhere in the world, he gave to the SCLC; almost all book royalties went to the movement, too, some $230,000 in a good year. From the SCLC itself Martin drew only a $1-a-year salary. "He felt that much of the corruption in society came from the desire to acquire material things," Coretta wrote. If he did not have the money, he could not desire the things.

Coretta told herself she was fine with this as well. "I knew he was searching for a balance between asceticism and materialism," she wrote. It was her job to make do. So she did. On that April morning in 1963 she settled baby Bernice and hugged and kissed the three other children who had missed her while she was at the hospital. Hearth and home and her life within it. Soon Martin was at the door, telling her he had the flight to Birmingham to catch. Coretta was a woman who would ultimately write more than seven hundred pages about her time with her husband, but about this pivotal moment, the moment of departure before Martin's most important campaign, she wrote nothing. We don't know what he told her, or she him. We don't know if they embraced, or for how long.

We do know she wanted to go with him. "I was deeply concerned that I would not be there to comfort him," she wrote. She understood him so much better than the men—the donors and pastors and lawyers, all of them "close advisors" of the SCLC—who huddled around Martin wherever he went now. Martin put on a show of toughness for these guys, but she knew that even though he'd been arrested twelve times in eight years, he'd never gotten used to imprisonment. He'd told her about the isolation of a lonely cell or the claustrophobia of an overcrowded one, and always the sneering, threatening deputies who sauntered past the bars. He didn't like jail, not one bit, but there was another reason Coretta wanted to go to Birmingham. Her "desperate desire" to be "near my husband" was also her desire to stand next to him once more. "I am an activist," she wrote, and "for the longest time, way before I married Martin, I believed that women should allow our essence and presence to shine."

She told herself hers would again, and soon. But on that April day in 1963 Martin walked out the door after having walked in only a few hours earlier, and Coretta watched from the window as the car drove off to the airport and to Project X beyond.

She turned back to the children.

Hearth and home and her life within it.

She told herself she was fine.

6

ARRIVAL

King boarded the plane with Ralph Abernathy. Flight time to Birmingham was estimated at a little under an hour. Were they ready?

It seemed so. Wyatt Walker was in Birmingham with charts and lists and more blueprints. In fact, since Dorchester the man had basically abandoned his home in Atlanta, which was the SCLC's base, to live in Birmingham, planning, endlessly planning, going on so many one-man reconnaissance missions that Walker could now report to King how many stools, tables, and chairs were in every department store where they might stage sit-ins. Walker knew every street in Birmingham and had sketched out where Bull Connor's police force might position itself, and then imagined how protesters could move around the force and hit what Walker called "tertiary targets." Walker had even timed, to the second, how long it took an old man to walk from a Black church to Birmingham's downtown, and how long it took a child to walk the same distance. It was impressive, Walker proving once again why King relied on him, but it was also a little much, the granularity showing a guilt Walker still felt about the Albany campaign a year ago, when the SCLC's executive director had failed to foresee all the problems King and the rest would face. Every Birmingham memo and checklist from Wyatt Walker could be read as a plea for absolution: *This time I will not fail you, Mr. Leader.*

There was another reason Walker planned this much. Birmingham was foreign. Another country, really, vastly different from even Atlanta, the southern city of comparable size where King, Abernathy, and Walker all lived.

For one thing, Birmingham wasn't a southern city. Not exactly. In the Civil War, when Union general William Tecumseh Sherman burned Atlanta to the ground and torched the rest of the South in his famed March to the Sea, Birmingham didn't exist yet. It wasn't formed until after the war, and only then because southern prospectors and northern railmen found that this stretch of hills in Jefferson County, Alabama, contained a bounty of coal and iron. It was seen as the lone spot in the world holding *all* the mineral deposits needed for the manufacturing of steel. Southern entrepreneurs and northern financiers bribed the voters of Jefferson County to charter a new city in 1871, and those industrialists named it after Birmingham, England, as if to signify this new place's distinction from surrounding southern cities and their loyalty to cotton.

Birmingham very quickly became a southern outpost of northern interests. The black smoke that belched from the steel mills served as an unceasing homage to the owners of those mills in Pittsburgh and their financiers in Boston or New York. The elites abused Birmingham. Raped it, the smoke blotting out the skies, the coal mines carving up the earth, and the low wages for such work attracting desperate people, poor whites whose fathers had lost the war and their livelihoods, and the first generations of freed Blacks, who sought any sort of money on which to build a better existence. It was a lawless place. "The Murder Capital of the World," wrote *Harper's* magazine, and by 1935 home to the second-highest rate of venereal disease in the nation. The elites who managed the mills and mines did not live in Birmingham. They stayed up north or settled in Mountain Brook, a Birmingham suburb at a safe remove from the smog and violence. They had no ties to Birmingham. They cared little about it. No one did. Birmingham well into the twentieth century had more illiterate people than any other city in the nation and the lowest spendable income per citizen, too. For generations neither the Blacks nor whites got ahead, serfs to their bosses in Mountain Brook or their bosses' bosses up north. The whites couldn't lash out against their managers and keep their jobs, so they lashed out at Blacks.

The Klan grew to monstrous proportions in Birmingham. In 1920, its chapter had twenty thousand members, the largest klavern in the nation. Whites flocked to it not because their granddaddies had lost at Gettysburg but because they themselves were hardly better off than Blacks in the here and now. That fact humiliated white people. That humiliation, while never voiced, nonetheless fueled a hatred of Black people distinct from that found in every other southern city. *This* was why Birmingham was foreign, a different country from the rest of the South: It hated along class lines, along economic lines, because of ongoing embarrassment and not historical "honor." Slavery had actually been uncommon here, amid the hills of northern Alabama. "As the Civil War broke out," the author Scott Horton wrote, "this area bitterly resented the secessionist slaveholding planters of the state's south." Birmingham's bigotry, then, was learned. But it seethed and pulsed all the same, became an almost tactile presence, there every time a Black man was lynched or a Black church burned or a white Girl Scout beaten for teaching Black children to read. And never any repercussions: The Klan often marched the streets with police escorts. Politicians sought the local Klan's endorsement.

Bull Connor, then, was never quite the disease of Birmingham but a symptom, a *product* of the city. In fact, a quintessentially white Birminghamian: raised in a broken home on the north side of town, never graduating from high school, listless and itinerant, working odd jobs until he realized—and this was where he distinguished himself—that a hatred of Blacks *and* drawled-out populism toward whites could propel a political rise. The white people of Birmingham came to love Bull. That's why they kept voting for him from 1937 on, over the objections of the managerial class in Mountain Brook who thought Connor was as dumb as an actual bull, and despite the scandals that accompanied his unchecked reign. The extramarital affairs. The instances grand juries viewed his police force to be as violent and thieving as any villainous enterprise. Bull survived these scandals, survived the name-calling in widely circulated criminal indictments—"dictatorial, immoral, autocratic"—and the subsequent impeachment proceedings against him, too. He concentrated his power in Birmingham because he made one promise to its white citizens: He would always remain just like them.

"They all know me," he once told a local newspaper reporter. "I've been Bull Connor. I'm still Bull Connor. . . . If they wanted to start treating me any other way I'd get worried and figure they didn't like me any more."

Across a generation of elections, he never worried much.

Today, April 2, was another election for Bull. The man was running for mayor in the city's new mayor-and-council system, which was supposed to be less dictatorial than the city-commissioner system under which Bull had thrived for decades. Bull's name at the top of the mayoral ballot, though, was meant to serve as a reminder: Nothing had changed. And nothing would.

Bull's mayoral opponent was Alabama's former lieutenant governor, Albert Boutwell, an educated lawyer and the chamber of commerce's candidate.

The outcome of the election was on King's mind on the flight. Fred Shuttlesworth had told King that Boutwell "was just a dignified Connor." A man who may have spoken eloquently but as a state senator and then lieutenant governor remained a segregationist. Boutwell had authored a pivotal Alabama bill called the Pupil Placement Act, which, when it passed in 1956, meant the state did not have to abide by the U.S. Supreme Court's *Brown v. Board of Education* ruling. Shuttlesworth had tried to assuage King's worries about going ahead with Project X, telling him that if Boutwell won, "there isn't a whole lot of difference between Mr. Bull and Mr. Boutwell."

So on that flight to Birmingham, King and Abernathy discussed how they would proceed with Project X in the unlikely event that Bull lost the mayoral election.

Talking about the mayoral election was another way for King and Abernathy to talk about the SCLC's own preparedness. Wyatt Walker was on the ground, clipboard in hand, minutiae in his head, ready to bark orders. James Bevel had told King he would tolerate Walker's officiousness and abide by the plan Walker had proposed: the four-part escalation of conflict. The SCLC had bail money for mass arrests, thanks to Harry Belafonte's fundraiser. King himself had Abernathy, his closest friend, by his side for the campaign that would either define or break them. And both men knew they had the most courageous activist in the movement in Fred Shuttlesworth, the Birmingham pastor who had promised King he could corral all Black preachers and their congregants to support Project X. "Don't worry, Martin," Fred had told King in the preceding weeks. "I can handle the preachers."

The plane touched down in that strangest and most hostile of American cities.

King and Abernathy stepped into the airport's lobby, where they saw Fred Shuttlesworth but not the other reverend who was supposed to be there. "Where's Ware?" King asked Shuttlesworth.

Ware was J. L. Ware, one of the prominent Black pastors Fred had promised he could corral, who represented the city's Black establishment and was the de facto head of Birmingham's Black Baptist Ministers' Conference.

"He's holding a meeting at the Conference," Fred said, a little reluctantly. "The others"—meaning the large contingent of pastors aside from Ware who were also supposed to be here to greet Martin and Ralph—"are probably there, too."

King and Abernathy exchanged uneasy glances. This was not the plan. The plan was for a big show of bonhomie, a grand welcoming party at the airport. Could Ware's absence mean he and other local church leaders did not stand with the SCLC? The question bothered King so much that when they got into Fred's car for the ride to their motel, Martin told Fred to drive instead to the Ministers' Conference.

"If I can speak to the whole group today, maybe we can get them to pledge their support," Martin said. That would ease his mind: an assurance from Ware that he and the other pastors were in fact prepared to endorse King and Project X.

The meeting was at a Baptist church. Martin and Ralph entered and saw Ware presiding. When Ware saw them, he stopped speaking mid-sentence. All heads turned toward King and Abernathy. No one broke into applause. No one smiled. The room was suddenly colder than Boston in December. Martin asked reluctantly, deferentially, if he could speak. Ware in turn asked everyone if that was all right. A few ministers muttered *Okay*, so Ware ceded the floor but did not welcome King to the meeting.

Martin explained the need for the Black leaders of Birmingham to unite. Ralph Abernathy noticed how the pastors looking at King did not utter *Amen!* in agreement or even nod. They remained frosty. They remained noncommittal.

Why?

If this lasted, what would it mean for the protests?

Martin and Ralph left the church and got back into Fred's car. Without the dozens of other Black ministers and their thousands of congregants, the SCLC would be on an island in Birmingham, voyagers to a stranger and even more antagonistic land than they'd anticipated.

No one said a word on the way to the Gaston Motel.

The motel rose above the tree-lined Kelly Ingram Park on Fifth Avenue North, a cornerstone of Black Birmingham and its business and entertainment district. It was owned by A. G. Gaston, a World War I veteran and Black entrepreneur who'd opened a small funeral home and made an empire out of it. Gaston these days also owned an insurance company, a bank, and a technical college. He was well on his way to becoming the richest Black man in America and looked the part, too: overfed, gray-haired, in exquisite suits, and in every photo from the era carrying the satisfied smile of the self-made man. His motel was the only one in the city open to Blacks, which meant it catered to world-famous entertainers and dignitaries traveling through town. It was nearly as renowned as the performers themselves. The Gaston never slept—and wasn't fancy either. Just two stories, with an open-air courtyard where the doors to the rooms faced each other. Gaston gave King and Abernathy number 30, a suite above the lobby, with two beds and a separate sitting room with tables and chairs.

There had been talk, even plans, of Gaston giving the SCLC's leaders the suite for free. He didn't. He told King and Abernathy when they arrived that they'd pay full rate. The way he said it, without that satisfied smile—the implication was that King and Abernathy were like any other customers. The implication was that Gaston, like the local pastors, was not their friend.

What was going on? That was what King and Abernathy wondered in their rooms and what they debated, especially after Fred Shuttlesworth left. Had Fred overpromised whom he could deliver to the cause? Were Wyatt Walker's memos and checklists based on reality or aspiration? Forget white people: How many Black Birminghamians were opposed to the Birmingham campaign?

They would find out tomorrow, with the first planned sit-ins.

7

IT BEGINS

Unfortunately, the next morning, April 3, confronted them with something else they hadn't expected. Albert Boutwell won the mayoral election. He beat Bull Connor. The *Birmingham News* carried the shocking results. Of Birmingham's 340,000 people, some 51,200 ballots had been cast in the election, setting a new record for the city. Boutwell received 29,630 votes. Bull got 21,648. Nearly all of the 10,000 Black people registered to vote went for Boutwell. His victory was seen as a repudiation of Bull's hardened tactics—his men terrorizing Blacks and beating up Freedom Riders in 1961 while CBS's camera crews rolled—and also a reflection of how the manufacturing sector had rotted out due to the city's image. In recent years, Birmingham had lost 10 percent of its job force to other southern cities. Birminghamians, it seemed, could stomach the occasion when Bull's police force formed their own burglary ring or the time Bull allegedly placed five sticks of dynamite in the car of a political opponent, but those same voters could no longer stand the city's declining job prospects after twenty-five years of Connor's reign. In Boutwell's victory speech, the mayor-elect said, "We are on our way to better things." The *Birmingham News* was so taken by Boutwell's win, it paid extra for a color drawing on its front page: a golden sun rising over the city, under the headline "New Day Dawns for Birmingham."

The *News'* editors weren't alone in their belief that ridding Birmingham of Bull Connor would grant the city a new identity. When Bobby Kennedy read about the election results in Washington, he signed off on his civil rights chief, Burke Marshall, phoning the Gaston Motel, where the SCLC's leadership team had headquartered itself for the mass protests. Burke Marshall rang and rang the Gaston until he got Wyatt Walker on the line. Marshall said it was the wish of Attorney General Kennedy for Walker and King to delay the SCLC's protest in Birmingham. The civil rights leaders should give the mayor-elect and his new government a chance to succeed, Marshall said.

Walker thanked Marshall for the call and said he would "pass the message on to Dr. King."

When Walker found King, the two talked as if the election changed nothing. Boutwell was still a white Birminghamian. He was still the former state senator who'd authored that racist Pupil Placement Act. Bobby Kennedy or the *Birmingham News* could tout all day long how 10,000 Black voters had gone for Boutwell yesterday. But there were *135,000* Black people in Birmingham. That meant 125,000 of them had no voice in the city. If almost all of Birmingham's Black voters were for Boutwell, almost all of Birmingham's Black residents were not. That was how King saw it. Boutwell, King later wrote, "showed that he understood nothing about two-fifths of Birmingham's citizens." Nor did Boutwell care to learn.

King told Walker Project X was still on.

Walker nodded and breathed out. Privately, though, he wondered what the campaign would look like now. Wyatt Walker had composed Project X in January on the notion that Bull would be in office in April, that Bull would in fact always have power. Bull's power made him the necessary antagonist in Walker's four-act play here in Birmingham. Now, with Bull a lame duck at the end of his term as city commissioner, who would serve as the SCLC's enemy? Without Bull, who would demand that Birmingham unleash its violence upon the SCLC's protesters? Would the city even remain violent? Walker assumed so—his research over the past few months showed the residual strength of the Klan—but how many Black

Birminghamians had woken up this morning thrilled that Bull Connor was at last out of office? A happy state of mind did not make for agitated, dedicated mass protesters. Walker had spent so much time canvassing the city, gathering assurances from Black people that they would protest because they'd wanted a new day for Birmingham.

Now the *Birmingham News* said a new day had dawned.

Walker wondered how many Black people believed it.

Many, apparently. Walker had compiled a "jail list": all the Black Birminghamians who had told him they were prepared to protest and go to jail for Project X. He had 350 names on his jail list, but come the first day of the protests, only sixty-five showed to fulfill their pledge. Almost all appeared out of loyalty to Fred Shuttlesworth. They were deeply religious adults with ties to Fred's church or his local civil rights organization. What that meant for the days ahead Walker chose not to dwell upon. Not yet.

Instead he briefed the sixty-five "like an air commander before a bombing mission," as one writer later put it, with all of Walker's meticulous logistics chalked out on a blackboard behind him, as the assembled protesters listened to Walker in the basement of a movement-friendly church.

Walker had the sixty-five sync their wristwatches, and then they all met King and a bevy of national reporters with whom Walker had been currying favor at the 16th Street Baptist Church, a block from the Gaston Motel. Fred Shuttlesworth dispersed to the press something he called the Birmingham Manifesto: "This is Birmingham's moment of truth in which every citizen can play his part in her larger destiny." King then gave a benediction on nonviolence to the sixty-five. He intoned what they represented to Birmingham and to history. When he finished, the protesters moved out across the city.

Without any other fanfare, Project X was under way.

From 16th Street Baptist, the protesters walked to five downtown stores: Britling Cafeteria, Woolworth's, Loveman's, Pizitz, and Kress. The stores had segregated lunch counters, serving whites near the front, Blacks near the dingy back. The plan was for the sixty-five to sit in the white sections and request a meal. The protesters would not shout and demand service. They would not throw punches to get it. They would act as if all this were normal, and in their quiet composure the sixty-five would face whatever white Birmingham threw at them, perhaps literally.

While the sixty-five set out on their fifteen-to-twenty-minute walks to the various downtown stores, the store owners prepared themselves as well. Word had spread throughout the city of King's protest. When the Black activists in their Sunday best approached the entrances to four of the counters—Woolworth's, Loveman's, Pizitz, and Kress—the waitresses simply told the white customers they were closing for the day. The diners' cooks went home. The protesters had barely opened the doors and now those same doors were shut on all customers.

This had not been the plan for Project X, either. The protesters didn't know what to do.

Only at Britling's did the lunch counter remain open. Seven activists entered there, led by Rev. Abraham Woods Jr., a friend of Shuttlesworth's. Woods and the others sat in the whites-only section. The white waitresses refused to offer them a glass of water or a menu. Store managers appeared and asked that they leave. Woods and the rest politely stayed put. White customers then poured hot coffee on their heads and laps. The protesters stayed where they were. Then the Black people who'd attempted to sit-in at other counters sauntered into Britling's and sat amid their fellow activists. Now the store owners threatened to press charges. Still the Black people sat where they were.

At last the cops were called. By the early afternoon, thirteen people had been arrested.

When it was over that first day, twenty protesters had been thrown in the Birmingham Jail. They had remained nonviolent, courageous, dignified, and yet what bothered King back at the Gaston Motel was something more quantifiable.

Sixty-five protesters and twenty arrests? Those were terribly low figures. There had been around 265 people arrested on the first day the SCLC had joined the campaign in Albany.

And Albany had ended in complete failure.

8

WHO WILL RISE FROM THE PEWS?

The SCLC would get the best gauge of Black Birmingham's reluctance toward Project X at the mass meeting. Given how nothing had gone according to plan yesterday or today, it was impossible for King to guess what might happen at that first mass meeting the night of April 3. Black people could picket it, for all he knew. Or worse, and far more likely, they could stay home.

What a welcome sight then, late that afternoon, when King and Abernathy and other executives approached St. James Baptist Church, some eight blocks from the Gaston and the site of the mass meeting. People lined the sidewalks, both sides of 24th Street North, and cars jammed around the church, everyone hoping to get inside.

It filled quickly. Five hundred people jostled for seats in the auditorium or balcony, and when they couldn't find seats there, they stood. They sang hymns and freedom songs loud enough for Bull Connor to hear. One of the favorites was the call-and-response number "Ain't Gonna Let Nobody Turn Me Round."

It started with a single singer, calling out: *Ain't gonna lehhht noooobahdy . . .*

The chorus, in response: *TU-URN ME ROUUUND, TU-URN ME ROUUUND, TU-URN ME ROUND . . .*

Again the single singer, calling out: *Ain't gonna lehhht noooobahdy . . .*
And the chorus: *TU-URN ME ROUUUND . . .*

Finally all singers: *I'm gonna keep onnn a-walkin', eh . . . Keep onnn a-talkin', eh . . . Marchin' up to FREE-EH-DOM LAAAAND.*

They sang with a yearning that raised gooseflesh on the arms of the meeting's headliners waiting to take the pulpit. This was what King had hoped for. This was what Fred Shuttlesworth had expected. St. James had been one of the few Black churches that supported Shuttlesworth's activism in Birmingham, going back to the Christmas Day bombing in 1956. The man who quieted the music and opened the mass meeting, the meeting's master of ceremonies if you will, the Reverend Ed Gardner, had been part of the patrol over the years guarding Fred's parsonage and church. Gardner did it with his Winchester rifle. "My nonviolent Winchester," he'd said with a smirk to any white person who asked. Tonight, when the crowd settled, Gardner preached about how "freedom bells will ring in Birmingham as soon as we all get together and pull together."

The evening, like Project X itself, was building toward something grand. Fred Shuttlesworth spoke next. These were Fred's people. Many of the assembled were members of his local civil rights organization, the Alabama Christian Movement for Human Rights. The ACMHR never had more than a few thousand members, but if Project X was to succeed, Fred would need the support of his own, the fearless few, especially if Fred had overpromised in telling King he could deliver all 135,000 Black Birminghamians to Project X. To those in the pews, Shuttlesworth high-lighted his alliance with King. "Follow him to jail!" he said of King. "In the end he will lead us to freedom!"

Then King took the pulpit. He opened by saying he had known Fred for years; they had met in 1954, two pastors involved in the civil rights movement in a state that abhorred it. That was their initial bond, this shared struggle. It helped Fred and Martin to become "close," as Martin put it, and even though Martin had never lived in Birmingham, he was, thanks to Fred Shuttlesworth, no stranger to it. Being here tonight was like "coming home." And so "we are embarking on a mission to break down the barrier of segregation in Birmingham," King said. "Hard segregation is entrenched in Birmingham. We in Atlanta have come to the aid of Fred Shuttlesworth. He called on us and we were glad to come because of the injustice in Birmingham."

The crowd warmed to King, and so he turned it on, unleashed that distinct incantatory style of his: "If there is injustice in Birmingham, then New York City is not right. If there is injustice in Birmingham, then the world is not right. We are here because your problem is our problem.

"Some people have told us to wait," King said, without mentioning the call the SCLC had received that morning from Bobby Kennedy's office. "But we have waited too long. Now is the time to get rid of injustice. The time is always right to do right."

The applause, the shouts. This was the mythic King, and if there was any doubt how long his almost ethereal presence would remain in Birmingham—because there had been such doubt during the Albany campaign; even in this moment in Birmingham, Albany remained the ghost in King's life—then King was out to put Birminghamians' minds at ease with a story of his lovely wife, Coretta, and the baby girl he'd left back in Atlanta. "I told [Coretta] that I was coming to Birmingham and it might take three days and it might take three months, but however long it took that's how long we'd be gone."

He had them. He decided to affirm what they knew, to show how their struggle was his. "Birmingham is the last big city in the United States that is segregated. Birmingham has the worst record for police brutality in the United States." The only way to deter the violence was through action counter to it, he said. King spoke about the need for nonviolent direct action. "To present life, soul, and body to show people you are ready. If you create enough tension you attract attention to your cause. The direct action may mean sit-ins. . . . It may mean going to jail. . . . We are not out to defeat the white man but to save him. We are struggling to set 20 million Negroes free. In so doing we will set 80 million whites free. . . . When you create enough tension to cause attention to your cause then you get to the conscience of the white man."

This was the whole of Project X's ambition and, really, of King's, too. To demand equality through marches and sit-ins and economic boycotts, everything peaceful, nothing carried out with a closed fist or concealed gun. In King's vision of Birmingham, Black people would be the agents of change but the change itself would occur within white people. White people would initially fight against this change, very likely literally, very likely brutally, but if Blacks remained peaceful even as the blows fell, then their calmness would, with time, form a placid pool in which the white people could at last see, reflected back at them, their terrible actions. White people who had any conscience—and these could be the white people striking Blacks or the ones witnessing such violence, either on the streets of Birmingham or on the evening news with Walter Cronkite—would reconsider their own actions toward Blacks. They would see that the demands of Martin Luther King Jr. and the SCLC strove only toward one thing: Black people akin to white people. Once whites realized this, well, it was a short walk of conscience to King's ultimate aim: new laws, passed by Congress and signed by the president, that ensured Black people's civil rights and would at last treat them with the dignity that was theirs but had been denied them for 350 years in this country that called itself the land of the free.

"Suffering," King told the crowd, returning them to what would win them their victory, "has a way of getting to our opponent's conscience."

It was the night's signature line, in its way similar to Shuttlesworth's "You have to be prepared to die before you can begin to live" in New York. There was nothing rah-rah about it. "Suffering has a way of getting to our opponent's conscience" meant it would take time, and blood, to see change. Birminghamians knew this. Hell, they lived in Birmingham. By speaking so honestly, King refused to talk down to these men and women or make over-the-top promises. If anything, King signaled he was prepared to suffer alongside them.

As if to affirm that point, Ralph Abernathy rose now to headline the evening. His aim was simple: get people to join the protests he and King had helped to organize. "Alabama is my home," he said as his opener, to show his bona fides. Ralph had been raised on a five-hundred-acre farm in Marengo County, some 120 miles south of Birmingham, raised with a self-sufficiency that informed the Abernathys' every action. They butchered forty hogs a year, grew all the vegetables their family of fourteen could eat, wore clothes sewn from the cotton grown in their fields. Ralph grew up during the Great Depression, but it never reached the acreage; he was barely aware of it as a kid. It was very much God's country there in Marengo County, a haven from the world, and the sense that Ralph could sustain in life what God provided on the farm was what led him next to the ministry and ultimately to the cause of civil rights. The dignity Ralph felt, he wanted for all of Black America—for all of America. This was why he had joined Martin Luther King a decade ago. This was why he was in Birmingham now. "The eyes of the world are on Birmingham tonight," Ralph told the assembled in the pews. "Bobby Kennedy is looking here at Birmingham. The United States Congress is looking at Birmingham." Who sitting here would at last look within themselves? Ralph asked. Who would join King and Abernathy? Who would join the movement? Who was ready to march, to suffer? "If you are afraid then don't come with us," Abernathy said.

One by one they rose and walked down the aisles of St. James, old and young, male and female, looking to the pews to their left and right for other people to join them. Others rose and trickled toward the committed, who stood alongside Abernathy near the pulpit. In waves, still more came, and when at last those waves receded, perhaps eighty people looked at one another near the front of the church.

Abernathy stared at the four hundred who remained almost shoulder to shoulder in the pews and would not stand, no matter how much he cajoled them. He worked some quick math. If you took the eighty who had come forward and added them to the sixty-five who had volunteered that morning to march, the Birmingham campaign had begun with 120 fewer protesters than Albany, and thousands fewer than what he and Martin had assembled in the halcyon days of Montgomery's bus boycotts.

Here in Birmingham, the largest civil rights campaign of their lives, Ralph and Martin were beginning with the smallest number of volunteers they'd ever assembled. At the pulpit, Ralph did his best not to sneer at the four hundred who sat. Mostly he did his best to mask his rising panic. How could he and Martin and the SCLC win if almost no one joined them?

He would keep that question to himself until he got back to the Gaston and could talk honestly with Martin.

"Not encouraging," Ralph later wrote.

9

EXPLANATIONS AND ACCUSATIONS

Weeping may endure for a night but joy cometh in the morning," the Good Book said. Wyatt Walker knew the Psalms just as well as he knew Paul's letter to the Philippians: "I can do all things through Christ who strengthens me." Even more than the Bible, Wyatt Walker knew himself, trusted himself. He told himself he would not worry. He repeated it almost as a mantra as he stalked the halls of the Gaston Motel Thursday morning, April 4. He had made a grand show when he'd come to Birmingham, the executive director of King's SCLC with that four-stage plan of escalation. He had cultivated the press. It was all in the approach. It was "the tone of the voice or hang of the head . . . or sharpness of the tongue," Walker later said. He'd told the press he'd come to Birmingham to "ride the Bull." The press liked that line. They liked a man who had Walker's confidence.

King did, too.

So Walker must continue to project it now, in the Gaston, he thought. The confident man can will anything into existence if he acts like everything is under control. This thinking, informed as much by "I can do all things through Christ who strengthens me" as by Wyatt Walker's faith in himself, also did the important work of masking how Walker truly felt in Birmingham. Deep down, he wanted no part of this city. He might have announced he planned to ride the Bull, but hours before that, "when I kissed my wife and children goodbye down on Carol Road in Atlanta," Walker later admitted, "I didn't think I would ever see them again. I didn't see how I . . . could get out of Birmingham alive." So what he told himself now, on this second morning of the campaign, was that if he could push down his fear of death and joke with the press about Bull, he could proceed with Project X after what was, surely, only its opening-day missteps.

When the second day's protesters headed to the lunch counters that Walker had ordered them to target, those counters once again closed for the day. Britling's even posted three bouncers out front.

Walker then had four teenagers attempt to sit in at a drugstore. When the manager refused to press charges, the kids just left. Desperate, Walker turned to a lunch counter at another pharmacy he'd researched, the Lane-Liggett drugstore downtown. There, the activists got in. There, Birmingham cops arrested four protesters.

Four.

Wyatt Walker had said Project X would fill the jails (plural). The campaign instead could not fill a jail cell (singular).

That night at the mass meeting, King and Abernathy spoke again, but as Walker watched from the corner of the church—tall and gaunt, with the eyes behind those big black-rimmed glasses of his reading the room and its every nuance of body language—he saw a lot of fear. He saw, ultimately, even fewer people walk forward to volunteer: Just fifty. Day two and they were already at the point of diminishing returns?

The press began to excoriate the SCLC. The *New York Times*, hinting at how much Walker had guaranteed the paper by way of protests and bloodshed, wrote that the campaign featured "much less than the 'full-scale assault' that had been promised." The "mass demonstrations" had "failed to materialize." The city was "quiet."

It got worse for Walker. The *Birmingham World*, the city's Black-owned newspaper, opposed the interventionists from Atlanta meddling in the city's affairs and said, "This direct action seems to be both wasteful and worthless." Even more humiliating, A. G. Gaston himself "argued against the demonstrations," as one writer put it. This placed Walker's boss, Martin Luther King Jr., in the very awkward position during that day's press conference at the Gaston Motel of explaining why the SCLC was so intent on defying the wishes of its literal host. After all, what A. G. Gaston wanted—to call off the protests and negotiate calmly, in the months ahead, with Mayor-Elect Boutwell and his new government, a mayor *whom Black voters had elected*—Gaston's wish was also Bobby Kennedy's, and the *Birmingham World*'s, and that of the city's only bi-racial committee, the Alabama Council on Human Relations. Every Bir-minghamian wanted to slow down and give the city a chance to resolve its differences on its own, without the help of King and his acolytes from Atlanta.

Wyatt Walker was a man who knew optics—it was why he always ap-peared so self-assured—and he knew this was a terrible one. King sitting at that press conference in the Gaston, A. G. Gaston and the whole of Birmingham against him, and King answering questions from a frustrated press, not about *what* King planned to do but *why* he was doing it. "We feel Birmingham will never desegregate Birmingham voluntarily," King said in response to questions from reporters at *Life* and the *New York Times* and NBC News, among other national outlets. Boutwell's victory "does not appear to materially affect the life of the Negro." Out of view of the clustered microphones, Wyatt Walker knew King sounded pomp-ous and condescending—*De Lawd comes to Birmingham*—an appearance that contradicted everything the SCLC actually believed.

Explanations became the lingua franca that week. They were all the SCLC wanted and would discuss. Explanations of failure, however, have a tendency to turn into accusations of who failed whom. To many, Fred Shuttlesworth was to blame. The (very few) Black pastors who agreed to join King and Project X whispered to Martin how Shuttlesworth had always been a "dic-tator" in Birmingham. He'd told even the Black pastors friendly to him that Birmingham's push for civil rights was a "one-man show. . . . 'This is my movement,'" Fred had said. "'You get in line or you get out.'" In his way, Shuttlesworth was as bad as his enemy, Bull Connor: "headstrong and wild for publicity, almost to the point of neurosis," one observer put it, "willing to do almost anything to keep [the] spotlight on himself."

Fred countered that *of course* the spotlight was on him. He was the only one willing to lead the fight for civil rights in Birmingham.

In the summer of 1957, he'd said he was going to integrate Phillips High School. Was just going to walk right in and enroll his oldest daughters, Pat and Ricky. The weekend before enrollment opened, six members of the Klan ambushed a Black man named Edward Aaron on a road outside the city. Pistol-whipped him. Took him to their "lair." Took down his pants and took out a razor. The Klan told Aaron they had a message for Shuttlesworth: "Stop sending nigger children and white children to school together." Then they cut off Aaron's balls. Castrated him right there. Poured turpentine on the wound, which cauterized it, and then told Aaron to go tell Shuttlesworth.

Aaron survived, somehow, and word of what happened reached Fred. Fred responded much as he had after the Christmas Day bombing. He would not be intimidated. He said he would integrate the school *and* he would bring Pat and Ricky along with him. Fred told his girls the Shuttlesworth family set the example for the rest of Birmingham.

That was leadership, Fred argued years later. *Your own actions* showed how others should act.

Which led to Fred's other point: There wasn't anybody who had wanted to come to Phillips with the Shuttlesworth family in 1957. Pat's and Ricky's boyfriends didn't want to. No "leader" from the Birmingham civil rights movement did, either. Fred got one friend of his, Rev. J. S. Phifer, to chauffeur the Shuttlesworths—Fred; his wife, Ruby; and their daughters—to the school that day. When they arrived, they saw camera crews and four cop cars waiting for them. Suddenly, a mob of eight to ten white men with bats and chains and brass knuckles descended on the car even before it could stop. They rocked it. Attempted to upend it. Shouted, "Niggers go home!"

Ricky Shuttlesworth wondered, *And now we're supposed to go into the school?* But that's exactly what her dad did. Fred got out of the car.

The mob tackled him. "This is the son of a bitch," they shouted as the blows fell on Fred. "Kill the motherfuckin' nigger!" "Kill him, god-dammit!"

They tried. Fred drifted in and out of consciousness. He heard a cop halfheartedly say, "Now you ought not to bother him." As Fred under-stood it, Ruby came to his aid and tried to break up the mob. She got stabbed in the lower back. Eventually Fred heard the cops push aside the mob, and he heard something else, too. The voice from the Christmas Day bombing. "You can't die here," it said. "I've got a job for you to do."

And so God did. Most of Fred's skin had been scarred off his face in the melee, but he checked himself and Ruby out of the hospital that afternoon. After all, the enrollment period at the school had fallen on a Monday, and Monday meant Mass Monday for the Shuttlesworths' civil rights group.

Fred led the meeting that night.

Leadership. Bravery. No one in town but Fred had it. "No other man would dare to take Fred's place," his own bodyguard, Colonel Stone Johnson, later said.

The spotlight was on Fred because no one else would step into it, Fred said now, at the start of the Birmingham campaign.

Today, we don't know the order of the discord—who accused whom and how the accused in turn responded—because Wyatt Walker, for all his meticulous note-keeping as executive director of the SCLC, did not chronicle the fallout of the first week in Birmingham in meeting minutes. There are broad outlines of the frustration and anger of that first week, and personal remembrances and interviews from much later, but the absence of detailed notes is striking. In fact, the absence sketches its own picture. Wyatt Walker had to have been somewhat ashamed that week of the accu-sations he and his colleagues leveled at each other.

Because another way to see Fred Shuttlesworth's bravery was that of a man who relied on bluster instead of a blueprint to lead his flock. What had been gained, to use Fred's example, from his integration attempt at Phillips High? Was Phillips integrated in 1963? Of course not. Phillips remained as segregated as the lunch counters downtown. All Fred had really done was alienate the people closest to him. Take his lawyer, Oscar Adams, who worked with Fred on civil rights suits. Adams had told him the weekend before Fred drove to the high school, "Fred, there ain't any point in going down to Phillips. You won't do nothin' but get in trouble." Adams had argued they should instead stay the course with lawsuits they'd filed demanding that Phillips and other local schools integrate. Fred didn't care about the suits. "*I* might get it desegregated," he told Adams, which Adams saw as not only boneheaded but also a rebuke of Adams's own work as the ACMHR's lawyer.

Or take the Shuttlesworth children. He alienated them, too. Pat and Ricky didn't have a choice whether or not to go to Phillips. "Fred essentially announced to the girls that they were going," one writer later put it. Fred's home was no place to argue with him. He could be ruthless with his kids, a "life and death" environment, as Fred Shuttlesworth Jr. later explained. "You might seriously consider whether or not you were going to make it through the next confrontation you had with Dad's belt." To the public, Fred's actions may have been comparable to those of Superman, as Fred Jr. said, and even Junior sometimes saw his dad as a comic book hero, but Fred Sr.'s rule at home was so absolute, so scary, "the family would just quit talking when he came home," Fred Jr. said.

Or take Ruby Shuttlesworth. Fred's actions were brutal on her. She and Fred had married because of their shared passion for civil rights, but she had gone to Phillips High for another reason: to protect their daughters. She never, not fully, got over how Fred was willing to risk his life *and* his children's for the movement. She relocated the family to Cincinnati in 1961. ("I am sure that is the reason we're alive today," Fred Jr. said.) Ruby and Fred later divorced.

Fred's actions with his loved ones fit a broader pattern with his friends and associates. He alienated them, too. That's why, for all of Fred's national and international headlines through the 1950s and '60s, his local civil rights group, the ACMHR, never had more than a few thousand members and often no more than a few hundred. He behaved stridently, insufferably, dangerously. Friends of the Shuttlesworths would tell Fred Jr., "Your old man ought to leave these white folks alone before he get hisself and all of us killed."

And now, in the spring of 1963, for the SCLC to align with that man? To see Fred Shuttlesworth as the gateway, even, to Birmingham's Black Christendom and to Project X's success? It cast doubt not only on Fred Shuttlesworth's promises during the planning of the campaign here but on Wyatt Walker's, too.

Walker should have known. With all those planning memos timed down to the second, Wyatt should have known Fred Shuttlesworth was toxic. Hell, a few days into the campaign it wasn't hard to recognize that Fred had a difficult relationship, at best, with A. G. Gaston; with Emory Jackson, the editor of the *Birmingham World*; with J. L. Ware and his Black Ministers Conference, which still hadn't offered its support to Project X because Fred had basically, and over a span of years, called the group Uncle Toms. How could Walker have missed all this?

Walker bristled at the idea that he had missed anything. He knew what Fred was like. They all did. They all saw those national and international headlines with Fred's name in them, stories that described Fred's courage and push for freedom. Those pieces, every one of them, had carried a single message: Fred pleading for support from other Black people. The SCLC had at last answered that call. King himself had said "we owe it to Fred" to come to Birmingham.

Walker argued they should stand by Fred when Birmingham wouldn't. If Fred alienated so many Birminghamians, it was because, as Walker later said, "[Fred] made Black people ashamed of themselves . . . talking about Uncle Toms. I don't blame him, because that is what they were." Walker admired Fred because of his actions and words and argued that the rest of the SCLC should, too. What was the alternative? To go along with the accommodationists, who would integrate at the pace white Birmingham set? To believe that the eloquent Albert Boutwell would be a good mayor and not just a dignified racist? Fred "made Black people uncomfortable," Walker said, and discomfort was the point of this campaign. Walker had grown up in Merchantville, New Jersey, with a portrait of Frederick Douglass on the wall. What Douglass wrote still resonated with him: "It is not light that is needed, but fire; it is not the gentle shower, but thunder. We need the storm, the whirlwind, and the earthquake." Damn right. Fred was not the problem. Black Birmingham was the problem. Segregation was the problem. As Walker put it: "See, it was the uncomfortableness that the presence of a Fred Shuttlesworth created. You have to understand how segregation is like a stain and it's on everybody, and Fred represented the person who had the task of going around trying to wash the stain off."

They would succeed, Walker argued, when Black Birmingham started scrubbing, too.

They *would* succeed then, they most certainly would, James Bevel said. Bevel had been Wyatt Walker's nemesis for more than a year now. The youngest member of the SCLC's executive team, Bevel still wore a yarmulke on his shaved head because the Torah's prophets still summoned his own strength. Still appeared in his attire (the country bibs) and in his speech ("Thus saith the Lord") as idiosyncratic as ever. Above all, Bevel still disliked Wyatt Walker. The SCLC would most certainly succeed when Black Birminghamians started scrubbing, Bevel said. How many were scrubbing now? Twenty protesters arrested the first day, four the second, ten the third. And Wyatt Walker's solution to increase the number of volunteers was to—what?—*shame* them into the movement?

King had talked at the Dorchester conference of the need to work *with* their fellow Black brethren. In that "with" was a worldview, King had said. Where was the *with* in browbeating? When would Wyatt Walker learn that clipboards and multipoint action memos don't inspire people? When would King learn, for that matter, that to be truly *with* the community here you had to march alongside them? King hadn't done it yet.

If the SCLC couldn't learn to be *with* Black Birminghamians, James Bevel said, well, he couldn't be with the SCLC.

Bevel left Birmingham that first week, amid all these heated debates about what was going wrong. The man whose job it was to organize Birmingham's demonstrations just left and drove back to his native Mississippi.

The intimation was that Bevel would come back to Birmingham when King lived up to his rhetoric.

They were fracturing. They had done this a year ago in the Albany campaign, too, when the city government there wouldn't negotiate with King and Albany's police chief, Laurie Pritchett, was clever enough—had read enough Gandhi—to arrest King and every other protester with kindness, and then release them from their cells quickly, so that the SCLC could never reach its goal of "filling the jail." The SCLC had bickered in Albany among themselves, had broken privately as much as they had publicly with other civil rights groups.

The SCLC had decided to do two things in the wake of Albany. First, they would no longer pressure southern governments to change. Southern governments were hard to alter, so the SCLC would instead apply pressure to the South's economic institutions. That's why they were targeting the lunch counters in Birmingham. That's why they were asking Black Birminghamians to not shop at white-owned stores during this Easter season of 1963: If the SCLC could harm Birmingham financially, the city might be compelled to respond morally to its Black citizens' demands.

The SCLC convinced itself that pressuring the city's economic institutions could break segregation in Birmingham. But it would break only if the SCLC united. That was the second major lesson from Albany. "We must have unity," King kept saying in the wake of that campaign and throughout the planning of Project X. They had planned Birmingham as fervently as they had prayed over how they would remain together.

And now here was James Bevel, leaving town.

And now here was the whole of the SCLC, come Saturday, April 6, on the fourth day of the protests, debating whether they should leave aside their economic boycott and target Birmingham's government.

It was Albany all over again.

The city's lunch counters still closed themselves off to all Black customers, Fred Shuttlesworth argued. The SCLC needed a "broader scope of activities than lunch counters," he said. Fred had long wanted to protest everywhere: at the parks, on the buses, and especially at City Hall. Now he repeated the demand he'd made in the planning sessions. They should protest in prayer at the seat of Birmingham's government.

Wyatt Walker must have winced here, too, but there is no account of how Walker felt about Fred Shuttlesworth, his friend and like-minded activist, saying that Wyatt's blueprint for Project X should be abandoned.

We are left only with external actions—what the SCLC did that Saturday, April 6, in Birmingham, Alabama.

The SCLC officially discarded Walker's blueprint.

They marched toward Birmingham's Federal Building.

10

OPTICS, OPTICS, OPTICS

Fred Shuttlesworth led the way, without Wyatt Walker but with a local activist pastor, Charles Billups. Some thirty protesters walked in pairs behind Shuttlesworth and Billups down Fifth Avenue and toward the Federal Building in the noonday sun. They passed uniformed officers who scowled at them. They arrived at the seat of power to see a bored Bull Connor already waiting for them, flanked on the steps of his kingdom by a barricade of police officers and Police Chief Jamie Moore. Any protester needed a permit to picket in Birmingham. Bull had denied Fred his earlier in the week. (Connor still presided as a city commissioner and would do so for nine more days, until Mayor Boutwell's government took office.) Bull turned to Chief Moore. "Let's get this over with . . . I'm hungry."

Moore put a megaphone to his lips. "You are parading without a permit."

"We are taking an orderly walk," Shuttlesworth shouted back.

Moore had the phalanx of cops move in to arrest the protesters. Shuttlesworth and his crowd dropped to their knees and began to pray. Cops cuffed everyone as the protesters sang "The Lord Will Help Us" and "We Shall Overcome."

When the paddy wagons came, they hauled twenty-nine protesters to jail, Shuttlesworth included. When word reached Wyatt Walker back at the Gaston, he knew the SCLC's money for bail bonds would free Fred. The money almost highlighted the problem. They had more bail bond cash than they had protesters needing to be sprung from jail. The meager show of civil disobedience today, like the days preceding it—the optics in Birmingham had not improved. Walker knew they'd only gotten worse. This campaign had the makings of a more humiliating defeat than Albany. "Promised mass demonstrations have not been held," the *Times* wrote Saturday. If this continued, Walker knew, there would be no more SCLC. There might not even be a civil rights movement.

"Wyatt," King said to Walker Saturday night, King's voice straining, pleading. Mr. Leader wanted to talk optics, too. The SCLC needed the mass demonstrations Walker had promised, and bloody ones at that. It was through such optics that they might reach their larger goals. "You have got to find a way," King told Walker, "to create a crisis, to make Bull Connor tip his hand."

The way he looked at Walker, the implication was clear: *You've got to do this right now.*

"Mr. Leader," Walker said with an air of confidence, because especially in this moment of desperation he needed to project it, "I haven't found the key yet, but I'm going to find it."

King studied him, then nodded. He looked weary. Every choice the SCLC had made in Birmingham, he said, had only led to harder choices and worse options. King understood he should lead a protest, as James Bevel wanted, and tomorrow was Palm Sunday, a day rich with images of people walking for their beliefs. But King would not lead the masses. If he marched tomorrow and only a couple of dozen people followed him, as they had Shuttlesworth today, it would prove the press's suspicion that the SCLC had no support here. That the SCLC was done. Martin and Ralph Abernathy agreed that the problems of Birmingham "were the work of the Devil," and the movement could not have such an evil narrative overwhelm the good Project X would carry out.

For the movement's sake, King could not march.

Wyatt Walker studied King.

Mr. Leader's unspoken message to Walker echoed through the night.

Even Martin Luther King was distancing himself from the terrible optics of Birmingham.

11

"I'VE GOT IT!"

Although King would not lead the march Palm Sunday, he decided to have his little brother go in his place. This was not an appealing proposition for Wyatt Walker.

Alfred Daniel King, known as A.D., was the kid brother in every sense. Rougher than Martin, angrier than Martin—A.D. suffered, in fact, from the constant comparison to Martin. He'd abandoned Martin's alma mater, Morehouse, and also the ministry to which Martin had been called, to sell insurance and start a family while still a teenager with his young wife, Naomi. Eventually M. L. King Sr. coaxed A.D. to return to Morehouse and then the church, with A.D. helping the senior King with services at Ebenezer Baptist. Some said A.D. was little more than a janitor there. But King Sr.'s pull within the Black Baptist world—Ebenezer was among the most powerful churches in the South—helped his son A.D. land positions as head pastor. By 1963, A.D. led his own flock at First Baptist Church in the Ensley neighborhood of west Birmingham. Stories of how much he drank became better-known than his sermons. What caused A.D.'s alcoholism seemed to be the sense of self he lacked, living in his brother's shadow and with his father's temper. Still, A.D. welcomed a role in Martin's movement. He staged sit-ins with Martin, got arrested with Martin. By 1963, A.D. worked for Martin. A "detail man," his

SCLC job description went. A charitable title, Wyatt Walker snickered to himself, because if A.D. truly were so detail-oriented, Martin would have called on his brother as Project X's Birmingham liaison. Instead Martin called on Fred Shuttlesworth to colead the campaign here. Fred Shuttlesworth was Martin's and Wyatt's and every other Atlantan's guide to all things Birmingham. Even in the city where he pastored, A.D. remained in the dark corners of Martin's shadow.

Today, though, it was Wyatt Walker's job to push A.D. into the light. Into the light and onto the street and against the bright backdrop of Palm Sunday, where the metaphor of a leader and his followers would be unavoidable for the waiting press. To place the lesser King as the SCLC's Palm Sunday messiah put even more pressure on Walker. If today's march failed as every other day's had, there would be a new round of public ridicule and serious questions about how much longer Project X could go on. Walker saw it already in the media. The *New York Times* wrote how the campaign "might be temporarily abandoned." It was true enough, and Walker took what comfort he could from the more embarrassing facts he could still keep from the papers. The SCLC had so few volunteers that it sent the same people to prison day after day but dressed them in different clothes, so they might appear as different people and Project X's supporters might seem more numerous than they were. Couple that secret with the publicly available facts—last night's mass meeting had attracted just two hundred people, the smallest crowd yet—and a desperate energy coursed through Wyatt Walker that Palm Sunday morning. Today might be his last chance to salvage Project X.

Walker recognized something else, too. Bull Connor *had* responded to yesterday's march. He'd stood on the steps of the Federal Building, the first time Bull himself had appeared to oppose Project X since its debut. This intrigued Walker. "Bull Connor had something in his mind," Walker later said, "about not letting niggers [through]."

Walker could exploit that. He decided the Palm Sunday protesters should march to another government building. Sure, the move went against Walker's own blueprint for Birmingham, but Walker's intelligence lay in part in his dexterity. He'd learned to adapt to life's humiliations—so poor as a kid he'd used cardboard to cover the gaping holes in the bottom of his shoes—which meant he was never quite the arrogant asshole James Bevel portrayed him as here in Birmingham. In fact, if Walker were to tell his life story (a proposition that *did* appeal to him), he would say his was a narrative of adaptation: surviving the sort of childhood poverty that killed five of his siblings, turning from his bachelor's degrees in physics and chemistry to answer God's call in the ministry, and then answering Martin Luther King's call to leave his pastorship in Virginia and helm the SCLC as its executive director.

Wyatt Walker shifted to the circumstances around him and found a way to thrive. He could thrive here in Birmingham.

He could find a way to incite Bull Connor.

How to anger the Bull? And how to anger him while utilizing the lesser King? These were Walker's questions that Sunday morning. Walker worked toward his answer by returning to everything he'd learned in the last few months about Bull Connor. Walker knew Connor was a control freak. Governing had always been the means for Connor to centralize power. From his perch as city commissioner, Bull Connor oversaw many agencies, but foremost among them was the police department. He effectively *was* its chief. The chief of police himself "had absolutely no power," one twenty-five-year veteran of the force later said. Bull put a new man in the job often, and then ran that man out, so that no police chief could ever assume the potency of his station. To then tighten his control over the department, Bull had a more permanent collection of cronies beneath the chief whom Bull called "my niggers." These were white sergeants and detectives loyal to Bull, a loyalty born as often as not from the kickbacks Bull gave them. One cop later said 45 percent of the police department was receiving some sort of under-the-table cash. Bull intentionally set an officer's base pay low, and when one cop, James Parsons, complained to

Bull that he was trying to do his job on his base pay alone, Bull laughed and said, "Well, that's your problem."

Bull fashioned the police force in his own image—white, corrupt, and racist—which was another way on this Sunday morning for Wyatt Walker to consider Bull's vanity. A high school dropout who thought himself cultured, Bull banned "unwholesome" films from Birmingham cinemas and yanked over fifty comic books from newsstand racks. The press hated the one-man censorship—were the "thought police next?" the *Birmingham Post-Herald* wrote—but Bull kept winning elections because he cared about his voters more than his kin, Bull's wife later said. The voters gave Bull the power and constant affirmation a vain man needs. Bull in turn gave the voters spectacles. He patrolled the streets of Birmingham not in a police cruiser but in an armored riot car, which Bull referred to as his "tank," and which he painted white so it would further announce itself on the streets. He said any sort of incendiary thing he could, at any time of day, and to anyone who would take it down. He governed cruelly. Take the food-sharing incident from a year prior. Black Miles College students had organized boycotts of white-owned department stores downtown. In response Bull withdrew all of the city's funding for a low-income food-sharing program that fed some twenty thousand Birminghamians, 95 percent of them Black. "A boycott can work both ways," Bull said. It was merciless. Most of all it was spectacle.

Spectacle was what Bull had always known. Walker knew that before Bull's political career, he had done the play-by-play for the Birmingham Barons minor-league baseball games. He called them in a gruff and somewhat contrived voice that earned him statewide adulation and the nickname "Bull." In other words, radio had been Bull's first foray into making a spectacle of himself. He'd been doing it ever since.

So the way to incite Bull, Walker realized, was to create a spectacle around him. If this spectacle threatened Bull's power and image, Bull would try his best to snuff it out. Bull's actions would create a new spectacle, which the press could capture.

Walker thought the best way to goad Bull was to march to City Hall.

Yes, Walker would up the ante from yesterday's march to the Federal Building. Everything must escalate, after all. At the mass meeting last night the suggestion had arisen that they might go to City Hall, and Bull had his usual crony detectives in the crowd, transcribing every word. But to ensure Bull knew Walker's intent on Palm Sunday itself, Wyatt issued press releases announcing that afternoon's march to City Hall. That way Bull would be unavoidably aware the SCLC was coming for him.

The protesters congregated in St. Paul Methodist Church on Sixth Avenue North that Palm Sunday afternoon. Walker needed a mass of protesters, which would look to Bull like the spectacle that threatened his power. "We were supposed to march at something like 2:30," Walker later said. But two thirty came and Wyatt didn't have a mass of people. He had twenty. So he waited. He hoped more protesters would come in off the streets. Two thirty became three, and inside St. Paul only twenty-two people stood ready to march. Walker put off the start again. Three became three thirty and Walker peeked out the window. Hundreds of Black people lined Sixth Avenue North, ready to watch. Word had spread about where the protesters were heading and many thought as Walker did: There might be violence. The hundreds outside wanted to gawk at it.

They did not want to join it though. This exasperated Walker.

At four o'clock, with maybe thousands lining the streets as witnesses but only the twenty-two inside St. Paul's, Walker knew he couldn't put off the march. Since the sheer number of protesters couldn't create a spectacle, and since A. D. King himself couldn't create it, perhaps Walker's delayed start had developed the sort of tension that might lead to a spectacle. Walker didn't have answers. He knew he could only adapt to Bull's actions.

Walker gave the signal.

A. D. King, in his black ministerial robes, opened the doors of the church and led the twenty-two protesters down Sixth Avenue North. They sang "Hold My Hand While I Run This Race." The thousands of spectators on the sidewalks let the protesters pass and then bunched behind them. They started walking themselves, the better to see how bad the twenty-two would get it. Walker moved among these thousands, watching, neck craning, alert.

The procession of twenty-two walked two blocks, to 17th Street North and the corner of Kelly Ingram Park, where they encountered scowling cops and the man of the hour, Bull Connor. Bull halted A. D. King and the twenty-two. A crony of Bull's reminded A.D. that his people were picketing without a permit. No way in hell could they move beyond this point to City Hall, three blocks away. In response A.D. and the twenty-two dropped to their knees and began to pray. Bull, eyes rolling, gave the signal, and his officers moved in to arrest the faithful few.

Now the crowd grew restless. *They're just gonna cuff 'em?* This was not the bloody show the crowd had spent two hours waiting for. Wyatt Walker heard shouts of "Fight 'em!" and "Do something!" from the onlookers around him, people who wanted the protesters to engage in a violence they'd been trained to forswear. A.D. and the twenty-two continued to pray as cops handcuffed them. When the paddy wagons arrived, the scattered cries turned into angry shouts. *Do something! Fight back!* The scowling white Birmingham cops took this anger as Black onlookers mouthing off. Disrespecting white authority. And in Birmingham, Alabama.

The cops turned on the crowd. Swung their billy clubs at them, corralled them, cuffed them. Shouts, slurs, shoving, punching—*like that* it escalated into a scene.

Wyatt Walker's face lit up in that sea of onlookers.

Bull Connor saw these Black Birminghamians wresting control of the afternoon from him, and, much as Walker predicted, Bull did not abide that. He unleashed the K-9 corps on the crowd, six snarling German shepherds. Hysterical shouting now. Chaos. Hundreds of people running in all directions.

And some staying put. Some wrestling with the dogs. One eighteen-year-old spectator, LeRoy Allen, pulled a large knife on the German shepherd that tried to bite him. Nearby cops saw the flash of the blade and rushed Allen, tackling and kicking him. Elsewhere, other dogs bit other Black people, and Bull Connor shouted over the din, "Look at them dogs go!" More Black people fought with German shepherds or cops or both. At least one other Black man pulled a knife on a dog. "I don't know whether I cut him," he later said, "but I hope I did." And still the hysterical shouting, the running, the chaos. Still the billy clubs raised high in the air smashing down on someone new, someone else, someone Black. This was mayhem. A descent into violent spectacle.

In the crowd, Wyatt Walker beamed.

Little had gone as expected, least of all the way the gawking crowd had incited Bull Connor, but as Wyatt Walker took stock of the afternoon, he realized one thing had gone as planned. The press had witnessed everything. *Life* and the *New York Times* and the camera crews from the television networks—they'd been there on Sixth Avenue North. Now, hours later, they wanted a comment from Martin Luther King Jr. and the SCLC. Walker arranged for a press conference at the Gaston Motel. There, something else unforeseen occurred.

The press assumed the gawking spectators were part of the SCLC's march. Walker could hear it in the questions the members of the media asked. These white northern reporters—thinking themselves liberal or at least enlightened—couldn't distinguish protester from peanut gallery. To them all Black people were the same.

Walker did not correct the reporters. He saw right away how their mistake might help the movement. The press might grossly enlarge the protester count. When those stories aired that night and appeared in the first editions of the next day's papers, Walker was right: the northern media had reported that the Palm Sunday march numbered in the thousands.

Wyatt Walker thought about how he could exploit this. If racist Birmingham cops *and* northern white reporters saw all Black people as the same, that meant they assumed all Black people acted the same, too. And *that* meant Wyatt Walker could manufacture a spectacle in Birmingham whenever he wanted. All he had to do was follow Sunday's blueprint: Make sure a protest started hours late, so a mass of spectators could grow in number and grow restless as they waited. When the church doors at last opened and the protest began, the onlookers would trail close behind the few actual protesters, as they had on Sunday. No white person would be able to tell the difference. Certainly not Bull Connor, who would see what he had always seen: masses of Blacks who threatened Bull's very identity.

Walker phoned King.

"I've got it!"

The terrible optics of Birmingham could be solved, Walker said, by an optical illusion.

King loved it.

Walker's Palm Sunday revelation—his shouts of "We've got a movement" after the press had left the Gaston—were so central to his understanding of Birmingham that he renamed the campaign.

Project X became Project C. The C stood for "confrontation," because confronting white people through the spectacles of Walker's creation would lead to the change the whole of the SCLC sought.

But another way to view Project C was as a double entendre.

Wyatt Walker could see everything now. He could see what Bull Connor could not: how Bull's hatred could be used against him. He could see what the "good" white people could not: their own subtle racism. Project C would escalate in its tension and violence until Wyatt Walker took the blinders off those good white people. Then they would see for themselves the humanity of every Black person protesting and suffering before them.

At that point, at last, everyone would see real change in America.

Part III

THE GOOD FRIDAY TEST

12

"... THE RIGHTEOUS ARE BOLD AS A LION"

Here was the truth: Almost everyone thought Martin Luther King Jr.'s pacifism equaled timidity. But they didn't understand pacifism. Or King. Because King had never been timid. King had always been bold. And that boldness stemmed from the rage he felt. This surprised even his parents, who saw Martin, then as now, as an intelligent and introspective son, one who loved church and Grandma Williams. They could not comprehend their middle child's occasional turns to vengeance. One summer day when they were boys, A.D. and Martin were playing in the house, which mostly amounted to A.D. teasing the boys' older sister, Christine. A.D. wouldn't quit. When Martin saw tears well in Christine's eyes, he decided he'd had enough. Martin grabbed a nearby telephone and conked A.D. over the head with it.

A.D. yelped so loud it brought his parents, Martin Sr. and Alberta, into the house. Martin Jr. had struck a blow for justice, and for striking it they laughed at Martin. "The great little negotiator," King Sr. said, as if wrath were a response Martin's precocity didn't allow. It was humiliating, emasculating in its way, but instructive, too.

With time Martin learned to turn people's beliefs about him to his advantage.

By the second week of the Birmingham campaign, Martin Luther King Jr. was emboldened. Wyatt Walker's optical illusion on Palm Sunday had lured 135 foreign correspondents to Birmingham to cover for their own outlets what Walker now called Project C. The city soon swarmed with journalists. They buoyed King to act as he hadn't so far.

A week into the protests, the SCLC still had to do the work of Birmingham without the help of Birminghamians. That upset King. He did not have the support of the city's Black leaders, not A. G. Gaston and none of the ministers beyond Fred Shuttlesworth's tiny band of freedom fighters. King remained convinced that if Black ministers aligned with him, their congregations would, too. Early in that second week King walked into a meeting of two hundred Black pastors. He strode before them just like he had one week prior, when he'd asked for their support at the Black Ministers Conference. Just like last week, the pastors remained frosty. Unlike last week, King lit into them.

"I'm tired of preachers riding around in big cars, living in fine homes, but not willing to take their part in the fight," King shouted, staring the reverends down. "If you can't stand up with your own people . . . you are not fit to be a leader!"

The abrasiveness shocked everyone. King intended to flatten the pastors with the heavy blast of shame they themselves deployed on Sundays. Shame had worked for Baptist pastors since 1638, with the founding of the denomination's first church in Providence, Rhode Island. King waited on the dais for it to work now.

The Reverend John H. Cross Jr. stood up. Cross pastored at 16th Street Baptist Church, two blocks from the rooms at the Gaston Motel. The church touched the border of Smithfield, the Black neighborhood where the homes were expensive and the culture the Harlem of the South. As a result, Cross breathed the air of Black high society. It intoxicated him. Cross's 16th Street Baptist was snooty, "the most exclusive Black congregation" in the city, according to one Birminghamian. Its members were educated, rich, and conservative, and the church had a history of opposing not only labor unions but also Fred Shuttlesworth. Cross's predecessor, Rev. Luke Beard, had seen the north-side-living Fred as gauche and his ACMHR as dangerous. When Fred had formed his civil rights group in 1956, Beard had phoned him and attempted to stop him.

"The Lord wants you to call it off," Beard had said.

Fred had seethed. The patronizing sanctimony of these so-called elites.

"Pray for me," Fred had hissed, and hung up the phone.

The dynamic between civil rights groups and 16th Street Baptist had not improved since then. For Cross to rise now, during the second week of the Birmingham campaign and moments after King had laid into him, well, it could only mean the good Reverend Cross was about to show more of the "tremendous resistance" he held for the SCLC, King later wrote.

Instead, Cross surprised King by saying Martin's speech resonated.

By Cross's own admission, he did not have a protesting bone in his body, but even he, the well-off pastor of Birmingham's most well-off congregation, had experienced the diminishment of racism. The day he'd first stepped off the train in Birmingham and hailed a cab, the taxi driver had slowed, said, "Don't drive coloreds," and then sped off. It had stunned Cross: He had joined the army in 1944 to defeat an orthodoxy of white supremacy in Europe only to see the battle remain pitched here, twenty years later, in the city he now called his own.

Cross lived in a nice home and drove a fancy car, but King was right, Cross said. The time had come for him and his congregation to stand with Martin Luther King Jr. Cross and 16th Street Baptist would support the protests.

With that, King struck another blow for justice.

Martin realized that 16th Street Baptist joining the movement sent both an unstated message—other elite churches could now follow its lead—and a visual one: a second base of operations for the SCLC, and just two blocks from King's own at the Gaston. To have these twin bases facing Birmingham's downtown would give the illusion of mass support.

King thought his turn toward vengeance and righteousness had worked so well that he tried it out next on A. G. Gaston. The millionaire convened a meeting early that second week for a hundred Black business leaders at his motel. The Palm Sunday melee at Kelly Ingram Park, feet from the motel, had alarmed Gaston. It had alarmed other Black business leaders, too. At the meeting, some talked about stopping the protests and giving Mayor-Elect Boutwell "more of a chance." Others said there should not be picket lines orchestrated by outsiders.

These were the tired arguments King had heard before. Martin was about to speak when Dr. James Montgomery stood up. He was Fred Shuttlesworth's physician. He'd been educated at Morehouse, where he'd met King. He'd trained at Howard Medical School and then taken a cardiology residency at Harvard before returning to Birmingham to practice. To the elites around him, Dr. Montgomery said, "Have all y'all lost your minds? We've been trying to get these things done all these years and someone comes in to help"—Montgomery pointed to King—"and y'all want to get rid of him?" Montgomery looked at his fellow Birminghamians. "Y'all just want to go backward."

In the silence that followed, King stood and addressed the business leaders. Birmingham's racism was the South's, and America's. "We *have* to stick together if we ever hope to change its ways," Martin scolded.

Here was the truth of what he'd learned in life: When he was perhaps eight years old and two friends of his in their well-to-do neighborhood in Atlanta said they couldn't play with Martin because they were white and he was not, Martin's "heart broke." The pain he felt, even at eight, wasn't just his own but any Black person's, especially after he asked his mom, "Why don't white people like us?" and Alberta had told him about America. Every Black person must feel as he did, and all the time, the young Martin reasoned. That was the day he'd begun to resist. That was his origin story. King's motivation since was to soothe his pain and that of every Black person he encountered. His empathy for others informed his righteousness now. He wanted the Black people in this room in the Gaston to *live* the truth Alberta had told him at eight: "Don't you be impressed by any of this prejudice you see. And never think there is anything that makes a person *better* than you are, especially the color of his skin."

That's what was really going on here. They could debate all they wanted about the leniency they should extend to the new mayor's administration, or deride "outside agitators" like King. But the conversation they were not having in this room was the one that mattered: the inferiority they felt, even as business leaders, the whole of them "skillfully brainwashed," as King put it, by Birmingham's segregation.

To the Black elites staring back at him in the Gaston Motel, King said, almost sneering, "Man cannot ride your back if you can stand up."

The blast of rhetoric flattened this room, too.

He was not done shocking people. He went next to that night's mass meeting, held at his brother's church, First Baptist, in Ensley. Martin walked in to a standing ovation and a crowd larger than any before. The campaign seemed realer now because of the mayhem on Palm Sunday and all the people who sat in jail: ninety-four in total, including Fred Shuttlesworth and A.D. King. The crowd jostled for seats, and Martin told all of them he did not pity his brother. Let him sit in jail. Jail was the point. "We are going to fill *all* the jails of Birmingham," Martin shouted.

Martin said he did not want to look at a congregation like tonight's, packed to the very eaves of the church, if that body couldn't step forward as one and join this fight. "Any of the people who are not willing . . . get up and leave the church so somebody can have your seat who wants to go to jail for freedom!" he thundered.

His deputies internalized his anger and spouted it themselves. "Get rid of the Uncle Toms!" shouted Ralph Abernathy, who spoke following Martin. "Get out of the church! Let someone in who is willing to go to jail for freedom!"

It worked. All of it.

In this city of Baptist churches, where Blacks and whites bragged about having more Sunday schools than any other place in America, the guilt King leveled everywhere he went did his bidding. He picked up new volunteers. For the first time since the campaign had begun, Birminghamians cheered the protesters who sat in at lunch counters. More business leaders stood behind King, and more pastors followed Reverend Cross's lead and joined the movement. A. G. Gaston himself issued a statement: "We want freedom and justice; and we want to be able to live and work with dignity in all endeavors where we are qualified." By the middle of the week, the hundreds of pressmen in Birmingham noticed the change. "Negroes Uniting in Birmingham," read the headline in the *New York Times*. The story went on: "Some Negro leaders were said to feel that the city's entire Negro population of 150,000 had now been committed, whether they liked it or not."

Whether they liked it or not.

About as Baptist a sentiment as you could find.

13

WHEN BULL SAID NO TO ALL THAT

There was one thing King did not anticipate that week: Bull Connor's response to the new legions of people in the movement.

Bull himself had been on the receiving end of many a stern come-to-Jesus from Birmingham's power structure. White elites told Bull that releasing the hounds on Palm Sunday had been exactly what King and his people wanted. Couldn't he see that?

Bull had long boasted to voters that a childhood playtime accident with an air rifle had blinded him in one eye but allowed him to see the truth of white power with the other. The racism and hatred that defined his life had also propelled his career. It was hard for him to see anything else. So white Birminghamians phoned Laurie Pritchett, the chief of police in Albany who'd had all that success deterring King last year. Pritchett agreed to speak with Bull.

Pritchett said Bull needed to operate as Laurie himself had: No guns, no billy clubs, and certainly no K-9 corps. Just careful, even tender arrests. A nonviolent campaign like King's could not work, Pritchett said, if white cops themselves practiced peace.

Bull scowled and glared at Pritchett with his one good eye, so Pritchett changed his tactic.

The superiority of the white man lay in his cunning, Pritchett said. If

Bull would back off and quit acting so, well, bullish, then Connor and really the whole of the white South could win the streets of Birmingham from King. A win there would prove, once again, the advantage of the white race.

This line of thought seemed to reach Bull. He soon told his police captains to back down, and they in turn told the patrolling officers at roll call, "If a camera catches you beating anyone, you'll be in [prison] in 24 hours." Bull then reached out to Governor George Wallace and Captain Al Lingo of the Alabama State Police. They'd wanted to increase the police presence in Birmingham after Palm Sunday, militarize it, even morph it into the kind of marauding renegades Lingo favored, the state troopers of his who kept knives and sawed-off shotguns at the ready.

Bull said no to all that. He and his police force would handle Birmingham.

Connor next tracked down his friends in the Birmingham Klan. "Stay out of town," he told them.

This confused the leaders of the local klavern. With King himself in the city, they assumed Bull would continue to need their help. But Connor was steadfast. Through an emissary he said: "We want to keep our friendship with the Klan but if you try to help us you'll be arrested."

The result was striking. The Birmingham police force that previously had no compunction about abducting and raping Black women, the force that had rewarded officers who'd shot and killed Black men with extra days off for a job well done, this same police force by the second week of the Birmingham campaign showed the discipline of samurais. No arrests Monday. Just eight Tuesday at Loveman's in the heart of the city, where hundreds over the lunch hour watched the police carefully, tenderly cuff the picketers.

It was hard for Bull to witness this new force. He remained a vain man who loved his spectacles. Terrorizing Blacks was his favorite—his voters', too. "Give 'em hell, Bull!" they'd shouted. To be this restrained, this *peaceful*, this close to the end of his tenure? Was this how he'd be remembered? As if to pacify him, two city-father types, Hayes Aircraft chief

Lew Jeffers and federal judge Clarence Allgood, took Bull to dinner at La Paree, the downtown steakhouse where the people who ran Birmingham dined. Dimmed lights, wood-paneled walls, expensive entrées Bull didn't have to pay for, and Jeffers and Allgood telling him to stay the course. Back off and the demonstrations "would peter out on their own." Bull nodded and no doubt ordered another drink.

Restraint, he said. He would continue to show restraint.

His officers' greatest test of it came Wednesday that week at the Birmingham Public Library. There, Black adults and children walked into the whites-only sections, pulled biographies and magazines from the shelves, and sat down to read. As if they could just do that. This horrified white patrons. "Why don't you go home?" And: "It stinks in here." The Black people ignored them and stayed where they were.

Library staffers called the cops.

Officers arrived but, perhaps realizing that a roughing-up of Blacks was what King and the SCLC wanted, chose to do nothing. They watched the Black protesters as they read. After about an hour, the protesters walked back out into the bright light of the April afternoon, confused as to why the officers had never arrested them.

Wyatt Walker tried to spin the protest as a successful integration. Not even the Black press fully bought it. "Southern Policemen Adopting King's Non-Violent Method," read a *Jet* magazine headline.

The whole of Black Birmingham may have been behind King, but Bull Connor showed the power he held when the whole of white Birmingham refused to engage.

14

THE COUNTER TO THE COUNTERMOVE

As the week wore on, King wondered if he would need to act even bolder. He huddled with Ralph Abernathy and Wyatt Walker. If everything must escalate, he asked, what was the appropriate escalation here?

Perhaps the answer lay in the Al Hibbler incident.

On Tuesday Bull had personally overseen the arrest of Hibbler, the Black activist and baritone who'd sung with Duke Ellington and now recorded under Frank Sinatra's label. Outside of King, Hibbler was the most famous Black man in Birmingham. That notoriety brought Bull close to Hibbler, close enough to shout epithets at him when Hibbler was cuffed during Tuesday's sit-in at Loveman's. "Bring that nigger over here," Bull had said. Bull then threatened violence against Hibbler, chomping on the bit of his own restraint. A lieutenant in the police force had had to intervene Tuesday. "Mr. Connor, you can call him all the names you want to, but don't lay a hand on him."

The lieutenant would follow Bull's order for peaceful arrests even if Bull wouldn't himself. The cop became so distrustful of how an angry Connor or his praetorian guards at the city jail would treat the famous Hibbler that the officer instead drove Hibbler back to the Gaston Motel, where he uncuffed him. The lieutenant didn't want to risk any Palm Sunday–style headline about white violence on Black protesters.

King and Abernathy and Walker looked at each other: What was the lesson of the Hibbler story?

Well, there was only one activist in town more famous than Al Hibbler.

Maybe the time had come for that man to march. Maybe that was the way to release Bull Connor from his own restraint.

Wednesday night of that second week, with the protesters confused by the cops' civility and the press bored with it, Martin Luther King Jr. took to the pulpit at the mass meeting. King told the crowd at St. James Baptist that two days from now on Good Friday, "Ralph Abernathy and I will make our move."

The crowd leaned forward. Was King himself about to march? King saw amid the attentive congregation the pale white detectives from Bull's police force, scribbling furiously now in their notepads.

Good. He had Bull's attention, too.

Yes, in two days' time, King said, he and Abernathy would make their move, and "I can't think of a better day than Good Friday for a move to freedom."

This crowd was flattened, too. It was King's boldest action yet. "We are not here to do something *for* you," King roared, "but to do something *with* you!" In that "with" was a whole worldview, you see.

They saw it. Men and women, Black and white, saw a Baptist pastor who could not only shame them into the movement but lead them into harm's way.

It was the week's most electric message, and even before the meeting's end it lit up the city.

On Good Friday, Martin Luther King Jr. would march.

15

UPPING THE STAKES

N ot long after King pushed open the doors of St. James Baptist that night, an aide relayed a troubling message. An Alabama court had just ordered him to stop his campaign in Birmingham.

The order was drafted by two city attorneys and signed by Alabama circuit court judge W. A. Jenkins at 9:00 p.m., literally within the hour of King's Good Friday announcement.

That's how quickly word had spread of King's coming march. And been acted on.

King sighed.

The order was labeled a "temporary injunction." King knew about injunctions. "The leading instrument of the South to block the direct-action civil rights drive," he later wrote. "You initiate a non-violent demonstration. The power structure secures an injunction against you. It can conceivably take two or three years before any disposition of the case is made. The Alabama courts are notorious for 'sitting on' cases of this nature. This has been a maliciously effective, pseudo-legal way of breaking the back of legitimate moral protest."

The injunction issued that Wednesday night against King and 138 others—including pretty much all who'd been jailed thus far, the senior staff of the SCLC, and "John Doe," to cover any unnamed protesters—

accused the activists of "provoking breaches of the peace," "threatening the safety, peace and tranquility of the City," and disregarding the law. The last accusation was the most damning. King and the SCLC had "unlawfully" picketed Birmingham the past two weeks, with the full knowledge that they needed approval from the city to demonstrate. But the SCLC had never gained that approval, the injunction argued.

And the man who had the authority to approve demonstrations in the city of Birmingham was one Eugene "Bull" Connor.

Failure to gain his signature for the SCLC's mass protests meant King and his acolytes were "in violation of numerous ordinances and statutes of the city of Birmingham and state of Alabama," the injunction stated.

Should anyone break the city's laws again by protesting, they would face 180 days in prison.

Back at the Gaston Motel, King summoned his top deputies. Fred Shuttlesworth had just been released from jail on bond for leading one of last week's protests. He said to Martin he was ready to go behind bars again. This injunction was ludicrous. They had to fight it.

They would, Martin said. The SCLC's legal team in New York would start tomorrow. They'd write an appeal to continue the protests, to fight on.

Why not fight now, though?

This became *the* question of that lengthening night.

The idea was simple. The chief defendants—King and everyone else in the SCLC—still had to be served to show they were in violation of the law. A sheriff's deputy would very likely serve them that injunction tonight, if the city wanted to stop the SCLC from protesting tomorrow. If Bull's spectacles had become his city's, why not create a counterspectacle? If everyone here agreed the injunction was bullshit, well . . .

King saw where this was going and his face lit up.

In no time, Walker had called every contact of his in the press and told them to rush to the Gaston Motel.

• • •

Around 1:15 a.m. Chief Deputy Ray Belcher of the Jefferson County Sheriff's Department walked into the Gaston carrying a copy of the injunction. Belcher, a friend of the Klan, was hostile not only to Blacks but to northern types.

That's all he saw in the Gaston.

Shuttlesworth, Abernathy, and King waited for Belcher in the motel's restaurant, and behind them stood dozens of unruly camera-popping national pressmen. For King it was brilliant stagecraft. He and Shuttlesworth and Abernathy sipped coffee in shirtsleeves, "as if they were not sitting amid a crush of reporters and it was not 1:15 in the morning," as one writer later put it.

The civil rights leaders took the injunction from the sneering Belcher and, making sure the press's eyes were on them, read from it. They were outraged—genuinely outraged. They also accentuated their fury for the notebooks and microphones surrounding them.

Fred Shuttlesworth called the injunction "a flagrant denial of our constitutional rights."

King said the SCLC would defy the order. The force of his statement made the early morning "electric," *Newsweek* wrote. "One knew that the talk was over, that people were going to get hurt, possibly killed."

The injunction's spectacle had just been matched by counterspectacle.

16

THE GARDEN OF GETHSEMANE

hat King had not said was whether he would still march.

If he did, he would be arrested and thrown in jail for six months. More than enough time to snuff out the Birmingham campaign. To ruin it, and the SCLC, and perhaps the whole of the civil rights movement.

King spoke with the SCLC's lawyers not long after dawn on Thursday. They said they would attempt to convince a court to lift the temporary injunction, allowing protests to continue on the streets. But no promises.

The lawyers told King: *However you proceed, do so carefully.*

That morning, King thought again about the Albany campaign. An injunction had been issued against the SCLC there, too. King hated the passive position the order had forced him to adopt. An aide later said that when a Georgia court issued the Albany injunction, "it was the angriest I'd ever seen Martin."

One of the core activists in Albany had begged Martin to defy the injunction.

"Martin, you are the symbol of spiritual integrity," the activist had said. "If you say this injunction is a tactical move to co-opt the movement, then everybody will listen and follow you to jail. And you then change the rules . . . We are at a point where you have to provide the leadership, even for the Kennedys. . . . So let's go to jail, bro'."

But King felt he had no choice but to obey the Albany order. So he had. It'd taken a long time for the SCLC's lawyers in Albany to get the injunction lifted, and by the time they succeeded, the Albany campaign had lost its momentum. King left town.

His actions haunted him one year later.

He vowed he would not make the mistake of Albany in Birmingham.

That afternoon, King told the press that surrounded him in the Gaston's open-air courtyard: "We cannot in all good conscience obey an injunction, which is an unjust, undemocratic and unconstitutional misuse of the legal process.

"In the past," King said, "we have abided by federal injunctions out of respect for the forthright and consistent leadership [of] the Federal judiciary. . . . However, we are now confronted with recalcitrant forces in the Deep South that will use the courts to perpetuate the unjust and illegal system of racial separation."

So they would march, King said. He and Ralph Abernathy and Fred Shuttlesworth would march tomorrow, on Good Friday.

When King finished reading from the statement, he put down the paper. He stared deep into the television cameras.

"I am prepared to go to jail and stay as long as necessary."

It should have ended there, that defiant moment. If the Birmingham campaign had been the televised drama Wyatt Walker wished it to be, the camera would have cut to the next morning and the protest on Good Friday, rich with the symbolism of marching one's cross toward one's demise and possible rebirth. Instead on that Maundy Thursday, even as Ralph Abernathy delivered the script-ready line "Almost 2,000 years ago Christ died on the cross for us; tomorrow we will take it up for our people and die if necessary," the reality of Bull Connor's Birmingham imposed its own vision on events.

Bull had learned a tremendous amount that second week of the campaign. With Laurie Pritchett's guidance, Bull had become quite wily. That Thursday afternoon Bull phoned the bondsman the SCLC used, James Esdale of the Esdale Bonding Company. Bull informed Esdale the city would no longer secure the bonds Esdale's company issued. The city of Birmingham suddenly considered Esdale's assets insufficient to warrant the bonds.

Bull's thinking here was clever: Without a bondsman, the SCLC would have to pay the full amount of bail to release any of its protesters from jail. The injunction itself doubled the price of any prisoner's release from $50 to $100. Bull thought that if King wanted to stay in jail, fine. But would he want to protest tomorrow if he knew that each person who marched with him would face six months behind bars? And that the release for any prisoner before that date would cost $100, which the SCLC would have to pay because no bondsman in the city could help to defray the costs?

When Martin received word from Esdale that he could no longer assist the SCLC to post bail, "it was a serious blow," King wrote. The SCLC didn't have the cash to cover its operations in Birmingham *and* pay in full to release protesters from imprisonment. "There were our people in jail," Martin wrote, "for whom we had a moral responsibility. Fifty more were to go with Ralph and me [on Good Friday]. This would be the largest single group to be arrested to date. Without bail facilities, how could we guarantee their eventual release?"

Hours after he'd stared into the cameras at the Gaston, King considered calling off Friday's protest. Maybe fly overnight to New York and do an emergency fundraiser at Harry Belafonte's home? Maybe delay the protests for a week and tour the North, delivering speeches for hard cash? Desperate, he phoned the SCLC's lawyers in New York. Could the legal team help him stage fundraisers?

They were busy, they said, appealing that morning's injunction. Now King wanted help fundraising?

Martin hung up.

King Sr. arrived from Atlanta. This was a planned trip, but the crises of the last day meant Martin was in no mood to visit with his father. Martin holed up in room 30 of the Gaston, seeing no one, ruminating. *If he went forward with tomorrow's protest, he and Ralph and the fifty others would bankrupt the SCLC. How could they succeed without money?*

Aides knocked on room 30's door, telling Martin the time had come for the nightly mass meeting. Martin didn't respond.

But if he called off tomorrow's protest and obeyed the injunction, he and the SCLC would lose all credibility. How could they succeed without their reputation?

The mass meeting opened, and King Sr. spoke. He said tomorrow was a big day, and "whatever you do, try your best to be a Christian." The crowd at Sixth Avenue Baptist wondered when his son would speak. Martin remained in room 30.

If he went forward with tomorrow's protest, he could be held in prison for months. How could the Birmingham campaign succeed without its leader?

Ralph Abernathy eyed the side entrance and did not see King, so he took to the pulpit at Sixth Avenue Baptist. "We ain't afraid of white folks anymore!" he shouted. "We are going to march tomorrow." The crowd cheered, but it wasn't as deafening as when King spoke.

But if he called off tomorrow's protest he would be ridiculed by the press that had broadcast today's promise to march. Breaking his promise with the press was breaking his promise with America. How could he succeed if no one in America trusted what he said?

Martin stayed behind the door of room 30 until well after the meeting's end. On that Maundy Thursday evening, the suite seemed to take on the dimensions of the Garden of Gethsemane.

That whole night room 30's door never opened.

17

THE GOOD FRIDAY TEST

King emerged in the morning. He hadn't slept. He hadn't made up his mind, either.

By Good Friday, not only the executive staff but also every member of the SCLC's advisory committee had arrived in Birmingham. King wanted all twenty-four of them present for a meeting at 8:30 a.m. at the Gaston.

King looked terrible. His face bore the exhaustion of the sleepless night and the stress of the decision before him. Aides who saw him later said their leader was enduring the hardest test in his decade of activism. The hardest test in his life.

King asked the staff and advisory committee to come to room 30. They positioned themselves in the suite's living room, twenty-five people standing and sitting and breathing in a room meant for perhaps eight. King took a seat at the living room table and dragged on a cigarette. He wanted to hear what everyone thought.

One by one they said they understood the impossible choice. Was there a way to find a less-terrible option? Could Harry Belafonte help again?

King said he'd reached Belafonte last night, asking about the possibility of an emergency fundraiser in New York at Harry's apartment, to cover the now-exorbitant costs of bail. Harry had told Martin they could raise funds, but to be most effective, fundraisers needed Martin's presence.

"This means you can't go to jail," someone said now. "We need money. We need a lot of money. We need it now. . . . If you go to jail we are lost. The battle of Birmingham is lost."

The conversation turned to all the reasons King should cancel the day's protests. Just that morning eight Alabama clergymen, Christian and Jewish, had written an op-ed in the *Birmingham News* calling King's march "unwise and untimely." Wasn't at least one thing in that op-ed true? Couldn't King benefit from more time now?

Fred Shuttlesworth and Wyatt Walker argued he couldn't. To delay the Good Friday march even for the campaign's well-being was to capitulate. What Martin would gain in money over the weekend he would lose in reputation. Who would follow the leader who does not follow his own words?

If anything, "you should have gone to jail earlier," Walker said.

Walker's response showed a certain punchiness: King was not the only executive in the SCLC who had gone without sleep last night, worrying over the fate of the campaign.

Some members of the SCLC's advisory committee spoke plainly. This body included A. G. Gaston and King Sr. himself. Almost as if they'd rehearsed their lines in advance, the advisory committee said:

> You march and things might get out of hand, Martin. The violence against Black people. The possible retaliation from Black people. Better to uphold the sanctity of the Easter season.
>   Better to delay the march, Martin.

King inhaled on his cigarette and nodded. He tried to hide from the two dozen what his best friend saw immediately. Ralph Abernathy later wrote how the advisory committee's recommendation "damage[d] our morale."

And yet capitulation seemed the prudent play here. No one else, not

Shuttlesworth or Walker or Abernathy for that matter, volunteered to march alongside King. Perhaps that was due to their fear of a possible six-month jail sentence. Perhaps that was due to the understanding that only King could lead today's march, if a march was going to happen.

The point was, nobody wanted King's crown.

He rose.

"I was alone in that crowded room," he later wrote.

He told the two dozen he needed to pray. He walked out of the suite's cramped living room and into the adjoining, and empty, bedroom.

He closed the door behind him.

He had never wanted this. For years now he'd told his wife, Coretta, he'd wanted someone else to lead the marches or give the speeches. When the movement had begun in Montgomery in 1955, King wrote, "I neither started the protest nor suggested it." He was pushed into leadership simply because he spoke well, he said. Once out front, he decided to apply the nonviolent resistance alluded to in the Gospels and practiced millennia later by Gandhi. He did not know what he was doing in Montgomery, but because no other protester did, either, he became the bus boycott's leader.

Early in that Montgomery campaign, when almost all Black protesters chose to walk to work and withhold their fare from the city's buses, Martin and Coretta began to get threatening phone calls at home. At first he thought nothing of them. "The work of a few hotheads," he told himself and Coretta. *They'll stop phoning the house when they realize we aren't going to fight back.*

The calls increased. Specified the bodily harm to be done to Martin and his young family. One night after a long day of marches, Martin climbed into bed next to Coretta and the bedside phone rang.

Martin had learned to pick up, to leave Coretta out of it entirely. He put the receiver to his ear.

"Listen, nigger. We've taken all we want from you. Before next week you'll be sorry you ever came to Montgomery."

Martin hung up.

This one got to him. Maybe it was the anger in the man's voice; maybe the forewarned date: *before next week*. Martin couldn't sleep, and on that night it was worse than insomnia. "It seemed that all of my fears had come down on me at once. I had reached the saturation point."

He got out of bed. Paced. Went to the kitchen and made a pot of coffee. When it had brewed and he'd poured his cup, he'd reached a conclusion. "I was ready to give up. . . . I tried to think of a way to move out of the picture without appearing a coward." He couldn't figure how, though, so he took his problem of saving face to God. With his head in his hands and cup of coffee untouched before him, King prayed aloud: "I am afraid. The people are looking to me for leadership, and if I stand before them without strength and courage, they too will falter. I am at the end of my powers. I have nothing left. I've come to the point where I can't face it alone."

He'd come to the point where he couldn't face it at all.

At that moment he experienced the rush of God's presence "as I had never experienced Him before." A voice called to him or, rather, issued from within him. "Stand up for righteousness, stand up for truth," it said with quiet assurance. "God will be at your side forever."

The fears dissipated. His self-confidence returned. He could endure this night. He could lead this movement.

"I was ready to face anything. The outer situation remained the same but God had given me the inner calm to face it."

The warning turned out to be far from idle—his home was bombed two days later—but how King continued to lead in Montgomery despite his fear was why he was still leading today, and often against his inclination.

What he sought in room 30 in Birmingham was that same inner calm. That assured voice that would tell him what to do in a situation even more threatening than the late-night phone calls in Montgomery.

The noise of his inner monologue this morning—*If I proceed, the campaign will die; if I delay, the campaign will die as well*—quieted as he relayed his struggle to God. "I sat in the midst of the deepest quiet I have ever felt," King later wrote. A moment more and he found himself standing in the center of the room, eyes open. "I think I was standing also at the center of all that my life had brought me to be." He thought of the two dozen next door, the 150 already in jail, the hundreds more who might join them today if the thousands of Blacks lining the streets were any indication. All of them waiting on this Good Friday to see what Martin Luther King Jr. would decide. His mind then leaped beyond Birmingham, and Alabama, to the twenty million Black people in America who yearned for the freedom Martin promised—if only he would lead them.

Suddenly, "There was no more room for doubt."

He took off his suit jacket and dress shirt.

From Montgomery until today he realized he had prayed to God for leadership but then faltered in his own execution. Why had he been an observer during the Freedom Rides in 1961? Why had the organizers in SNCC called him "De Lawd" last year? Why had James Bevel abandoned just last week the Birmingham protests that he was meant to organize?

King took off his dress slacks and put on a pair of blue jeans and a green denim shirt.

Bevel had left, and SNCC had sneered at King, and the Freedom Riders had dismissed his speeches because Martin's actions as a leader had never risen to the level of his rhetoric.

He stared in the mirror, in these "work clothes," as he called them, which were suddenly as rich in symbolism as Good Friday itself.

He opened the door to the other room.

Martin looked at the two dozen.

"I have decided to go to jail."

The room gasped. The firmness of King's voice, even what he wore: Many of those assembled had never seen Martin in anything but a suit and tie. To dress like the working-class Blacks who would inevitably want to march behind him showed the conviction King held regarding his own martyrdom.

"I don't know what will happen," he said. "I don't know where the money will come from. But I have to make a faith act."

Some in the room smiled. Many of them were horrified. The most horrified was Martin's own father, King Sr.

"Son," he said, "I think at this time my advice would be to you to not violate the injunction."

The words unspooled a gnarled history. King Sr. had always been overbearing: forcing his way into Morehouse despite failing its entrance tests; proclaiming he would marry Alberta Williams before he met her. But because King Sr. had willed his way through life (Morehouse grad, husband to Alberta), he also thought he could will into existence the life he wanted for his older son.

In 1934, after a visit to Germany and the birthplace of Protestantism, King Sr.—born Michael King—changed his name to Martin Luther King. *And* changed his five-year-old son's to Martin Luther King Jr.

As soon as he was old enough to understand its significance, Martin Jr. shrank from his name. He wondered if he could ever "earn" it, he said. He lacked his father's self-confidence. He was too aware of mankind's limitations. Maybe King Sr. was right that Martin read too much. Martin found strength in books that he could not find in himself.

Through the years other coping mechanisms emerged. Martin often dressed in a suit and tie because his dandyism pleased his father. Martin relinquished his dream in college to become a professor because King Sr. told him he should pastor his own congregation. Martin learned to tell himself the same thing. Ultimately that congregation became King Sr.'s own at Ebenezer Baptist, with Martin a co-pastor and in line to inherit the family business, but even now in 1963, and despite Martin's worldwide recognition, Martin did not usurp his father. Martin's name still appeared below King Sr.'s in each Sunday's bulletin. That was how King Sr. advised the secretary to draw it up. Martin didn't question it.

To compound the problem of expectations, Martin did not share King Sr.'s beliefs. King Sr. lived life as if it were a daily practice of manifest destiny. To the extent that he discussed civil rights—and he almost never did—King Sr. knew that "he was right, segregation was wrong, and the hatefulness of white people was a mystery best left to God," as one observer of both men put it. But Martin, perhaps because he'd read too many books by Marx or Gandhi or Plato, wanted to push more people than himself across the line of freedom.

So what King Sr. said to Martin in room 30—"My advice would be to you to not violate the injunction"—really meant: *Listen to me again, son.*

Martin looked his dad in the eye. His whole life had been an act of loving God and loving his father, the two sometimes hard to extricate from each other and even harder to defy.

But he did not agree with King Sr. "If we obey it," Martin said of the injunction, "then we are out of business."

His father stepped back, as much baffled as amazed by the insubordination.

Martin didn't try to placate him, not today.

At last King Sr. said, "You didn't get this nonviolence from me." He would turn his humiliation into a joke if he had to. "You must have got it from your mama."

But this was no day for jokes. "I have to go," Martin said softly, but looking his father in the eye, meeting that gaze, expanding beyond the parameters of King Sr.'s expectations because Junior was setting his own.

"I am going to march if I have to march by myself," he told his father.

In the end he did not march alone. Martin asked Ralph Abernathy to join him.

Abernathy had planned to lead the Easter services at his own church in Atlanta, but said to those in room 30 now, "Let me see if I can get in touch with my deacons, because I'm going to see if I can spend Easter Sunday in the Birmingham jail."

Fred Shuttlesworth said he would march, too. This was his city, his people. He had asked King to come to Birmingham, and by God, to return the favor Fred would walk beside Martin, whatever the costs, start-ing with Fred's own pastoral responsibilities on Easter Sunday.

An hour earlier no one had wanted to walk beside King. Now, as if to unify the decision, King asked the two dozen in the room to join hands. Martin led them all, even his father, in their anthem, "We Shall Over-come." Some sang with tears in their eyes.

This moment in room 30, one aide later said, was the emergence of King's "true leadership."

18

"WHY HAVE YOU FORSAKEN ME?"

Then they waited. Wyatt Walker planned to do on Good Friday what he'd done on Palm Sunday: delay the march by hours. He wanted the power of King marching and the optical illusion of Birmingham following in his footsteps. Wyatt sent out releases and worked the phones, telling the press to be at Zion Hill Baptist Church, on the corner of 14th Street and Sixth Avenue, as soon as they could get there. King was about to march.

Footage later emerged of cameramen beating even King to the church. Martin was seen walking in with forty-odd protesters filing behind him. Then the doors to the church closed.

They remained shut for a long time.

The midday sun beat down on the waiting press and Birminghamians outside the church. Come afternoon, more people filled the streets, sweating now. At last, after three hours, King and Abernathy and Shuttlesworth walked out of Zion Hill Baptist, all of them in work clothes, walking down the church's flight of steps and hitting the street, with King out front.

A man in the crowd yelled, "There he goes! Just like Jesus!"

The march was to be four blocks, and King expected Bull Connor and his men to stop it at any point; Wyatt Walker had told the police where the march would head, in order to escalate the tension. The forty or so protesters behind Martin were soon joined by more, hundreds more. Walker trailed the movement of people, snapping photos to enhance the optical illusion.

But this was no illusion. Today was not Palm Sunday. The people trailing King were joyous, singing, shouting for Martin and for themselves, the liberation he might yet make possible for everyone in Birmingham.

The power of the moment transcended even these optics. As King and the rest marched together, Black Birminghamians by the thousands dropped to their knees along the protest route. They kneeled in solidarity, singing "Talkin' 'Bout Freedom" and "We Shall Overcome," as King walked by them.

Shuttlesworth and Abernathy smiled—the whole of Birmingham with them! and because Martin had *acted* on his words!—but King himself remained stoic. You see it in the footage from that day: the leader thin-lipped and grimacing as he passed the Black Birminghamians on their knees. Perhaps he felt the solemnity of the moment. "We Shall Overcome" on these crowded streets was as much a yearning moan as an anthem. Or perhaps King's tight-lipped strain showed the responsibility he carried.

Or, just as likely, it revealed the future he envisioned from his foreboding, forewarning God.

Because here came a cop on a motorcycle, cutting hard in front of King on the street, forcing him and Abernathy to stop just before they reached the Federal Building.

The pair dropped to their knees and began to pray.

The cop got off the bike, scowled, and looked around. The hundreds of Birminghamians and the unblinking eyes of the television cameras stared back, then moved still closer to the officer.

He glanced down at King. As if positively identifying him, the cop said, "Right here."

Without taking off his helmet the officer bent down, grabbed King's belt beneath the small of Martin's back, and hoisted King to his feet.

With the belt in his grip, the cop then frog-marched King, roughly, to the paddy wagon.

Martin passed the television cameras that, in turn, tightened their focus on his face. His eyes showed everything: satisfaction for at last leading as he should have, and uncertainty of what lay ahead. The days and longer nights in Bull's jail. All the time that others, in the churches and on the streets, would have to lead in his stead. God had directed him to this moment, and yet in his brief encounter with the television cameras, one can see the outline of panic on Martin Luther King Jr.'s face, King questioning even the faith that had delivered him to this paddy wagon on Good Friday.

Had he miscalculated?

Or, given the day and hour, had God just forsaken him?

Part IV

THE WRITING ON SCRAPS
OF NEWSPRINT

19

THE HOLE

They wrote a song called "Birmingham Jail." The rednecks Tom Darby and Jimmie Tarlton recorded it as a country ballad for Columbia Records in 1927 after Birmingham cops arrested Tarlton for bootlegging. The stripped-down arrangement and in particular the song's opening verse—*Down in the valley / Valley so low / Late in the evenin' / Hear the train blow*—made it a sensation. The record sold more than two hundred thousand copies.

Tarlton, the son of sharecroppers in South Carolina, had always loved as a kid the slide and open-tuned guitars he heard from the Black musicians on acreages next to his own. The sound of some of those guitarists lived in "Birmingham Jail." That strain of soul was what Lead Belly heard. The bluesman covered Tarlton's song and returned it to the music of the Black South. This was in the mid-1930s, just as Bull Connor came to power in Birmingham. Lead Belly renamed the song "Shreveport Jail" for his native city, but unmistakable in his rendition was its full-bodied ache. Lead Belly's guitar and vocals sounded like a man who had been to jail numerous times, each trip unjust, each one terrifying.

His song, in other words, still stood for Birmingham. This was especially true after the reputation of Bull Connor's jail began to extend beyond its perimeter.

As far back as the 1930s people understood that the Birmingham Jail could hold inmates "incommunicado for months at a time," two union organizers reported. "A lot of them just disappeared. Nobody knows where they went, just died or killed or thrown in the river." Guards at the jail sometimes beat Black suspects to death. Emory Jackson, the publisher of the Black-owned newspaper the *Birmingham World*, demanded in his pages that the killings at the jail be investigated. To the extent the coroner or court system examined the murders, they'd declared the victims "niggers" and their deaths mysteries. Jackson wrote how he wanted, if nothing else, to *number* how many people Bull's guards killed. Connor in turn demanded Jackson be subpoenaed, and perhaps questioned at the jail, "since he seems to be so interested in seeing an investigation made."

The threat signaled to the national media that Bull Connor and his jail guards were a nasty story. In the early 1960s, the *New York Times* and *Saturday Evening Post* noted how fear permeated the city and the movements of its Black citizens. Bull's "favorite technique," the *Times* said, was to arrest Black men on the flimsiest of vagrancy charges and then hold them in jail for three to five days. If Black suspects didn't die there, they were sometimes "tortured" there. Guards beat them with rubber hoses, sliced them open with razors, but never officially charged them with a crime or offered them bail. "We kept them," one guard rather icily said under oath, "until we'd completed our investigation."

The stories shocked the nation and attracted still more attention. Under Bull Connor's leadership, the Birmingham Jail was a "small-time Gestapo," in the words of one Alabama radio broadcaster. In the words of CBS's Edward R. Murrow, there was nothing small-time about it. Birmingham was as bad as anything he'd seen in fascist Germany, he said.

Martin Luther King Jr. knew all of this. He had Wyatt Walker's planning memos and Fred Shuttlesworth's firsthand accounts of his experience in jail. Bull and the guards could be brutal to anyone but tended to be heinous to the lesser-known offenders, the ones without the bold-type prestige of Fred Shuttlesworth. The jailers felt that to maim or kill Shuttlesworth was to risk a race riot. So time after time Fred had been arrested, and time after time he had been released on bail. Shuttlesworth had argued to King that the same would happen to the Birmingham campaign's protesters. The campaign would focus too much attention on the city for its guards at the jail to treat the incarcerated Blacks as they might wish.

It took a while for King to come around to Shuttlesworth's view. It took longer still, as King sat in the paddy wagon on Good Friday, to think he'd be unscathed, especially as the three-story concrete mass of the Birmingham Jail rose before him.

The nerves he felt. Not just to enter the Birmingham Jail as Martin Luther King Jr. but to be processed and to stand this way and that for a glum mugshot, and all the while thinking his imprisonment here might harm the movement even more than any harm that might come to his body. Ralph Abernathy had been arrested as well; this brought King some comfort. At least Ralph would be in the cell. They could talk out their fears as they had the year prior, in the Albany campaign, when they'd been incarcerated together.

But Birmingham Jail administrators quickly separated King from Abernathy. "For their safety," the warden declared. Guards directed King down a narrow passage away from Abernathy and stopped him before a cell far too cramped to be habitable. Just eight paces across, barely wide enough for the metal slat of a concrete bed bolted to the wall. The bed had no linen or pillow. The cell had only a small window high up, which cast a wan beam of light into the unit. Guards unlocked the iron door and shoved King in.

They slammed it shut and the clang of metal echoed down the hallway. Flakes of rust fell from the cell bars. King understood: His home, for an indeterminate time, would be in solitary confinement.

The day passed. He watched it through the arc of light on the wall. That light shadowed with the late afternoon and then blackened into a terrible night.

"You will never know the meaning of utter darkness until you have lain in such a dungeon," King later wrote.

That evening, without light, without lawyers to advise him, without his best friend or wife to soothe him, Martin Luther King Jr. fell apart. He had thought a beating would be the worst of it. No beating came. No one came, in fact, and this made it unendurable: What his mind could do to itself. How it could turn as dark as this cell. "I was besieged with worry," he said. "How was the movement faring? Where would . . . the other leaders get the money to have our demonstrators released? What was happening to morale in the Negro community?"

He was in hell that Good Friday night.

"Those were the longest, most frustrating and bewildering hours I have lived."

20

WHO CARES ABOUT
PRISON REFORM NOW?

Because of the months he'd spent in Birmingham, because of the pressmen who now flocked to him at the Gaston, Wyatt Walker had as many contacts in this city as his enemy Bull Connor. It did not take Walker long to learn King was being held in solitary. It took even less time for Walker to see what Bull planned to do with King: Treat Martin as Connor had so many prior inmates. Deprive him of visitors, if not food and water. Keep him in that cell for days, incommunicado.

Walker would not allow that. It was time for another counterspectacle.

He phoned Harry Belafonte in New York. Harry could get to the Kennedys faster than Walker or King could. Walker said to Belafonte that perhaps Bobby Kennedy, in his capacity as attorney general, would like to know that a decent American was being denied his constitutional rights in the Birmingham Jail.

"I called Bobby Kennedy," Harry later wrote. Harry asked him: "'How can you sit by while Martin is suffering in these barbaric conditions?'"

Bobby paused. Harry could almost hear Bobby's mind at work: the righteous Catholic who saw a clear line separating good from evil, the protective brother who considered every political angle before pursuing any.

"Tell Reverend King we're doing all we can," Bobby said, his tone shifting to the wry paternalism he'd learned from the WASPs at Harvard. "But I'm not sure we can get into prison reform at this moment."

Belafonte hung up, furious.

He did not relent, though. With Walker's help, Belafonte crafted a telegram to be sent to the president. "In these times," it read, "there is a great need of moral leadership to strengthen those like Dr. King who are leading the fight for all men and to make clear the knowledge that this land will not permit the continuing denial of freedom to any of its citizens or the abuse of those who are lawfully seeking such freedom." In a matter of hours Belafonte got not only religious emissaries like Dr. Emerson Fosdick to cosign the telegram but friends such as Marlon Brando, too.

Harry sent the telegram to Jack *and* Bobby Kennedy's offices. Then, with Wyatt Walker's assistance, he gave the *New York Times*'s man in Birmingham, Foster Hailey, access to the telegram, so that Hailey might pressure the Kennedys by asking them about it.

When Walker in Birmingham and Belafonte in New York opened the Saturday edition of the *Times* they saw a most curious fact: a suddenly concerned Kennedy administration telling Foster Hailey that the president himself had phoned the Justice Department from his Easter weekend vacation spot in Palm Beach. He asked about the fate of King in that Birmingham cell.

The story also noted, in what was surely not a coincidence, that Birmingham Jail administrators had done an about-face and would now allow defense attorneys to visit King.

Looks like the Kennedys are *concerned about prison reform*, Harry told Walker when he phoned him.

Another successful counterspectacle.

21

"THIS WILL BE ONE OF THE MOST HISTORIC DOCUMENTS. . . ."

In his jail cell, King heard the hard clack of boots echo down the hall and thought another guard would soon stand before him, ready to hurl epithets. Perhaps this time, if King could persuade him, this guard could hint at news from the outside, for which King was starved. His worrying had not ceased from the night before.

Instead King saw Clarence B. Jones with the guard.

Martin smiled.

The cavalry had arrived.

Jones was one of the SCLC's lawyers, perhaps its best, but not always Martin's favorite. Gregarious, loud, a chaser of tax credits and women, Jones was a northerner, Philly bred, a man who had scandalized the society pages in the 1950s by marrying a white woman—an heiress, in fact: Ann Aston Warder Norton, the scion of the W. W. Norton publishing fortune. They'd moved to L.A. so Jones could practice entertainment law. That's where King had met him, back in 1960. Martin was on a speaking tour and in real need of a lawyer who knew contracts and tax codes; King had been indicted by the state of Alabama for perjury on a tax charge. Jones agreed to meet with King at Clarence and Ann's modernist mansion in Altadena. The accommodations stunned Martin. A palm tree grew in the middle of the expansive living room. A retractable ceiling overhead showed puffy clouds drift past during the day and then at night the Milky Way. The San Gabriel Mountains were in view everywhere. Just as stunning was how Jones had gotten to this station in life. His parents, both domestic servants, had been so poor in Philadelphia they'd briefly given up Clarence as a child. An orphanage helped to raise him. It operated a mission on a Navajo reservation, too, and, "I vividly recall being in school with young boys seven or eight years old whose names were Running Deer and Little Bear," Jones said.

To go from that upbring to this mansion? King had asked. Certainly Jones would understand the need to help someone like Martin, someone in a position as precarious as Clarence's had been.

Jones refused. "Just because some Negro preacher got caught with his hand in the cookie jar, it's not my problem," he'd said.

King left the mansion muttering to himself and shaking his head, but the next day Martin's secretary called Jones and invited Clarence and Ann to Friendship Baptist Church, in well-off Baldwin Hills, as guests of honor. Martin was to be that Sunday's preacher.

Jones did not want to offend King further. He accepted the invitation but let Ann stay home.

It turned out to be a wise decision.

King lit into Jones in the sermon.

There was a young Black man in the church that day who was a great lawyer, Martin preached, perhaps the finest the SCLC knew. But he was a "young man who lives in a home, in the suburbs of Los Angeles, with a tree in the middle of his living room and a ceiling that opens up to the sky. He has a convertible car parked in his driveway. . . . [T]his young man told me something about himself. His parents were domestic servants. His mother worked as a maid and cook, his father a chauffeur and gardener. I am afraid this gifted young man has forgotten from whence he came."

Martin never named Jones in the sermon. Never looked in his direction.

Jones sank deeper in the pew all the same. When King quoted from the Langston Hughes poem "Mother to Son," an allegory for Black women who longed to educate their children by means they never gained themselves, Jones winced. His own mother, a dear and lovely woman, had died a few years prior. All she'd wanted was the life Jones had.

He bawled in that pew.

After the sermon, Jones found King in the church parking lot, signing autographs.

He extended his hand. "Dr. King, when do you need me to leave for Alabama?"

"Soon," King said, smiling and taking Jones's hand in his. "Very soon."

From then on they were a pair. King liked him, after that initial impression. Jones helped Martin beat the tax case in Alabama, but more than that, Clarence was Martin's age, with Martin's passions, and a family about the size of Martin's. Once Jones remembered whence he'd come, he never forgot it. He advised King during the Freedom Rides. Literally stood by King's side in Albany. Was among the anointed few at the Dorchester Academy, setting the course for the campaign in Birmingham.

Jones was smart, wily, just the right degree of paranoid—"During my time in the military I had some experience with the people who make the rules, and I knew they did not play by them"—and by 1963 a bona fide movement man. At Martin's request Clarence relocated his family out of that mansion with its retractable roof to an apartment in Harlem so that Clarence could better handle the SCLC's legal work.

Now, in the Birmingham Jail, Clarence Jones waited until the guard had passed out of hearing. Jones spoke quickly, saying he didn't know how long this legal visit would last and—

Martin asked if he'd brought the day's newspapers.

Jones smiled and snuck out from under his dress shirt the two Birmingham dailies and the *New York Times*. Martin snatched them through the bars.

Jones began to talk about the mass meeting last night (the turnout had been meager) and the real trouble about raising enough funds. But King was distracted—or, rather, absorbed—by a story in the *Birmingham Post-Herald*: "White Clergymen Urge Local Negroes to Withdraw from Demonstration." The piece was a reprint of an op-ed from the day before, authored by eight white religious leaders, Christian and Jewish. It was the "untimely" argument Martin had heard in room 30 Friday morning. Reading the full argument today transfixed King.

"In Birmingham . . . we are now confronted by a series of demonstrations by some of our Negro citizens, directed and led in part by outsiders."

Led in part by outsiders? King *knew* some of these pastors. He *worked* with them. They were liberal. They'd praised King and condemned Governor Wallace's "Segregation forever!" inaugural address a few months earlier.

"Just as we formerly pointed out that 'hatred and violence have no sanction in our religious and political traditions,' we also point out that such actions as incite hatred and violence, however technically peaceful those actions may be, have not contributed to the resolution of our local problems. We do not believe that these days of new hope are days when extreme measures are justified in Birmingham."

Incite hatred and violence? Extreme measures? So King's actions were the equal of Bull Connor's? This letter was insane. Infuriating.

Above all, it was wrong.

Forget everything else before him. "I have to respond to this," King told Jones.

Jones was baffled by King's urgency, but King dismissed him and started writing on scraps of newspaper. When he'd filled those margins he moved to strips of toilet paper. Within these scribblings King shaped a letter, both for the Alabama clergy and a more universal *us*, in the style of Paul's epistles in the Bible. A piece of writing for a named group and everyone outside it, too. Yes, *that* letter would both convey his pique and please the theologian in him.

Too often as a pastor he had to corral his ideas within the borders of the average life, the simple faith, the relatable experience. Here, though, with a response to his fellow clergymen, King could call upon the full array of his intellectual powers. He could cite Christian rhetoric, ancient philosophy, world history, because his readers would be familiar with these volumes. Here in his jail cell Martin Luther King Jr. was unbound.

Maybe that's why he wrote so feverishly, with lines crossed out, phrases scribbled above them, and directional points wending and looping around the margins of newsprint to connect broader ideas. More likely he wrote for the reason any writer does: Because he had to. Because, in this case, the Alabama clergymen represented a flaw in thinking common to Christian theology, to liberalism, to the Deep South, and to any nation that considered itself free and democratic.

It assumed that power yielded to superior ideas.

King had once assumed this, too. While a student at Crozer Theological Seminary fifteen years earlier, he'd read Walter Rauschenbusch's *Christianity and the Social Crisis*. The book argued that salvation lay in what you could do for your community as much as your spirit. "A religion that ends with the individual, ends," King wrote of the book. He loved it. Rauschenbusch had ministered at the turn of the twentieth century in Hell's Kitchen in New York City, and by looking at the depravities of his neighborhood and the disparities a ruthless capitalism imposed on it, Rauschenbusch found that souls could be enriched if man came together as one, reached a Christian ideal of "love perfection." Rauschenbusch developed a Social Gospel movement in American Christianity, and the social justice reforms of that movement—the abolition of child labor, a shorter work week, factory regulations—showed a young King how better ideas could become fairer laws. "Rauschenbusch had done a great service for the Christian Church by insisting that the Gospel deals with the whole man," King wrote, "not only his soul but his body; not only his spiritual well-being but his material well-being."

For the college-aged King, Walter Rauschenbusch's Social Gospel also alleviated a point of tension in Martin's life. He had been embarrassed by his own riches. King Sr. had turned Ebenezer Baptist from a two-hundred-member congregation with a padlock on its foreclosed doors into a four-thousand-person megachurch. He'd done it by preaching the prosperity gospel. Ebenezer's Sunday congregants, many of them shopkeepers or entrepreneurs, became each other's customers the rest of the week under King Sr.'s guidance. Material success expanded the client base and then the congregation that showed up Sunday. All of this was done in a segregated Atlanta in the middle of the Great Depression. King Sr. took pride in it. His son saw the materialism of his surroundings—the big car out front, the piano in the living room, the leather-bound books—and wondered what kind of God would allow him to have so much and his friends so little. "I could never get out of my mind the economic insecurity of many of my playmates and the tragic poverty of those around me," King wrote. Rauschenbusch assuaged King's guilt by showing him how good works could do what even donations to the poor could not. Good works could unite a community. So bound, everyone could rise. Rauschenbusch argued people would stand up as one when they'd been enlightened by greater truths.

For a long time at Crozer Theological Seminary King lived out Rauschenbusch's Social Gospel. He ate lunch with students from all over the world, the better to understand their corners of it. He read Marx, and over the Christmas break no less, because Marx's view of communion on earth was closest to Rauschenbusch's. He defied his Baptist upbringing and drank beer, smoked cigarettes, and played pool at the halls on campus and the ones off it, too, because to uplift mankind you had to live among its lowest people. When King Sr. visited, Martin showed him how much of a pool shark he'd become. Aghast, King Sr. said he'd better get right with God.

Martin said serving God meant knowing how His people acted. To a certain extent Martin channeled the Victor Hugo line: "If the soul is left in darkness, sins will be committed. The guilty one is not he who commits the sin but the one who causes the darkness." Martin refused to cause the darkness.

His father, suspicious, and very much a Baptist preacher, told his son that what he learned in books was never an excuse to sin.

But what Martin learned in books was how to live. Even on a Saturday night, whether he was on campus or at a pool hall or babysitting a professor's children, he could be found with a stack of thick tomes under his arm. At Crozer, he began "a serious intellectual quest for a method to eliminate social evil," he wrote. "I spent a great deal of time reading the great social philosophers," Aristotle, Rousseau, Nietzsche, Hobbes, and always, more than anyone, Rauschenbusch.

Then, in his last year at seminary, he read Reinhold Niebuhr.

Niebuhr upended everything.

Niebuhr had once been like Rauschenbusch. A German American theologian who ministered to the poor and oppressed. In Niebuhr's case, he ministered to those in Detroit in the 1920s, when the city was the fourth-largest in the country and deluged with immigrants from Europe, and Blacks from the South, all of them intent on improving their lives by working at Henry Ford's factories. Niebuhr's own congregation at Bethel Evangelical Church featured many workers from Ford's plants. A young Niebuhr preached Rauschenbusch's Social Gospel to them: the real change they could make through the spread of superior ideas. The congregation loved it. Word of this fierce Niebuhr and his righteous sermons helped Bethel Evangelical grow from sixty-six members to nearly seven hundred.

As the church grew, Niebuhr went on tours of the factories where many of his congregants worked. "The foundry interested me particularly," he later wrote. "The heat was terrific. The men seemed weary. Here manual labour is a drudgery and toil is slavery. The men cannot possibly find any satisfaction in their work. They simply work to make a living."

This trip and others had a profound impact on Niebuhr. What good was a Social Gospel doctrine? Put another way: What good were union dues, shorter workweeks, and the collective bargaining his Black and immigrant congregants enjoyed if the labor itself remained exploitative? A Social Gospel disciple would say, "The goal is to make the work ever less exploitative." Niebuhr dismissed this now. An unreachable utopia. Almost childlike in its hopes.

No, Niebuhr now saw that the world tilted on power. Who had it and how they wielded it and what small concessions they would make to obtain more of it. Power decided everything.

Over the next few years Niebuhr moved from the softheaded liberalism of the Social Gospel to a more centrist, realistic, and hardened position callused by what he saw in the foundries and the fallout from the peace treaties of World War I. In 1932 he distilled his neo-orthodoxy into a book, *Moral Man and Immoral Society*, which made him an international celebrity and, decades later, altered everything a young Martin Luther King Jr. believed.

What King loved about the book was its stark understanding of human motivation. A man could be moral, Niebuhr argued, and as an individual assist the poor and disadvantaged through acts of God's grace. But that same man, when placed in a collective, could not impose his morality on the group. Groups of people seek one thing: power. Once they have it they want to hold on to it. This is true of the smallest groups (a manufacturing oligarchy, say) and the largest (a nation of people in conflict with another). Every struggle in life is some form of a collective struggle, and *that* struggle is a battle for power.

"Insofar as this treatise has a polemic interest," Niebuhr wrote in *Moral Man and Immoral Society*, "it is directed against the moralists, both religious and secular, who imagine that the egoism of individuals is being progressively checked by the development of rationality or the growth of a religiously inspired goodwill and that nothing but the continuance of this process is necessary to establish social harmony between all the human societies and collectives." Bullshit, Niebuhr said. He could say that, he argued, because he was someone who had once held such views. People like the sort he used to be "do not recognise that when collective power, whether in the form of imperialism or class domination, exploits weakness, it can never be dislodged unless power is raised against it."

That seemed true to King. Sitting in his seminary dorm room in 1951, six years after World War II, he noted how democracy hadn't defeated fascism in 1945 so much as the Allies' military forces defeated the Axis's. Even the nations fighting on the same side weren't bound by the same ideas. A communist Soviet Union joined a capitalist United States because both nations lusted after power: the destruction of two other countries and the increased dominion over many more.

Martin's own life, too, played out within spheres of power, so ubiquitous they were almost invisible. He was here at Crozer, in Pennsylvania, and integrating with students of other races because he could never do so at a seminary in his native Georgia. The Social Gospel doctrine would argue he could seek integration in Georgia through accommodation: Black students negotiating with white administrators. Niebuhr thought that was ridiculous. "Will not even its most minimum demands seem exorbitant to the dominant whites, among whom only a very small minority will regard the inter-racial problem from the perspective of objective justice?" Niebuhr wrote in *Moral Man and Immoral Society*. "What is lacking among all these moralists, whether religious or rational, is an understanding of the brutal character of the behavior of all human collectives."

Niebuhr was abrasive reading, but he was honest, too. You obtained power by taking it, wholly, from others.

"The prophetic and realistic elements in Niebuhr's passionate style and profound thought were appealing to me," King wrote a few years after first reading *Moral Man and Immoral Society*, "and I became so enamored of his social ethics."

It returned King to a Baptist faith. Niebuhr argued what King Sr. did: Mankind is inherently sinful, and grace comes through a daily acknowledgment of lived evil.

Like Niebuhr, King began to distance himself from Rauschenbusch's

Social Gospel. But King needed a framework to apply Niebuhr's teach-ings, which diagnosed the problem for any disadvantaged group but did not necessarily offer solutions.

Around this time, King read Mohandas Gandhi.

Gandhi was different. Gandhi's life showed how minorities might obtain power. King read about Gandhi's Salt March in 1930. Salt was a staple of the Indian diet. The imperial British had not only banned Indians from collecting it but also mandated they buy salt from the ruling colonials, and pay a heavy tax. Gandhi thought the best way to challenge the whole of British rule in India—to make a metaphor of an oppressed people's will—was to march to the Indian Ocean and collect the salt himself.

King read how Gandhi didn't do it alone. In 1930 Gandhi was sixty-one years old and had developed a large following: people inspired by the protests and demonstrations he'd waged for Indian independence. Gandhi set out from his ashram at Sabermanti with seventy-nine people trailing him. The sea was 240 miles away, and each day more Indians joined the procession. This was civil disobedience on an increasingly massive scale. By the time they reached the Indian Ocean some sixty thousand people marched behind Gandhi—far too many for British law enforcement to beat back. Gandhi and others collected the salt that day but, more im-portantly, the protest led to ever-wider acts of civil disobedience in other parts of the country. Soon millions were demonstrating. The British ar-rested tens of thousands across various cities, Gandhi included, and vi-ciously beat still more protesters with steel-tipped batons. Almost all of the protesters followed Gandhi's lead and did not fight back. These beatings, recorded by the Western press—"the sickening whacks of the clubs on unprotected skulls"—sparked foreign leaders to question British rule in India. A push for Indian sovereignty increased, both within the nation and well outside it. In 1947 India gained independence, and the Salt March, when King read about it in the 1950s, was portrayed as the first battle in India's struggle for self-rule.

And none of it violent. That amazed King. He began to read more of

Gandhi, to try to understand his peaceful philosophy and how Gandhi developed it. King grew obsessed with knowing everything he could on the topic of nonviolent disobedience.

King learned that Gandhi had discovered peaceful protests by reading Leo Tolstoy. Years after writing *War and Peace* and *Anna Karenina*, Tolstoy professed his strain of Christianity in a book titled *The Kingdom of God Is Within You*. It argued, "Christ's teachings . . . can only be diffused through the world by the example of peace, harmony, and love among its followers." All Christians knew this but none lived it, Tolstoy said. If they did, there'd be no more war because Christian soldiers would simply "refuse to serve."

Tolstoy's argument distinguished itself from a woozy utopian tract through its knowledge of the endurance of love. Tolstoy wasn't the only one to understand this. No less a military genius than Napoleon had said at the end of his life that he had lived it the wrong way. He was like all great military leaders before him, building empires through conquest. But Caesar's empire, and Alexander's, and Charlemagne's, and Napoleon's own had crumbled, he said, because any nation built through violence invites more of it and ultimately collapses beneath it. But two thousand years ago, "Jesus built an empire that depended on love, and even to this day millions will die for him," Napoleon wrote. That truth was at the core of Tolstoy's *The Kingdom of God Is Within You*. Love wins everywhere, and every time, if people have the courage to practice it.

Gandhi was no Christian, but Tolstoy's book changed his life. In the early 1900s, editing a journal called *Indian Opinion*, which focused on civil rights and Indian sovereignty, Gandhi struck up a correspondence with Tolstoy. Some of these letters informed the essays Gandhi wrote or published in his journal. Gandhi became ever more convinced of Tolstoy's truth and issued a call to action for Indians seeking independence: "If someone gives us pain through ignorance, we shall win him through love," he wrote in *Indian Opinion*. The whole of Gandhi's crusade was to be nonviolent. "Love must be at the forefront of our movement if it is to be a successful movement," he wrote. He believed in Tolstoy's message so completely that as Gandhi moved from words to action he named his first ashram, where he taught the principles of nonviolent protest, Tolstoy Farm.

It worked. Oppressed Indians gained their independence without war. British officers ordered to snuff out the peaceful protests got nauseated when they struck unarmed picketers; many officers resigned. The British secretary of state for India, William Wedgwood Benn, wrote that terrorism was easier to defeat than nonviolence. Gandhi showed that violent power could be used against itself if it was met with peace. Peace neutered violence. Benn and other British officials saw this themselves. If they attacked the protesters and upheld colonial rule, Britain's morality would be questioned by British officers in India and dignitaries and leaders outside the country. If Benn and others ceded ground to Gandhi, Britain ceded nothing less than its authority in India.

The power of peace and love in Gandhi's actions transformed a young Martin Luther King Jr. "True pacifism," King wrote, "is a courageous confrontation of evil by the power of love." King began to develop a worldview informed by Niebuhr's raw honesty about mankind's motivation and Gandhi's core truth of how oppressed people could counter it. This philosophy depended not only on a reading of Niebuhr and Gandhi but also a deepening, an accentuation, of King's lifelong beliefs: the Southern Baptist's understanding that humanity is inherently flawed, and Jesus's lesson about turning the other cheek to oppose such sin.

That's what he wanted to relay to the Alabama clergymen as he sat in his cell in the Birmingham Jail: these truths, from which sprang everything he'd learned and everything he'd lived for in his last decade of nonviolent activism.

"You may well ask: 'Why direct action? Why sit-ins, marches and so forth? Isn't negotiation a better path?'" King wrote in the letter, confronting head-on what he'd heard from the clergymen and other white leaders in Birmingham (and some Black ones, too), a series of questions that King interpreted as some Rauschenbuschian argument for gradualism and accommodation. No; true freedom wasn't gained that way. King wrote instead what he believed: "Nonviolent direct action seeks to create such a crisis and foster such a tension that a community which has constantly refused to negotiate is forced to confront the issue. It seeks to so dramatize the issue that it can no longer be ignored."

He then name-dropped the person from whom he'd learned this: "Individuals may see the moral light and voluntarily give up their unjust posture; but, as Reinhold Niebuhr has reminded us, groups tend to be more immoral than individuals. We know through painful experience that freedom is never voluntarily given by the oppressor; it must be demanded by the oppressed."

By 1963, after Montgomery and the Freedom Rides and Albany and amid the campaign here in Birmingham, King's life experience had taught him Niebuhr's truth. As King sat in that jail cell he found more and more of his own life spreading across these scraps of paper, too.

To the clergymen's point that his demonstrations in Birmingham during the Easter season and with a new mayor seated were poorly timed, King wrote: "Frankly, I have yet to engage in a direct action campaign that was 'well timed' in the view of those who have not suffered unduly from the disease of segregation. For years now I have heard the word 'Wait!' It rings in the ear of every Negro with piercing familiarity. This 'Wait' has almost always meant 'Never.' We must come to see, with one of our distinguished jurists, that 'justice too long delayed is justice denied.'"

Then he turned it on.

We have waited for more than 340 years for our constitutional and God-given rights. . . . Perhaps it is easy for those who have never felt the stinging darts of segregation to say, "Wait." But when you have seen vicious mobs lynch your mothers and fathers at will and drown your sisters and brothers at whim; when you have seen hate-filled policemen curse, kick and even kill your black brothers and sisters; when you see the vast majority of your twenty million Negro brothers smothering in an airtight cage of poverty in the midst of an affluent society; when you suddenly find your tongue twisted and your speech stammering as you seek to explain to your six-year-old daughter why she can't go to the public amusement park that has just been advertised on television, and see tears welling up in her eyes when she is told that Funtown is closed to colored children, and see ominous clouds of inferiority beginning to form in her little mental sky, and see her beginning to distort her personality by developing an unconscious bitterness toward white people, . . . when you take a cross-county drive and find it necessary to sleep night after night in the uncomfortable corners of your automobile because no motel will accept you, . . . when you are forever fighting a degenerating sense of "nobodiness"—then you will understand why we find it difficult to wait.

It was good. It was possibly great. When Clarence Jones returned to King's jail cell King blurted out to his lawyer, "I need more paper."

King showed Jones what he'd been writing, how the fragments of thoughts across margins of newsprint and toilet paper connected. He drew arrows from one piece of scribbling to the next.

"I thought it was crazy," Jones later said, and tried to turn King to more pressing matters: the SCLC's money problems, King's upcoming criminal trial for marching Friday and violating Birmingham's laws.

Martin seemed not to care. He wanted his writing transcribed.

"Have Dora type it up, okay?" King told Jones, referring to Martin's secretary, Dora McDonald.

Jones sighed. He then looked at the broken nub of a pencil in Martin's cell, its point dulled from overuse. He saw in Martin's eyes how "the eight white clergymen had truly upset him, and this was a man who had been nothing but forgiving when he had faced down police dogs or been stabbed in the chest"—in Harlem in 1958—"while autographing books."

A bit reluctantly Jones handed over notepaper he had with him. King took it and gave Jones the scraps of newsprint and toilet paper.

"Take this out of here," King whispered, as if guards might overhear and seize his precious writing.

So Jones did. He walked out of the Birmingham Jail with newsprint and toilet paper stuffed under his shirt and falling down his pants, with the understanding that he should come back tomorrow to do the same thing.

Because in that cell King set about writing more.

Decades later, two things still seem to distinguish this letter, especially when you're aware of King's fifteen-year intellectual trek to reach the point of writing in that tiny cell with that nub of a pencil. The first is how tightly King wove Niebuhr's and Gandhi's arguments into his own. You see this throughout, certain passages carrying some of Niebuhr's motif *Better notions do not equal better lives* and Gandhi's idea *Be the change you want to see in the world*.

The second thing is more amazing. King quoted from so many more than these two, without reference books around him or notes of any kind. King braided through his letter the wisdom of the Apostle Paul and T. S. Eliot. Allegorized the fate of revolutionaries, from Socrates to Jesus. Distilled the dense writing of Jewish philosophers (Martin Buber) and Christian theologians (Paul Tillich).

Day after day Clarence Jones walked to the cell and day after day King told him: *More paper. I need more paper.* He seemed, as he wrote, to realize that what he was scribbling was not only exceptional but his manifesto on the life he had chosen. When Jones would ask him about other concerns, King was anxious to return to the letter. By the end of each visit Jones would tuck a few more pages under his dress shirt and leave Martin with his thoughts, more loose-leaf pages, and a pen that Jones had given him.

Clarence Jones was no dummy—he would serve as King's chief speechwriter in the years ahead—but as he returned to the Gaston Motel day after day, he would hand King's scribblings to Dora McDonald and mutter how Martin had once again delayed the urgent matters of Project C. It took Wyatt Walker picking up King's ongoing letter to realize its significance.

Walker was a theologian, too, and not a lawyer. That helped. He was also the lone SCLC executive as well-read as King. So as Martin produced pages and Jones handed them over, Walker sensed, increasingly, he was reading something that would outlive him, and King, and define the movement. It was that powerful.

Injustice anywhere is a threat to justice everywhere.

And:

One day the South will recognize its real heroes. . . . One day the South will know that when these disinherited children of God sat down at lunch counters, they were in reality standing up for what is best in the American dream. . . .

And:

In your statement you assert that our actions, even though peaceful, must be condemned because they precipitate violence. But is this a logical assertion? Isn't this like condemning a robbed man because his possession of money precipitated the evil act of robbery? . . . We must come to see that, as the federal courts have consistently affirmed, it is wrong to urge an individual to cease his efforts to gain his basic constitutional rights because the quest may precipitate violence. Society must protect the robbed and punish the robber.

The first draft wasn't flawless. Editing it, Walker asked King to strike a specious section on how the civil rights movement in Alabama could increase U.S. morality abroad in the Cold War. King also had St. Augustine's penchant for overripening his metaphors until they fell to the page and scattered his thoughts. "There comes a time when the cup of endurance runs over and men are no longer willing to be plunged into the abyss of despair." Still, what astounded Walker was how King could channel—from memory!—all his influences, a discordant chorus of voices that King then set his own against, and somehow the whole thing harmonized. Walker was so taken with the letter that not only did he oversee its transcription despite all else he had to do in Birmingham, but when a secretary fell asleep at the typewriter one night—the letter ran to twenty pages—Walker gently pushed the woman aside and began transcribing himself.

> *Abused and scorned though we may be, our destiny is tied up with America's destiny. Before the pilgrims landed at Plymouth, we were here. Before the pen of Jefferson etched the majestic words of the Declaration of Independence across the pages of history, we were here. For more than two centuries our forebears labored in this country without wages; they made cotton king; they built the homes of their masters while suffering gross injustice and shameful humiliation—and yet out of a bottomless vitality they continued to thrive and develop. If the inexpressible cruelties of slavery could not stop us, the opposition we now face will surely fail. We will win our freedom, because the sacred heritage of our nation and the eternal will of God are embodied in our echoing demands.*

When it was finished, roughly a week after King began it, Martin said, "I had never been truly in solitary confinement; God's companionship does not stop at the door of a jail cell."

At the Gaston, Wyatt Walker sent King's letter to the pressmen and said because of its transcendence, it deserved the simplest of titles.

"Call it," Walker said, "'Letter from Birmingham Jail.'"

He was right: It outlived them both.

Part V

"... AND A CHILD SHALL LEAD THEM"

—Isaiah 11:6

22

THE PROPHET RETURNS
WITH HIS WIFE

The letter did not impress James Bevel as much as the act that preceded it: Martin Luther King Jr. marching straight into the Birmingham Jail. That's what Bevel wanted, the leader who lived out his sermons. So as King was processed and tossed into that tiny cell, James Bevel, the SCLC's youngest and most strident executive, the Black Baptist preacher who fascinated and even frightened others, and above all the one who'd left Birmingham a week ago because King refused to lead the campaign as Bevel saw fit, that same James Bevel returned now from his native Mississippi, gunning for Alabama in his '59 Rambler, impressed with King and ready to once again carry out the vision of the Birmingham campaign as the SCLC's director of operations.

Next to him in the Rambler sat Diane Nash, his young wife. They were an odd pair. It had shocked friends to learn they'd married. For one thing, the militancy of James's righteousness came in part from the pride he took in his skin tone, the deep brown, he'd said, of the Delta soil he'd worked as a child. Diane, by contrast, was a light-skinned beauty queen from the South Side of Chicago, her people too well-to-do to speak of race, only considering themselves an "American family." Bevel was an inveterate womanizer. Nash internalized from her grandmother that her dignity was "more precious than all the money in the world." But they had dated and then married and now sat next to each other in the Rambler because of the fearlessness that bound them.

They'd each learned it. The education took place at Fisk University in Nashville, which both of them attended in the 1950s. Walking the campus and, worse, abiding by Nashville's segregation codes had enraged Diane Nash in particular. She'd grown up without the overt promotion of racism. She sought out the means to correct it and walked into a campus workshop on nonviolent civil disobedience. It was modeled off Gandhi's success in India. One seminar became many. Meetings to plan protests broke into subcommittees that carried out certain tasks, and somewhere amid all that congregating she came across James Bevel. They began to work together. They were smart. Young. And in the beginning very scared about what would happen when they actually protested at Nashville's lunch counters.

That time arrived in the early spring of 1960. They had arranged the sit-ins in such a way that jail was the point. As one set of Black students was hauled off, another would enter the restaurant and take the first set's place in the whites-only section. Though Nash had helped to organize the protests, when her own turn came in that wave of students sitting down at the counter, she was petrified. Her whole life had trained her to stay out of jail. To be the good and pretty girl. When the cops threw her off her stool and into the paddy wagon, she nearly suffocated from the panic.

The fingerprinting at the station humiliated her. *I have fallen so far,* she thought. The two white cops who oversaw the processing glanced at her, her beauty, and began to talk to Nash as if she were better than the Fisk students around her. The cops joked about the way the others looked and smelled. The thickness of one "boy's" lips.

She realized an offer lay in these denigrating remarks. *Diane, honey, join our side.* She was light-skinned enough to pass; in the planning of the sit-ins even other Black students had mistaken her for white. However low her arrest had sunk her, though, she felt something else now at the base of her soul: anger.

What right do these cops have? she thought. This was a revolutionary idea for Diane Nash. Her life to date had been one long exercise in ceding to authority and to white culture. The same grandmother who had taught Diane her self-worth had also said how "white people have better things because they work harder and are better people." But now? At the police station? Nash knew Grandma Bolton was wrong, and so were these police officers.

Who are these white cops to judge me? And my friends and colleagues? she thought. *What is so grand about being white anyway?* If being white meant standing tall when Black people remained on their knees, she didn't want to think a day more about cultural assimilation or, worse, passing. White people were sick. Disgusting.

Nash turned from the cops. She walked toward her cell in the Nashville jail, surrounded by brave friends and James Bevel, too. It had taken her whole life, but she realized in that moment how proud she was to be Black.

She never forgot it.

Diane emerged as the leader. Everything in Nashville had thus far been planned by committee, but now, hardened by her days-long stint in jail, Nash showed a boldness and tenacity that perhaps no one but James Bevel possessed. Diane Nash flat-out got stuff done. She did it without ego and because she wanted to. That *wanting to*, especially since she didn't *have to*— her beauty and light skin offering her an easier life than almost any other protester—endeared her to the Fisk students all the more. Everyone liked Diane, Bevel included. He was the one to suggest in one of those central committee meetings that Nash be christened chairman of the Nashville sit-ins. That amazed her. His righteousness had brought him from Mississippi. He spoke in biblical phrases and everybody called him "The Prophet." And *he* was telling *her* to lead.

It emboldened her to accept, and it did something else, too: It attracted her to Bevel. As the sit-ins led to bombing attacks and ultimately, after four months of protests, the desegregation of Nashville lunch counters, and then later still, as the sit-ins spread to sixty-nine other cities, Nash and

Bevel began dating and, as a pair, rose together as leaders of the civil rights movement. They both aligned with John Lewis's Student Nonviolent Coordinating Committee, which had its roots in the Nashville sit-ins. To be a civil rights leader in the early 1960s was to stomach the assassination threats that came through the mail, the dynamite that detonated as you marched past. Diane and James's was a classic wartime romance, all the more intoxicating for how quickly it could be over. She adopted his militancy until it was her own. "Kill us or desegregate," she learned to tell the white leaders of any city in which they protested, while James smiled and nodded.

They married in 1961. He remained the eccentric one, with his country bibs and beautiful baritone voice, which he summoned in jail to lighten Diane's or other protesters' moods. (He sang so loud and so well in one Mississippi jail cell that the guard mistook Bevel for a radio.) But even as James came to the attention of Martin Luther King Jr., even as he landed an executive position in King's SCLC, Diane matched her husband's leadership and ferocity. She signed her own will and testament rather than bow to white supremacists outside Birmingham intent on bombing the Freedom Ride bus she sat in in 1961. A year later, in 1962, pregnant with their first child, Diane stared down a two-year prison sentence in Mississippi by saying, "This will be a Black child born in Mississippi and thus wherever he is born he will be in prison. I believe that if I go to jail now it may help hasten the day when my child and all children will be free."

"Who the *hell* is Diane Nash?" Bobby Kennedy asked an aide in the Justice Department at one point in James and Diane's activism in the early 1960s.

The answer was one-half of the fiercest duo in the civil rights movement.

Together, James and Diane Bevel sped to Birmingham to save Project C.

It needed saving. That was James's view. He and Diane arrived in Birmingham not long after cops hauled King to jail. Bevel watched the campaign falter without its leader. He saw membership at the nightly mass meetings dwindle. He saw the press lose interest. A campaign without King was a campaign of "doubtful utility," wrote the *Washington Post*, while *Time* said King himself was the problem: "To many Birmingham Negroes, King's drive inflamed tensions at a time when the city seemed to be making some progress." President Kennedy phoned Coretta Scott King while Martin sat in jail, but the Kennedys themselves remained distant. Bobby openly hoped for Mayor Boutwell to succeed. "The federal government has no authority to take legal action in Birmingham," Bobby's civil rights lead in the Justice Department said on Bobby's behalf. Mayor Boutwell was sworn in while King sat in solitary and James Bevel heard in the inaugural address how Boutwell wanted the "local problems" of Birmingham to be resolved by "local effort and local unity.

"We shall not submit to the intimidations of pressure or to the dictates of interference," Boutwell said. The Kennedy administration applauded the speech, as did the *New York Times*, saying the mayor's swearing-in ceremony was "like a picnic" where "the warm sun was shining." Worse, *Black people* liked it. They constituted one-fourth of the inaugural crowd. They didn't want to protest, either, not with King in prison. At one mass meeting, Bevel watched as nine people stepped forward to march out of a crowd of perhaps five hundred. "There are more Negroes going to jail for getting drunk," the Reverend J. S. Phifer scolded. Almost no one wanted to abide by the SCLC's economic boycott of downtown department stores, either. Wyatt Walker tried to set up a "Grapevine Squad" to rat out Black downtown shoppers and stem the defections. It did little good.

Bevel watched his old nemesis Walker get so desperate while King sat in jail that Walker asked the whole campaign to pivot to a voter registration drive, a request that Bevel heard as the campaign's death rattle. Registering voters meant nothing if the government itself remained racist and corrupt. And yet Walker held voter registration drives at 16th Street Baptist Church while King sat in solitary, and while other SCLC aides said stuff like, *This is the only way we can get the Justice Department in on this thing*—meaning the only way Bobby Kennedy could be convinced to intervene, even though he'd sworn he wouldn't.

It was magical thinking, all of it, Bevel said. Everyone had lost their God-given minds. One night Bevel took to the podium at the mass meeting to voice his frustration. "Birmingham is sick. Not only the white man but the Negro is sick," he said. "Some sick people don't want to get well."

Something about this sermon stirred the crowd, the first time this had happened since King's imprisonment. They called out *Amen!* or hollered their agreement, and now it was Diane's turn, sitting among the congregants, to smile and nod.

"You must ask if you really want to be free," James said from the pulpit. "You can if you want to."

The hollers and whoops turned to roars. Bevel pointed at the white detectives scribbling their meeting notes in the back of the church.

"Aren't you tired of getting walked on by white trash?" he said.

The church erupted. Even the white cops wrote how hard it was to make out what Bevel said from all the shouting.

The Prophet had indeed returned.

That same night, with Diane by his side, Bevel sized up the depleted core of SCLC leadership—basically Wyatt Walker and lawyers, what with King and Shuttlesworth and Abernathy in jail—and told them: "You guys are running a scam movement. . . . A movement is when people actually *do* out of conviction."

It was Bevel's long-standing belief. Movements could not be ordered on planning memos. When would the SCLC understand this?

Someone asked Bevel, *Well, what would* you *do?*

James and Diane already had an answer. It was an idea too radical to be voiced.

23

EMERGENCE

Harry Belafonte found the bail funds: $50,000 in total. Martin and the fifty protesters who'd been jailed with him for marching on Good Friday could be freed. When Clarence Jones came with the news, it "lifted one thousand pounds from my heart," King later wrote. Belafonte had wired the money—"some of it raised, most of it my own," Harry said—with the hope that he'd get the cash back, "but you never knew for sure with southern bail bondsmen. Often weeks or months after a case had been settled . . . the money would somehow be stuck in the entrails of a southern city's court system." King knew that all too well. The generosity of Harry Belafonte moved Martin to silence. "What quieted me," King later said of his friend, "was a profound sense of awe." From New York, Belafonte had tended to Martin, just as James Bevel had from the pulpit and Clarence Jones had as he went to see Martin in solitary. "The life of the movement could not be snuffed out," King later wrote.

The other bit of good news was that Bull Connor wouldn't stand down. Mayor Boutwell had been sworn in the day after Easter, April 15, and Connor had refused to cede power to him. Connor and other ousted city commissioners argued that their terms ended in October 1965. It wasn't just their wish to serve out those terms; it was mandated by the laws of Alabama, they insisted. Connor's argument ignored the referendum on the mayor-council system of governance that Birmingham voters had approved in 1962, which trashed the city commissioner system Bull had presided over for thirty years. Connor's argument also ignored the reality that Bull himself had run for mayor just months ago in that new mayor-council system and lost to Albert Boutwell. Bull's refusal to cede to Boutwell now, in the days after Easter 1963, wasn't so much an argument as an old man's desperate grab for the power he'd thought would always be his. Boutwell saw it as such. He didn't complain while Bull filed his appeal within the Alabama courts, because Boutwell, a lawyer himself, was confident Bull's appeal would be overturned. Still, that appeal could take weeks if not months to be ruled on. That meant Bull would remain in office and in power. King saw it as a post-Easter miracle: For at least a few weeks more, Project C's antagonist, the man so openly hateful he was like a comic-book villain, would remain on the stage. The job for King now was to make sure Bull acted within Project C's ongoing play.

That work began Saturday, April 20. King and Abernathy were released from jail. They'd been incarcerated for eight days and looked the part. Each had grown a beard. Jail administrators had refused them razors, along with pillows and linen. Wyatt Walker saw how the optics of such a scraggly look might reinforce the pair's plight, and quickly arranged a press conference before either of them could shave. At that press conference Abernathy joked with reporters how they were part of the "Castro brigade" for their bushy faces, but King sent a message to Bull and white Birmingham that he was not backing down, not after Harry Belafonte had posted the bail money, not after King had written his letter. This weekend, King said, the SCLC would discuss "the strategy for future actions."

In those weekend chats in room 30 at the Gaston, Martin listened as Clarence Jones and other SCLC lawyers discussed the looming court battle. The SCLC had appealed the injunction that had led to Martin and Ralph and fifty other protesters being thrown behind bars on Good Friday. But that appeal would be heard by the judge who *issued* the injunction: W. A. Jenkins Jr., of the Alabama Tenth Circuit. If Judge Jenkins denied the SCLC's request to lift the ban against mass protests, Martin and Ralph and the others could be right back in jail. Worse, any new march or picket in the days ahead would subject *those* protesters to a long term behind bars.

It was absurd, this injunction, the lawyers argued. The First Amendment of the U.S. Constitution guaranteed the rights of citizens to march and protest the government. Many Americans outside Alabama understood this absurdity. College students and pastors throughout the nation now protested in prayer vigils against "the absence of justice in Birmingham." Twenty-five unions and civic organizations had started nationwide protests of the department stores—Woolworth's and Newberry—whose Birmingham locations refused to serve Black customers at their lunch counters. The SCLC's message was reaching people outside Birmingham. But a problem remained. Getting this Birmingham injunction before an appellate court outside Alabama, one that ruled as the SCLC wanted—that would take a lot of time. And in the interim? Judge Jenkins could rule against the SCLC and send everyone to jail for however long he saw fit. That meant more money for bail, more legal appeals, more pleas to a heartless Kennedy administration to intervene, more frustration.

In fact, frustration was the best-case outcome, the lawyers said. The worst case was Jenkins's court decree killing Project C.

Listening to it all, Martin nodded. These possibilities didn't surprise him. He'd considered them in solitary.

He said that, however sobering the reality, they had to proceed.

The big question was whether Birminghamians would march knowing full well they could be thrown in jail, and potentially for a long time.

They hadn't done that when Martin was in solitary. Would they now?

No. That's what King learned during the third week of Project C, the week of April 22. He could tell a mass meeting he was prepared to go to jail: "I would rather stay in jail the rest of my days than make a butchery of my conscience." He could allude to Scripture and say that God had given Black people not a spirit of timidity but one of love and power

and conviction. He could say of incarceration, "I will die there if necessary." And the crowd could be eager, even, to hear these words: One mass
meeting that third week was so packed, a standing-room-only affair that
flooded the aisles at St. James Baptist, that the Birmingham fire marshal
walked in to say they were in violation. Beyond capacity.

No one left the meeting that night.

Almost no one stepped forward, either.

The resulting sit-ins and marches that third week of Project C slowed
to such a "trickle," in the words of one writer, that picketed department
stores didn't even bother phoning the police. The protesters weren't
enough of a nuisance to report.

King grew depressed, and Coretta flew to him. She herself had been
"despondent" while Martin sat in solitary, she later wrote: "lonely and
worried" over how Bull was treating Martin while she tended to four
children—one a newborn—in the house they rented on Johnson Avenue.
So she'd phoned Harry Belafonte, and arrived in Birmingham the third
week of Project C with Harry's help. "Good friend that he is," Coretta
said, Harry had paid for a nanny to tend to the Kings' children, and a
secretary to oversee their household expenses.

While they were together in Birmingham, Martin told her how nothing, not his actions prior to imprisonment nor his letter while there nor
his words now, upon release, could convince the men and women of
Birmingham to protest as he did.

She consoled him. She consoled him, she later said, because she had
no answers, either.

But when Martin repeated his lament to his staff in one meeting,
James Bevel spoke up.

He had an idea. What if, Bevel asked, the SCLC was focusing on the
wrong people in Birmingham?

24

THE INDECENT PROPOSAL

Bevel had been around town since his return to Birmingham, he told King. Driven the neighborhoods in his '59 Rambler. When necessary, walked the streets. He'd talked to people, he and Diane. Done his James Bevel thing of understanding the community, becoming one with it, moving alongside it. Bevel had learned Black Birminghamians weren't afraid of going to jail. Hell, fifty or sixty of them got arrested *every day* on some BS charge. That wasn't Bevel's made-up math, either. That came from the city's own crime stats. Black people here knew the horrors of incarceration.

What scared them now were their bosses.

Half the Blacks in Birmingham were laborers. That wasn't Bevel's figure. That was the U.S. Census's. Black people could work the mines and steel plants like their daddies and granddaddies or tend to white children in Mountain Brook like their mamas and grandmamas. Either way, Black people here worked for white people. And white people didn't want Blacks protesting alongside Martin Luther King Jr. Whites would rather fire Black employees than listen to their demands. And once fired for causing "trouble"? Good luck getting good work again, Bevel said. It was just the way this city was. Wasn't limited to laborers, either. Even the minority of Black professionals had to work within the white caste system.

Black teachers reported to a white superintendent who hated them well before they uttered word one about civil rights. So how would a teacher-led protest go over? Black lawyers had to fight just to appear in Birmingham courthouses. A lot of times they still couldn't. And now the SCLC wanted them to march and risk disbarment? Even the richest of Blacks in Birmingham, A. G. Gaston, a self-made man with more millions in his bank account than any white mogul in Jefferson County, even A.G. had to abide by the white man's code. When Gaston ordered Chinese food from the white-owned restaurant that did a brisk business in take-out, he had to walk past the front door, around the building, and head down a flight of steps to the restaurant's basement, out of view of the white customers, and pay for his order there.

And he did it.

Bevel argued you couldn't help these generations of men and women in Birmingham. Either too much was on the line or they'd grown too accustomed to the dimensions of their cage. You couldn't reach them.

But you could reach their kids. See, what James and Diane had learned since their return to town was this: The kids here wanted freedom. Could be a straight-A student like one girl, who said she had an "inner calling" to be free when James and Diane spoke to her. Project C "appealed to something that was already there." Could be one young man who'd had trouble in school because of all the harassment he got from the Birmingham cops, whom he considered "torturers, murderers, masochists," someone whose own mama had forbade him to attend the protest thus far because of the threat to his young life: "I'd rather kill you myself than let the white folks kill you," the mama said. Guess what? This guy wanted to protest anyway. He loved the "courage" of it. How "Black people could be more than the buffoons on the *Amos 'n' Andy* show," he said.

As for the risks: "Hard times make hard people," he reasoned.

That's the sort they were dealing with, Bevel said. Birmingham kids who were fearless, who in some cases had even learned this fearlessness from their parents but had one thing, the best thing, going for them: no obligations.

No responsibilities, no jobs. They could march for change with less fear of their family's destitution. They could demand the freedom they wanted, that their parents wanted, and they could lead this movement.

The SCLC should switch its emphasis, Bevel said, reaching his conclusion and the idea that he and Diane had considered almost too radical to be voiced.

The SCLC should march Black children straight into the wrath of Bull Connor's Birmingham.

Children? King stared at Bevel.

Was the man crazy? Many people said so. Even *King* thought so on occasion, and this, judging from subsequent records, was one such occasion.

King didn't tell Bevel as much. That wasn't Martin's way. Instead, he asked others what they thought. He started with Fred Shuttlesworth. Fred's own civil rights group, the ACMHR, had formed a children's wing a couple of years ago. That group hadn't led marches, as Bevel proposed, but still: What did Fred think?

Shuttlesworth was too much a man of action to give weight to moral obligations, much less have any patience for meetings where these things were discussed.

"Whatever," Shuttlesworth responded.

It was the sort of non-answer that didn't help King, so he told Bevel that for something as bold as what he was suggesting, King would have to raise it with Project C's central committee.

This was effectively the death of Bevel's proposal. On that committee sat A. G. Gaston and Birmingham pastors like J. L. Ware, the sort who had always been cold to Martin and had only reluctantly joined Project C when Martin shamed them into the movement with his heavy blasts of Baptist guilt two weeks ago.

When King broached Bevel's idea with this committee, it appalled Gaston.

Why would the SCLC "use" children like that? Gaston asked. Bull

Connor had already sicced dogs on the adults. Wouldn't injured kids, wouldn't dead ones, reflect on Connor *and* the reckless parents who'd allowed their kids to protest? This idea, Gaston said, was manipulative at best, shortsighted and fatal at worst.

The others agreed. This Bevel guy, the Reverend John Porter said, "is a radical of the worst kind."

After that meeting King told Bevel as diplomatically as possible that his idea lacked executive support.

The Prophet wasn't much for diplomacy, though.

In the days ahead he continued to talk with children, even formalized these discussions into after-school sessions on civil disobedience. He'd hold these meetings at 16th Street Baptist or New Pilgrim Baptist, whatever movement-friendly church opened its doors to Bevel. These sessions weren't sanctioned by King, but because Bevel never sought King's approval, they weren't *not* sanctioned by King, either. That's how Bevel saw it. *Do what you want and you'll never need to ask to do it.*

The meetings began as history lessons the kids weren't getting in school. "Your grandmama went along with disenfranchisement," Bevel said, but in other cities in the North and South, when Blacks demanded equality, "'niggers' become 'colored constituents.'" As the sessions grew from a handful of attendees to a dozen or more, Bevel started to talk about the schools themselves. At one session held in the small but well-lit annex of New Pilgrim Baptist, Bevel did a roll call to see which schools the kids attended.

A lot of them shouted, *Parker!* or *Ullman!*, the two largest Black high schools in the city, the teenagers full of school spirit and a little competition, too.

"At Ullman High School, how many electronic typewriters do you have?" Bevel asked.

"We have one," boasted Janice Kelsey, an honor-roll student at Ullman who never missed a day at school. "I get to type on it because I'm a good typist."

"Did you know at Phillips High School," Bevel said, referencing the large all-white high school in Birmingham, "they have three *rooms* of electronic typewriters? They don't even *practice* on those things you use at Ullman's."

Kelsey did not know that. She was an outgoing and popular girl whose life was Ullman, her church, and the few blocks of her neighborhood. She'd gone to this session because she lived within walking distance of New Pilgrim Baptist and a girlfriend had told her cute boys might be there. She was stunned by what Bevel said, and a little humiliated, too. *How had she not known this?*

Other kids seemed to feel the same. The chatter and energy of the room quieted into something more somber.

"How many of you guys play football at Ullman?" Bevel asked.

A few hands tentatively rose, Kelsey's brother Alvin's among them.

"Have you ever wondered why your helmets are blue and white when you get them, but your school colors are green and gray?" Bevel asked.

"We always paint them the right colors," Alvin responded.

"Well, why don't they *arrive* in green and gray?" Bevel asked.

Alvin didn't know the answer.

No one did.

"It's because you get Ramsay's discards," Bevel said. Ramsay High School was the all-white high school six blocks from Ullman High.

The boys in the church annex looked at each other. They were playing with discarded football equipment?

Bevel kept going. He talked about other second-rate school supplies they received, how the textbooks themselves were out of date. "Check the copyright," Bevel said. This was not a harangue or a lecture. Bevel was something like a peer. Not much older than them, and not in the movement man's attire of natty suits and middle-aged sensibilities. Bevel attracted the kids *because* he looked so different from King: in denim overalls, with his shaved head and yarmulke. But talking like a friend.

The kids began to trust him in that church annex.

The deprivations at Ullman High existed at Parker, too, Bevel said, and *every* Black school in the city. As he talked, the silence of the afternoon acquired a new dimension: the unfairness of it all. Many kids were like the Kelseys and had no idea they lived such limited lives. Bevel was here, as their friend, to show them the wide and cruel world.

"Now," he said near the end of the session, "if you want to do something about it, you can. Your parents really can't because if they get in trouble, if they go and participate, go to jail, they're going to lose their jobs. There'd be no one to take care of you. But you don't have a lot to lose."

He smirked.

"After all, you're already getting a second-class education."

The kids snickered.

Janice Kelsey later said that session was her "wake-up call." Her brother Alvin said he didn't care that Ullman's football coach had just given his players an ultimatum: *If you protest this spring, you can't play football next fall.* Alvin was going to follow James Bevel's lead.

These sessions led to more, and at each the attendance increased, with kids at Ullman and Parker telling their friends about Bevel, and these friends telling more students, and suddenly the after-school sessions became large enough for field trips throughout the city, Bevel showing the students, who trailed him by the dozens and then hundreds, where the literal lines of segregation tracked through Birmingham. Many of the kids had parents who'd shielded them from the pain that they knew all too well.

Bevel and the kids went one day to a grave site.

"In 40 years you're going to be here!" Bevel shouted to the teenagers huddled around him.

Bevel studied their faces, one by one.

"Now: What are you going to do while you're alive?"

The sessions evolved into practical nonviolence workshops during which Bevel told them they could protest. That's what they could do. White kids might attack them if they marched. Cops might. So Bevel showed the kids how to get into a fetal position and protect their skulls from the billy clubs or metal pipes that could thwack across them. They must not strike back, Bevel said. Ever. They must embrace nonviolence. As if to emphasize this point, he or Diane or another colleague would walk among the students with a trash can and demand the kids throw in switchblades or Swiss army knives or any other bit of teenaged weaponry.

Violence met by violence means segregation without end, Bevel said. *Lash out with violence and you're harming your friends who have the courage when the blows fall to remain peaceful.*

And so—*thunk! thunk! thunk!*—the knives and brass knuckles fell into the trash can.

Bevel was "the most dynamic person for the young," one teenaged boy later recalled. "He knew how to really talk to us."

He mixed street slang with Old Testament Scripture and was "very charismatic," said one girl. The sort of leader who not only brought ever more kids to the workshops but took the time to *see* each of them. "Young lady," he told the girl once, "we're so glad you're here." And then he gave her a hug.

For the boys and girls, James Bevel was more than persuasive. From how he dressed to how he talked, he had an "almost mystical way" about him, one observer noted.

Who was *that guy?* the kids asked each other after leaving his sessions.

Many in the movement wanted to know that, too. Bevel played up his mysticism around colleagues because he saw how it granted him authority. The truth of his background, though, was almost as otherworldly.

He was the thirteenth of seventeen children born to Dennis Bevel, a father who had changed the family name from Beverly to wipe from the record the white grandfather in Humphreys County, Mississippi, who had owned slaves and impregnated some of them. The name Dennis chose for himself and his kin, Bevel, was also part of the Hebrew word for "God," and the Torah fascinated Dennis.

Dennis Bevel had an eighth-grade education and, like many ambitious yet impoverished people, was an autodidact, well read and serving as a guest minister at many ramshackle Black churches in the Mississippi Delta, often outdrawing the regular pastors. Dennis was fastidious in his manners and disciplined in his habits. The acreage Dennis owned— bequeathed from that slaveholding white grandfather—angered nearby whites not just because Dennis was a successful farmer but because he told his children they could aspire to lives far beyond this plot of land. He sent some of his kids to seminary. He sent others to Piney Woods, an early Black boarding school in Mississippi. The dreams Dennis Bevel built on that acreage began to threaten his white neighbors. Would he teach other Blacks to succeed as he had? In the early 1930s, the FBI approached him, alleging Dennis was some sort of revolutionary.

Dennis said he was a farmer.

The FBI agents didn't buy it. They said it would be in Dennis's interest to inform on his Black neighbors.

Dennis said he was no snitch.

So the FBI blacklisted him. Local banks a short time later refused to give Dennis the loans he needed to continue to farm.

He lost the acreage. He ultimately lost his wife, Illie, who was furious he hadn't done what was necessary to keep the land. She moved to Cleveland, and he to Itta Bena, Mississippi, where his son James grew up and where Dennis took the only work he could find, as a sharecropper. When James was old enough to ask his father about the time his life fell apart, Dennis said he had actually avoided collapse. "The worst thing a man can do is betray his own kind to people like the FBI."

No regrets, you see. That's the lesson a young James took from his father. *You will have no regrets for leading a principled life.* Dennis's principles came from the Bible, from the Old Testament prophets whose righteousness transfixed him, and from Jesus Christ, whose teachings opened a portal to the divine. A belief in Jesus was nothing less than the acquisition of God's conscience, Dennis taught James. God resided within you. Anyone who failed to recognize this and attempted to oppress you because of your race—this person showed his own frailty, and, more than that, his separation from God. So pay attention instead to how you treat others. In such treatment lies your self-worth. In such treatment lies God's grace.

James adored his father. He loved to work alongside him on that share-cropper's plot. There, Dennis taught James to transcend such mortal designations and to do the work that pleased them and God. For James that meant a life in line with his father's. James developed his own fascination with Old Testament prophets. He began to view himself, as his father did, as half Jewish, the pair of them descendants of a Jew from Bethlehem who turned Judaic practices into a new vision for the world. To honor that new vision, Dennis taught James that one had to first honor its source material. There were other ways Dennis influenced his son, too. Dennis played the banjo and soon enough, by singing in the church choir, James developed the same love of music. More than anything, James obtained his father's curiosity. He read widely. Newspapers and periodicals about the godless Communist menace—this was the early 1950s—captured his young mind, and at seventeen, in 1954, James enlisted in the navy.

When James told Dennis about his decision, his father scoffed. *Why serve man's silly fears?* Dennis asked.

James told his dad it wasn't just the Red threat. James thought by enlisting he could save money for college.

Dennis shook his head, but he let James go his way. *After all*, Dennis said, *if it's an education you want . . .*

One day, on a ship, James met a Black seaman with a PhD who served as that ship's cook. This confounded Bevel. Was it racism that held the man back?

No, the man said. He *wanted* to cook.

Why?

Every man should serve his country, but the cook didn't want to kill others to do it. Cooking on a naval ship was this man's compromise.

But the Red menace—

The cook cut Bevel short. He handed him a book: Leo Tolstoy's *The Kingdom of God Is Within You.*

Read it, he said.

Over the next week, James Bevel tore through the book. Tolstoy distilled his faith and, James realized, Dennis Bevel's, too: Serve God's truth. It lay in how one acted with others and how one refused to act. You should never kill anyone, Tolstoy wrote. This was in fact the book's abiding message: pacifism in all of life's encounters.

It so moved Bevel that within a few weeks he was out of the navy.

Within a few years he had enrolled at Fisk University, where he came across the writings of a man who had been just as inspired by Tolstoy's book, Mohandas Gandhi. In Gandhi's books, Bevel found what Martin Luther King Jr. ultimately did: a model by which to fashion his own work. Bevel sought out the seminars on nonviolence held on Fisk's campus, run by people just as riveted by Gandhi's life. That's where Bevel met John Lewis and, yes, Diane Nash, and set up the Bevel Lending Library on Fisk's campus. Bevel dispersed the books that his half-Jewish father would have been proud of. Books by a Hindu from India who'd been inspired by a Christian from Russia and who brought down the British empire in Asia by "wrapping a rag around his balls," as Bevel said, and living a life of peace.

The Bevel Lending Library was a huge success.

In a very real sense it led Bevel and the civil rights movement to Birmingham.

If Bevel didn't talk about who he was in Birmingham, it was only because he had so much else to tell the teenagers. He began to recruit them at school, he and Diane and other SCLC staffers. They found the leaders, the brave kids, the loud ones, basketball stars, Miss Parker High School—whoever believed in the message of nonviolence and could participate in the "whisper campaign," as Bevel put it, about upcoming workshops. Bevel gave them palm-sized leaflets to distribute between classes: "Fight for freedom. Then go to school." He thought the hushed tones, the concealed leaflets, would make the students "feel like they were doing something half-sneaky, half-devilish," he later said, and attract more kids to the movement. His interactions also *needed* to be sneaky. School administrators didn't appreciate James and Diane being on the grounds. No teacher or principal, even if they believed in civil rights, wanted to get fired.

The cloaked campaign worked. High schoolers, middle schoolers, and even elementary-aged kids began to show at Bevel's afternoon sessions. Whole broods of children walked to a movement-friendly church where Bevel welcomed them, welcomed them all, once again not asking King if it was okay to admit this many kids but just doing it.

He and Diane screened a film from NBC shot three years prior at Nashville, at the sit-ins where James and Diane had met and found the courage, like their colleagues, to embrace the blows that fell on them. The footage was stark. Punches, maulings, Black protesters thrown over lunch counters.

Birmingham will be worse! Bevel said to the wide-eyed children. *But look! Look how our bodies remained dignified, peaceful. It is the most power-ful of ideas to turn your body into a vessel for change, to turn your body into a story of the Black experience itself.*

The children nodded. They did not run out. They were not terrified of what might happen to them. Instead, when the film ended, Bevel asked them to walk to that night's mass meeting.

They did. At the end of it, when King put out his nightly call for volunteers, a great many kids stepped forward. Bevel wanted to see how King would respond when the children themselves, some as young as eight, made Bevel's case.

King repeatedly told the young people to return to their seats.

By this point, in the latter half of April, Bevel's actions weren't a secret. They were Project C's draw. So well known that some high schoolers were getting expelled for going to his workshops. King himself had heard from distressed parents. Two of them, John and Deenie Drew, were Martin and Coretta's friends dating back years. Martin stayed with the Drews on the nights he didn't stay at the Gaston during Project C. The Drews were so horrified by James Bevel's actions, they sent their eleven-year-old to a prep school rather than have him be seduced into marching.

A. G. Gaston, the Reverend John Porter, the Black Birmingham establishment—no one wanted these kids protesting. The movement shouldn't have any person younger than eighteen, they argued. They urged King to punish Bevel. Wyatt Walker wanted Bevel fired for insubordination.

But King didn't do it. He was torn.

In open staff meetings and private discussions he freely admitted his distaste for child protesters. *The Birmingham Jail is no place for children*, he said with the knowledge of a man who'd just been there. Other issues troubled him, too. Child protesters posed legal issues for King. To use kids in a march was to tempt Alabama authorities to charge the SCLC with contributing to the delinquency of minors. The truancy, the arrests of un-derage protesters—these could be wielded against the kids *and* the SCLC. The legal fees and fines would be exorbitant, exhausting the organization and once again exceeding its budget. Considering all it would cost to bat-tle the new bevy of charges, this was fraught stuff, using children.

And yet.

Who else did the SCLC have? Each day the protests shriveled in num-ber and not even Wyatt Walker's optical illusions could keep the marches from looking lifeless. The press was beyond the point of commenting on Project C's anemia. "The press is leaving," King told Reverend Porter in one briefing at which they discussed utilizing children. "We've got to get something going."

"And I looked at him," Porter recalled, "and I really couldn't believe my ears." As if civil rights were some *entertainment*, Porter said, some *feature attraction* to amuse white reporters.

Now it was King's turn to gaze in astonishment. *If we don't hold the press's interest*, he said, *we don't defeat segregation*.

And yet he didn't endorse Bevel's plan, either. King seemed, if anything, to move the other way. It was the calling of his nature; he felt the pain of others. He felt something else, too. A responsibility for everyone's lives.

He felt it keenly in Birmingham. "A continual series of blows to his conscience," one advisor later said. A story that had always troubled King was one that appeared in the *New York Times* before the protests, distinct among pieces of journalism because it had drawn a libel lawsuit from the city of Birmingham and shaped the civil rights movement far outside it. By 1963 everybody in the South, white and Black, had either read Harrison Salisbury's piece or had strong opinions about it. The story described the fear and terrorism of Birmingham. In one of its anecdotes a Black teenaged boy participated in a prayer vigil for civil rights. For praying publicly and requesting equality, seven carloads of white men roared into his neighborhood and found the home where he lived with his mother and sister. They stormed the house. They beat the boy with iron pipes and leather blackjacks, and then his mother and sister, too, when they tried to defend him. The men broke the mother's leg, "smashed open her scalp and crushed her hands," Salisbury wrote.

It took the police a leisurely forty-five minutes to show, more than enough time for the assailants to flee.

The next day, in the hospital, the mother was awakened by two sheriff's deputies who said they wanted to take her statement.

When the mother, woozy from painkillers, focused on the deputies' faces, she recoiled.

They were two of the men who'd beaten her the night prior.

"She is afraid to say anything about it," a friend told the *Times*.

Which was, of course, the point of the deputies' visit. Not just the pain they could inflict but also the terror they could impart. They could reach her again, and her family, too, whenever they wanted, and act as they wanted.

The *brazenness* of it—*of course we'll visit her in the hospital and of course she'll stay silent afterward*—that's what bothered King. No repercussions for sin. Unchecked evil. A city where even the church bells chimed "Dixie."

And now King was thinking of subjecting hundreds more children and their parents to that brand of barbarity?

25

THE PROPHET AND THE PLAYBOY

B evel never stopped meeting with children. It didn't matter who questioned his actions or told him no. He expanded his mission and, at one point in April, Bevel and others sought out a deejay the kids loved: Shelley "The Playboy" Stewart. He spun records at WENN, an AM R & B station whose studio was on Fifth Avenue North, not far from the Gaston Motel. The red car Stewart parked in the lot had "Shelley 'The Playboy' Stewart" emblazoned across the side. Birmingham children—Black and white—loved Stewart. He refused to speak like other broadcasters. Stewart was goofy on air. He was loud. He said stuff like, "Ooohee! Good googly moogly!" and "Timberrrr, let it fall!" when he played a top hit.

Bevel walked into the studios one day and thought it would take serious work to focus Stewart on the children's campaign and then convince him to play a part in it. After all: *Good googly moogly?*

Stewart was bright, though. Ambitious. Above all, Stewart was aware of the injustice Black children inherited, he told Bevel and others, because he himself had endured so much as a kid in Birmingham. When he was five, he watched his father kill his mother with an ax. The cops didn't investigate. "Nigger crimes," as the police called them, seldom were. Shelley and his three brothers continued to live in a home where their father raged at them, drunk from his shift at the local iron company and where his father's girlfriend caught rats and fried them for dinner. When Shelley's dad got so violent one night that he broke Shelley's arm, Shelley ran away from home, as one of his brothers had done earlier. On the outskirts of the city he found a horse stable, where he would work and live over the next few years and from which he would continue his education.

That was the point of his travails (and there were many more travails): how an education could erase the pain. Stewart realized this with time, and he broke into radio broadcasting so that he could make a contribution to the city. "Being on the air you had music as the bait," he later explained, by way of elucidating his philosophy as a deejay. Sure, he said "Good googly moogly," but he also loathed Bull Connor and called him on air by his given name, a mocking "*U*-Gene." Like the hits he played, Stewart had his own refrains behind the mic: "Get some education" and "Someday we may want to drive the bus instead of riding in the back of the bus."

Each time he had an opportunity, he later said, "You talk about freedom. You talk about rights."

So, yeah, he told Bevel and other SCLC members, he was down for whatever. The Klan had already tried to cut down the station's radio tower. Stewart was still here, still broadcasting. As Stewart later told his station's owner, "I am a man. My people are suffering. I would rather eat shit with a toothpick than stop the drive for freedom."

Bevel liked him immediately.

The two devised a plan. Its goal was to attract even more kids to Bevel's workshops without getting them expelled from school or beaten at home by fearful parents. Stewart and Bevel settled on a series of code words Stewart would use on air. Bevel hoped the code words would work like the palm-sized leaflets he'd asked kids to distribute when their teachers weren't watching. A clandestine movement was, after all, an irresistibly attractive one.

Bevel left the studios and told the bravest kids—the teenaged leaders—to listen the next day to Stewart with all their friends, especially those who hadn't yet come to Bevel's sessions. The kids nodded.

The following day, Stewart took to the air in the afternoon. "Well, let's check the time," he said. "It's 3 o'clock. No, wait: It's 9 o'clock." This meant the next workshop would happen at 3:00 p.m.

As for where it would happen: "Hey, you know I saw Reverend Gardner up on 16th Street?" Stewart said. This told the kids listening that the workshop would be at 16th Street Baptist Church.

They came in droves. Children from all over Birmingham and even ones outside the city, who'd hitched a ride in. That's how quickly a secret spread. Bevel quit recruiting children and started recruiting SCLC staffers to help him handle all the kids who needed an education about nonviolence.

Inevitably, this got back to King. He wasn't angry at Bevel so much as shocked. Thousands of children willing to protest, and at a time when the SCLC could not find dozens of adults. Were the kids aware of what might happen to them?

In the meetings at which Bevel forced the SCLC to continue to debate his plan, he also continued to scoff at any resistance to it. The children lived in the same city as their parents, he said. The very ubiquity of terror here meant parents couldn't shield their children from all of it. The facts remained: The kids showed up to Bevel's sessions. They curled into the fetal position. They practiced protecting their skulls. They said after their training that they were willing to march. Their willingness was not born of ignorance.

King said the early Christians did not throw their children to the lions in the Colosseum, a point the middle-aged board seconded. They were a *Christian* organization, the SCLC. Christian leaders. Christian *pastors*. What would God think of the shepherd who led his young flock to this kind of slaughter?

God accommodates the righteous man, Bevel said.

He spoke from personal knowledge.

When James was ten, he and his younger brother Charles followed their father, Dennis, into a grove behind their sharecropper's plot to cut trees for firewood. Young Charles wandered off into the quiet of the woods and fell asleep. Dennis and James kept working, unaware. Dennis labored over a large tree and when it at last began to fall, he noticed a sleeping Charles in the tree's path.

"Don't let that tree hit the boy!" Dennis yelled to God.

The tree seemed just then to slow in its fall, to hesitate. Charles woke from his nap in that moment and lurched out of the way before the tree thundered to the ground.

James, mouth open, stared at his father. *How did you do that?* James asked. *How did you get the tree to stop?*

Dennis Bevel eyed him. "A man should live his life in a way that God will obey him," he told James.

The truth of that experience was what James relayed in Birmingham to his fellow freedom fighters. No action of theirs could be wrong if they lived right. The SCLC's intentions in Birmingham were pure: freedom for all of God's children. That purity meant God would listen to, even abide by, the actions of the SCLC, and of all of its protesters, whatever their age.

King didn't immediately dismiss Bevel. He asked Bevel what he would propose as the cutoff age for protesters. This set off another fierce discussion across multiple meetings because Bevel didn't think there should *be* a cutoff.

Any child old enough to walk to church was old enough to march for freedom, Bevel said.

26

THE END OF THE "ENDLESS" DELIBERATION

Meanwhile, the rest of the campaign floundered.

By April 26, the largest and most important newspaper in the country, the *New York Times*, pulled its reporter Foster Hailey from Birmingham and directed him to other locales throughout the South. The wire services carried less and less coverage of the adult-led protests in Birmingham. One piece ran at three paragraphs and, frankly, didn't warrant that space. It described a protest in which few adults showed up, all left quietly, and no one was arrested. The Birmingham dailies either ignored the protests or gloated over the movement's demise. "For the agitators," the *Birmingham Post-Herald* wrote, "things are going awry."

The whole of the movement now lay with the kids whom King did not want to protest. Wyatt Walker saw that much as he sat at the Gaston and fretted over Project C. His eight-page memo and its four-act plan of escalation had failed. No optical illusion of his could save them now. To accept that children were the best hope for Birmingham was to accept another truth, too: that Walker was wrong and Bevel was right. James Bevel had been right all along about this place.

That burned Walker. He loathed Bevel and had wanted him fired as far back as the Albany campaign. But Bevel had the attention of thousands of Birminghamians, thousands more than Walker had ever drawn.

Walker hunted down King.

Walker said not only did the protests have to continue, but "we need something new." The SCLC had "scraped the bottom of the barrel of adults who could go," as he would later remember saying.

King seemed to sense what Walker was really implying: *I was wrong, and Bevel was right.* Walker admitted Bevel had "one of the best tactical minds in our movement."

King was impressed, but still he equivocated: the morality of using kids . . .

Walker dismissed it. Think of the optics, he said. Bull Connor attacking children? Every news outlet in the *world* would cover that.

Everything must escalate, Walker reiterated.

Walker sensed that part of King's concern also had to do with violating Judge Jenkins's ruling and subjecting children to weeks if not months in jail for protesting.

"Six days in the . . . jail," Walker later recalled saying, "would be more educational to these children than six months in the segregated Birmingham schools."

King didn't give his blessing to the use of child marchers that day, but he did allow them to continue to congregate and learn from Bevel and like-minded staffers. These staffers now included Wyatt Walker.

We don't know how Walker made his peace with Bevel—Walker controlled a lot of the SCLC's messaging—and Walker would later attempt to portray his about-face in a light most favorable to himself: "Without being immodest, I think the combination of James Bevel and Wyatt Walker was unbeatable." But with Bevel's fiercest critic now in favor of it, Bevel's plan moved ahead.

He started to talk about a big protest in May. "D-Day," Bevel called it: children marching and singing and, most of all, accepting with grace and courage whatever happened to them. This grace and courage would inspire their parents. The northern press. The whole of America.

That was how they would break segregation in Birmingham. And by breaking it here, Bevel said, they would be able to break it anywhere.

Some board members remained resistant, some outraged. But A. D. King said children from his own congregation ached to march. Fred Shuttlesworth said simply, "We've got to use what we got."

Bevel gave D-Day a date: Thursday, May 2. He then appeared at a mass meeting on Saturday night, April 27, with a blackboard and chalk, and began to literally illustrate for the congregation—and Bull Connor's detectives in the audience—what he planned to do. Segregation was like a water tank, he said, "built to withstand storms and tornadoes," but as he and other staffers remarked that night, a march on City Hall, unlike any Birmingham had seen, was about to take place.

Expect four thousand marchers to knock over that water tank.

The detectives scribbled their notes; the SCLC filed paperwork to march on May 2; Shelley Stewart used more code words on air; and Martin Luther King Jr., well, he flew to Atlanta on the twenty-ninth for an opera and then on to Memphis for an SCLC meeting on the thirtieth, but mostly he deliberated as April flipped to May and he returned to Birmingham.

He never stopped deliberating. An "endless" deliberation, as even he later lamented: "I question and soul-search constantly."

He weighed and judged and stayed quiet for so long that on the eve of D-Day, King's silence provided its own answer. It was, ironically, one that he had foreseen all those months ago, at Dorchester.

The time had indeed come when James Bevel would lead them.

Part VI

D-DAY AND BEYOND

27

D-DAY

They tuned in by the thousands that Thursday morning, May 2, Black children who listened for the latest coded message on their radios from Shelley "The Playboy" Stewart, broadcasting live from his booth at WENN. In the hour before school began, children throughout Birmingham heard it: "Kids, there's gonna be a party at the park. Bring your toothbrushes because lunch will be served."

A party at the park meant the protest was on, and would be carried out at Kelly Ingram Park, across the street from 16th Street Baptist Church. The *toothbrushes* and *lunch* bit meant the kids should expect to be arrested and go to jail.

D-Day had arrived.

It was both a fiercely held secret and an openly acknowledged truth. James Bevel had talked about D-Day in nightly mass meetings for almost a week. Fred Shuttlesworth had requested a parade permit from the city for May 2. (It was denied.) There were few white cops or Black parents unaware *something* might happen. Bull Connor had even said that any child who walked out of school today would be "summarily and permanently expelled." And yet almost none of the adults knew *what* would occur or *when*. The children of Birmingham held that secret. The children of Birmingham and James Bevel and Shelley Stewart.

So they went to school. Thousands of children that Thursday morning went to school because that was the plan: to give the day the veneer of any other. On the bus to Parker High "my heart was pounding," one sophomore girl later wrote, thinking of all that lay ahead. Other students later recalled the hot flash of shame for lying to their parents when asked if the kids planned to do something. Other children remembered the illicit thrill that rose within them for keeping their plans to themselves. Some kids were terrified of what might go down. Others were terrified of what might happen to their parents when they—and their white employers—learned the children had protested. Would the parents lose their jobs? Go to jail themselves? What would happen to the *kids* in jail?

No one knew.

They proceeded anyway. "It wasn't the fear that kept us from doing it," one student later recalled. "It was the fear that made us want to do more."

At 11:00 a.m., a few students at Parker High snuck outside and held up a sign for all to see: "It's Time."

Inside the school they rose and walked out. The hallways became so crowded and chaotic that some kids hopped out the first-floor windows of their classrooms. The school's principal, R. C. Johnson, had earlier in the morning locked Parker's front gates in preparation for what might take place. This didn't stop the students now. They climbed over the gate and kept walking. An amazing sight: hundreds of teenagers, perhaps more than a thousand, suddenly on the street, walking and some singing the freedom songs they'd learned at James Bevel's workshops. Just as stunning was the remaining sight at Parker. It was the largest Black high school in the city—it had been the country's largest years prior—but on that May morning in 1963 the classrooms were empty. A school with 2,200 students where suddenly a straggling few remained, wide chasms of space between them.

A similar scene played out at Ullman High, Parker's biggest rival, and at Carver High and Western High and even at middle and elementary schools in Birmingham: Student leaders (whom Bevel had handpicked) telling other students, *Let's walk*. The kids then sneaking out front doors or jumping out windows and all the while the student leaders moving deeper into the schools, telling the willing children, *It's time*, until these schools were empty, too.

"The job is to get this file [of kids] out, get that file, get the football team, basketball team, get the cheerleaders, the band," recalled one young organizer of how he approached his work that day. Some teachers seemed outraged, but many were pleased by the disobedience. Silently pleased, because "I didn't want to lose my job," in the words of one such teacher. Some even subtly aided their students. One teacher at Ullman heard the disruptions coming from other classrooms and turned her back on her own. Just turned her eyes to the chalkboard and stayed like that, staring at the board, giving the kids whatever time they needed to walk out.

En masse they filled the streets of Birmingham, all these kids, from all directions, marching toward 16th Street Baptist Church, the rendezvous point.

Wyatt Walker and others within the SCLC had convinced enough members of the press to return to Birmingham and to set up around 16th Street Baptist. This was how media footage later emerged of James Bevel pacing in a tight circle outside the church that morning in his overalls, denim jacket, and yarmulke, waiting for the kids to arrive and wondering, in his darker moments, if they even would.

Here they came: a few at first, then dozens, then a deluge of hundreds, thousands, some running toward the church, laughing and shouting, and Bevel and the SCLC opening all doors—the front entrance, side, basement—to accommodate the flood of children.

As noon approached, the church was as loud and disorderly as the schools had been, the difference being no one wanted to leave the church.

In fact, more begged to be let in. One of Bevel's young deputies within the SCLC, James Orange, heard that a few kids from Fairfield High, in Fairfield, Alabama, needed a ride to D-Day. Orange drove his car—a big stretch of a sedan—to Fairfield, about seven miles from the church. When he got to the high school it wasn't a few kids. "The whole campus was outside the building," Orange later recalled. Some kids ran up to him. "We going to Birmingham! We going to Birmingham!"

Orange stuffed twenty kids into the seats and onto the roof and trunk of his car. He set off for Birmingham slowly, slow enough for eight hundred more kids to walk behind the sedan.

It was later reported that other children, from other suburban or rural schools, walked up to eighteen miles that day to 16th Street Baptist.

What did they see when they got there, if they calmed their excitement enough to look around? Police barricades across the street, at Kelly Ingram Park. Cops milling there, shotguns and rifles in hand. German shepherds from the K-9 corps prowling the park on loose leashes. Six fire engines blocking streets and avenues around the park. Bull Connor's white tank and even "army tanks," one student later wrote. "No one had said anything about army tanks."

Because Kelly Ingram Park stretched across a block of the city and divided Black Birmingham from white, and because D-Day was both a well-kept secret and a plainly acknowledged truth, the park quickly, and literally, assembled itself into a battle site. The cops with long guns and battle helmets on their heads looked at the Black adults watching them from across the street as the children ran into 16th Street Baptist, the adults glancing from the park to the church, their faces lined with anxiety, and the television cameras from the networks capturing it all.

Inside the church, many children experienced what one later described in writing: "Goose bumps of terror rose on my arms. *Are those tanks going to shoot bullets at us, like in a real war?*"

There was another question, just as pressing: Where was Martin Luther King Jr?

He was not in the church. No child or member of the press who'd been allowed in saw him. He was not on 16th Street North, which separated the church from Kelly Ingram Park. Local members of the campaign's organizing committee went looking for him on the sidewalks, irate over what the children were to march into. Only when they went to the Gaston Motel a half block south of the church did Black civic leaders or pressmen learn that King was in his suite, in room 30. He was not seeing visitors.

A. G. Gaston burst through the door anyway.

"Let those kids stay in school!" he shouted at King. Gaston had seen combat in World War I, and out that window looked like the makings of combat, he told King. Gaston had already said to the press, "I deplore the invasions of our schools to enlist students for demonstrations during school hours. I do not condone violence or violation of the law on the part of anyone and I am sure all responsible Negro citizens share this thought."

Now Gaston implored King. The kids—"they don't know nothing."

King remained calm. He later wrote, "The children understood the stakes they were fighting for." Bevel had convinced King of that.

To Gaston, King said, "Brother Gaston, let those people go into the streets where they'll learn something."

This appalled Gaston and he stormed out of the room. Perhaps the words even appalled King. He remained behind the door of room 30 long after Gaston slammed it shut, unable to lead the movement in its most decisive moment, unwilling to walk with the children or even bless them before they marched.

We don't know why King stayed in his suite that morning. In all his subsequent writings he never broached the subject. Press accounts from that day found it baffling that he never emerged. He was no doubt terrified of what he'd set in motion; people close to him said he stayed in the suite, "wrestling with his conscience." A less charitable view from other aides had it that distancing himself from D-Day allowed King to shirk responsibility for it, too. It's just as likely that remaining in room 30 gave him the chance to waffle about his decision even as it played out on the streets. As one of his lawyers, William Kunstler, later said, "Martin was about the most indecisive man I've ever seen." His uncertainty over what was right might have effectively paralyzed him that morning.

His absence affirmed one thing to his deputies, waiting for him at 16th Street Baptist. This day was theirs. Specifically, it was James Bevel's.

• • •

To quiet any nerves, Bevel strode to the altar at 16th Street Baptist a little before noon and turned the morning into "one big pep rally," as a teenager later put it. *Who's all here from Parker High School? Who's all here from Western?* Shrieks and applause and Bevel prowling the front of the church, a huge smile on his face. Music was central to the adults' nightly mass meetings, and Bevel wanted it to carry the same buoying effect for the kids. That morning, the moaning, somber "Ain't Gonna Let Nobody Turn Me 'Round" became—thanks to the organist taking his cue from Bevel—a fast-paced, jaunty pop number.

In the pews the kids swayed and clapped and belted out the song. The church was almost comically beyond capacity, children sitting or perching or standing wherever they could, all of them sweating from the surrounding body heat and the song's fast tempo. And all of them happy. That's the other thing you notice from the footage of that morning: the sheer number of kids with smiles on their faces. The girl who worried about the army tanks and bullets outside wrote that once she was inside the church, "the friends I had known all my life . . . stood around me. They gave me the courage I needed."

Bevel's workshops the preceding weeks had provided the children with knowledge many felt they had to act on. "The reality of it was that we were born Black in Alabama," another teenaged girl later said. "And we were going to get hurt if we *didn't* do something."

In the minutes before 1:00 p.m. the songs quieted and the preparation began. Charts and timetables emerged: when students from this church organization or that high school were to march, the names of the children within any protesting group, and each group's leaders. Everyone's mission was to walk to a destination in the city or be arrested trying. The meticulousness of these plans, timed down to the minute and almost compulsively organized, bore the mark of Wyatt Walker, the executive director who loved a good planning memo, and suggested how simpatico he and James Bevel had become in the last week. The children were to sing certain songs as they marched. They were to hold signs.

At all times do not fight back, Bevel said now, steps from the church's closed front door, the whole of this young congregation staring back at him, thousands of kids ranging in age from six to twenty. *Be nonviolent no matter what is said or done to you.*

Bevel saw the suddenly steely-eyed children nodding.

In that congregation as well were Bevel's dozens of SCLC colleagues. Ralph Abernathy viewed what was about to happen as a "battle." Fred Shuttlesworth saw it as a "miracle," given where the protests had been weeks earlier. Wyatt Walker considered this moment as his to shape alongside Bevel. He grabbed a walkie-talkie, with plans to retreat to the upper reaches of the church, high enough to offer a bird's-eye view of Kelly Ingram Park, and guide the events that happened there.

At the front of the church James Bevel nodded.

God accommodates the righteous.

He opened the doors to the glare of the afternoon.

Fifty children marched two by two. They sang "We Shall Overcome" as they moved straight into the phalanx of cops across the street in Kelly Ingram Park. When officers told them to halt, they did. When officers told them to return to the church, they did not. The officers said the children were in violation of the city's code for parading without a permit. The children dropped to their knees and prayed, as they'd been instructed. In the filmed footage from this day, some cops looked puzzled, they in battle helmets, unarmed children praying at their feet, the cops glancing at each other as if asking, *How do we do this?*

Gently, it turned out. The cops carefully lifted the kids one by one and walked the arrested children to a waiting paddy wagon. Whether out of their own concern or because of the national press corps a few yards away that recorded this encounter, the cops seemed to breathe a sigh of relief when the fifty children were driven off, as if their work were done.

It was at that point that Bevel had the next fifty march out.

It went like this for an hour. A freedom song; *You're in violation of the city's code*; children praying on their knees; a paddy wagon; a lull when it looked like these were the last of the child protesters; then another fifty stepping out of the church. Some groups held signs that said "Freedom," "Segregation Is a Sin," or "I'll Die to Make This Land My Home." Some groups walked to different corners of the park before being stopped. One group tried to avoid the park entirely and headed up Sixth Avenue North, which gave them a straight shot to City Hall. Bull Connor watched that group closely and had his officers arrest the kids before they made much headway. "Bull had something in his mind about not letting niggers get to City Hall," Wyatt Walker later said with a dry chuckle. Some praying kids refused to walk to the paddy wagon, and so the cops took them by their limbs and dragged them there. Almost every group sang "We Shall Overcome," or "Ain't Gonna Let Nobody Turn Me 'Round" or, more pointedly, and a song seemingly meant for the gathering adults who watched from the street: "Will You Join Us or Will You 'Tom' for the Big Bad Bull?"

The cops began to run out of paddy wagons. Officers crammed ever more kids inside the remaining few vehicles. It became a two- or three-cop job just to shove the doors closed.

And then another fifty walked out of the church.

Around this time, one officer approached Fred Shuttlesworth, standing outside 16th Street Baptist.

"Hey, Fred. How many more have you got?"

"At least a thousand."

"God a'mighty."

Bull Connor brought buses in from the Jefferson County school district. Soon those brimmed with children, too, who waved to the adults on the streets or to their friends about to be arrested alongside them in the park. Some kids sang as the buses drove to jail.

"Sing, children, sing!" one elderly woman shouted back, watching it all. Overwhelmed by it all.

Maybe five hundred kids had been hauled off by this point, and cops looked worn down from the cuffing and cramming. James Bevel halted the next group of protesters and walked out of the church and into the park. He walked straight to Bull Connor, who had spent a good portion of the afternoon with his hands on his hips and exasperation on his face.

Your men have to take a break, Bevel said.

Bevel's directness with Bull suggested two things: the sympathy Bevel held for even his enemy's needs, and how thoroughly Bevel controlled events here, able to dam the flood of protesters whenever he wanted and change the dynamic of the afternoon simply because he felt like it.

"Yeah," Bull said, a little cowed by Bevel, "we need a break because my officers—they've been out here and they haven't had anything to eat."

Bevel nodded. As if it had been ordained by God, food trucks came into view and parked on 16th Street North and Sixth Avenue.

The police department ordered so many sandwiches and Coca-Colas that they were set down in big cardboard boxes. Bevel and the SCLC placed their own orders for the kids, but Bevel then walked back outside and crossed the street. He took a sandwich from one of the cops' boxes. He unwrapped it and ate within view of Connor.

"Hey!" Bull shouted. "What's that nigger doing eating our sandwich?"

Bevel laughed. In response, he walked back into the church, and moments later the next group of fifty marched out.

The cops had to rise from the curb and guzzle down their Cokes and start cuffing again.

By the end of the afternoon, 973 children had been arrested.

The mugshots that day showed cool, unfazed boys and girls with the glare of defiance in their eyes; smiling teenagers and shy tweens who hunched their shoulders; young men in newsboy caps and girls with their hair wrapped; bespectacled kids; kids caught mid-laugh; kids caught in the midst of a terrible thought; kids too young to know they should look at the camera, their pupils drifting up to the flash of the bulb while they held their booking placard before them.

They had prepared for this eventuality; they had been told by Bevel they were doing God's work. Some, all too aware of Bombingham's reputation, even saw their coming martyrdom. "They'd tell me, 'Well, I know you gonna kill me,'" Detective James Parsons later recalled. "'But I wanna call my mama first.'"

It was a fevered situation that afternoon in the city and county jails. A lengthy line at the booking areas. Just too many kids to process: kids flushed with daring or beaming with pride for the fear they'd overcome. Some succumbed to that fear and bawled in their cells. Still more kids crowded in next to them.

Many were concerned that the protests might lead to their parents losing their jobs. Bevel had instructed the children to say nothing when asked who their parents were. The cops arrested eight-year-old Margaret Givener that afternoon, and when the officers asked her for the names of her parents, she told them, "No comment." Later that night at the juvenile jail, Margaret sat in a cell with her twelve-year-old sister and other young people when law enforcement agents approached the Givener girls again. "They asked us who our parents were and where we lived. They said they wanted it so they could call our parents," Margaret later said. The cops tried to position this phone call as an act of goodwill: Letting the Giveners know their daughters were safe. Young Margaret saw through the ruse. "We didn't tell them anything."

Almost to a child the kids followed the SCLC's training. Janice Kelsey sure did. She was the honor student from Ullman High who'd attended Bevel's earliest workshop. She'd had her life altered when Bevel told her and other teenagers how their school supplies were white schools' discards. Kelsey did not come from an activist household. She had taken Shelley Stewart's coded message about toothbrushes so literally this morning that she'd smuggled her family's tube of toothpaste out of her home. Kelsey had surprised herself today, first by finding the courage to march and then by feeling excited when a yellow school bus came to haul her away. She'd always dreamed of riding in a Jefferson County yellow school bus; Black students in Birmingham weren't allowed to. "I sat down in the front seat," Kelsey later wrote. No one would tell her to sit in the back today. "We started singing freedom songs again and had the greatest time." At the booking station, officers took her and other students' jackets and purses and wallets—all their personal effects—and moved the kids to a jail cell, which wasn't a proper cell but a holding area. Other children occupied all official cells. Some of those cells jammed in seventy-five kids. The units had been designed for eight. Kelsey's holding area, not quite as crowded, turned cold that night. There were no beds. Kelsey and her friends slept on the chilly concrete floor. It sounds as bad as it was but for one thing, a thought that Kelsey and almost all other children considered that day.

They had done it. They had filled the jails.

"The whole world is watching Birmingham!" Fred Shuttlesworth shouted at that night's mass meeting, held at Sixth Avenue Baptist. More than two thousand people looked back at him, rising and *amen*-ing and applauding, the largest crowd yet for any mass meeting. Fred was almost too jittery to speak. He had *never* been part of *any* protest as successful as today's. He had woken early this morning and headed straight to the church to see that deluge of students rushing in. Fred had darted from one group of kids to the next, interrupting the final training sessions Bevel or other SCLC colleagues led to give short bursts of inspiration: "Freedom fighters," he'd told the kids. That's what they were. "As much so as those in the army. But without weapons." Oh, it was wonderful to witness. The student leaders whom Bevel had handpicked—Shuttlesworth had guided Bevel to many of them. Fred knew these kids. Knew their character. Their parents. Birmingham was *Fred's* town, and to see what happened today made the years of struggle—the Christmas Day bombing; the beating at all-white Phillips High; his endless encounters with Bull, many of them faced alone or with his tiny band of congregants—today redeemed all that pain. "Our little folks," he said to the crowd at Sixth Avenue Baptist, emotion coursing through him. Those children had damn near filled the jails. *No one* had done that. Not one civil rights group in the whole of the movement stretching back to the 1950s. But they'd done it today in Fred's town of Birmingham, Alabama.

Amazed himself, he repeated the number for the audience: "one thousand kids."

James Bevel spoke, too. "There ain't gonna be no meeting [like this] Monday night because *every* Negro is going to be in jail by Sunday night," he said. He asked for a show of hands: Who'd been inspired by the children? It seemed almost two thousand arms shot up.

Then go to jail, Bevel said. He'd been many times. His wife, Diane, was incarcerated now; she'd been arrested for protesting days earlier. Bevel said he wanted everyone in jail over the weekend, "so that I can be back in Mississippi chopping cotton by Tuesday."

Like this morning, Bevel then helped to lead the congregation in song. Two thousand people rose to their feet and the church erupted in freedom anthems. The adults left the pews and marched up and down the aisles, as if practicing what they planned to do over the weekend.

King spoke as well. "I have been inspired and moved today," he said. He meant that literally: He'd pushed himself from his room in the Gaston in part because the afternoon could not have gone better. Peaceful protests, mass arrests, no counterviolence, no injuries. And the greatest of God's beneficence: They were close to *filling the jails.* "I have never seen anything like it!" King shouted to the crowd.

For every child arrested, two or three more had come in through the back of the church, hoping to protest. "Some of us might have to spend three or four hours tonight planning our strategy for tomorrow," King said. "If they think today is the end of this, they will be badly mistaken."

28

DOUBLE D-DAY

Friday, May 3, and 1,500 kids not even bothering with the veneer of heading to school. Fifteen hundred kids who skipped it entirely and didn't give a damn about Bull Connor's decree of permanent expulsion—or, judging from subsequent accounts, their parents' finger-wagging to stay away from Kelly Ingram Park. Today was Double D-Day. That's what James Bevel and Wyatt Walker were calling it. That's what Shelley "The Playboy" Stewart alluded to on WENN this morning. Fifteen hundred kids walked straight to 16th Street Baptist, a move that, frankly, may have helped their teachers. Governor George Wallace had threatened overnight to have any educator charged with criminal collaboration for aiding a child's truancy today.

They poured into the church. Fifteen hundred, two thousand, more: One report stated that only 887 of the city's 7,386 Black high school students attended school that Friday. Of the thousands who appeared at 16th Street Baptist were children who'd come yesterday but had not made it to the front to be arrested. There were kids who'd seen the arrests on the news and wanted to play their part in Double D-Day. A lot of children were new to nonviolence. Bevel started the training and passed a trash can through the ranks, and soon that can was half full with knives the kids had discarded.

Not so much as a peach pit *should be on you when you march*, Bevel and other workshop leaders said.

Meanwhile, around 10:00 a.m., King and Shuttlesworth held a press conference in the open-air courtyard of the Gaston Motel. "We intend to negotiate from strength," King told the crush of reporters crowded around: local columnists, national outlets, European camera crews. "If the white power structure of this city will consider meeting some of our minimum demands, then we will consider calling off the demonstrations."

The SCLC had talked about this last night and into the morning: The jails were close to bursting, with even more kids primed for incarceration this afternoon. Where would Mayor Boutwell and Bull Connor put them all? King argued it was in the city's best interest to sit down with him and Shuttlesworth and negotiate the terms of desegregation in Birmingham.

"We want promises, plus action," King told the reporters.

What he didn't say was what he knew and had known all along, what Wyatt Walker even hoped for in that initial planning memo in January. If the goal was to leave Bull Connor no good option, then the result might be Bull lashing out, turning his terrible vengeance on the protesters, in this case children. The SCLC had to be prepared for that. Which meant King had to make his peace with it.

He didn't say this to the newsmen, in part because he didn't know what sort of pain Bull Connor might inflict today. As the morning wore on it became clearer. Across the street at Kelly Ingram Park were not only the cops in battle helmets and K-9 corps and the tanks on display but also something new. Firefighters unfurled water hoses and trained the nozzles on the church.

Since April, Birmingham fire chief John Swindle had heard Bull Connor bellow about his fear: a mass of Black protesters marching into the white-owned downtown. Connor had demanded Swindle turn the hoses on any Black protester who tried to march there. The suggestion appalled Swindle. He'd been able to deter Bull, had even argued that the firemen's national union strongly disapproved of fire hoses being used as "crowd control."

But with the deluge of protesters yesterday, Bull had ordered Swindle to unfurl the hoses today. Swindle had again argued against it just this morning: *Fire engines are tied to hydrants; protesters can simply walk away from you*, he'd said.

So Bull had ordered Swindle to put even more fire engines in the park. Bull said no one was walking or marching anywhere today. The jails were damn near full.

The message was clear: Bull would beat back the crowds because he could not afford to arrest them.

Swindle could either obey Bull's order or be fired.

Chief Swindle was not fired that day.

The pep rally, the freedom anthems, the kids sweating from the exertion of singing and the surrounding body heat: Today felt a bit like yesterday inside 16th Street Baptist in the final moments before Bevel opened the doors to that glare of the afternoon. Today was also different. There were too many cops outside, for one. Hundreds of them, as if the whole force had shown up. Cops and tanks and all those fire trucks: It looked like a battle against the apocalypse when the kids peeked out the windows. For the kids who'd been inside the church yesterday, they saw so many more onlookers on the street today, too. One estimate later put it at three thousand people, most of them Black, some of them parents of the kids in the church, all of them staring at the show of force Bull Connor assembled.

"Bull Connor had ordered the white army tanks onto the streets," Carolyn McKinstry, a fourteen-year-old who'd been at the church yesterday but hadn't marched, later wrote. "If [Bull] meant for them to surprise and frighten us, his plan worked." She found strength in the school friends around her, clapping and singing. She told herself she would not back down. She would march today. She would right the wrongs Bevel had highlighted in the workshops she'd attended: Why there were "white" and "colored" lines in the city; why she couldn't go to Kiddieland, the local amusement park, when she begged her parents to take her. McKinstry was just a child, but she vowed to do something today that might make *her* children's lives better.

Martin Luther King Jr. came to the pulpit. "If you take part in the marches," King said, "you are going to jail, but for a good cause." King still clung to jail as today's best-case outcome. He did not share with the kids the worst.

The time came.

No violence, Bevel said, the whole of the congregation eyeing him, just like yesterday.

Then, much like yesterday, the church doors swung wide.

The first group of fifty marched out. These children saw how police barricaded certain streets around the park, while thousands of onlookers and hundreds of pressmen effectively cordoned off the other side of the park's avenues. There was one place for the children to march: Toward the fire trucks ahead. The kids tried to be brave as they approached. They sang a call-and-response number: *"We're going to walk, walk, walk / Freedom, freedom, freedom."* One girl noticed the firefighters dressed in their full suits and helmets, holding giant hoses. She thought, *Where's the fire? It must be massive.* Then she watched as the nozzles leveled at her fellow protesters. *Bevel never said a* word *about water hoses*, she thought.

Bull Connor stood in a suit and tie just behind the line of firemen, squinting at these children with his one good eye. Captain G. V. Evans of the police department, a few feet from Connor, put a bullhorn to his lips.

"Disperse!" he shouted. "Or you're gonna get wet."

The kids had been trained not to disperse. They inched forward again. Some children saw how it took three or four firemen just to hold a hose. Other firemen quickly mounted their hoses on massive metal tripods, as if the water that would rush out carried the force of a cannon.

Last chance, Evans said through the bullhorn. The kids did not move. Evans told the firemen to turn the nozzles to "fogging." This would drench the kids, at perhaps half the strength of the hoses' potential.

Evans watched the children.

They inched forward again.

Like a geyser the water shot out. The force was strong enough to send many children fleeing and screaming in pain. "That water *stung*," one teenaged boy later said.

After the dousing, the shouts and fleeing, and then the mist that spread in the water's wake, onlookers saw something amazing. About ten kids had refused to move. These teenaged boys and girls, completely soaked, held their ground and even continued to sing as more sprays of water hit them. They grabbed each other's hands for balance. They raised those hands as one and belted out a single word of a song, over and over, until everyone in the park could hear it.

FREEDOM!

The defiance, the *plea* of their one-word anthem: Still photographers had the presence of mind to capture this moment, one as instantly iconic as the Marines raising the flag on Iwo Jima.

Bull Connor saw these ten kids as something other than freedom fighters. He saw them as degenerates trying to wrest control of the day from him.

"*Blast* them with that water!" one protester heard Bull shout.

Some firemen hesitated. The nozzles on full strength? One firefighter later said, "Good Lord, I was scared to death" about what might happen if they turned the nozzles to full power.

But an order from Bull was an order from Bull. Obey it or be canned.

The moment of indecision stretched out.

In the end what can be said is that no firefighter had the bravery of those ten children, standing no more than thirty feet from them. No fireman walked away from the job.

Instead, as one, the firefighters cranked up the pressure and steadied themselves.

The water lashed out.

. . .

The singing stopped immediately. As if "from automatic machine-gun fire," the force of the water flattened the kids, in the words of one writer. One teenaged boy tried to rise again, and a stream hit him square in the face and back-flipped him. These fire hoses, either held by four men or mounted on metal tripods, so highly pressurized the water that its power could knock bricks loose from mortar or strip the bark from trees at a distance of a hundred feet.

The water struck down some children at perhaps thirty feet. It stripped the shirt off one boy. Just kind of disintegrated it. The kids shouted in agony as they began a slow retreat. Slow because some children kept trying to stand against the water's wrath. They did not want to leave the park.

It was at that point that James Bevel sent out the next fifty kids.

Reinforcements.

From then on, the day showcased an almost otherworldly bravery—and savagery. One girl walked into the water and it cartwheeled her through the park, end over end. When the water hit another girl it flattened her on the sidewalk. The firemen then had the cruelty to focus that hissing stream on her exposed back. The water slid her perhaps fifty feet down the street as she screamed in pain and fear. Elsewhere, children huddled behind trees or light poles, or just attempted to use each other as shields against that rushing, stinging fury.

"We could hear the firemen yelling, 'Knock the niggers down,'" one girl later said.

The crowd—some three thousand people and, again, some of them parents—retaliated. They threw whatever was near at the firefighters: bottles, rocks, even the bricks the fire hoses had dislodged.

Bull didn't like that. He ordered the firemen to train the water on the crowd, too. This only increased the debris thrown at the firemen.

The fight was on now.

Mass arrests, cops cracking people across the skull—footage showed victims bleeding from their temples—and Bull antagonizing the crowd by hopping in that white tank of his and driving it up and down 16th Street North as more bottles and bricks rained on it. And still the next group of fifty protesters, the hissing water, the screaming children, the freedom songs between the screams, Bevel rushing out another fifty, because what was a metaphor of the Black experience in America if not this moment? And fourteen-year-old Carolyn McKinstry being in this group, trying to act bravely, trying to sing, marching into the park as the water leveled the kids in front of her and now her, too, hitting her in the face and hissing across her hairline, pulling it from the roots, scalping her, effectively, and making her cry in pain.

And then the K-9 corps, Bull trying to grab control of the afternoon by unleashing the chaos of the police department's six German shepherds, the dogs snarling, biting whomever they wished, as adults fled or children tried to avert them like bullfighters. One of the dogs, a black German shepherd named Nigger—"vicious," in the words of one teenaged girl who saw him that day—lunged at a small boy, a child protester, and clamped its teeth around the boy's throat and shook its head from side to side until eventually it let the boy go and the child was rushed to the hospital. And still another fifty marching out of 16th Street Baptist, then another. And one group of firemen training their hose on a huddled mass of children, on their knees, on the sidewalk, completely defenseless, at a distance of perhaps fifteen feet. The wails from those kids. And elsewhere in the park, the overwhelming power of a hose such that the four firemen holding it could no longer contain the thing, the hose freeing itself, spraying water and twisting wildly, like some angry venomous serpent, until one firefighter tried to grab hold of it and the nozzle slapped him hard across the face and knocked him out cold. And the press capturing all of this, those hundreds of pressmen from across the world filming everything, the afternoon shading into something darker still, a white man driving his car into the crowd and a Black teenager fighting a cop and grabbing that cop's gun from his holster and the cop reclaiming it by beating back the kid before he could shoot. And elsewhere, or rather everywhere, the streams of water and the dogs, crazed now, one German shepherd named Leo attacking a fifteen-year-old boy named Walter Gadsden, Leo leaping in the air and clamping down on Gadsden's exposed right core, his ribs and obliques, like the dog was *feasting* on the boy. Good lord the *carnage* of this day. NBC's reporter R. W. "Johnny" Apple, stopping to just gather himself in one moment and saying to *Life* photographer Charles Moore, "I've never seen anything like this in my life," a sentiment that Apple would repeat for decades after, even when reporting from war zones: Nothing distressed him, nothing *frightened* him, like Double D-Day in Birmingham, Alabama. And in that moment as Apple spoke to Moore, Moore thought about his own life—three years as a photographer in the *Marines*, for chrissake—and agreed with Apple, commenting that the dogs were the worst of it, at least for him, the snarl of the German shepherds, how they ripped flesh, how the victims screamed in equal parts pain and terror. It was "revolting," Moore said. And neither man knew that at various street corners around the park Wyatt Walker had enlisted his SCLC deputies to blow dog whistles, blow them as hard as they could, because Walker wanted this scene, *wanted* these optics—*everything must escalate*. But he hadn't okayed the idea with King; he just did it. Walker helped to instigate a white rage and the consequent Black suffering that were in fact native to Birmingham, and had been since its founding, and America's, too, and the quicker Walker could show all that to the press, who would in turn show it to the nation—hell, the world—the sooner Walker could get what he wanted from that nation, and world.

Equality.

A bitch of a line to draw in America's dirt. And yet what was Project C if not the filmed pain of Wyatt Walker's fellow Black people? That had been his rationale all along. And everyone else's in the SCLC, too. But now that the day was here and those doing the suffering were children, James Bevel went outside at 3:00 p.m., two hours and a lifetime after the protest had begun, and shouted at the kids to move back into the church. Bevel had seen enough. Around this time a police inspector, William Haley, walked into 16th Street Baptist and found King. The cop looked queasy and told King both sides needed to call it off for the day. It was unclear if the cop was negotiating with Bull's approval. King, who had been watching the last two hours himself, was "only too happy to accept the truce," as one writer later put it.

He had seen enough, too.

He stood by what he had allowed, though. If anything, King sought to take advantage of it. Within an hour of the protest's end, King phoned Clarence Jones and gave the lawyer a lengthy list of people who should be notified of the afternoon's events, starting with Jack and Bobby Kennedy. They were to be sent a telegram demanding that the federal government intervene in Birmingham. King would use this day for the cause's benefit. King wanted that telegram sent immediately because he wanted Jack and Bobby to hold it as they watched the nightly news. Wyatt Walker was sure all networks' lead story would be Birmingham.

He was right. CBS, ABC, every radio station and broadcast syndicate: They showed the footage of those furious hoses and aired the piercing screams of the children. NBC's story—with R. W. Apple's reporting—was so stark that the network ultimately decided to lengthen the format of the nightly news itself, from fifteen minutes to thirty. For the television networks, this was coverage unlike any they had broadcast. Violence, lurid violence, but capturing a terrible truth, rooted in the events of the last few hours and the hatred that stretched back centuries. "No one had seen anything quite like it in America," one writer later said. One SCLC executive in New York called May 3 "television's greatest hour."

The wall-to-wall coverage invigorated King. He went to the nightly mass meeting at 16th Street Baptist and said the children who'd come back to the church this afternoon with their clothes stripped from them, with dog bites puncturing their skin, were doing God's work. These children highlighted how it had been a "dark day" for the police force. King had heard from parents all afternoon. One of them, Nims R. Gay, who'd been an activist alongside Fred Shuttlesworth since the 1950s, said watching his oldest son, Cordell, "being washed down the street with a hose . . . was one of the hardest things to accept." And yet King told the crowd, "Don't worry about your children; they're going to be all right."

Only some *amen*-ed to that. The early media reports said at least three kids had been rushed to the hospital. There had been two hundred more arrests today, almost all of them children. "Your daughters and sons are in jail, many of them, and I'm sure many of their parents are here tonight," King said. He had heard the rumors at the jails of roaming rats and overwhelmed latrines. "They are suffering for what they believe and they are suffering to make this world a better place. . . . Don't worry about them.

"And dogs?" Here King's tone turned even more defiant. "Well, I'll tell you. When I was growing up, I was dog bitten." He paused and drew out the moment for the congregation. The picture of a young King being attacked—or, more likely, the crowd's own children—led some in the audience to gasp and shriek. King said he was bitten "for *nothing*! So I don't mind being bitten by a dog for standing up for freedom!"

This was a colder King, a recalcitrant one. If yesterday he had second-guessed his decision, today he stood resolutely beside it. He quieted his sensitive nature and allowed for a detached, almost clinical logic. Double D-Day was the inevitable outcome of everything this movement had striven for.

He was, in his way, only affirming with his actions what he'd written in his "Letter from Birmingham Jail." "Nonviolent direct action seeks to create such a crisis and foster such a tension that a community which has constantly refused to negotiate is forced to confront the issue. It seeks to so dramatize the issue that it can no longer be ignored."

Today they had dramatized the issue.

Tomorrow, King assured the crowd, no Black person in Birmingham would be ignored.

29

THE VIEW FROM WASHINGTON

They had seen it, almost all of it. Jack and Bobby Kennedy had watched the news programs that Friday night and Bobby had then released a statement in response: "An injured, maimed, or dead child is a price that none of us can afford to pay." For all the footage from Friday, though, it was a still photograph on Saturday morning, May 4, that really got to the Kennedy brothers.

It appeared on the front page of the *New York Times*. Above the fold and across three columns of newsprint. It was the photo of a dog attack, specifically of the German shepherd named Leo, the one who had leapt through the air and bitten the ribs and obliques of fifteen-year-old Walter Gadsden, of Parker High. Associated Press photographer Bill Hudson had taken the photo. In the carnage outside the frame, Leo continued growling and biting, as if the dog were feasting on Gadsden, but Hudson's still photograph captured something else.

Serenity.

In the photo, a snarling Leo is about to close its jaws around the midsection of Gadsden, but the boy's face is somehow peaceful. His body is at ease. He is not fighting the dog or even protecting himself. His arms remain at his sides. It is as if Walter Gadsden is giving himself to the German shepherd—as if he has some notion the moment would live beyond the attack. (And it would.)

It was that juxtaposition—of the dog's ferocity and the boy's whole-body offering—that arrested the Kennedy brothers Saturday morning. The image made President Kennedy "sick," he said. It captured everything: the unleashed rage of the white South; the brave demands of King and his protesters; the government of Birmingham's attempt to snuff out those demands, a snuffing out itself symbolic of every southern seat of power—and, in its subtler forms, of white authority everywhere in America.

When Secretary of State Dean Rusk saw the photo that day, he worried it would "embarrass our friends abroad and make our enemies joyful." The Kennedys agreed. It was another concern for Jack and Bobby: the purposes to which the photo could be used by the Soviets. The Cold War was not so cold in the spring of 1963. The Cuban missile crisis had played out just the previous fall.

This photo was a huge advantage for the Soviets, published in almost every American newspaper. The Kennedys knew they needed to act. They *wanted* to. It was the right thing to do, but there was another reason, too.

"In this family we want winners," Joe Kennedy had told his sons almost every day when Jack and Bobby were boys. The will to win that they'd learned in Hyannisport, less a childhood home than a rough field of play, lived now at 1600 Pennsylvania Avenue. Chester Bowles, the U.S. ambassador to India, said the Kennedys saw governing as a game. Whenever the brothers suffered a setback administering America, both of them, but particularly Bobby, could become "emotional and belligerent," Bowles said. "Neither Jack nor Bobby was accustomed to setbacks. For years they moved from success to success."

That's what the brothers needed now: another victory.

The problem was neither of them knew how to win on civil rights.

This was their own doing. They were, for all their liberal polish, apathetic toward Black people. As a senator in the 1950s, Jack had not given "much thought" to civil rights, one aide said. If anything, he'd considered

Reconstruction "punitive" to the South. Mississippi's governor J. P. Coleman liked him: In 1958 Coleman told the press that on the issue of Black equality, Jack Kennedy was "no hell raiser or barnburner."

Bobby—the "Puritan," in Jack's words, the one with the "high moral standards"—was no more passionate about Black people's struggles. "I won't say I stayed awake nights worrying about civil rights before I became Attorney General," Bobby said. Even after he took office as AG, "Robert Kennedy was not learned in the intricacies of civil rights," the Kennedy administration's own historian, Arthur M. Schlesinger, wrote. Jack and Bobby had that patriarchal air about them, particular to the northern ruling class, and to many liberal whites of the 1960s. The brothers understood segregation was wrong. They didn't understand what they could do to fix it.

This was in part Washington's fault. The Kennedy administration sent a voting rights bill to Congress in February 1963, but it went nowhere. Southern politicians controlled the House and Senate. "Nobody paid any attention," Bobby later said. He was so resigned to the bill's demise that even as he oversaw it Bobby shielded his brother from it. "I don't think we ever discussed [the legislation]," Bobby admitted. Both Kennedys viewed civil rights bills as hopeless and wondered at times about changing the South through an executive order.

Jack and Bobby debated this with Justice Department lawyers: how to strike down segregation with a stroke of the president's pen. The DOJ lawyers argued that the administration couldn't demand that the South desegregate. An executive order didn't work like that. If the Kennedys tried, they'd get too many challenges in southern federal courthouses before the order became policy.

Even court-approved law had its problems. The Supreme Court had integrated schools in 1954 and yet almost all of them in the South remained segregated in 1963. The problem for the Supreme Court was the problem for the Kennedys. Despite the federal government's power, state and local institutions throughout the South did what they wanted through the passing of their own legislation. This legislation countered Washington's. So long as local police and sheriff's departments enforced southern law and not the federal government's, segregation remained the way of life. The Kennedys' only possible solution was to send in the national guard and mandate integration at the point of a gun. Of course, if the Kennedys did that, they'd have to do it in each municipality in each southern state that was breaking federal law.

That meant a nationalized police force. And *that* looked like a police state, and not just to paranoid southerners. Liberal Supreme Court justice Robert H. Jackson had prosecuted cases at the Nuremberg trials and later warned Congress that "the establishment of the supremacy of the national over the local police authorities" was a central feature "in every totalitarian state."

All of this was why the DOJ lawyers didn't like an executive order. They argued the Kennedys should return to their first dead end: legislation passed by Congress.

And *that* was why the Kennedys couldn't win—or rather, didn't know how to win on civil rights. Come the morning after Double D-Day, though, the brothers were convinced they had to try again.

Bobby called Burke Marshall. Marshall was the lead attorney in the civil rights division in Bobby's Justice Department. Marshall was a Yalie, taciturn, having learned to keep a tight lip as a partner at Covington & Burling, the D.C. megafirm that specialized in corporate law, where Marshall had worked antitrust cases before joining the DOJ and reporting to Bobby. Marshall had spent almost every day of the last three years around Bobby Kennedy, and over the phone this morning Marshall could hear Bobby's stress, how beleaguered he was.

We've got to do something here, Burke.

Marshall wanted to be helpful but told Bobby that Birmingham was a tough problem, and half-suggested a more formalized meeting at the White House.

Bobby brushed that aside. Formality wasn't his way. This was a guy who brought his Labrador to the DOJ and conducted meetings with his necktie loosened, hair askew, while sitting cross-legged in his chair or on one of the office's sofas. Bobby cared about the result, not how the work was done. Today, Bobby said he wanted the work done immediately.

He and Marshall stayed on the phone, talking about their options.

Well, they could send in the U.S. Army, Marshall said. He had thought about it not long after King's campaign in Birmingham started. The army had been used in the past. Eisenhower sent one thousand troops from the 101st Airborne Division to ensure that nine Black students could attend Central High School in Little Rock, Arkansas. The problem with sending the 101st to Birmingham was that the city's leaders were not violating a *single* federal law. They were violating *all* of them. The army wasn't useful against pervasive violations, as the ubiquity of the violations made federal law itself invisible. The army couldn't go down to Birmingham and enforce an entire invisible world, Marshall argued.

The only thing the Kennedy administration could do was change that world bit by bit, until the invisible was made visible.

So the issue before Bobby Kennedy this morning, Marshall said, was really how to help King.

Bobby repeated that he did not want to help King. He just wanted to end the protests.

Marshall said the best way to end the protests was to mediate the negotiations. Marshall volunteered to go down to Birmingham. Serve as a liaison between the city's negotiators and the SCLC's. A mediation would place the federal government in a neutral position, favoring neither King nor Bull Connor.

Bobby liked that idea. It was the swiftest, most direct path to what Bobby wanted: no more Double D-Days.

Within a half hour, Burke Marshall was on a plane to Birmingham.

30

BURKE GOES TO BIRMINGHAM

Burke Marshall was ill-prepared for this job. He was only vaguely familiar with King's demands, much less the particulars of what had occurred over the last five weeks in Birmingham. He kept a voluminous correspondence with Bobby Kennedy across hundreds of pages of letters, memos, and strategy suggestions in the first few months of 1963, and yet no more than a dozen of those pages dealt with the Birmingham campaign. One letter Marshall wrote to a friend three days before he flew to Birmingham showed Marshall having only a cursory knowledge of the week King spent in the Birmingham Jail and joking how Marshall himself would need "further training in the tenets of civil disobedience" if he was to deal with King and Alabama governor George Wallace much more.

Marshall's portfolio *was* massive. Oversight of what the SCLC did, the NAACP, SNCC, CORE, and Malcolm X, too. Every law-flouting southern politician. Each effort for fair housing or employment. And always, every southern voter registration drive, which Bobby Kennedy saw as the best path to a more equitable future. It was a big job.

From the start, though, Burke Marshall had been questioned about why he had it. An "enigmatic" hiring, the NAACP had said. Marshall had never lived in the South. He had never argued a civil rights case prior to his appointment in the Kennedy administration. He cared personally about civil rights—"You've got to treat people in accordance with the Constitution; you've got to get the police to go along with it; get the courts to go along with it"—but had been so soft-spoken in his interview for the civil rights job, "so terribly nervous," as one aide put it, that Bobby Kennedy himself nearly rejected Marshall. Bobby reconsidered him because Marshall had a reputation in D.C. as a rigorous lawyer and the other leading candidate for the job, Harris Wofford, was an outright advocate who had advised Martin Luther King Jr. "I was reluctant to appoint [Wofford]," Bobby later said, "because he was so committed to civil rights emotionally and what I wanted was a tough lawyer who could look at things . . . objectively."

Marshall had learned that an objective view was the one that helped the administration's aim. In other words: Now that Bobby seemed to care about Birmingham, Burke Marshall would, too. He was a Kennedy loyalist, enthralled with the brothers not just because their gilded paths paralleled his own—from Exeter to Yale to the army to Yale Law—but because his road and the brothers' led straight to D.C., the city that housed the central belief of their lives.

Noblesse oblige. Ask not what your country can do for you but what you can do for your country. That wasn't just a clever line. Burke Marshall lived it. Jack Kennedy's call to arms for "the best and brightest" meant Burke Marshall had to find a way, and fast, to honor the Kennedy brothers and the ideal they all shared.

He stepped off the plane and into Birmingham.

He settled in a motel alongside another DOJ lawyer, Assistant Deputy Attorney General Joseph Dolan, who would work with Marshall to hurry along the negotiations.

The first thing Marshall did was call the Gaston. He tried to get King on the phone but settled for Wyatt Walker.

"I said that we thought they should put off the demonstrations," Marshall later recalled telling Walker. Marshall was in Birmingham, he said, to meet with King and then the city's leaders and begin the process of a truce. *Let's act in good faith*, Marshall argued. *Hash out differences at the negotiating table and not the streets.*

Walker, wily as ever, fully aware the demonstrations were the SCLC's leverage, said he would pass along word that Marshall wanted to speak with Dr. King.

He did not call off that day's protest.

And so Burke Marshall watched from his motel room as more hoses sprayed more kids. Screams, epithets, two girls' dresses ripped from their bodies—the water disintegrating them—and the girls running from Kelly Ingram Park in their white slips, crying. Marshall called the Gaston again to halt the demonstrations, but King was not interested.

The SCLC was carrying out a new plan today.

Walker and Bevel staged a subterfuge campaign. When the protests started Saturday at the park and the first group of kids marched from 16th Street Baptist into the hoses' fury, a separate group of twenty-five children casually assembled near City Hall. The kids then raced to the steps of white power, where a few of them unfurled a banner: "Love God and Thy Neighbor." The children fell to their knees and began to pray. This sent members of the press scurrying to City Hall, to capture the guerrilla tactics and movement victory: The children had made it to the very home of Bull Connor!

Bull himself came out of the building, irate. He ordered the kneeling children arrested. He then cuffed any Black person anywhere near City Hall. The press captured the children laughing at what they'd pulled off. Angry cops frog-marched them and unsuspecting bystanders to a waiting bus to take them all to jail.

Back at the park, and perhaps because of what had just occurred at City Hall, the afternoon turned uglier than it had yesterday. It was not only the debris from the bystanders; or how the firefighters once more leveled the hoses on the crowd and brutally kept them there; or the prowling of the K-9 corps; or the skirmishes between Blacks and whites, the raised billy clubs, spilled blood, and taunts, one young Black woman shouting, "You don't like us but you like our Black pussy!"

No, this Saturday afternoon turned uglier because of the guns. More than an hour into the protest the cops unclipped their handguns from their holsters and angry bystanders began to flash their own. If *everything must escalate*, then guns were indeed an escalation, the only logical escalation. James Bevel, marching out another group of fifty kids, saw at least two dozen bystanders openly carrying near the northern edge of the park, letting the cops know they had their own firepower. It looked to some like a standoff. Who would fire first? Bevel raced into the park and grabbed a bullhorn from a cop.

"Everybody get off this street corner!" he shouted. "If you're not going to demonstrate in a nonviolent way, then leave!"

They didn't, not at first, and so Bevel just halted the protests right there. Marched the kids who hadn't been hauled off to jail back into the church.

The Saturday protest ended like that, on the cusp of a lethal showdown.

For Burke Marshall that meant one thing: He had to move quicker.

The good news about the protest's early end was it provided Marshall more time. It was still the middle of Saturday afternoon when he began to contact all parties: the SCLC again, local law enforcement, Mayor Boutwell's office, and downtown merchants affected by the protests and the economic boycotts.

Marshall noticed right away how "the politicians in Birmingham were not in a position to make any sort of accommodation with Martin Luther King. They wouldn't talk to him. They wouldn't talk to anybody that *would* talk to him."

Compounding matters, nobody liked Marshall's boss. Bull Connor took every opportunity to emasculate Bobby Kennedy. Bull called him "Bobby Sox." King had a long-standing wariness of Bobby, for all the times the AG had placed politics above principles in the civil rights struggle. Birmingham's so-called Big Mules, the 150 or so merchants and CEOs who were their own negotiating faction—basically employing everyone in Birmingham—didn't like the money they were losing because of the protests and wished Bobby would do *something* to stop King or Bull or both of them. "Kennedy was . . . the source of trouble," Marshall later recalled, "and not the source of a solution."

Marshall wondered how he would find any solution here.

31

HOW NOT TO NEGOTIATE
WITH THE KING

*T*he hubris of this Burke Marshall, thought King. First to come down here and demand a halt to the protests, and then, when King reluctantly agreed to meet with him Saturday night, to not understand what the SCLC wanted.

"What are you after?" Marshall asked King.

It baffled King. "Martin was constantly amazed at the naivete . . . coming out of the White House," one aide later said. Had Marshall misplaced the Birmingham Manifesto the SCLC released way back on day two of the protests? A manifesto that spelled out the SCLC's demands? Had Marshall not read *any* of the press accounts roughly a week later, when those same demands were reprinted? For that matter, had Marshall not read *today's* papers? They had paraphrased last night's mass meeting, where King had repeated the SCLC's call for desegregation and fair hiring practices.

No, Burke Marshall had not read any of this. In that first meeting with King on Saturday, Marshall asked Martin and his deputies to state plainly their negotiating points for him. "I thought it was a bad sign that he was the broker," Wyatt Walker later said. "He was weak, naive, and uninformed."

And then, when the SCLC restated what it wanted, Marshall had the gall to act as if he had "saved the day," as one author later put it, because at last someone had gleaned from King his wishes for Birmingham.

The white savior complex of this guy. The patronizing smugness of the Kennedy administration—it was all so clichéd.

Take Bobby Kennedy's statement to the press the day before. It carried the classic notes of the well-intentioned white liberal: "I believe that everyone understands that [Black people's] just grievances must be resolved. Continued refusal to grant equal rights and opportunities to Negroes makes increasing turmoil inevitable." Then there was the *but*, the familiar, hectoring *but*. "However . . . School children participating in street demonstrations is a dangerous business. An injured, maimed, or dead child is a price that none of us can afford to pay."

As if it were *King's* fault Bull Connor had turned the hoses on the kids. King wanted to know if Bobby and his ilk had forgotten the entire *centuries* "when our segregated social system had been using and abusing Negro children." It disgusted King. The truth was, Bobby could tsk-tsk him and Mayor Boutwell could say, "I cannot condone . . . the use of children," and Malcolm X could even chime in from the peanut gallery of Harlem with "Real men don't put their children on the firing line." But where had any of these people been, "with their protective words," as King later put it, "when, down through the years, Negro infants were born into ghettos, taking their first breath of life in a social atmosphere where the fresh air of freedom was crowded out by the stench of discrimination?"

King would not apologize for his actions in Birmingham. His actions reflected the centuries of actions against people like him.

So, no: King told Burke Marshall that he would not call off future protests. King knew Marshall was in Birmingham *because* of the protests' effectiveness. Let the images from these marches sicken Jack and Bobby. A sickened administration was the point. It meant King had the Kennedys' attention.

And now that Burke Marshall "at last" understood the SCLC's demands, he could go about trying to meet them.

32

AND LO, THE PHARAOH SHALL WEEP

King flew to Atlanta to pastor his flock at Ebenezer Baptist that Sunday, May 5. The move showed the growing confidence he had about the Birmingham campaign: He could leave it for a day. "In a few days we will have everything we are asking for and maybe more," King said. Many other bold-type names flew into Birmingham overnight: the comedian Dick Gregory, from Chicago, ready to march; the white folk singers Joan Baez and Guy Carawan, from New York. They'd all been appalled by the images from Kelly Ingram Park and wanted to see for themselves the bravery of the protesters here.

Gregory, Baez, and Carawan planned to do more than watch. Baez said she'd give a free concert Sunday night at Miles College, Birmingham's historically Black institution of higher education. Carawan, meanwhile, planned to record upcoming movement meetings and turn their freedom songs into an album.

For all of Baez's fame, Carawan was the folk singer movement executives admired. He had introduced "We Shall Overcome" at SNCC's inaugural meeting in 1960. Soon the song spread and "We Shall Overcome" became the civil rights movement's anthem.

So when Carawan tried to walk into Sunday's mass meeting at New Pilgrim Baptist and police arrested him for attempting to integrate, the

SCLC leaders got hot. One executive, Andrew Young, interrupted the meeting to say Carawan "taught us many of the songs that we sing in the movement." To arrest Carawan meant the police were acting like the cornered pigs they were: nervous and nasty. James Bevel got so upset at Carawan's arrest that *he* interrupted the meeting minutes after Young. Bevel said they should put aside all other items and protest right now.

"Let's just walk," Bevel said.

As if on cue, the music from the choir and backing band soared to the rafters. Many people moved toward the exits.

This is not good, Wyatt Walker thought. *An unscheduled march? Without King present? And against all those nervous and nasty cops?*

Walker strode toward Bevel while signaling to Fred Shuttlesworth and other SCLC executives to join him near the altar.

When the preachers huddled around, the music still rising above them, Walker lashed out at Bevel. *What are you doing? Most of the people here are adults; they've not been through the nonviolence training. You can't just decide unilaterally when we'll stage our next protest.*

Bevel said the movement could not let the police dictate action. The police could not seize the upper hand and make the protesters fearful.

Those present in the huddle later said Walker "fumed." *Big marches are planned for next week. A march tonight, with all those untrained people, could turn bloody. Could turn into a riot. The movement is on the cusp of something huge. We cannot have it all ruined by bad headlines.*

Some of Walker's arguments were justified. But some stemmed from his anger over what Bevel had done yesterday: calling off the protests when he saw bystanders flash their guns in that corner of Kelly Ingram Park. Walker had wanted to continue the protest. Or had at least wanted King to make the call about shutting everything down. What Bevel did yesterday, what he was doing now: It showed how he didn't give a shit about hierarchy, Walker said. Walker, as executive director, embodied the SCLC's hierarchy.

Bevel stared at Walker. As if to show that *he* was the hierarchy, Bevel brought Bernard Lee into the argument. Lee was a young SCLC deputy and Wyatt Walker's mentee, "practically Walker's ward," as one writer later put it. Bevel asked Lee what he thought, and Lee said he agreed with Bevel.

This was a not-so-subtle power move: Bevel showing Walker he could shape not only this movement but even Walker's mentee when he felt like it.

Walker looked away, toward the church doors, furious.

There he saw people leaving. They were beginning to walk without anyone from the SCLC directing the charge.

As if to reclaim some authority, Walker told Bevel and the other preachers gathered around that Bevel could not lead this march tonight. The SCLC couldn't have Bevel arrested; they needed him in the days ahead. Walker chose Charles Billups, New Pilgrim's co-pastor, who'd been protesting alongside Fred Shuttlesworth since pretty much the Christmas Day bombing in 1956.

They would all walk tonight, Walker said. But Billups would lead the way.

Bevel nodded.

When the SCLC executives emerged from New Pilgrim Church, they saw perhaps another thousand ready to march. That pushed tonight's protest to three thousand people, the largest yet of Project C. Even more surprising, almost all of tonight's marchers were adults. Some would later say they had been inspired by the bravery of Birmingham's children the last few days.

The leaders announced they would head to the Southside Jail, where Guy Carawan had presumably been processed. The crowd walked west on Sixth Avenue, toward the jail and the setting sun.

James Bevel inched his way toward the front of the procession. He was not about to stand back, no matter what Wyatt Walker said. He soon marched alongside Charles Billups.

They made an odd pair. Billups, a diminutive movement man, all short build and slight frame and well-tailored conservative suit, taking his cues from Fred Shuttlesworth and Martin Luther King Jr.; Bevel looking like, well, Bevel: tall and broad in his country bibs, answering to no one but Yahweh.

But Bevel panicked first. As the massive procession full of untrained protesters approached the jail, Bevel saw what appeared to be machine guns up ahead, mounted on metal tripods, flanking the side streets. With a few more steps, Bevel saw that those guns were actually massive fire hoses situated on tripods and connected to a half dozen fire trucks.

The police department had, as always, attended tonight's mass meeting. When the SCLC decided to carry out its impromptu protest, the cops had rushed ahead and quickly assembled a bulwark against it: The fire trucks with hoses on metal tripods and, now, closing off Sixth Avenue, the blue line of hundreds of police officers in riot gear, and dozens of Birmingham firefighters in their red slickers, lining themselves up amid the cops and holding still more fire hoses.

Bevel must have gasped when he came within view of the opposition. The next thing Bevel knew, Charles Billups was grabbing Bevel's shoulder and telling him perhaps he should bring up the back of the line. Billups said he did not need to get arrested, injured, or worse.

Without waiting for Bevel's answer, Charles Billups strode forward alone.

Billups began to sing, "I Want Jesus to Walk with Me."

The lyrics drifted back and were picked up by Bevel and Shuttlesworth and the thousands of people surrounding them. The echo of it, the force of three thousand people singing: It was awesome to hear.

When they reached the blue and red line of cops and firefighters barricading Sixth Avenue, Billups halted everyone.

Bull Connor was here, and next to him tonight was Captain Evans of the Birmingham Police Department. Evans ordered the marchers to disperse. He was the same cop who had risen before the first group of children on Double D-Day and told the kids to leave Kelly Ingram Park or "get wet." He clearly had no qualms about using brutal force on unarmed civilians. Tonight, however, carried an even more sinister edge than Double D-Day.

The Birmingham Police Department had stopped all members of the media as they'd walked alongside the protesters. The cops had pulled out the reporters and cameramen and, effectively, corralled the media behind a barricade of still more BPD officers a few hundred yards back from where Charles Billups stood now.

It seemed the cops did not want the press to have any clear sight lines of what was about to happen.

In response to Captain Evans, Billups said: "We're not turning back. We haven't done anything wrong."

Evans smirked at Billups: *Who the hell are* you?

It's true: Charles Billups was no leader of the SCLC, wasn't even the lead pastor of his Baptist church. He was the associate at New Pilgrim. From his glasses to his shoes he embodied the unassuming man. But Charles Billups had also served in World War II and Korea and then applied a similar fearlessness within the movement. One year earlier, in 1962, the Birmingham Klan had kidnapped Billups for protesting alongside Fred Shuttlesworth. The Klan drove Billups into the woods. Beat him with chains. Demanded to know what Shuttlesworth and his civil rights group would do next. Billups wouldn't say. So the Klan branded the letters "KKK" onto Billups's stomach.

When the Klan at last released Billups and returned him to his house, the sight of his bloodied body terrified his family. For the next fifty years, his daughter Helene would be too traumatized to discuss the incident or, more broadly, the civil rights movement. But Billups himself was not scared. When Fred Shuttlesworth talked to him in the hours after the Klan attack, Billups told him: "I know you want to know what I felt. I felt sorry for them."

That was the man who stood before Captain Evans and the barricade of cops and firefighters: the small, bespectacled, but almost transcendent Charles Billups.

He said to Captain Evans: "All we want is our freedom."

Evans remained unmoved by Billups's answer.

So Billups knelt to pray. Others behind him did the same. When he rose again, Billups seemed to have resolved something within himself.

He shouted: "Turn on your water! Turn loose your dogs! We will stand here till we die!"

He yelled the lines again, and then a third time, and soon they morphed into a chant that the thousands of others behind him picked up and shouted themselves. This was even more awe-inspiring to hear. *Turn on your water! Turn loose your dogs! We will stand here till we die!*

The sound seemed to fill the whole of Birmingham. As Billups listened, tears dropped down his cheeks.

Bull Connor looked at the men closest to him and shouted: "Turn on the hoses!"

The firemen around him just stood there.

"Dammit! Turn on the *hoses!*"

The firemen wouldn't budge. Some of them began to cry themselves.

Charles Billups saw their tears and yelled, as if in a trance, "Let us proceed!"

He walked around the line of resistance on Sixth Avenue, brushing shoulders with cops and firefighters, stepping over the hoses meant to level him. The protesters behind him did the same, by the thousands walking past and sometimes through the white authority out to harm them.

None of them were harmed. The thick blue and red line watched them go and even parted for them.

The marchers gathered at a public park across the street, where they knelt and prayed.

Was this a miracle? What could explain it all?

There *was* a practical explanation. Wyatt Walker later said that as Billups and the thousands behind him shouted their refrain, Walker broke from the crowd and approached two officers near Bull Connor. Walker whispered to them that the protesters could go to the park across the street and pray there. Walker seemed to be worried still about the violence untrained protesters might resort to if the hoses hit them. Walker later said he told the officers that if Bull would allow the marchers to head to the park, there would be no need for the protesters to march on to the jail.

Bull told some members of the press that he had granted, on the spot, an emergency request to let the marchers pray in the park.

But the problem with this version was it saved Bull from embarrassment while aggrandizing Wyatt Walker, a man as vain as Bull. This version of events provided a bow-tied reason for why no firefighter had followed Bull's order about the hoses: Bull himself had quickly changed his mind, with Wyatt Walker's help, and that about-face was immediately understood and acted on by thousands.

But Bull didn't about-face with Black people. He had spent *years* refusing their requests to protest. Particularly in the last few days, Bull had shown no remorse for brutality against peaceful Black marchers. He'd turned loose the hoses and the dogs on Double D-Day and then laughed and shouted, "Look at those niggers run!" Why Bull would have acted in a way so diametrically opposed to his nature on this Sunday night was an explanation Connor himself never offered.

So another explanation of events emerged in the minutes and hours after the prayers in the park. This version came from multiple witnesses: Billups, the pastors and other protesters behind him, and some of the firefighters opposite him. This version began with the tears that streaked down the faces of the firefighters as Bull yelled, "Turn on the hoses!"

One fireman said, loud enough to be heard by many others: "We're here to put out fires! Not people!"

For the firefighters to bawl as freely as Charles Billups did was to acknowledge God's grace. That was what the pastors behind Billups later said. The firemen had caught the movement's "spiritual intoxication," as

Nelson Smith, the lead preacher at Billups's New Pilgrim Church, put it. Billups knew this. The firemen had "frozen," he later said. Which is why, in this version of the story, he led the protesters around the cops and firefighters, over the fire hoses, sometimes through the line of blue and red resistance, which parted like the Red Sea. This was nothing less than the "hand of God" at work, some protesters said. And to settle at the park, pray there, while the fire hoses stayed trained on the protesters but no water rushed out? That was a lasting, triumphant display of peace defeating violence, of God's love conquering all.

This was the version of events Martin Luther King Jr. came to believe when he heard the story. People felt "the pride and the *power* of nonviolence," King later wrote. Sunday night, May 5, 1963, was "one of the most fantastic events of the Birmingham story," he said.

33

MARSHALL'S INTERPRETATION

It was more than that. It meant they were getting through, breaching the conscience of the white authority figures in Birmingham. That was how Burke Marshall interpreted the Sunday night march.

The progress he had made. He'd spent the last couple of days meeting with anyone he could, learning all he could. Marshall learned the phones were tapped, for one thing. Anything he said about King on a private call got repeated back in some manner by some white figure at the negotiating table. Marshall began to use the tapped phones to his advantage. He made benign comments on the phone that he knew the white authority listening in would like, so that Marshall might then gain an audience with the mayor's staffers, or the business community, or the sheriff's department.

That's how Marshall's peace brokering began.

"We had a series of meetings on a marathon basis with different groups," Marshall later said. "There were groups that would meet with each other; and there were groups that would meet with some people and not with other people; and then there were groups that wouldn't meet."

The caste system within Birmingham's segregation was itself a lesson for Burke Marshall. He was a quick learner. "The white political leaders and business leaders, generally speaking, wouldn't meet with Negroes," he later said. "None of them would meet with Martin King or Fred Shuttlesworth." But some of these white folks would meet with "local people": the A. G. Gaston crowd of longtime Black Birminghamians who didn't have the outspoken gall of, say, Fred Shuttlesworth. "So we got groups of people together who would talk to each other. . . . Store owners, who had a stake because they were being boycotted and losing money. Politicians, because it was costing the city an awful lot of money. . . . The law-enforcement people . . . who had a stake because their men were on duty 24 hours a day." He got these people to see, even if they wouldn't see King himself, that all the SCLC wanted was "recognition of what was right and what was fair."

Marshall made a study of hearing people out, of not being forceful. "I have a constant recollection," one business executive later said, "of Burke Marshall sitting off in a corner with his arms folded, and *soooooooo* quiet."

Patience: That was something else Marshall learned in Birmingham. The more patience he showed all sides, he hoped, the quicker they might resolve their differences.

34

UNINTENDED OUTCOMES

Then Bull Connor threw Black kids in the concentration camp.

It wasn't technically a concentration camp, but even the sheriff's department said it looked like one. The jails were so crowded by Monday, May 6—with over 4,000 arrests, 2,500 of them children—that Bull Connor transferred some 800 kids to the county fairgrounds. He stuck them in cattle yards, behind chain-link fences, with wire above that was, optically, not too far removed from concertina wire.

The kids who stared out from behind the fence were already malnourished. Some had subsisted on a lone meal a day since Thursday, five days ago: a single bologna sandwich jail guards gave them around noon. Or jail staff had fed them "something that looked like grits; something that looked like soup; we couldn't tell," one child prisoner later said. She and her friends refused to eat it. And then kids like these were transferred to the yards and razor wire and weren't given anything to eat at all.

It began to rain. There was no shelter from it out there in those cattle yards that still stank of cattle. The prison staff abandoned the kids on the other side of the fence and went back to their cars. They just left the children there, in a downpour.

Camera crews arrived. Their footage showed kids hugging each other or shielding themselves beneath loose pages of newspaper. Word reached

Martin Luther King Jr. He and Coretta drove to the fairgrounds and CBS later showed her throwing loaves of bread over the fence and the kids catching them. With King present, more and more members of the media gathered to witness the scene at the fairgrounds: parents now tossing blankets or candy bars to their children.

King addressed the media. He said the Kennedy administration must find a way to attend to these "political prisoners."

The quip was an indirect shot at Burke Marshall. But the footage behind King was so appalling, so embarrassing for the city of Birmingham, that it only quickened the pace of mediation. It brought more powerful white people to Marshall's negotiating table.

Bull Connor may have hated the Kennedys, but as Marshall himself noted, Bull was sure helping Jack and Bobby's man in Birmingham.

35

"MARTIN, THIS IS IT!"

For seven years Fred Shuttlesworth had fought the Birmingham Klan, and Bull, and the racist local courts, and twice he nearly died trying to convince other Black Birminghamians to fight alongside him. Few would.

Until now. Now it was like a dream, Fred thought. Not only were millions of people witnessing the blatant evil of Bull Connor, stuffing kids behind a fence, but back at 16th Street Baptist, away from the cattle yards, one thousand protesters were arrested Monday, the largest single-day total yet. Fred watched them stream out of the church. At the front of the procession: Dick Gregory, the famous comedian who'd flown from Chicago just to march from 16th Street into a paddy wagon near the park. At the back, among the last to be hauled away two hours later, some white lady—some white lady!—from the *Nation* magazine, Barbara Deming.

Incredible. Surreal, even. And around 60 percent of the protesters jailed Monday were adults. The children were getting through, Fred thought. They were convincing every Black Birminghamian to demand the integration Shuttlesworth had wanted since 1956.

The *joy* Fred felt at this almost brought tears to his eyes when he went to Monday's mass meeting. It began at St. James, but too many people wanted in. So the meeting itself spread to Thirgood Memorial Christian Methodist Episcopalian Church, one block over on Seventh Avenue North. Fred and other preachers moved between the two, but more people kept appearing until both churches were beyond capacity. So the mass meeting then spread to St. Luke's Baptist. But the same thing happened there. Too many people rushed inside. The meeting spread to St. Paul. A mass meeting held simultaneously at four churches. Fred had never seen anything like that.

Nor had Martin. When King at last addressed the crowd at St. James, some three hours after the meeting began, he said that what was happening this month in Birmingham was historic. "There are those who make history," King said. "There are those who experience history. I don't know how many historians we have in Birmingham tonight. . . . But . . . you will make it possible for the historians of the future to write a marvelous chapter. Never in the history of this nation have so many people been arrested for the cause of freedom and human dignity!"

Shuttlesworth thought: *Just a few more days.*

With all these thousands of people following Fred and Martin now, with all those millions watching the protest on the news, it would take just a few more days of pressure and white Birmingham would fold. Fred was sure of it.

He wasn't the only one. Shuttlesworth walked into 16th Street Baptist Tuesday morning, May 7, and got word from James Bevel that today's protest would be different. Bevel hoped to break white authority's will for good. Today's march even carried a code name: Operation Confusion. Shuttlesworth laughed with delight when he heard the particulars and then helped Bevel and Walker and other executives shape the final dimensions of the plan.

The SCLC had gathered its most trusted recruits. Fifteen groups lined up within the church, each line holding at least a dozen volunteers, some up to fifty. Shuttlesworth paced from unit to unit, telling its leaders—many of them children, many of them protesters Fred himself had groomed—to prepare their minds and bodies for what lay ahead.

"A movement has a way of crescendoing," Fred said.

The church doors opened earlier than expected, a little before noon. Fourteen children streamed out and surprised the cops across the streets. The officers weren't anticipating any protesters before one o'clock. From the church, Shuttlesworth saw the officers on the scene radio for backup and try to keep the first group of children from marching downtown. The cops had just corralled the kids and confiscated their signs when Shuttlesworth and Bevel sent out the next group.

This rushed even more cops to the scene, and Shuttlesworth smiled.

Now Operation Confusion could begin in earnest.

There were more protesters than those inside the church. These hundreds more had discreetly gathered throughout the city since the morning, hiding picket signs in movement-friendly cars. And now, at the appointed time, high noon, they began to run toward downtown from all parts of the city, grabbing their signs from the cars where they'd hidden them, and keeping a double-time pace until, almost as one, they emerged: six hundred Black protesters streaming into the white downtown.

The white downtown: where Bull Connor had never wanted mass demonstrations. The white downtown: where Birmingham's so-called Big Mules, the store owners and CEOs, were holding an emergency meeting at the Chamber of Commerce, to see how they could end these protests. By marching downtown, the SCLC wanted to show the Big Mules they could end nothing.

And it was at this point, with more than six hundred Black protesters downtown, that Operation Confusion opened its second line of attack. Back within 16th Street Baptist, well more than one thousand protesters watched the cops leave Kelly Ingram Park and head toward the city's core. The protesters then burst out all the doors of the church and sprinted toward downtown themselves. Fred Shuttlesworth hurried outside just to witness it all. Children and adults running around the few remaining cops, making a mad dash for downtown to join the hundreds of their brethren already there. Fred watched as what seemed like the whole of the city sprinted for its core: the protesters on foot, the cops chasing after them, the firefighters near the church quickly wrapping up their hoses and the trucks then screaming away.

Fred ran after them all, too, joyous at the anarchy he'd helped to create.

When he got downtown, it stunned him: Some four thousand protesters, maybe more. On the sidewalks, on the streets, sitting in the aisles of downtown stores, standing outside them with picket signs. All of these people singing freedom songs. And even better: the Big Mules emerging from their chamber meeting, coming out for their lunch break and seeing "square blocks of Negroes, a veritable sea of Black faces," as one writer put it.

It was too perfect. *And the cops can't do anything!* Fred thought. They couldn't break up the crowd for the mass of people. They couldn't arrest that mass because the jails were already full. Fred moved among the protesters, barked instructions to stay strong, stay nonviolent, saw a cop on a motorcycle overturn his bike just trying to maneuver among the masses, while those people sang "We Shall Overcome."

Martin has to see this, Fred thought.

He rushed as quickly as he could back to the Gaston. He sprinted up to room 30, where he saw King and Abernathy.

"Martin! This is it! You need to come out!"

They got in a car and headed back downtown, Fred narrating as they drove. He had never witnessed anything like it: not just the mass of Black protesters but the impotence of white authority.

"All we got to do," Fred said to Martin in the car, Fred's finger stabbing the air, "is hold it like this a few more days!"

A few more days and they would win everything.

Martin nodded and smiled.

36

"PUT SOME WATER ON THE REVEREND"

After the tour, Fred dropped King and Abernathy at the Gaston and returned to 16th Street Baptist. Thousands more protesters had assembled there. They were the next wave, ready to charge. At Shuttlesworth's entrance, Wyatt Walker gave Fred "a hero's introduction," as one observer later put it. The assembled stood and shouted their ovation. This was their fearless pastor who'd waited for this day since 1956.

Fred quieted the crowd and said, "You are as good a soldier as any that go across the water. Because you are fighting for what your country is and what it will be."

Around this time a white cop burst into the church. He begged them not to march. The jails were full.

But a white cop pleading like this only reinforced how much power Shuttlesworth and the SCLC held. Now was the time to utilize it.

Shuttlesworth and Bevel sent out two thousand more marchers.

Some three hundred cops and firefighters had reassembled near Kelly Ingram Park, to block these protesters from making it downtown. The hissing water hoses, the unleashed K-9 corps, and now the bottles and rocks thrown at the white authority from spectators gathered on street corners: Shuttlesworth and Bevel exhaled with weary about having to rush outside once more to stop the onlookers.

Striking them only sets us all back, Shuttlesworth said. *We can't have that when we're so close to winning.*

He settled the scene enough to walk back toward 16th Street Baptist. A group of firefighters there now trained a hose on the church door, flooring any Black people who dared to step out. The desperate fury of these white people. When Fred moved within feet of the firefighters, one of them said, "Hey! . . . Put some water on the Reverend!"

Its force hit him in the back of the shoulder and ribs, knocked him from his feet and rolled him, hard, into the brick wall of the church. The firefighters moved closer. Kept the water on Shuttlesworth. Pinned him against that wall until Fred lost his breath. Then his consciousness.

Fred thought, *I'm going to die.*

When he came to, the water had abated and the firefighters had redirected their hose back at the park. Shuttlesworth was in a fetal position against the brick wall of the church. A voice came to him, the voice he'd heard in '56 during the Christmas Day bombing: "Not here; not yet."

He tried to get up. Three nearby protesters saw him struggle. They rushed to him and helped Fred to his feet.

He thanked them.

"Let's go!" he said. "I'm ready to march!"

But he wasn't. He was woozy, wincing from the pain. Someone called for an ambulance.

When it arrived, Fred was put on a stretcher into the back of the truck.

37

THIS TIME, SOMETHING NEW

The facts of Fred Shuttlesworth's injury spread beyond the park and into downtown. When Bull Connor heard, he said, "I wish they'd carried him away in a hearse."

And perhaps it was the news of this injury or perhaps the course of the day, with thousands of protesters downtown and Governor George Wallace himself afraid, sending 250 Alabama state troopers to Birmingham to reinforce the cops and sheriff's deputies: Whatever the case, the day turned hostile. All these men of the law drew even more people downtown until traffic stopped the whole district. Cars idled where they were. Some were then rocked side to side by onlookers. Many white people were angry. They didn't like any disruption of "our way of life."

In front of one of the department stores, white onlookers threw punches at the Black people who congregated there.

This time the Blacks fought back.

Brawls broke out.

Cops took them as a cue to barrel through crowds. Nightsticks crashing on heads, stones hurled in response, Alabama state troopers marauding with sawed-off shotguns, bricks and bottles from civilians crashing onto the troopers' helmets, the fire hoses hissing on the packed mass of humanity, and for the journalists watching it, the precipice of protests passing into something else, something new.

"Rioting Negroes," the *New York Times* headline read when the first editions rolled off the press.

38

WISHFUL THINKING?

When did success ruin you? When did people no longer heed your words? This was what King wondered now. The protests attracted so many people that King could no longer manage them all. The *New York Times* reporter Claude Sitton wrote of Tuesday's "riot" that King "appeared to have little control over the demonstrations."

King sensed this himself and looked uneasy when he took to the pulpit at that night's mass meeting. It was held once again at multiple locations, 16th Street Baptist and St. Paul, a metaphor of Project C's triumphs and its increasing unruliness. Literally too many people for King to watch over.

He delivered a disjointed message. King said he had heard the news of "your president," Fred Shuttlesworth, as if Fred were somehow a separate entity, removed from Project C's planning and not central to it. But stranger than the "your president" comment was King's reference to Shuttlesworth's "foot injury." The doctors at Holy Family Hospital were in truth worried about Shuttlesworth's ribs and chest. They were worried about internal bleeding. King didn't tell the mass meeting this. Instead he said, "God works in mysterious ways."

He seemed to regain some control at the pulpit when he isolated what he saw as the problem of that afternoon's protest: "Our movement is a nonviolent movement. Go to your friends, your neighbors, your brothers, and your sisters and your children and tell them that we can't win with weapons of violence." He said that their children had been hosed, bitten by dogs, kicked in the stomach, and yet they had found the courage last week to restrain themselves. Today, however, whites had done nothing more than punch Black adults and "riots" had broken out. "We don't need to throw rocks," King said. "If you have a knife, get rid of it."

Was this wishful thinking? Even as he spoke, King knew he had never overseen a campaign this large. As it metastasized day by day, could he still lead it? At what point did a well-trained group of people ignore its lessons and heed the mob mentality coursing through it? Was it three thousand people? Five thousand? King could put that many on the streets tomorrow. What would it take to provoke them? Spectators joining the ranks? The hoses? The state troopers who carried sawed-off shotguns?

Were more bad headlines in store? Were deaths?

At what point was a protest too large for its own good?

39

THE SEATS AT THE TABLE

King wasn't the only one alarmed by the mass of protesters. Jefferson County Sheriff Mel Bailey attended the emergency meeting at the Chamber of Commerce. There was a reason only twenty-eight people had been arrested Tuesday, despite the thousands protesting and rioting downtown, Bailey said. Law enforcement had nowhere to put people. Bailey said to the business leaders in the meeting, the hundred or so Big Mules, as well as to Mayor Boutwell and his staff, that law enforcement was considering moving beyond the cattle yards at the fairgrounds to incarcerate people at Legion Fields, the fifty-four-thousand-seat football stadium in Birmingham where Alabama played Auburn in the Iron Bowl. *If we have to put people at Legion Field*, Bailey said, *we'll have to erect barbed-wire fences around them.*

In other words: If the press thought the cattle yards looked like a concentration camp . . .

Bailey admitted what everyone in attendance knew. *We cannot counter the protests anymore*, he said.

It silenced the room.

Mayor Boutwell at last spoke up. Birmingham needed to "act honorably in the situation," he said. The people gathered here needed to reach a resolution with King.

Burke Marshall, watching it all, tried to suppress his smile.

• • •

It went like this.

The people who ran Birmingham would not put their names to a desegregation agreement, so they agreed to outsource all negotiations to a subcommittee. Heading that subcommittee was a white lawyer named David Vann, who'd negotiated on behalf of the city thus far, and Birmingham's Chamber of Commerce president, Sidney Smyer. Smyer, an avowed segregationist, agreed to sit on the subcommittee because, as he said in the Chamber of Commerce meeting, he was "not a damn fool." Nobody was shopping downtown anymore, Black *or* white. The city's business district was a "ghost town," in the words of one writer. In the words of *Business Week*, it was the site of an economic depression. Sales had plummeted 10 percent in April, when King launched the campaign. They'd fallen another 15 percent in May, when Bull brought out the fire hoses and dogs. Tourist spending had plummeted 40 percent thus far this spring. Smyer knew that most downtown businesses operated on margins of 10 percent or less, which meant they wouldn't make it through summer unless revenues picked up now.

Smyer told the Big Mules that if an agreement was reached, he alone would sign it. He alone would take the heat for coming to terms with King. Whatever it took to get business back to normal; that was Smyer's rationale.

He and Vann and two others—one of them Mayor Boutwell's executive assistant—agreed to be the city's subcommittee in its direct negotiations with the SCLC.

The white contingent met Tuesday night at John Drew's insurance company. Drew was part of the city's Black elite. Educated at Morehouse, living in the tony East Thomas neighborhood, and the president of the Alexander and Company General Insurance Agency, Drew had become friendly with King nearly a decade ago, when Drew was the only man in Alabama willing to insure the station wagons that King's protesters used during the Montgomery bus boycott. King wasn't at the negotiating table tonight.

The white subcommittee refused to meet with him. Instead, they agreed to meet with the SCLC's Andrew Young, the executive who had been incensed at Guy Carawan's arrest Sunday night, and a man whom many saw as the SCLC's most socially conservative leader. Also present were old-line Black Birminghamians A. G. Gaston and the Reverend Lucius Pitts, the president of Miles College.

Burke Marshall mediated. Just before the subcommittee negotiations opened, an ecstatic Marshall placed a call to Jack and Bobby while the brothers ate dinner at the White House.

"We're over the hump!" Marshall said.

Bobby asked how long before a settlement was reached.

"A day or so."

But when the negotiations actually began, a day or so seemed too optimistic. The Black contingent had four demands. They'd written them out:

1. The "desegregation of all store facilities, Lunch Counters, Rest Rooms, Fitting Rooms."
2. The "immediate upgrading of employment opportunities available for Negroes, and the beginning of a nondiscriminatory hiring policy."
3. That the "merchants request the City Government drop all charges against those persons arrested while exercising their Constitutionally guaranteed right to peaceful protest."
4. That the "merchants request the City Government to establish a Biracial Committee to deal with future problems of the community and to develop specific plans for: hiring Negroes to the police force, alleviation of obstacles in voter registration, school desegregation, reopening all municipal facilities on a desegregated basis, desegregation of movies and hotels."

The white contingent balked. They agreed to only two demands: the desegregation of downtown stores and the establishment of a biracial committee.

Marshall took progress where he could find it and told both sides it was good they were at least talking.

They kept talking that night. They talked until the white negotiators agreed to upgrade employment opportunities for Blacks.

At this point it was nearly midnight. Both groups wanted to stay at it but knew that from here on in any conversation would need to include Martin Luther King Jr.

John Drew offered his own house as a site of negotiations. King had known John and Deenie Drew for so long that John called Martin by his birth name, Mike, and Martin called John "Mr. Beefeater" for all the steaks John served whenever Martin was in Birmingham. The idea tonight was to make the remaining talks as comfortable for the negotiators as the Drew house had been over the years for King. Deenie Drew would even make cocktails and sandwiches.

Mayor Boutwell's representative, chief assistant Billy Hamilton, said neither he nor the mayor's office could be seen at a Black man's home. Hamilton refused to go. The remaining whites—Smyer and Vann, and Roper Dial, a downtown merchant whose revenues had been in freefall because of the protests—agreed to continue on.

They would negotiate without Hamilton.

Within moments of the negotiators parking at Drew's house, there were so many pressmen suddenly crowding around that Burke Marshall drove past, parked a block behind the home, and approached it through an alley, to avoid the throng. That throng doubled in size after King arrived. Soon it was not only press but also Fred Shuttlesworth's friends and local activists. Deenie Drew had to keep "sweeping the porch clean of groupies," she later said.

Inside, Sidney Smyer opened the midnight negotiations with a group prayer. But after they all concluded with an *amen*, the white contingent wouldn't budge on the Black contingent's remaining demand: dropping the charges against the Black children and adults in prison. It also became obvious that the previously agreed-upon points were less than agreed-upon.

The Black contingent wanted desegregation of the lunch counters immediately; the whites wanted it after sixty days, or, more broadly, after King
and his "rabble-rousers" had left town. This left King and the Black negotiators suspicious. Would Birmingham desegregate anything if King
wasn't there to enforce it?

The Blacks wanted details in the draft of the truce. The whites wanted
generalities. David Vann later said, "How could a settlement be announced
in terms specific enough for the Negroes to know that their demands were
being fairly met, and yet vague enough so that white leaders would not
be subject to attacks and their stores not subject to demonstration from
the other side?" The question troubled Vann to the point that he fell to
the floor that night and cried. The negotiations seemed to be moving
backward.

Both sides regrouped. Vann and the rest of the white contingent
agreed to desegregate either the lunch counters or the schools in sixty
days, whichever came first. This appeased King, but the Black contingent
also wanted an assurance in writing that certain downtown merchants
would agree to hire at least one Black employee.

Any negotiation is a compromise. But as Burke Marshall guided that
night's, he kept thinking something he didn't voice: that King was compromising too much. King had come to Birmingham with a promise to
"break segregation or be broken by it." Yet his demands tonight were far
more malleable. They were in fact diminished. Marshall wasn't alone in
thinking this. When he'd presented the general demands to one downtown merchant earlier in the day, the merchant had gasped.

"That's all they want?" the merchant asked.

And now, in the small hours of Wednesday morning, even those demands were being pruned back. Instead of the desegregation of all store
facilities, the desegregation of some. Instead of the upgrading of employment opportunities for all Negroes, the hiring of at least one Black at
certain downtown stores.

As Marshall listened to the negotiations, he understood King's plight.
Any progress was progress in Birmingham. "In part he was just trying

to accomplish something," Marshall later said of King. Marshall knew, though, that King could continue the protests. King could force more bloody spectacles on everyone, and thereby force the city's and Washington's hand. He could force the federal government to send troops to Birmingham. "But I do not think that [King] wanted . . . troops in Birmingham or that he was trying to create a situation where the troops would be sent in," Marshall later said.

So as Marshall kept his thoughts to himself that night and studied King, he considered what was driving the civil rights leader.

It became clear to Burke Marshall as 2:00 a.m. wound its way to 3:00 a.m. that King wanted a victory. The Albany campaign last year had been a disaster. The Freedom Rides the year before that had gained no freedom. *Nothing* had worked for the civil rights movement since the Montgomery bus boycott in 1956. That was seven *years* for King without a win. "He wanted it for himself," Marshall later said. "He, King, as a Negro leader, wanted to be the Negro leader who had a success."

In Marshall's view, that was why King accommodated, and accommodated, and accommodated at the Drew house.

King himself would later say he was pained by how much he was compromising. Just that afternoon he'd nodded when Fred Shuttlesworth said, *Just a few more days and we win everything.* But now Fred was in the hospital, and the *New York Times* was calling King's protesters "rioters," and here tonight was a chance for desegregation, in some form, in the most racist city in America.

Should he take it?

Put another way: What would happen elsewhere if a truce was signed here? Where else might southern Blacks rise up? How else might northern Blacks demand equality? How could a victory here lead to victories everywhere?

Even though such questions weren't part of tonight's negotiations, they were very much part of King's aim. "The system to which [the segregationists] have been committed lies on its deathbed," King later wrote of the negotiations. "The only imponderable is how costly they will make the funeral."

It was an even larger gamble to hash out a truce in Birmingham while imagining its ripple effects across the nation. But King had made a career of imagining a better future. King had made a life of keeping the faith.

At 4:00 a.m. on Wednesday, King thought they had the makings of a truce and would need a few hours' sleep before they could finish it off.

40

THE BETRAYAL

Fred Shuttlesworth slept poorly in his hospital bed. It wasn't just the discomfort from his cracked ribs. It was trepidation. Why had Martin not visited him? What work was urgent enough to keep King away?

Shuttlesworth's doctors called it a "mild delirium," but when Ruby Shuttlesworth got to her husband's bedside the next morning, Wednesday, May 8, he was fully conscious and no better. A spidey sense made him restless, unhappy. Doctors gave him three hypos of sedatives, but still Fred did not calm down. Ruby called his longtime physician, Dr. James Montgomery, and Montgomery recommended Fred return to the Gaston, where he might relax once he saw for himself that nothing was amiss in the campaign.

Ruby helped Fred get dressed. He still wore his hospital bracelet as they left in Ruby's car. At the Gaston, Ruby settled Fred in one of its rooms. She tucked him into bed while the morning sun shone in. Just then they heard a knock at the door.

It was Andy Young. He said Fred needed to come to John Drew's house for an emergency meeting.

Emergency meeting? Fred said.

Young wouldn't elaborate.

. . .

In the car Fred's suspicion shot to anger. Why had Martin sent a deputy to Fred's room? Why had Martin himself not come? And why was there any sort of meeting at John Drew's house?

Drew and Shuttlesworth didn't get along. Drew found Shuttlesworth uncouth. Leading a movement—even leading it courageously—but leading always from the front. "Fred wanted to be sure that you recognized Fred Shuttlesworth," Drew later said. Drew had soured on Shuttlesworth at the outset of Birmingham's civil rights push. Just after Fred's parsonage was bombed on Christmas Day in 1956, Shuttlesworth had spoken with Black leaders and the press. King had come to Birmingham to offer his support and stayed at the Drews' house. When Shuttlesworth learned this, he'd phoned John Drew and asked to speak with King.

Martin grabbed the receiver.

"Dr. King, talk to me," Fred said. "Did you see me on television?"

"His quest for the limelight . . . annoyed me," Drew later said. "And of course he was not a Martin Luther King."

Shuttlesworth interpreted comments like that as class warfare. For Fred, here was the truth of John Drew. He was well-off enough to go to Morehouse, where he was a classmate of Martin Luther King Sr. John and his wife, Deenie, did not attend the sort of working-class Black Baptist church Shuttlesworth ministered. John and Deenie were Methodists, members of an A.M.E. church that attracted Black Birmingham's elite. Deenie was a northerner, raised outside Philadelphia, and so light-skinned she'd gone on a spying mission amid southern Dixiecrats at their political convention. The Drews *were* civil rights activists—Deenie had her voter registration drives and John's porch light was always on when King needed a place to stay—but they embodied a sphere of Black Birmingham that Shuttlesworth, with his childhood poverty and hard-knocks education, could not pierce. He had no interest in piercing it. "He had no patience with the wealthy segments of Black society," one observer later wrote. "He believed they were greedy, cowardly, and untrustworthy." The Drews didn't think much of Shuttlesworth, either. "They thought Fred was a country preacher," Wyatt Walker later said. "Right out of the rural." There was a reason the Drews were friends with King and not Shuttlesworth.

Which meant there *must* be a reason, and not a good one, why King was holding an emergency meeting at the Drews' house now, Fred thought.

When the Shuttlesworths arrived, King did not walk out to greet them. Ruby helped Fred out of his seat and then, with Fred still woozy, helped him into the Drews' home.

King was in the living room, along with members of the SCLC's executive leadership, among them Wyatt Walker, Ralph Abernathy, and Andy Young. The Kennedys' men were here, too: Burke Marshall and Joseph Dolan.

Fred plopped into an armchair. "Martin, why did I have to get up out of my sickbed to come out to John Drew's house? What's so important?"

King stood near the window with his back to Shuttlesworth, looking out onto the Drews' yard. King didn't speak.

He couldn't.

Shuttlesworth, getting agitated, said, "You and Ralph didn't even come to see me" in the hospital, "whether I was dying or living."

Still King stood there with his back to Fred, his hands in his pockets, thinking.

At last King turned from the window. He looked Shuttlesworth in the eyes.

"Fred, we got to call off the demonstrations."

"Say that again, Martin?"

The statement shocked him so much that Fred wondered if the morning's sedatives were taking effect and he'd somehow misheard King.

King's face remained grave.

"Who's *we*?" Fred asked.

The two sides were close to a settlement, King said, close enough that he had agreed earlier today to put a moratorium on future protests. "The merchants say they can't negotiate while we are demonstrating."

Shuttlesworth seethed. Birmingham was his town, and this campaign had been his as much as King's. Hell, Martin had *proclaimed* it to the press.

"Well, Martin, it's hard for me to see how anyone could decide that without me," Fred said. Besides, he added, King's rationale was illogical. "The merchants have been negotiating [for weeks] with Burke Marshall." Shuttlesworth pointed to Marshall, sitting in the corner of the room.

Marshall didn't respond. Neither did King.

Deenie Drew filled the silence. "I want to know why we can't call them off."

Fred turned to her. Now *Deenie Drew* was going to chime in? "You can't call them off," he snapped at Deenie, "because you ain't called nothing on and ain't got nothing to call off. Besides, I didn't come out here to talk with you."

Fred returned his scorn to Martin. "We're not callin' anything off."

"Well, uh—"

"You know they said in Albany that you come in, get people excited and started, and you leave town. But I live here. The people trust me. And I have the responsibility after the SCLC is gone, and I'm telling you it will not be called off."

"Now, Fred, you ought not to say it like that," King said.

"I have to say what's on my mind and speak the truth."

King sighed.

"I've been here," Shuttlesworth said. "People have been hurt, and I've been here to help heal. That's why I'm respected in Birmingham. They know I'm not going to change. We came in with the idea to say to Birmingham and the world, and we agreed before we got here that we wasn't gonna call it off no matter what, even if we had to go to jail. So if you want to go against that, go ahead and do it. But I will not call it off. And I don't think you can call it off without me."

Shuttlesworth rose to leave but was too dizzy. He plopped back into the chair.

Ralph Abernathy walked over and kneeled down until he was eye to eye with Shuttlesworth. "Now, Fred, we friends, ain't we?" Abernathy asked. "I can talk to you, can't I, Fred?"

"Ralph, get off your damn knees. You can get on your knees or get on your damn belly, it won't make no difference. We're not gon' call it off."

"But," Burke Marshall said from his corner of the room, "I made promises to these people."

"Burke, any promise you made that I didn't agree with is not a promise. You go back and tell [the Kennedys] that."

Those *promises* were a press conference, someone said.

"Oh, you called a press conference, huh?" Shuttlesworth sneered, looking toward King. "I thought we were going to make joint statements." It seemed King *was exactly* what those SNCC leaders had warned Fred about: De Lawd, coming in and taking credit for all that wasn't his. "Go ahead, Mr. Big, and call it off. I'm going back home and get in the bed," Fred said. "I'm gon' wait until I see on TV that you've called it off, and then with what little strength I have left, I'm gon' get up and lead those three or four thousand kids back in the streets. And you'll be dead."

In the adjoining room Burke Marshall's assistant, Joe Dolan, whispered into a phone, "We've hit a snag. . . . The frail one is hanging things up."

The frail one? Shuttlesworth turned toward Dolan and spoke loud enough for Jack or Bobby on the other end of the line to hear. "I guess you're talking to the president or his brother! Well, tell them they don't live down here, and I'm frail but not that frail, and we're not gon' call it off!"

King thought they couldn't break like this with Shuttlesworth. He turned to Marshall. "Burke, we got to have unity. We just got to have unity."

Shuttlesworth snorted. He gave King his most withering look yet. "I'll be damned if you'll have it like this. You may be Mr. Big now, but if you call it off, you'll be Mr. Shit."

King didn't respond.

"I will not compromise my principles," Shuttlesworth said, "and the principles *we* established."

With that he rose and left.

41

THE UNRAVELING

Had Fred heard what Burke Marshall called after him?

"Don't worry, Fred," Marshall had said as Fred and Ruby left the Drews' home. "They're gonna agree to your demands."

Shuttlesworth had been too hot to respond. Marshall wasn't trying to mollify him, though. Marshall knew what Shuttlesworth did not—what King did not.

The president himself was negotiating for a settlement now.

In the last few days Jack Kennedy had personally called three or four white business leaders in Birmingham, "very conservative men," as Marshall later put it, and pressured them to reach an accord with King. "And the president also saw to it that all the members of his cabinet . . . helped," Marshall said. Bobby Kennedy called some of the Big Mules. Defense secretary Robert McNamara called still more. When treasury secretary Douglas Dillon got on the phone with Edward Norton, the chairman of Royal Crown Cola was so in awe of someone that close to the locus of power calling *him* that Norton not only agreed to settle but agreed to pressure other Birmingham executives to do the same. William Pritchard, a lawyer for those executives, who had said in a CBS documentary on Birmingham in 1961 that Black people were "savages" and any effort to integrate his city would result in "violence," nevertheless supported integration two years later, after Kennedy cabinet members wooed and pressured him, too.

"We felt," Bobby Kennedy later said, "that if we could get the substantial white citizens who owned the—ran the financial life of Birmingham behind the department store heads, that perhaps we could get the department store heads to [integrate]."

For the Kennedys, integration was equitable, but these negotiations were also another of their games of government: to get cracker whites to agree to actions that were against their long-held beliefs, and to do it quietly. Neither Jack nor Bobby publicly endorsed King's settlement demands. They even refused to acknowledge phoning Birmingham executives. The administration remained wary of federal intervention, whether in the form of troops or legislation. The brothers just wanted a settlement. They wanted that more than anything. Bobby was phoning King all the time now, too, pressing for a truce. With a settlement, Martin could leave Birmingham, and the media could follow, and the Kennedy brothers could go back to ruling the world.

The administration's reticence to publicly own up to its negotiating tactics created a curious side effect. It allowed white executives to save face. These Birminghamians could say that for the good of their city they were willing to listen to King, and leave out how they'd been awestruck by the treasury secretary or scolded by the attorney general. Burke Marshall saw this happen in various confabs with the Big Mules. They'd drawl on about how the jails were full and the northern and international press a cancer, and how it was time to do something about all this for the betterment of Birmingham. These executives would then keep to themselves what they and Marshall knew, even as they looked Marshall's way: the Kennedy administration had told them, "You have no way out" but settlement.

So when Marshall called after Fred Shuttlesworth as he left the Drews' house and said, "Don't worry, Fred," he also meant: *The president will press your demands, too.*

Fred kept walking away, though.

. . .

It got harder for Marshall to reach Shuttlesworth. This was a problem. Fred Shuttlesworth was now the key to a deal. Sure, King could announce to the media a one-day moratorium on protests, in the hopes a truce might be reached, which then led President Kennedy to open his own afternoon press conference with the news: "I'm gratified to note the progress in the efforts by white and Negro citizens to end an ugly situation in Birmingham, Alabama." But Marshall knew Shuttlesworth needed to be placated.

The problem was, he was still pissed. Andy Young tried to talk to him at the Gaston: "Now, Reverend," Young began.

"Don't give me none of that 'Reverend' shit," Shuttlesworth interrupted.

Fred worried about truce talks that got international exposure for the movement but, if an accord was reached, might not change Black Birminghamians' lives. Fred had no reason to trust white Birminghamians' promises. Just last fall, after Miles College students launched an economic boycott of downtown, white merchants agreed to take down their "Whites Only" signs from drinking fountains. King had hailed it as progress when he came to Birmingham for the SCLC's annual convention. When King left the city, though, Bull Connor ordered the signs back up. The merchants did Bull's bidding.

That's why Shuttlesworth was so hot about the protests continuing now: They were the loaded gun. They would force the city's leadership to agree to the SCLC's demands. They would put that capitulation in writing. Anything less than written capitulation wouldn't work in Birmingham, Shuttlesworth said. White people couldn't be trusted.

As if to prove his point, Wednesday afternoon brought fresh hell for truce talks.

King, Abernathy, and twenty-five others headed to Judge Charles Brown's recorder's court for a trial on the Good Friday charge of parading without a permit. There Brown not only found the SCLC's protesters guilty, not only sentenced them to 180 days in jail, but also set appeal bail at

$2,500 per person. Everyone found that sum exorbitant; previously bail had been set at just $300. The bail figures carried a political message, too: The city was pressing its dominion over the SCLC. The $2,500 bail was a new maximum penalty meant to bankrupt the organization. Bull Connor himself rubber-stamped Brown's order. He said he did it out of spite. Bull didn't like any of these settlement negotiations excluding him. "They haven't talked to Bull Connor," he told the *New York Times*.

Brown's decision and Bull's seal of approval showed Shuttlesworth that it was the "same old shit" in his city. He wanted to march that afternoon in protest, get thousands of kids to follow behind him. It took Wyatt Walker and James Bevel to talk Shuttlesworth down.

The SCLC decided the smartest response was to refuse to pay the bail. King and Abernathy offered themselves up for incarceration for a reason: Jail was its own negotiating tactic. Soon after their booking, Walker told the press that if King and Abernathy were not released from prison *and* a settlement reached by the next morning, Thursday, May 9, the SCLC planned to "pull out all the stops."

42

THE YOUNGER BROTHER'S COMPLEX

The next morning came. King remained in prison. The settlement remained in negotiations. Shuttlesworth had had it. He stormed past
Burke Marshall and walked deeper into room 30 at the Gaston and told
Andy Young and Wyatt Walker he was putting on his "marching shoes." He
would organize the protest at 16th Street Baptist himself. Walker told Shuttlesworth to hold back—they would march on King's orders—but Fred kept
moving toward the exit. Young had to restrain him from leaving. The grap-
pling became the physical manifestation of the last forty-eight hours of talks:
Shuttlesworth trying, and failing, to obtain the full power of the movement.

Young, a larger man, began to wrestle Shuttlesworth to the floor.
Burke Marshall and Joe Dolan, watching all this, dialed Bobby Kennedy
in a panic.

"Fred's sort of gone off the deep end," Dolan whispered into the receiver. "Could you try to calm him down?"

Then Dolan looked up and said, "The attorney general would like to
speak with you, Reverend Shuttlesworth."

Fred relaxed. Young released him from his grip. Dolan handed over
the phone. Fred took it and retreated to the suite's other room, receiver
to his ear.

• • •

We don't know what exactly was said. Neither Bobby nor Fred would talk about it afterward, as if the point of placating Fred were for the pair to share secrets. Perhaps they did. Perhaps Bobby told Fred Shuttlesworth about the private talks he and Jack Kennedy were having with white Birmingham executives, pressuring them to settle, a fact that not even King knew. Perhaps Bobby heard on the phone what Burke Marshall had told him as well: about the pain Shuttlesworth felt at being left out of the negotiations at the Drews' house, and how any negotiations were far more personal for Shuttlesworth than for Atlantans like King and Walker, or a Mississippian like James Bevel. They could lead lives away from here. Fred Shuttlesworth could not. He would not. More than that, a settlement here held the promise of redeeming all of his choices in life. Bobby certainly understood that much. This was not the first time the two of them had talked on the phone. In 1961, during the Freedom Rides, as the Klan bombed buses outside Birmingham and then attacked the riders inside the city, Bobby and Fred had called each other almost every hour. In one mass meeting during the Freedom Rides, Shuttlesworth flaunted the sudden access he had to the attorney general: "Excuse me," he'd said from the pulpit after an aide had whispered in his ear, "I have a long distance call from Bob." Minutes later, when he returned, Shuttlesworth told the crowd, "Bob told me, 'If you can't get me at my office, just call me at the White House.'" The stunned crowd erupted into a roar. Some soon felt possessed by the Holy Spirit. Ushers had to restrain them from flailing about.

Fred liked that. The power to shape events; the access to still more power. Bobby understood that much, too. It was the younger-brother complex. Both men were overachievers, lusting for prestige within a code of strict righteousness. They worked so hard and achieved so much and held such an absolute line because they had to, because that was the only way to be seen, by parents (in Bobby's case) or the public (in Fred's) whose attention kept drifting to the more glamorous brother. Bobby Kennedy and Fred Shuttlesworth were alike in more ways than either cared to acknowledge. And perhaps on the phone they talked about how close Fred was to the biggest day of his life, to a lasting power. All Fred had to do to obtain it was distance himself, for once, from his tendency to overachieve, his drive to shape events.

Relax. Let the day come to *him*. Have the sanguinity, for once, of the older brother.

While we do not know what the pair discussed when Fred took the phone into the adjoining room, we do know that when he returned to Andy Young, Wyatt Walker, Burke Marshall, and Joe Dolan, he was a different man. Calmer, more assured of his standing.

In fact, later that day *Fred* was the one to tell Wyatt Walker to remain patient. When Walker told passing members of the press, "Plans are being made for the biggest demonstrations this city has ever seen," Shuttlesworth butted in and said that jailing King "does not destroy our faith in the people we are dealing with. . . . We hope the latest incident will spur the merchants to reach a settlement by tomorrow."

And with that, and perhaps with the support of Bobby Kennedy, Fred Shuttlesworth moved the final negotiating deadline to Friday, May 10.

43

"WHAT I'M ABOUT TO TELL YOU WILL NOT BE REPEATED"

King didn't want out of jail. Not exactly. From jail King had leverage. He could threaten more protests unless Bull Connor freed him on bail. He could highlight the plight of the roughly eight hundred children still incarcerated alongside him. He could argue *they* should be released by the city, too.

So it shocked him when, on Thursday afternoon, his cell door opened and a guard said he and Ralph Abernathy were free to go.

What? Why?

A. G. Gaston had bailed them out.

It was true. A. G. Gaston had sent a check for $5,000 for King and Abernathy's bail. Gaston hadn't cleared the action with anyone in the SCLC. He'd just done it. Paid it. Immediately rumors started. *Bobby Kennedy pressured Gaston to use his own money to bail King out; Bobby didn't want the SCLC or the city to have leverage in negotiations; Bobby just wanted a settlement.* Gaston would later say that wasn't why he paid King's bail. "More militant splinter groups of the Movement were whipping the Negroes into an ugly mood. . . . [King] was needed to calm and control the colored community."

King didn't buy it. Not one bit. Upon his release he gave the press an oblique critique of the White House: "The President said that there were no federal statutes involved in most aspects of this struggle," he said, "but I feel that there have been blatant violations." Privately, to Burke Marshall, he was more direct: *The administration can't argue any longer that the government's role is mediator. If Jack and Bobby are going to work to bail me out of jail, then Jack and Bobby need to bail out the eight hundred kids still there.*

Or else I'll march again.

The cost of bailing out every Black protester amounted to more than $250,000.

This was not an idle threat. Bailing out all protesters was the only outstanding demand on which white negotiators had refused to compromise. So King wanted Washington to compromise instead.

Bobby Kennedy balked when Marshall told him of King's demand. When King wouldn't listen to Bobby's rationale for why the federal government couldn't pay the child and adult protesters' bail, Bobby phoned Harry Belafonte in New York.

"I'm in an extremely vulnerable position," Bobby told Harry. "For me to show any favoritism in this case could become highly problematic." Bobby argued that *Harry* had to talk with King. Get Martin to see Bobby's view.

Harry wouldn't do it. "I told him this," Harry later recalled of the conversation. "If he didn't deal with the situation today, it would be twice as bad tomorrow. There would be twice as many children [protesters] and the potential for violence would be far, far greater. Helping to get these children out of jail, as part of the larger solution to the whole quagmire, was something he simply had to do."

Bobby didn't like that answer: Just when he had placated Shuttlesworth, now King needed to be appeased.

Bobby hung up.

In Birmingham, as new negotiations started at the Drews' house—

this time with the input of Fred Shuttlesworth—Burke Marshall stuck to the administration's position. *We can't intervene.*

Yes, you can, Wyatt Walker said. The administration had no problem raising $60 million in ransom for the political prisoners in the Bay of Pigs fiasco.

Marshall didn't have an adequate counter to that.

And soon, in New York, Harry Belafonte's phone rang again. It was Bobby. This time, and for reasons he didn't explain, he was ready to work with the SCLC.

"What I'm about to tell you will not be repeated," Bobby told Harry. "You're about to get a call from Mike Quill."

Quill served as the head of the Transit Workers Union and was a Kennedy administration consigliere of sorts to various other labor unions. Bobby told Harry that the Kennedy administration was pressuring national labor unions to pony up $160,000 for bail. Harry didn't ask what was in it for the unions. The answer seemed obvious enough: a chance for more preferential treatment from an attorney general who had often, and loudly, attacked the unions for their alleged ties to the mob. That's how much Bobby Kennedy, the Puritan, wanted a settlement in Birmingham. He would engage in a round of quid pro quo with union leaders he'd called "hoodlums" and sometimes prosecuted.

To the extent Harry Belafonte dwelled on these facts, he kept them to himself. He stayed quiet and learned Bobby was calling the United Automobile Workers, the United Steelworkers, the AFL-CIO. As the day wore on the unions all agreed to help.

That was where Harry came in. The unions could not send this money to the Kennedys. No, the money needed to be handled through a third party; and perhaps the only word here is "laundered." Like the mob bosses he loathed, Bobby Kennedy could never be seen touching this money directly. So Harry would get the money from the union bosses. And Harry would then take the money and deposit it in the SCLC's account.

"I did check with Martin," Belafonte later recalled, "to make sure he was on board. He was."

Bobby rang incessantly that afternoon. In one call, Bobby asked Harry if any of the couriers delivering the money had arrived. Just then Harry's intercom buzzed.

"That might be one now," Harry said.

"I'll wait on the line," Bobby responded.

Harry went to the apartment door and opened it. A courier handed Harry a black satchel and walked off.

Inside was $50,000 in cash.

Harry moved back to the phone in the living room.

"Okay," he told Bobby, "it's in my hands."

Bobby said Harry should plan on more courier visits like that.

Then Bobby hung up.

The unions raised roughly half the money to bail the children out of jail. The other half came from an unlikely source: A. G. Gaston.

Back in Birmingham, Gaston paid roughly $160,000 of his own money "to secure the protesters' liberation," as he later wrote. He did it, he said, because he could, because he was a self-made man worth millions, but also as a form of apology. He saw how bailing out King earlier had ruined "the bargaining chip" King had with white negotiators. Helping to meet King's demands on the children's bail was a way for Gaston to say *I'm sorry.*

King would ultimately write at length about Project C and the eight hundred children freed from jail, but never about Gaston's role in securing their release.

King's gratitude, in other words, was just as coded.

44

WRESTLING WITH ITS CONSCIENCE

They staggered, all of them, from Thursday night into Friday morning. Bobby in D.C., hovering near his phone, waiting for the latest update from Burke Marshall. King taking his own updates from Andy Young, who sat at the negotiating table with the white lawyer David Vann, while King attempted to work out a separate truce with Fred Shuttlesworth, still "bitterly angry," one aide later said, at being excluded from the negotiations two nights before. Both King and Shuttlesworth, notably, missed the mass meeting, and James Bevel's eyes widened when nineteen Jewish leaders from New Jersey walked in, comparing Bull Connor to the Stasi in East Berlin and teaching the overflow crowd of two thousand a hymn in Hebrew.

No one slept well that night. No SCLC executive had slept well in days; King got at most two hours a night now. "That first week in May was the time of our greatest stress," King would later say.

The negotiations continued: from Thursday night into Friday morning, and then past the 11:00 a.m. deadline when the truce was to be struck and the press conference called. The media huddled in the open-air courtyard of the Gaston, waiting for King, Shuttlesworth, and Walker, and perhaps Bevel, to emerge.

No one showed.

Noon became 1:00 p.m., 1:00 p.m. became 1:30, and still no one.

• • •

A little after 2:00 p.m. Wyatt Walker appeared. Behind him walked King, Shuttlesworth, and Abernathy. Those three took seats before a phalanx of microphones at a round metal table. Despite their dapper suits, they looked exhausted. It was Shuttlesworth, not King, who sat in the middle of the three. It was Shuttlesworth, not King, whom Walker praised by way of introducing the press conference.

And it was Shuttlesworth, and not King, who cleared his throat to speak first.

"The city of Birmingham has reached an accord with its conscience," Shuttlesworth said, reading from a statement, thick glasses perched on his nose. A settlement had been finalized. "Birmingham may well offer for twentieth-century America an example of progressive racial relations," Shuttlesworth said.

He then discussed the truce's terms:

1. Within three days, fitting rooms will be desegregated.
2. Within fifteen, an integrated Committee on Racial Problems and Employment will be established, to improve employment opportunities for Black Birminghamians.
3. Within thirty days of the court order affirming Mayor Boutwell's government, signs on washrooms, restrooms, and drinking fountains will be removed.
4. Within sixty days of the new city government, lunchroom counters will be desegregated.
5. Within sixty days, the integrated Committee on Racial Problems and Employment will see to it that certain downtown stores employ at least one Black salesperson or cashier.

King spoke next. "We have come today to the climax of a long struggle for justice, freedom, and human dignity in the city of Birmingham.

"Credit for what has been done must go to many persons. Without question, of course, the name of the Reverend Fred Shuttlesworth stands clear as the magic name in this Magic City. He has walked a long and often lonesome road to reach this day—and even now his health is impaired—but he has just reason to be thankful and glad for all of his great sacrifices. . . . And, without a doubt, the world will never forget the thousands of children and adults who gave up their own physical safety and freedom and went to jail to secure the safety and freedom of all men."

It was stagecraft, every bit of it. Shuttlesworth not only in the center of the camera's frame, not only speaking first, but Shuttlesworth being praised before the child protesters whose bravery had brought the world's attention to Birmingham. King's actions were as tightly edited as the script from which Shuttlesworth read.

King believed what he said about Fred. All of it was genuine, but some of it was another of King's coded apologies, too. As he'd told Burke Marshall Wednesday at the Drews' house: He and Fred just had to have unity.

Shuttlesworth and King took questions.

The press noticed that the terms were not immediate actions. They were promises to act. What assurance did Shuttlesworth have that white people would keep their word?

"They are dealing in good faith," Shuttlesworth said. His response was almost whispered, as if he were physically ill. "And I wouldn't double-cross my people. They know that."

Soon Fred's head began to dip. Shaking, he rose from his seat and said, "Gentlemen, I hope you'll excuse me. I have to go back to the hospital."

Shuttlesworth stepped away from the table . . . and fainted.

People shrieked. It was, as Shuttlesworth's doctor would later say, "complete physical and mental exhaustion."

For the movement, the moment in some sense allegorized the last two months, too. Pitching yourself against such an overwhelming foe that, even in victory, you collapse.

Was this a victory? Shuttlesworth kept asking himself that from his bed that afternoon in Holy Family Hospital, which, like all Birmingham hospitals, and even after today's truce, remained segregated. Shuttlesworth fixated on the idea of how much he had given up to obtain this settlement. It was not the total win he had promised Black Birminghamians. The *New York Times* wrote as much. King and Shuttlesworth, the paper said, had "accepted promises of progress from white business and civic leaders in lieu of immediate action. . . . There was speculation among observers that, despite the apparent sincerity of the negotiators, the situation might deteriorate into the pattern set in a similar dispute in Albany." Fred had wondered this himself. He'd grown so concerned about the final wording of the agreement that it'd taken another call from Bobby Kennedy just before the press conference to literally put Fred in line between King and Abernathy as they walked out to meet the cameras. Bobby had said that *any* agreement was a good agreement, any truce a victory. "The alternative to discussion is going to be great violence," Bobby later told the *Times*, while Burke Marshall added: "For a city like Birmingham . . . to reach a settlement like this . . . is a tremendous step forward for Birmingham, for Alabama, and for the South generally."

But would the victory last? Or, put another way: Would a win here, however tenuous, only grow in scope as King retold it so that Birmingham's integration served a national movement more than it did the people who lived here? This was Shuttlesworth's greatest concern in that hospital bed: that he had been duped by King. That Birmingham's plight had only ever been a platform for King's national exposure. Even if it was brought about by the near delirium of exhaustion, the idea of betrayal clung to those closest to Shuttlesworth that Friday afternoon. Ruby Shuttlesworth stood watch at Fred's hospital door and refused Ralph Abernathy entry. Only those who'd known Fred from before Project C could see him.

One of them was Rev. Herb Oliver, a longtime Birmingham civil rights activist. Fred awoke when Oliver entered.

"I tried to do a good job," Shuttlesworth said.

Oliver told him he'd done a great job. He'd accomplished what no one had thought possible just three months ago.

Shuttlesworth nodded but, as if he didn't fully believe Oliver, asked what else the papers were saying about the agreement.

Oliver stared at him for a moment. He told him not to worry what the papers said.

Shuttlesworth sighed.

Soon he drifted back to sleep.

That night at the mass meeting, hours after he'd been denied entry to Fred Shuttlesworth's room, Ralph Abernathy worked the crowd of two thousand at St. John's Church into a fevered state. "Tonight is victory night!" Abernathy shouted. "All these preachers are great men, but there isn't but one Martin Luther King! God sent him to lead us to freedom! Are you going to follow him? Is he our leader?"

The crowd chanted yes over and over, and Abernathy shouted: "Then say 'King!'"

Two thousand Black Birminghamians shouted, "King! King! *King!*" The chant became, in the words of one writer, "deafening."

King took the pulpit.

"Do not underestimate the power of this movement!" King shouted. Referring to the terms of the truce, he said, "These things would not have been granted without your presenting your bodies and your very lives before the dogs and the tanks and the water hoses of this city!"

Thunderous applause and more shouts and chants for King.

Thanks to the Birmingham protests, "the United States is concerned about its image," King said. "When things started happening down here, Mr. Kennedy got disturbed. For Mr. Kennedy . . . is battling for the minds and the hearts of men in Asia and Africa . . . and they aren't going to respect the United States of America if she deprives men and women of the basic rights of life because of the color of their skin. Mr. Kennedy knows that."

More shrieks and applause, and then King built to his point: What started here was now everywhere. Harry Belafonte had phoned just this morning to say three thousand New Yorkers were ready to walk to the White House to gain an agreement in Birmingham.

"Now this is an amazing thing!" King said. A local movement, whose local plight had grown into a national platform: "It should make us all feel very happy!"

Part VII

"BUT FOR BIRMINGHAM . . ."

45

"THIS WHOLE TOWN
HAS GONE BERSERK"

settlement assumes just that: a settled point. Nothing remained settled in white Birmingham. According to white Birmingham, nothing had *ever* been settled. City Hall did not agree to the truce. "I'm
unwilling to make decisions virtually at gunpoint or as the result of agita-
tion," Mayor Boutwell said. "I regard it as an unwarranted presumption
for anyone to infer or suggest that there has been a 'truce' with any who
have violated the law." The lead negotiator, Sidney Smyer, could hold a
press conference Friday afternoon at the Bankhead Hotel and say how
the settlement's terms avoided a "holocaust" and "reestablished racial
peace"—but Smyer also stood alone at that press conference. For all Smyer's backroom discussions with the Big Mules of Birmingham, where were
the Big Mules now? Those business executives whose interests Smyer said
he represented and who apparently signed off on this agreement? Why
were the Big Mules not flanking him for the cameras? Smyer would not
even release their names to the press.

"Why are they ashamed to release the names of those on the negotiating committee?" one enraged politician asked. "They call themselves
negotiators. I call them a bunch of quisling, gutless traitors!"

The *Birmingham News*, in an editorial hours after the settlement, wrote that when King's protests upset the city's order, "non-official" white businessmen met with the SCLC as individuals speaking "only for themselves . . . they knew they could not agree with Negroes for you—the citizen—to do anything. They knew they could not do so for any elected city official. . . . Negroes obviously accepted that basis for the discussion. They obviously knew nothing that anyone 'agreed upon' was binding."

And even if it were, even if King said the federal government had brokered this peace, which meant Bobby Kennedy had blessed it, even if Washington thought white Birmingham was now bound by a new set of laws, white Birmingham could still decide whether to live by them. "If this self-appointed committee is all hopped up over the idea" of a settlement, one white man told a radio reporter, "and they want to use the restroom with them . . . well that's fine, just as long as I don't have to do it."

The SCLC, Bull Connor said, "didn't gain a thing."

King told the press otherwise on Saturday, May 11, but wasn't absolutely sure of it himself. "The Klan is meeting today," King said. "We'll have to see what they do."

They met in an open field that Saturday night in Bessemer, fifteen miles southwest of Birmingham: thousands of racist Birminghamians and Grand Dragons and their retinue from Alabama, Georgia, Tennessee, South Carolina, and Mississippi. By the glow of two flaming crosses, the Klansmen and their wives and children huddled ever closer to the flatbed truck atop which the night's speakers paced, microphone in hand.

With their hoods on they thanked Bull Connor, Governor Wallace, and the Birmingham fire department, which had injured Black leaders like Fred Shuttlesworth. Birmingham cops were scattered throughout the grounds. Whether they wore their own hoods was irrelevant. They later wrote notes of the meeting. The leaders on that flatbed truck spoke of an "integrated" future that would produce "mongrel" children unless, of course, those assembled had the courage to stop that future tonight. "We are facing the greatest darkness that this nation has ever faced," one speaker said. "But tonight, we as God's people, can turn Alabama upside down."

They tried.

Around 10:45 that Saturday night a BPD cruiser, car 49, stopped in front of the house of Martin Luther King's brother, A.D., in the Ensley neighborhood of Birmingham. The driver threw what was likely a pack of dynamite into the front yard, but when he saw that the still-sizzling package landed short of the house, the passenger in the police cruiser got out. He cursed the driver—"son of a bitch"—raced to the front porch, and placed a second bomb there, lighting the fuse. The man then raced back to the cruiser.

The explosions, when they came, blasted through the house. One blew an opening three feet deep and five feet in diameter through the home's brick exterior. The roof collapsed, and the walls, too; part of the floor gave way and widened into a chasm that bared the foundation beneath. Splinters from the front door, suddenly shrapnel, stuck into the back wall of the living room. A.D.; his wife, Naomi; and their five children had little protection from this destruction. And yet, as A.D. later said, by the grace of the same God to which the Klan prayed, his family was not injured, though the blasts destroyed 80 percent of their home.

He kept thinking there were more bombs. He had the police and fire department, when they at last arrived, search the premises. Roughly an hour later, A.D. and the authorities heard a thunderous crack. So loud A.D. thought his own church had been bombed, just blocks away. But no: This explosion erupted some four miles distant, in the downtown core.

In the Gaston Motel.

Members of the Klan had placed a bomb in the Gaston's reception area, directly below room 30, where Martin Luther King Jr. and the SCLC had stationed themselves for the past six weeks. The explosion blew out the lobby and knocked down the water and electrical lines. It sent metal flying through the air, which then damaged cars and homes three blocks away. It injured four people, one fatally—the invalid mother-in-law of the Gaston's night manager—but none of those people were Martin Luther King Jr.

Martin had flown back to Atlanta hours earlier to see his newborn, Bernice, and to prepare a sermon for his home church, Ebenezer Baptist. The Klan did not know that. And yet with these two bombings suddenly the whole night came into focus.

The Klan had just staged two assassination attempts on the King family.

This understanding spread quickly, and it spread just as the bars let out. Within minutes, perhaps two thousand people crowded round the Gaston, half of them drunk, everyone furious. When the cops arrived in their patrol cars, or with their German shepherds to sniff for more bombs, the images and memories of the past two weeks came alive before the Gaston's destruction. "You'd better get those dogs out of here!" one man yelled.

Members of the crowd hurled rocks at the cops. Then came the glass bottles they'd been drinking from all night, and soon the bricks from the Gaston's ruins. Shoving and pushing and curses followed, pockets of brawls in front of the Gaston that spilled into the alleyway adjacent. Wyatt Walker arrived from A. D. King's house. He'd spent the last six weeks escalating scenes just like this but knew tonight's would do the movement no good. He grabbed a megaphone from a cop and climbed onto the hood of a patrol car. He asked the crowd to please go home.

They didn't listen. They continued to hurl debris at the cops. "Please do not throw any of the bricks anymore," Wyatt said.

Just then one hit him in the ankle. He hobbled down from the hood and tried to break up fights spreading along the front lines.

But the violence was its own force, and the crowd turned from the Gaston now to fully unleash its fury. It roved, gained speed, morphed into a mob, and upended a car near 16th Street Baptist and set it on fire. Then people moved to an Italian grocery on 15th Street and Sixth Avenue and hurled debris through the windows, storming it and setting it ablaze.

More smashed windows now, more looting, more fires along the streets of Birmingham, the mob growing to 2,500 people. The newsmen who'd heard the blasts from their own motel rooms watched a new and different story of this night take shape. They trailed the mob as its members shouted: "Let's go get Bull Connor's house!" "Let's kill him!" "An eye for an eye and a tooth for a tooth!" "I said there'd be a race riot and this is it!"

The violence spread, worsened: Bottles like hurled rockets smashed against police cars that tried to prevent the mob from advancing; a Black man stabbed a cop three times in the back; another Black man wielded a four-by-four and a knife at a fireman, who fled from him; a reporter using a pay phone called in what he saw and that phone booth, reporter and all, was shaken to and fro by mob members until it upended; Bull Connor's white tank barreled down the streets in response, and did not stop, just spread tear gas; more hurled bottles; more brawls; more epithets; more flames; the city on fire suddenly, "Let the whole fucking city burn!" one man said.

A. D. King took to the streets near Kelly Ingram Park, grabbing a megaphone and saying: "Our home was just bombed. . . . Now if we who were in jeopardy of being killed, if we have gone away not angry, not throwing bricks, if we could do that and we were in danger, why must you rise up to hurt our cause? You are hurting us! You are not helping! Now won't you please clear this park."

What was obvious to A. D. King was obvious to Wyatt Walker, who stalked the streets alongside him, and to Fred Shuttlesworth, who heard reports of that night's violence from his bed at Holy Family Hospital, and to James Bevel, too, who would the next day be quoted in the *New York Times* saying how victory was possible only if Blacks remained "righteous" and "nonviolent," and above all it was obvious to Martin Luther King Jr., whom A.D. called in the middle of the night, not long after A.D. phoned the Justice Department and said, "This whole town has gone berserk."

If the bombs did not kill King, Martin's accord could die on the streets of Birmingham, amid the response to the bombs.

46

SHAPING THE POSTSCRIPT

King didn't share such misgivings the next morning with his congregation at Ebenezer Baptist in Atlanta. That Sunday morning he talked of how he thought the agreement would hold, but his actions belied his words. Minutes after the service, he prepared to fly to Birmingham.

The headlines from there ("Negroes Attack Police After Blast Rips Home of King's Brother," in the *New York Times*), King's conversations with Burke Marshall from the White House, the administration suggesting how Black people were to blame for the riot and Bobby outright saying it between calls ("The people who've gotten out of hand are not the white people but the Negroes by and large")—all this spurred King's sense of urgency. He had to shape a postscript to the settlement, lest the whole written truce fall apart.

None of this was fair. None of the narrative-shaping King had in mind would get at the whole story of what happened. How Colonel Al Lingo of the Alabama State Police had barreled through the streets with a sawed-off shotgun at 2:30 that morning, he and his 250 troopers beating SCLC staffers within the Gaston who begged Lingo to put away the guns. Lingo and his men rifle-butted Wyatt Walker's wife in the face and fractured Wyatt's wrist when he tried to defend her. When Birmingham cops came to the Walkers' aid and said such violence might kill someone,

Lingo screamed, "You're damn right it'll kill somebody." The beatings continued, the heavy *thonk* of billy clubs on skulls heard across the street.

But even that deputized violence was not the full story. The real narrative was that the vast majority of Black people had remained peaceful. At one point in those long hours before dawn, A. D. King phoned Martin to update him. "My brother described the terror of the streets," Martin later said of the phone call. How Black people, "furious at the bombings, fought whites. . . . Then, behind [A.D.'s] voice, I heard a rising chorus of beautiful singing."

The singing grew louder. Martin could hear the song through the receiver.

"We Shall Overcome."

Hundreds of people sang out the words. It was an impromptu performance on the streets of Birmingham.

"Tears came to my eyes," Martin said.

Despite the power of that performance, King knew when he landed in Birmingham Sunday afternoon that relaying the full account of last night to the public would not help him. The city smoldered. Street after charred street, the remnants of houses, of an apartment complex. Six businesses had burned to the ground. At least fifty people had been injured. Early Sunday morning, Al Lingo's troopers sealed off a twenty-eight-block area of the city. No one inside it could leave. It was no coincidence, King realized, that the cordoned-off blocks fell almost exclusively in Black Birmingham. Throughout the city, and despite the agreement, King saw more evidence of racism. "The nigger King ought to be investigated by the Attorney General," said Art Hanes, a local politician, with reporters gathered around him.

When King got to the Gaston, he saw amid its ruins and busted water pipes how SCLC staffers had been quarantined without food or water. Wyatt Walker was in a cast and bandages. Walker's wife, Theresa, was at the hospital.

But this could not be King's narrative, either. So King invited what pressmen he could to that night's mass meeting at New Pilgrim Church, and while he said "We must not use second-class methods" to gain "first-class citizenship," King allowed his brother to deliver the lasting message. A.D., whose house was no longer inhabitable, said at the mass meeting, "You know when the Lord is with you even bombs cannot hurt you."

The congregation murmured, "All right" and "Amen."

"We are dealing with some very vicious people. . . . We've had some of our women beaten . . . and they have our friends blocked at the Gaston Motel without food or water. Now all of this is very bad but I want to say this regardless of how bad this is: If we turn to the same sort of thing, we've lost the victory that we've come so close to winning."

The crowd called back louder.

"If any violence must come, then let it come to *us*! And let us receive it in the spirit that Christ received it and say, 'Father, forgive them for they know *not* what they do!'"

Shouts of "Amen!" now.

"And if it means some of us must die, we still cannot afford to turn back violence for violence. And I feel that if we love this great cause as we proclaim we love it, if we love the cause of freedom, then we'll be willing to *die for it* so that other Negros will be able to enjoy the freedom that is due to *all* men!"

The congregation erupted. Martin saw the response himself, steps from the altar. Just as important, Martin saw the press recording and transcribing all of this.

One way to shape a narrative, after all, is to show how the story is not yours alone.

Another way is to show how actions outweigh words.

The next day, Monday the thirteenth, Martin made sure to have more members of the media follow him as he and Ralph Abernathy toured Black Birmingham. King stopped in bars and pool halls. He made a point of passing a hat through the crowd and asking the men and boys who were the businesses' patrons to deposit their knives and brickbats. Many did. The press cameras clicked as the hat sagged from the weight. Martin allowed the cameramen to keep clicking, take as many photos as they wanted of this voluntary disarmament. Then Martin moved to the next pool hall, the next bar, where similar scenes played out.

In one pool hall, King played a game with the men while lamenting he was not quite the shark he'd been in his seminary days. At another he said that those who had bombed the motel where he stayed, who had bombed his brother's house, "were trying to sabotage all that we are trying to do.

"We must not beat up *any* policeman, as brutal as they are trying to be," King said. As he spoke, more Black people crowded in and the press captured this, too: thirty men and women vying for spots in the hall to hear King. "Bull Connor is happy when we use force," but "we must not stab anybody," King said. "We must not burn down any stores."

The crowd nodded its agreement.

In a pause in King's speech, Abernathy asked all present to pledge to nonviolence with a shout of "aye."

"A great shout of 'aye' went up," the *New York Times* reported.

Martin smiled.

The crowd then followed him out of the pool hall, a "long retinue" of people, as the *Times* put it. They walked toward 18th Street and Fourth Avenue, a no-man's-land between white and Black Birmingham, and a road to Damascus, too: the recently converted in that long line behind King went out to spread the message of nonviolence within other pool halls and bars.

Two of Al Lingo's state troopers stepped from their car at the intersection and blocked King from moving on. "We are not going to have no band of men go into this area," one trooper said.

King turned around and began to head back to the Gaston, but these two state troopers were soon joined by more, all of them aggressive, shouting at Black people to disperse. King continued walking to the Gaston, and the long line stayed right behind him.

The troopers took out their carbines and used their butts to shove the marchers out of the line. The troopers slammed the peaceful protesters against storefronts.

The press captured all of that, too.

The peace must hold, the settlement must last, King said later that night when he took the pulpit at the mass meeting. "We are not going to allow this conflict in Birmingham to deteriorate into a struggle between Black people and white people. The tension in Birmingham is between justice and injustice!"

The crowd shouted, and the press recorded and transcribed everything.

It was a battle for "consciences," King said, and in that battle, no matter how many homes were bombed—and "they may try to bomb a little more"—no matter how many people were slammed out of a peaceful march like today's or rifle-butted as Wyatt Walker and his wife had been (with Walker present tonight, in his cast and bandages), no matter how many times Bull Connor called them "nigger" or how many fire hoses leveled them, no matter how many dogs bit them, "I will *never* teach *any of you* to hate white people," King boomed.

The crowd roared at this.

"I'm teaching you to *love* those who hate us!" King yelled, because when love is the message it triumphs over hate.

And so it did.

The press interpreted the narrative King shaped. These stories were informed by all the messages preceding it, too: the images from Double D-Day all the way to this one and what those photographs and video clips said about the South, and America; the pleas for peace in church congregations and now pool halls; and how those pleas were influencing the oppressed in Birmingham *and* the oppressors.

One day later, under pressure from President Kennedy to keep the peace lest the stories and protests continue, Sidney Smyer said in a press conference that he and the white delegation would agree to release the names of the white committee who'd brokered the deal.

Smyer said that, whatever would come its way, white Birmingham would abide forever more by the settlement.

With King's final show of peace, Project Confrontation had at last won.

47

CONSIDERING THE IMPOSSIBLE

By breaking segregation in Birmingham, Project C began to move beyond the city's borders. Marches and protests spread through the segregated South.

This was a problem for Jack and Bobby Kennedy. They had hoped the Birmingham truce would end the civil rights protests. Instead, the settlement showed Black people how segregation could be broken anywhere. Suddenly there were sit-ins in Greensboro, North Carolina. A freedom walk from Chattanooga, Tennessee, to Gadsden, Alabama. Demonstrations in Raleigh, North Carolina, where protesters challenged the cops to shoot. And none of these organized by King. Black people just took to the streets, inspired by what had happened in Birmingham.

And not just in the South. In Chicago, civil rights activists planned massive demonstrations. Chicago mayor Richard Daley phoned Bobby Kennedy and said Black people would not listen to the cops, would not cower before law enforcement anymore. Daley told Bobby about "a lot of trouble" in the days ahead, when Black Chicagoans planned to act like Black Birminghamians and demand justice.

Everyone demanded it now. Jackie Robinson flew to Birmingham to appear at a mass meeting and to say, "I don't think you realize down here in Birmingham what you mean to us up there in New York." *His* children wanted to protest. And not because he'd integrated baseball but because of what they'd seen on the news from Birmingham. The bravery of those child protesters, their peaceful dignity—Robinson could relate. "I can't help getting emotional about this thing," he told the mass meeting. He fought back tears. Massive protests were planned for Robinson's New York, too.

"Events in Birmingham in the last few days have seemed to electrify Negro concern over civil rights all across the country," Louis Martin, the deputy chairman of the Democratic National Committee, wrote to Bobby Kennedy in a memo two days after the Birmingham settlement. "As this is written, demonstrations and marches are underway or being planned in a number of major cities. . . . The accelerated tempo of Negro restiveness . . . may soon create the most critical state of race relations since the Civil War."

Bobby Kennedy agreed. He summoned Burke Marshall to the White House almost as soon as Burke flew back from Birmingham. Marshall later recalled that meeting with Bobby, saying, "My own judgment, the judgment of the Attorney General: we both saw it the same way. . . . This, after Birmingham, was already a terrible problem—with the sit-ins and everything—and it was going to get worse and worse and worse and had to be dealt with."

They could not mediate fifty Birminghams. They had to propose one solution for the nation.

They had to consider the impossible: civil rights legislation.

Many advisors in the White House still opposed legislation. Kenny O'Donnell, a special assistant to President Kennedy and close friend of both brothers, part of the Kennedys' "Irish mafia," opposed it. So did Ted Sorensen, Jack's speechwriter and the "intellectual blood bank," in Jack's words, of the administration. They both thought a civil rights bill would hurt Jack's reelection chances in 1964.

Jack thought the same. A big bill like that would tie up Congress until at least the reelection campaign, he said. Kennedy's pollsters would ultimately conclude that civil rights legislation would cost Kennedy 4.5 million white voters. Jack would lose his reelection bid.

Jack would lose anyway if he failed to address the massive spike in protests. That was the counterargument, the other truth of that late spring of 1963. By the middle of summer, there would be 758 civil rights demonstrations in 186 cities. Each protest carried a threat of violence. Race riots might erupt.

Bobby, the protective brother, the political animal, the Puritan, realized that by mediating in Birmingham the administration now had to mediate a larger solution. He asked Burke Marshall to fly to North Carolina with him, where Bobby was to give a talk on the Cold War, so that Bobby and Burke could think more about a civil rights bill on the flight down and back.

Once the air force plane took off, Bobby turned to Burke and said if there was to be a bill, he wanted one that got to "the heart of the matter."

Marshall nodded. "Something that didn't deal with pieces of the problem but . . . all parts of the problem," Marshall later recalled of the conversation. So that meant public accommodations—taking down all those "Whites Only" signs, for example—and also employment opportunities. Fair hiring practices and, once Blacks were hired, some form of recourse for workplace discrimination.

That would be a hard bill to pass. "The most difficult question, always in congressional terms, was in connection with employment rather than public accommodations and how to deal with that," Marshall later said. Congress didn't want to legislate fair employment. Hell, Congress didn't want to legislate civil rights. Politicians had tried. President Harry Truman had established a Committee on Civil Rights in 1946. "I want our Bill of Rights implemented in fact," he'd said. "We've been trying to do this for 150 years." Truman's legislation went nowhere. He had to sign an executive order just to integrate the army. In the intervening years various senators—Jacob Javits and Hubert Humphrey among them—had proposed numerous civil rights bills. All were pared back. Javits's in 1960 lost its school desegregation provision, its ban on workplace discrimination, its ban on poll taxes at the voting booth, even Congress's ability to make lynching a federal crime. And *even then*, weak as it was, Javits's bill failed to become law. Congress did pass a Civil Rights Act in 1957 on the strength of senators Paul Douglas and Lyndon Johnson's parliamentary maneuvering, but the bill was so thoroughly stripped of its parts by the time President Eisenhower signed it that the law changed nothing in America. That was the problem on this plane ride to North Carolina: Nothing had changed.

And yet Birmingham had changed everything. Its images each night, through that newest medium, television, which was also the widest-reaching, had "stirred the feelings of every Negro in the country," Marshall said, "and most whites in the country." Bobby and his brother heard all the time from voters, from Beltway insiders, from the press: *Why wasn't the president doing anything about civil rights?*

Doing nothing was now a liability. That's why this time was different.

Bobby had to hand it to King. He had turned Birmingham into a metaphor of America. And that story had compelled Bobby to act: to get on this air force plane and hash out with Burke Marshall the particulars of a bill to which Bobby had always been opposed. Bobby thought about his brother and the liability he faced in doing nothing, and decided that if the Kennedys were going to author any bill, they had to author the biggest one possible.

By the time Bobby and Burke returned from North Carolina, Jack Kennedy had an outline of the legislation on his desk. What it promised was the end of public segregation in the South. The end as well of workplace discrimination against Blacks across the nation, in every instance of hiring, promotion, and firing.

President Kennedy eyed the outline warily. He was a man who just three months earlier, at a White House celebration of President Lincoln's birthday, had spotted Sammy Davis Jr. and his white wife, May Britt, approaching him. "Get them out of here," Jack had hissed to an aide. He did not want to be photographed with an interracial couple. Too many headlines would come from that photo, and maybe bad polling numbers.

He remained opposed to integration at the start of the Birmingham campaign, too. But by the latter half of May, it seemed necessary to do something, and not just because of the nationwide demonstrations that mimicked Birmingham's. The United States was losing its standing in the world now. Many newspapers in Europe and Asia led their front pages with news from Birmingham. The head of Kenya's African National Union said, "If the United States wishes to maintain the respect and goodwill of the people of Africa, it must stand firmly by the fundamental principles of freedom and equality enshrined in its Constitution." *Pravda* distributed a story through Communist Europe and Asia titled "Monstrous Crimes Among Racists in the United States."

Domestically, members of Kennedy's own party sniped at him. Democratic Representative Emanuel Celler, who'd served Brooklyn for forty years, said President Kennedy couldn't hide behind a southern state's provincialism as the reason for not acting. "There is ample basis for federal intervention in the 13th and 14th and 15th Amendments to the Constitution," Celler said. New York's Republican governor, Nelson Rockefeller, talked about running for president in 1964 and making civil rights the focal point of his agenda.

And so Jack Kennedy looked at the outline of the bill before him and told his closest advisor to proceed. The president wanted to see if the bill could do the unthinkable: gain congressional support and, perhaps even more unlikely, the support of the American people.

Bobby Kennedy nodded.

48

THE GATHERING AT
24 CENTRAL PARK SOUTH

Bobby, faithful brother, worked the phones hard. Maybe his most important call was to James Baldwin, the Black intellectual and author. Baldwin had just published a searing book on the Black experience, *The Fire Next Time*. After Bobby called Baldwin, Baldwin in turn phoned Harry Belafonte.

"He'd like to meet with a group of us," Baldwin told Belafonte.

"What's the agenda?" Harry asked. He loved Baldwin like a brother but remained wary of Bobby Kennedy's angle. If the secret payment to free the jailed Birmingham kids was an indication, Bobby always played an angle.

"There's so much anger out there," Baldwin said. "Even Martin can't get his hands around it. Bobby wants to understand that anger better, to know how to respond."

Harry thought: *With all the history between Bobby and me, what does he not yet know about anger in the Black community?* He asked, "Who's going?"

Baldwin said he planned to reach out to lawyers and activists but also

Black performers like Lena Horne and writers like Lorraine Hansberry. Her play *A Raisin in the Sun* had recently been turned into a film.

Belafonte thought it over.

"I'll go," he said at last.

After hanging up, though, Harry's suspicions grew.

"I [still] wondered what Kennedy's agenda was," Belafonte later wrote. "Perhaps the Kennedys were trying to ease us into taking a more moderate line."

Bobby Kennedy had high hopes for the meeting: a private and therefore honest conversation with a constituency he and his brother would need if they were to act on the impossible. Bobby wanted nothing official about this meeting. He held it Friday night, May 24, in the apartment in New York that Bobby's father, Joe, owned, which overlooked Central Park. Bobby wanted the night at 24 Central Park South to feel like a cocktail party, and so when the evening came his staff served hors d'oeuvres and a light buffet to a somewhat strange amalgamation of people: SNCC and CORE activists; James Baldwin and his agent and secretary; the SCLC lawyer Clarence Jones, who'd stuffed King's scraps of newsprint into his pants as King wrote his "Letter from Birmingham Jail"; Harry Belafonte, who kept his distance from Bobby; various other creative types, like Lorraine Hansberry; and a few Black academics. When everyone had finished eating, Bobby and Burke Marshall and a Kennedy press aide, Ed Guthman, asked them to move to the living room.

Bobby opened with the administration's efforts: its unprecedented commitment to civil rights and—

Unprecedented? Jerome Smith, a young CORE activist, asked. He told Bobby there was nothing unprecedented about Kennedy's commitment to civil rights. There was no commitment at all. Just being in this room made Smith "nauseous."

Bobby snickered, insulted. *Nauseous? When Smith'd been given a* private meeting *with the attorney general of the United States?* Bobby turned away from Smith, as if to ignore him and address the more mature adults. But those mature adults knew what Bobby did not. Smith had been on the Freedom Rides in 1961 and then beaten again in Mississippi for trying to integrate other bus lines. Even now he risked his life. Smith was in New York for medical treatment after the Birmingham campaign.

Lorraine Hansberry told Bobby, "You've got a great many very accomplished people in this room, Mr. Attorney General. But the only man you should be listening to is that man over there." She pointed back to Jerome Smith.

The room saw Bobby tense up. He didn't engage Smith. He said he wanted to stay on script. He wanted to figure out how he and his brother could win with a civil rights bill. Bobby thought mentioning the possibility of a bill would impress the crowd.

James Baldwin could see the angling. "For [Bobby] it was a political matter," Baldwin later said. "It was a matter of finding out what's wrong in the twelfth ward and then correcting it. . . . But what was wrong in the twelfth ward was something very sinister, very deep, that couldn't be solved in the usual way." Bobby coming here and applauding himself for reaching out to Blacks in the wake of Birmingham wasn't enough. "Bobby didn't understand that," Baldwin said. "And our apprehension of his misunderstanding made it very tense."

Baldwin redirected the conversation, forced Bobby to listen to Smith. Baldwin asked the young activist if he would ever consider enlisting in the army to serve his country.

"Never! Never! Never!" Smith said.

"How can you *say* that?" Bobby asked, his cheeks reddening. He believed absolutely in public service. It was all he'd ever known.

"These are poor people who did nothing to us," Smith said, referencing the Vietnamese against whom people like Bobby waged an escalating conflict. "They're more my brothers than you are."

Now Bobby was irate.

Such beliefs were treasonous, Bobby said.

At that, everyone in the room rushed Bobby. Why did he not see that Smith "communicated the plain, basic suffering of being a Negro?" as Lena Horne put it.

"Look," Lorraine Hansberry said, eyeing Bobby. "If *you* can't understand what this young man is saying, then we are without any hope at all. Because you and your brother are representatives of the best that a white America can offer; and if *you* are insensitive to this, then there's no alternative except our going in the streets . . . and chaos."

Bobby took that as an opening to say he did not want chaos. He understood their pain. His grandparents had come from Ireland and settled in the States amid all the "Irish Need Not Apply" signs. Two generations later a Kennedy was president. The same could happen, in time, for Negroes, Bobby said.

"Your family has been here for three generations," Baldwin sneered. "*My* family has been here far longer than that. Why is your brother at the top while we are still so far away?"

It went like this for hours. Bobby saying he and his brother were trying to help Black people. The assembled saying Bobby's help patronized them—and they were astonished that Bobby couldn't see his efforts for the pat on the head they were. Bobby getting ever angrier at being called distant and obtuse and blind. The Black guests furious at the gratitude Bobby wanted them to express.

The meeting turned "very ugly," Baldwin later said.

As the back-and-forth approached its third hour—"one of the most violent, emotional verbal assaults that I had ever witnessed," one observer later said—Bobby took to bottling up his anger. He just sat there, the tension building within him. The fair cheeks he'd inherited from those Irish grandparents betrayed him now, turning bright red.

"I had never seen him so shaken," Harry Belafonte later wrote.

Lorraine Hansberry said that given how Bobby had failed to act in Birmingham—after watching those news programs, reading those newspaper articles with Birmingham datelines—given all that, she had no choice but to ignore Bobby now.

She walked out of the meeting.

Others joined her.

Bobby rose, laughing hysterically, "the laughter of desperation," one observer later said.

Belafonte approached. Even with his suspicions, Harry had known Bobby the longest. He thought he might calm Bobby down while also leveling with him. "You may think you're doing enough, but you don't live with us," Belafonte said. "You don't visit our pain. . . . Those children in Birmingham are our children and—"

"Enough," Bobby hissed.

He turned away from Belafonte and briskly left the living room.

The meeting stayed with him.

They don't know what the laws are, Bobby thought, a strain of thought he later shared with the Kennedy confidant Arthur Schlesinger. *They don't know what the facts are. They don't know what we've been doing or what we're trying to do.*

Was anything worth doing now? Any bill at all? Especially if this were to be the reaction?

"They seemed possessed," Bobby said.

And Bobby Kennedy had his brother to protect.

49

GOD'S BENEFICENCE

Hours later, at about 12:30 a.m., Harry Belafonte's phone rang. It was James Baldwin.

"It broke in the *Times*," Baldwin said.

"What?" Belafonte asked.

"Our evening. With Bobby. It's in tomorrow's *New York Times*."

"How the fuck did that happen?"

Baldwin said he hadn't leaked it, but he'd spoken with the reporter.

The next day, Sunday, May 26, the story appeared on page one under the headline "Robert Kennedy Fails to Sway Negroes at Secret Talks Here." Belafonte read it and got a "sick feeling," he later wrote. It was all there: the heated exchanges, the hysterical laughter, Bobby failing to "get the point" of Black constituents' concerns, Baldwin said.

"I felt we'd done a great disservice to Bobby," Belafonte wrote, "not by saying what we felt, but by embarrassing him in print. We'd . . . hurt our cause." Yes, Harry was suspicious of Bobby, but the only thing worse than an angling Bobby Kennedy was a dismissive one. A silent one. "Whether Bobby would even talk to me again, I had no idea," Belafonte wrote. "I felt sure that the trust we'd built up was seriously eroded, if not altogether swept away."

Belafonte's phone rang again.

Martin Luther King Jr. He'd read the story, too. He wanted every detail of Friday night.

Belafonte sighed. "Disaster," he said.

He recounted for King the details of the meeting, and when he got to the part about Jerome Smith's fury, King stopped him. King seemed, if anything, pleased with how the meeting went.

"Maybe it's just what Bobby needed to hear."

King saw what Belafonte did not. How God kept rewarding King's faith. King had held the faith that they would succeed in Birmingham and that the protests there would lead to more in other cities. Both of these aspirations had seemed impossible three months ago. Yet both had occurred. Why not keep the faith, then, for the largest of the movement's hopes—that Birmingham would lead to civil rights legislation?

After all, here was Bobby Kennedy, in that "disastrous" meeting, talking about a bill. This story in the *Times* hadn't distanced the movement from its ultimate goal, King said. This story had drawn the movement closer to it. Now that talk of legislation was in the open, Bobby was going to hear a lot more from King, "if the President keeps dawdling on that civil rights bill," King told Belafonte.

King would press his advantage because it was the work of God. In Birmingham, Bull Connor had lost his court fight to stay in power against Mayor Boutwell on the same day that another southern court had ruled the Birmingham school district could not expel the Black children who'd protested. The worst southern racist dethroned on the same day a white court system saw Black children's education as worthwhile? What was that if *not* divine providence? That these actions had occurred on Friday, May 24, the same day that Bobby met with Baldwin and Belafonte and all the rest in New York, meant God's beneficence was real.

King saw it everywhere now. He had flown to Cleveland after the Birmingham truce and been mobbed at the airport. It had taken body-guards to usher him to the church. At that night's mass meeting, King couldn't believe it: For the first time, as many white people in attendance as Blacks. And ten thousand people in total. "I've never seen such an aroused response!" King boomed from the pulpit.

Until the next weekend, in L.A., when fifty thousand people filled Wrigley Field. The majority in attendance held programs that featured photos of snarling Birmingham dogs. The metaphor of America now. King spoke of how "there comes a time when people get tired of being trampled over by the iron feet of oppression," a speech so good, that built to such a crescendo, that a woman could be heard "shrieking like a wolf whistle," as one writer put it. At a fundraiser afterward at the home of actor Burt Lancaster, the SCLC received donations of $75,000 from celebrities including Paul Newman, Marlon Brando, Sammy Davis Jr., and the wife of L.A. Lakers legend Elgin Baylor.

"We Shall Overcome" rang out, *Jet* magazine wrote, "like Wings Over Jordan in Beverly Hills."

And even after that night, and elsewhere, the protests for still more change: 100 arrested in Albany, 400 in Greensboro, 1,000 in Durham.

Yes, it was time, King thought, that the Kennedys saw what he did. A faith that stared through death, where the Kennedy brothers would give their lives for what they believed in. "The president must be ready to take a stand," King said in Chicago before another crowd, pressing hard for a civil rights bill, "even if it means assassination."

50

THE BROTHER'S MESSAGE

I f Bobby Kennedy took any stand, it was for vengeance. When he saw the story in the *Times* he phoned J. Edgar Hoover and demanded to see the FBI's surveillance of James Baldwin. Baldwin had leaked the story; Bobby just knew it. When Bobby got the Baldwin dossier—ultimately stretching to 1,884 pages, the largest of any Black American writer—he forwarded it to Burke Marshall with a snarky, embittered note: "He is a nice fellow & you have swell friends."

Marshall and other aides "worried" about Bobby's "rage," they later said. That Friday night meeting stayed with him long after its recounting Sunday morning in the *Times*. "He was absolutely shocked" by the meeting and its press leak, Nicholas Katzenbach, the deputy U.S. attorney general, said. "Bobby expected to be made an honorary black." That he hadn't been, that he'd been mocked in the press by Black people like Baldwin, outraged him to the point of fixation.

And then the point of reflection.

Why had it gone wrong?

Far more than his brother, Bobby Kennedy questioned any situation by questioning his own actions. This was the Catholic in Bobby. In what way had he sinned? The more he thought about that meeting, the more he thought about its end point, and what Harry Belafonte had told him: *Those children in Birmingham are our children.* Bobby had stormed out of the room, but what Harry meant, what Harry seemed to be saying, Bobby realized days later, was for Bobby to begin to see Birmingham through a parent's eyes.

Bobby loved children. He and his wife, Ethel, had seven with an eighth on the way in the spring of 1963. He hung their artwork in his office, and "there wasn't a problem that the kids had that he wouldn't interrupt everything he was doing to solve," one Kennedy confidant later said. Bobby saw how he had approached the meeting at 24 Central Park South as the attorney general, as the politician out to protect his brother. He should have approached it as a father. As a father, to see fire-hosed children and segregated schools and restrooms—it changed the calculus. Birmingham was no longer a political problem to solve. It was a deeply familial one.

In the days after the James Baldwin flare-up, Bobby told press aide Ed Guthman that he actually sympathized with Baldwin. The same went for Jerome Smith, whom Bobby had called a traitor in the meeting. He now said, "I guess if I were in [Smith's] shoes, if I had gone through what he's gone through, I might feel differently about this country." To Burke Marshall, Bobby began to "talk about how he'd feel if it was his children excluded" from the American dream.

Bobby in these last days in May formulated something he would later repeat to a Senate subcommittee: "The United States is dominated by white people, politically and economically. The question is whether we, in this position of dominance, are going to have not the charity but the wisdom to stop penalizing our fellow citizens whose only fault or sin is that they were born."

That meeting at 24 Central Park South, much as King had predicted, became just what Bobby needed to hear.

From there Bobby went on a "warpath," one confidant later wrote. He met with educators, lawyers, businesspeople, church people, all within a span of days, and always with the aim of listening to what desegregation would mean to them. Not the particulars of a bill. The morality of a policy: *What would that do for you?* Bobby wanted to know. He appeared on May 29 at a meeting for the Committee for Equal Employment Opportunity, overseen by Vice President Lyndon Johnson. Johnson had been telling Bobby forever that the federal government did a good job of hiring Black people for open positions. When Bobby got to the meeting, though, he learned that only fifteen of Birmingham's two thousand federal employees were Black. That was less than 1 percent. And in a city that was 37 percent Black.

"He was furious," one friend wrote.

He saw, increasingly, the totality of oppression, how it minimized and even erased people from a nation's portrait. The seventh of nine children in a house more competitive than loving, Bobby had felt invisible throughout his own life. His experiences were not a Black man's, but he understood how "you have to struggle to survive." His parents had ignored him. As a child, he began to loathe himself, his shy nature, his awkward body. One day on a yawl on Nantucket Sound, still unable to swim, young Bobby threw himself into the water, determined to learn or drown.

Joe Jr. had to save him.

Bobby eventually learned to swim, like he eventually learned anything: through nerve and drive. But the episode demonstrated what he had felt throughout his life: a deprivation, a lack of respect, a person risking even his life to be seen.

Now, in the last days of May 1963 and the first days of June, he understood King and the SCLC. For the first time he *saw* them.

"The more he saw," Burke Marshall said, "the more he understood. And the more you learned about how Negroes were treated . . . the madder you became. He always talked about the hypocrisy. That's what got him."

The administration *had* to propose a civil rights bill, Bobby told Marshall now. Forget how it would poll. Forget how Congress would respond.

A bill was the right thing to do. The only thing.

• • •

Bobby just had to convince his brother of that. This would be no easy feat. *Everyone* in Jack's cabinet was still against a bill. The president was far closer to his aides' feeling about the legislation than his brother's. Bobby's argument for racial equality and a civil rights bill became so passionate in May and June that he literally sounded different in meetings at the White House. "He had a way of saying it, a certain lilt to his voice," said Louis Oberdofer, an aide of Bobby's in the DOJ. "I can still hear it, a little higher pitch, not in decibels, but in octaves." You can hear it in a White House recording from May 20 about Birmingham. The testiness in Bobby's voice, the high-pitched urgency. Almost in despair, Bobby noted how a Black college graduate in the South could dream of nothing more than a job at the post office.

"Pretty good job for a Negro in the South, though, letter carrier," Jack said, leaning back in his chair until it squeaked.

A long silence ensued. In that silence you can almost hear Bobby brooding. You can almost see Bobby shaming his brother for his uncaring flippancy.

He redoubled his efforts. He staged meetings at the White House with Jack's cabinet members. Bobby wanted them to see what he now saw. How America erased opportunities and then identities. *We can fix this*, Bobby said. *We must.* "I don't think there was anyone in the Cabinet," Burke Marshall later said, "who felt that way on these issues."

Bobby kept at it. He worked on his brother, the only one who mattered anyway. It didn't hurt Bobby's cause that King now called Jack out. "He has not furnished the expected leadership and has not kept his campaign promises," King told the *New York Times*. King wanted an executive order from President Kennedy that outlawed segregation, that established real civil rights. On May 30 King sent a telegram to the White House asking for a face-to-face meeting with the president to discuss this. Jack's staffers said he could not meet for a week, and in that time J. Edgar Hoover and the FBI once again wiretapped King's conversations. In one phone call with Stanley Levison, the SCLC lawyer, King said, "The greatest weapon is the mass demonstration." King understood how Birmingham had become a pattern that played out across the country: "We can mobilize all this righteous indignation into a powerful mass movement." Levison and King began to talk about a march to Washington. Tens of thousands of protesters crossing state lines and descending on the capital, on the Lincoln Memorial, where King would demand civil rights legislation and with it a second Emancipation Proclamation.

These conversations deeply alarmed Hoover. But they served multiple purposes for King and Bobby. First, for King: Martin no doubt knew he was being recorded. He'd used code words, after all, to plan Project C's New York fundraiser with Harry Belafonte. "We suspected all our phones were tapped," Belafonte wrote. Second, King knew the FBI and J. Edgar Hoover thought Stanley Levison was a Communist. Burke Marshall had warned King about Levison's political leanings in a private meeting in Washington in 1962. That meant Levison was being watched closely by the administration. So for King to not only get on the phone with Levison at that point in 1963 but to discuss mass protests throughout the nation—and plainly, with no code words—was effectively to announce his intention to the White House. It was, almost certainly, King's way to talk with President Kennedy without talking to President Kennedy.

The wiretaps served Bobby Kennedy's purposes, too. On May 30, a panicked Hoover notified Bobby that King and Levison were discussing even larger protests than Birmingham. Bobby knew he could use this. He was, as ever, an angling politician. This time, with these wiretaps, he could apply pressure not to any interest group but to the president of the United States himself. The following day, May 31, Bobby asked "that the FBI furnish an account of the crucial conversation to his brother." Bobby could persuade through compassion or fear, but either way it was persuasion. Jack had these wiretapped conversations "within hours," one author later wrote.

Then Bobby went to work on Jack again. The next day, June 1, he met with Jack in the Oval Office about the civil rights bill. "I think you could make a good strong argument on this," Bobby said. "We couldn't [legally] go into Birmingham. . . . We can't go into any of these other communities.

The result is that you have street demonstrations. The result of that is that someone is very likely to get hurt. It's bad for the country. It's bad for us around the world. . . . I think it's absolutely essential that we have legislation."

Bobby worked the fear angle hard: *Look at all the terrible things that could happen if we don't write a bill.* Coming out of that meeting, Jack said he would strongly consider authoring legislation. But saying this wasn't the same as actually writing it. To get something as definitive, as epochal, as a civil rights bill, Bobby knew he needed to persuade Jack through compassion, too.

What can we say about those first days in June? We know that Bobby's real work happened in private. Meeting with senators and numerous representatives and, above all, Jack himself in back rooms and White House living rooms, away from FBI bugs and Oval Office confabs where notes became official minutes, talking always about a bill that Bobby believed in absolutely now, just as surely as he trusted King. It was a remarkable transformation. The cynical politician who now favored a bill of softhearted equality. The attorney general, who had moved from being Jack's protector, the one who shielded the president from people like King, to being King's unabashed advocate. "We haven't accomplished what we should have accomplished," Bobby said in a radio interview on June 3. "I think the record is bad." If Bobby was calling out Jack publicly, he was also privately asking Jack to trust him once more. Jack had persuaded Bobby to become his AG over breakfast in 1960 by saying, "I need you in this government. . . . I need to know that when problems arise I'm going to have somebody who's going to tell me the unvarnished truth, no matter what." Now Bobby was demanding Jack put his faith in Bobby again, evolve as Bobby had, shed the club ties of their hidebound privilege and see that Birmingham and everything in its wake was not just a crisis but an opportunity.

They could write a second Emancipation Proclamation. They could begin to heal the nation's hundred-year-old wound.

And they could do it together. The brothers hadn't been tight growing up. It was the seven-year gap between them and then boarding schools and different tastes and friends. It was 1952 and Jack's first campaign that brought them close. "It was politics," their sister Eunice said. And it was politics, Bobby told Jack in early June 1963, which could show that the love the brothers had for this nation was the same they had for each other.

Now Jack saw what Bobby saw.

It didn't matter that high-ranking senators said a civil rights bill wouldn't pass. Or that Jack would lose the election for trying. Or even that the South would turn against Democrats for a generation.

"There comes a time," Jack told his commerce secretary, "when a man has to take a stand."

51

THE SPEECH

On the morning of June 11, Jack Kennedy called Bobby to say he wanted to address the nation that night.

Bobby knew what this meant. He began to draft a speech while simultaneously receiving updates from Tuscaloosa, Alabama, where Governor George Wallace had threatened to "stand in the schoolhouse door" rather than allow two Black students, Vivian Malone and James Hood, to enroll at the University of Alabama. President Kennedy had issued an executive order that federalized the Alabama National Guard, and Bobby watched the news on the eleventh wondering if he and his brother would have to announce "the occupation of Tuscaloosa or the arrest of the governor."

It didn't come to that. Wallace made a speech about standing in the door and then . . . stepped aside. Malone and Hood enrolled, trailed by Bobby's deputy Nicholas Katzenbach, with Bobby convinced in Washington that Wallace had moved aside because of the Alabama businessmen who now flooded the governor's office with calls, fifteen to twenty a day. All of them said they didn't want in Tuscaloosa the violence the state had experienced in Birmingham.

The ripple effects of Project C.

The ripples continued to spread well into the evening of June 11. The speech that Jack wanted to give would announce his sponsorship of civil rights legislation. Everyone in the cabinet was against Kennedy addressing the nation; a televised speech would throw toxins on a bill that would be radioactive enough.

Bobby Kennedy was the lone voice of dissent. He thought a national address was exactly the way to introduce a civil rights bill.

Jack nodded.

He said to tell the networks he'd give his speech at 8:00 p.m.

Bobby handed his brother a draft a few hours beforehand, but Jack didn't like it. Didn't sound like him. So the brothers instead talked about what Jack should say, with Jack outlining the speech "on the back of an envelope or something," Bobby later recalled. Ted Sorensen, the speechwriter, took his own notes and then rushed off to write.

An hour before the address, there was no speech. Jack remained composed. The intensity with which Bobby faced all encounters made him wish his brother had something prepared, but even Bobby said Jack could deliver the whole thing "extemporaneously." This astounded Burke Marshall. "I remember him sitting there, putting down these notes"—Jack had a notebook beside him—"without any speech, when he was about to go on television, on what I thought was [an issue] of momentous importance."

What Marshall didn't know was how much the brothers had been talking about a civil rights bill in private over the last week. They were comfortable with what Jack would say.

A few minutes before eight, Sorensen rushed into the Cabinet Room of the White House, holding a draft. Jack read the speech and began to tinker with it, cutting lines, adding dramatic flair. Then Jack dictated his changes to one typist while Sorensen dictated his own to another. Still the minutes ticked down. Marshall tried to hide his concern—it was 7:55—but Jack noticed his nerves.

"Come on now, Burke," Jack said with a smirk. "You must have *some* ideas."

The speech was not finished in time.

It didn't matter.

> *We are confronted primarily with a moral issue. It is as old as the scriptures and is as clear as the American Constitution.*
>
> *The heart of the question is whether all Americans are to be afforded equal rights and equal opportunities, whether we are going to treat our fellow Americans as we want to be treated. If an American, because his skin is dark, cannot eat lunch in a restaurant open to the public, if he cannot send his children to the best public school available, if he cannot vote for the public officials who will represent him, if, in short, he cannot enjoy the full and free life which all of us want, then who among us would be content to have the color of his skin changed and stand in his place? Who among us would then be content with the counsels of patience and delay?*
>
> *One hundred years of delay have passed since President Lincoln freed the slaves, yet their heirs, their grandsons, are not fully free. They are not yet freed from the bonds of injustice. They are not yet freed from social and economic oppression. And this Nation, for all its hopes and all its boasts, will not be fully free until all its citizens are free. . . .*
>
> *Now the time has come for this nation to fulfill its promise. The events in Birmingham and elsewhere have so increased the cries for equality that no city or State or legislative body can prudently choose to ignore them. . . .*
>
> *Next week I shall ask the Congress of the United States to act, to make a commitment it has not fully made in this century to the proposition that race has no place in American life or law. . . .*
>
> *I am, therefore, asking the Congress to enact legislation giving all Americans the right to be served in facilities which are open to the*

public: hotels, restaurants, theaters, retail stores, and similar establish-ments. . . .

I am also asking the Congress to authorize the Federal Government to participate more fully in lawsuits designed to end segregation in public education. . . .

Other features will also be requested, including greater protection for the right to vote. But legislation, I repeat, cannot solve this problem alone. It must be solved in the homes of every American in every com-munity across our country. . . .

My fellow Americans, this is a problem which faces us all—in every city of the North as well as the South. Today there are Negroes unem-ployed, two or three times as many compared to whites, inadequate in education, moving into the large cities, unable to find work, young people particularly out of work without hope, denied equal rights, de-nied the opportunity to eat at a restaurant or lunch counter or go to a movie theater, denied the right to a decent education, denied almost to-day the right to attend a state university even though qualified. It seems to me that these are matters which concern us all, not merely Presidents or Congressmen or Governors, but every citizen of the United States.

The speech nearly brought Martin Luther King Jr. to tears. He imme-diately left his house in Atlanta to send a telegram to the White House. "I have just listened to your speech to the nation. It was one of the most eloquent, profound, unequivocal pleas for justice and freedom ever made by any president," King wrote.

When he returned home, King sat next to Coretta, stunned.

The impossible. Everything that Walker and Bevel and Shuttlesworth and the SCLC and the whole of Black America had wanted. Real and meaningful civil rights legislation. On national television King had just witnessed a second Emancipation Proclamation.

They had done it.

52

"BUT FOR BIRMINGHAM . . ."

Jack and Bobby Kennedy invited civil rights leaders to the White House on June 22. Foremost among them were King and the man who had convinced him to come to Birmingham, Fred Shuttlesworth. Jack Kennedy told the assembled that he had sent the bill to Congress for debate three days earlier. The question now was what everyone in this room would do to help the bill along.

King said he would organize a march to Washington.

President Kennedy said he wasn't against a march per se, but "now we are in a new phase, the legislative phase, and results are essential. . . . To get the votes, we need . . . first, to oppose demonstrations which will lead to violence, and, second, give Congress a fair chance to work its will."

King granted that a march to Washington might seem ill-timed. "Frankly, I have never engaged in any direct action movement which did not seem ill-timed," echoing what he had said in his now-famous letter from jail. "Some people thought Birmingham ill-timed."

"Including the Attorney General," Jack said with a smirk.

Those in the room laughed, Bobby more than anyone.

They agreed to work together on a march and on a bill that Jack had nicknamed "Bull Connor's Bill." He said it would be the most consequential of his presidency.

The meeting began to break up, and soon various civil rights leaders moved to the South Lawn to pose for pictures with Bobby. King could still not get over how Bobby was the bill's biggest advocate in Washington. Everyone understood the import of this day, the need to capture it for posterity, so they smiled widely. Before he left the Oval Office, Fred Shuttlesworth turned toward Jack Kennedy and heard the president mutter something, as much to Fred as to himself, that would be even more lasting than the photos Fred would keep of this meeting.

"But for Birmingham," President Kennedy said, "we wouldn't be here today."

EPILOGUE

That bill became the Civil Rights Act of 1964, accomplishing what a hundred years of freedom had not. It gave Black people rights that should have always been theirs. That law led to the Voting Rights Act of 1965, which further enshrined equality and led, I believe, not only to King's martyrdom in 1968 but a new life for his country. From the vantage point of the present day, King's and the SCLC's activism in Birmingham allowed me to fall in love with a Black woman from Houston in 2004, to get married in Texas, a former Jim Crow state, in 2007, and to raise our three Black kids today on a shaded street where none of our neighbors, white or Black, harass us for who we are. From 1963 to 2023: a lifetime of difference in less than a life's time.

They're dead now, not just King but also Shuttlesworth and Walker and Bevel, Burke Marshall and Jack and Bobby Kennedy. They led monumental lives but, like Jack Kennedy said, that spring in 1963 inspired their most consequential moments. What they did in those ten weeks forever changed America.

Progress—drawn by an author, an activist, or an elected official—is never quite what it seems, though. The line skews off course. The images that portray advancement deceive.

It happened with James Bevel, who became literally mad with power in the wake of Project C's success and an abusive monster to his daughters. The deception happened even before that, though. It happened with the defining image of that spring, the one that obsessed me all those decades later: the photo of Walter Gadsden giving himself to the attacking German shepherd.

That photo is not at all what it seems.

First, Gadsden wasn't a protester. His conservative Black family owned two newspapers that had been very critical of King in Birmingham. Young Walter, then, was one of those infamous Birmingham spectators who on Double D-Day had come to sneer at the marchers. Instead, he got attacked by Leo, but even that attack is misleading. The way Gadsden opened his entire right side to the dog? Look closer. Gadsden is raising his left leg in the photo, about to knee Leo in the muzzle. Gadsden later said he'd lived around large dogs and knew how to protect himself when one turned mean. In the ongoing reality just outside the frame, some people said Gadsden broke Leo's jaw. This didn't keep the SCLC from using the photo for its purposes, a campaign geared as much for the movement as the media. "A picture's worth a thousand words, darling," Wyatt Walker said.

Like the Gadsden image, any family portrait I sketch is also out to hoodwink you. My wife, Sonya, and I may hope with a fervency that borders on the vicarious that our three kids will be as brave as the children in Birmingham, marching for what they believe in. But the truth is we have also hoped they never find that courage, because if they stay indoors they'll stay safe. We kept them from the Black Lives Matter protests we attended in 2020, out of concern they might be roughed up by counter-protesters or cops. It turned out to be an irrational fear, but we have lived at times these last three years with an anxiety those long-dead parents in Birmingham felt. We know, as they did, that America has always been home to both hope and hate.

In fact, in the last few years we have had to look closer at the movement of American progress. Skin-deep identities have become the nation's obsession. This fixation is as endless as it is exhausting, and our wish is to move beyond it all. Move beyond the culture that spews the racist tropes of alt-right forums *and* the mindset that fosters "safe spaces" at progressive colleges, where Black students have been encouraged to sit at a remove from white students in the cafeteria and white students have been encouraged not to question the policy. None of that is the future I want for my children. One where progress looks a lot like regression, where skin color is all we are trained to see and where segregation is its inevitable result. Better societies build themselves from a foundation of empathy. When its materials are stirred and heated by our imagination, we see another person's perspective, and troubles, and begin to love that person. That's especially true if the *other* is different from *us*.

So if I may speak directly: *This* is the future I want for you, Harper and Marshall and Walker. One where you fight for the dignity that lives within you and the empathy that connects all those around you. That is the march of true progress, the one that Martin Luther King Jr. dreamed about in his life, too—and in Birmingham.

Four months before he gave his famous address on the steps of the Lincoln Memorial in the summer of 1963, King tried out that speech's classic refrain in Birmingham. It is another instance in which Birmingham set in motion all that followed. At a mass meeting on April 9 at the 16th Street Baptist Church, King talked about the Black nationalists and white racists in the pews, and how he did not want a future where whites fought to reign supreme any more than he wanted one where Blacks did, where people of different opinions could find no common ground.

"We love integration," King said.

Then he spoke about a dream he had had that night. It was a dream of little Black boys and girls walking to school with little white boys and girls, where the kids played in parks together, swam together. Loved one another.

Yes, King told that crowd in Birmingham, "I had a dream tonight!"

May my children and yours always be guided by it.

ACKNOWLEDGMENTS

Good Lord was I blessed by the archivists and scholars who came before me. A special thanks goes to the Birmingham Public Library and Birmingham Civil Rights Institute, both of which have assembled and archived over the last thirty-five years sprawling oral histories with seemingly every person of consequence who lived through that fateful spring of 1963. I spent months working my way through all pertinent material. A fair portion of it has not been published in a book before, so I owe a special debt to my points of contact at each institution: Wayne Coleman at the Birmingham Civil Rights Institute and Jim Baggett at the Birmingham Public Library.

A thank-you as well to the numerous university and presidential libraries that house collections related to those ten weeks in 1963. The frequency with which I cite these libraries in the pages to come shows how fascinated I remain by their letters and artifacts and specialized scholarship. Then there are the authors, commercial and academic, whose works profoundly influenced what you just read. Among many others, I am indebted to the histories by Glenn Eskew, Andrew Manis, Diane McWhorter, Taylor Branch, and David Garrow.

This book could not have happened without the support of my agent, David Granger, who helped to shape the proposal and then, great man that he is, read multiple drafts of the manuscript. He wasn't the only one poring over it. I deeply appreciate the edits and suggestions I received from Jamie Raab and Cecily van Buren-Freedman of Celadon Books. They, and the rest of the team there, improved what you just read immensely. Thank you.

As I said in the prologue, this book started as a family project of sorts. To see it completed fills me with unending gratitude for the people who mean the most to me in life: Sonya, Harper, Marshall, and Walker.

I love you.

NOTES

Prologue

xi   *watched him as a tight end*   ESPN.com, June 11, 2020, video clip, "Yates High School Senior George Floyd," accessed October 25, 2022, https://www.espn .com/video/clip/_/id/29289363.

xi   *that made the state championship*   1992 Texas State Championship box score, Conference 5A, Division 2, accessed October 25, 2022, https://www.uiltexas .org/files/athletics/state-football/boxscores/19925AD2FBBOX.pdf.

1. A Point That Everyone Should Consider Carefully

3   *without even Martin Luther King Sr.'s knowledge*   Taylor Branch, *Parting the Waters* (New York: Simon and Schuster, 2007).

3   *January morning in 1963 by jet or train*   FBI file on Stanley Levison, accessed October 25, 2022, https://vault.fbi.gov/Stanley%20Levison/Stanley%20Levison% 20Part%2011%20of%20109/view.

3   *quiet and shaded acres*   ExploreGeorgia.org's history of the academy, accessed October 25, 2022, https://www.exploregeorgia.org/things-to-do/blog/the -remarkable-history-of-dorchester-academy.

4   *one-room schoolhouse for freed slaves*   ExploreGeorgia.org's history of the schoolhouse, accessed October 25, 2022, https://www.exploregeorgia.org/sites /default/files/listing_documents/Dorchester20Academy3.pdf.

4   *larger school*   A video history of the academy, found on the YouTube page of the Liberty County Convention and Visitors Bureau, accessed October 25, 2022, https://www.youtube.com/watch?v=yZ2NLYjuP8o.

4   *buy homes and open businesses*   Website of the Dorchester Academy's Improvement Association, accessed October 25, 2022, https://www.dorchesteracademyia .com.

4   *had been to Dorchester before*   Ibid.; also, the history page of that 1963 visit, accessed October 25, 2022, https://www.dorchesteracademyia.com/mlk-dorchester.

4   *huddled near one another*   The history page of that 1963 visit, accessed October 25, 2022, https://www.dorchesteracademyia.com/mlk-dorchester.

4   *"The Madison Avenue streak in me"*   Malcolm Gladwell, *David and Goliath: Underdogs, Misfits, and the Art of Battling Giants* (New York: Little, Brown, 2013).

4   *X marked the spot of confrontation*   Glenn T. Eskew, *But for Birmingham: The Local and National Movements in the Civil Rights Struggle* (Chapel Hill: University of North Carolina Press, 2000).

5   *"a devastating loss of face"*   Howard Zinn, "Albany," academic paper published in conjunction by Spelman College and the Southern Regional Council, undated; found online at the Civil Rights Movement Archive, accessed October 25, 2022, https://www.crmvet.org/info/6201_zinn_albany.pdf.

5   *"riding in the back of the bus"*   Charles E. Silberman, *Crisis in Black and White* (New York: Random House, 1966).

6   *took to calling King "De Lawd"*   David J. Garrow, *Bearing the Cross: Martin Luther King Jr. and the Southern Christian Leadership Conference* (New York: Open Road Media, 2016); also, James Forman and Julian Bond, *The Making of Black Revolutionaries* (Seattle: University of Washington Press, 1997).

6   *pomposity in dress and speech*   Harry Belafonte, with Michael Shnayerson, *My Song: A Memoir* (New York: Vintage, 2012). Even Belafonte, King's friend, talked about how pompous MLK Jr. could be.

6   *"You are a phony"*   Robert F. Williams papers, Martin Luther King Jr. Research and Education Institute, Stanford University, accessed October 25, 2022, https://kinginstitute.stanford.edu/king-papers/documents/robert-f-williams.

6   *earned 45 percent less than whites*   John Herbers, "Income Gap Between Races Wide as in 1960, Study Finds," *New York Times*, July 18, 1983, https://www.nytimes.com/1983/07/18/us/income-gap-between-races-wide-as-in-1960-study-finds.html.

6   *only 28 percent were registered to vote*   Carl M. Brauer, *John F. Kennedy and the Second Reconstruction* (New York: Columbia University Press, 1977).

7   *the joke about Birmingham*   Gladwell, *David and Goliath.*

7   *more than fifty residences and Black-owned businesses*   Eskew, *But for Birmingham.*

7   *bombed since the end of World War II*   Segregation in America report, "Beyond Brown: Opposition Intensifies," Equal Justice Initiative, undated, accessed October 25, 2022, https://segregationinamerica.eji.org/report/beyond-brown.html.

7   *The police raped Black women*   Fred Shuttlesworth papers, BCRI, Box 30, 35–3.

7   *The Klan castrated Black men*   Diane McWhorter, *Carry Me Home: Birmingham, Alabama: The Climactic Battle of the Civil Rights Revolution* (New York: Simon and Schuster, 2001).

7   *since Nazi Germany*   Ibid.

8   *eight typed pages that revealed*   Interview with Rev. Wyatt Tee Walker, *Eyes on the Prize* documentary series, Blackside Inc. (broadcast as part of the series *American Experience*, PBS, 1987). The full Walker interview is now housed in

the Washington University at St. Louis Libraries, accessed October 25, 2022, http://repository.wustl.edu/concern/videos/ht24wm403.

8   *spent about $4 million a week downtown*   Michael Cooper Nichols, "Cities Are What Men Make Them: Birmingham, Alabama, Faces the Civil Rights Movement, 1963," thesis paper, 1974, John Hay Library, Brown University.

9   *"one of the keenest minds"*   Wyatt Tee Walker papers, Martin Luther King Jr. Research and Education Center, Stanford University, accessed October 25, 2022, https://kinginstitute.stanford.edu/encyclopedia/walker-wyatt-tee.

9   *many staffers cry*   Robert Penn Warren interview with Walker, "Who Speaks for the Negro?" series, Robert Penn Warren Center for the Humanities at Vanderbilt University, 1964, accessed October 25, 2022, https://www.crmvet.org/nars/w_walker.htm; interview with Wyatt Tee Walker, "Dr. and Mrs. Wyatt Tee Walker Oral Histories," University of Richmond Libraries, June 29, 2016, accessed October 25, 2022, https://richmond.access.preservica.com/uncategorized/digitalFile_30fa411f-427f-418f-bad0–07b73ffc9030/.

10   *"alter my morality for the sake of getting a job done"*   Gladwell, *David and Goliath.*

10   *There was little discussion of it*   Walker's full interview, *Eyes on the Prize*; Branch, *Parting the Waters.*

10   *altered nothing of Walker's blueprint*   Branch, *Parting the Waters.*

10   *not Stanley Levison, the most liberal member*   Garrow, *Bearing the Cross.*

10   *not Andrew Young, the most conservative*   Howell Raines, *My Soul Is Rested: Movement Days in the Deep South Remembered* (New York: G. P. Putnam's Sons, 1977).

11   *gassing the place*   Ibid.

11   *as righteously committed to justice*   James Bevel bio, SNCC Digital Gateway, Duke University Libraries, accessed October 25, 2022, https://snccdigital.org/people/james-bevel/.

11   *Many in the movement called him "The Prophet"*   David Halberstam, *The Children* (New York: Open Road Media, 2012).

12   *light-skinned Wyatt Walker*   Ibid.

12   *ironed a crease into his blue jeans*   McWhorter, *Carry Me Home.*

12   *had read every day in Hebrew and Greek*   Fernanda Santos, "Wyatt Tee Walker, Dr. King's Strategist and a Harlem Leader, Dies at 88," *New York Times*, January 23, 2018, accessed October 25, 2022, https://www.nytimes.com/2018/01/23/obituaries/wyatt-tee-walker-dead.html.

13   *more a "boss" than a "brother"*   McWhorter, *Carry Me Home.*

13   *"getting hired hands to get something done"*   Ibid.; also, Halberstam, in *The Children*, talks about how much Bevel and Walker didn't get along.

13   *"to surpass others, to achieve distinction"*   Martin Luther King Jr., "The Drum Major Instinct" sermon, found in *A Gift of Love: Sermons from "Strength of Love" and Other Preachings* (New York: Beacon Press, 2012).

14   *"I want you to be first in generosity"*   Ibid.

14   *"Mr. Leader"*   Gladwell, *David and Goliath.*

14   *"and even his life for the welfare of others"*   King, *A Gift of Love*. See in particular King's "Drum Major Instinct" sermon.

15   *"I know it will be done"*   Interview with Wyatt Tee Walker, "Dr. and Mrs. Wyatt Tee Walker Oral Histories," University of Richmond Libraries, June 29,

2016, accessed October 25, 2022, https://richmond.access.preservica.com /uncategorized/digitalFile_30fa411f-427f-418f-bad0–07b73ffc9030/.

15   *He'd asked Walker a week earlier*   Garrow, *Bearing the Cross*.

15   *His persona meant he lived in absolutes*   Halberstam, *The Children*.

15   *Levison, the secret caucus's lone white man*   Levison, FBI files, accessed October 25, 2022, https://vault.fbi.gov/Stanley%20Levison/Stanley%20Levison%20Part%2011%20of%20109/view, part 11 of 109, page 2.

15   *"the toughest fight in our civil rights careers"*   Martin Luther King Jr., *Why We Can't Wait* (New York: Beacon Press, 2011).

16   *"A victory there"*   Ibid.

16   *refused to travel with a security detail or carry a gun*   Hampton Sides, *Hellhound on His Trail: The Electrifying Account of the Largest Manhunt in History* (New York: Anchor Books, 2010).

16   *"will not come back alive from this campaign"*   Branch, *Parting the Waters*.

2. "This Is Not Getting Any Better"

17   *The confidential memo reached the desk*   McWhorter, *Carry Me Home*; Levison, FBI files.

17   *met with a group of young women*   Arthur M. Schlesinger Jr., *Robert Kennedy and His Times* (New York: Open Road Integrated Media, 2012).

17   *agents in the bureau's field office*   Levison, FBI files, accessed October 25, 2022, https://vault.fbi.gov/Stanley%20Levison/Stanley%20Levison%20Part%2011%20of%20109/view, part 11 of 109, pages 1–4.

17   *surreptitiously snapped photos*   McWhorter, *Carry Me Home*.

18   *Bobby and his aides had warned King*   Garrow, *Bearing the Cross;* Branch, *Parting the Waters*.

18   *his own investigative findings stood up*   Terry Gross, "From 'Runt of the Litter' to 'Liberal Icon': The Story of Robert Kennedy," *Fresh Air* interview of Kennedy biographer Larry Tye, July 5, 2016, accessed October 25, 2022, https://www.wbur.org/npr/484780316/from-runt-of-the-litter-to-liberal-icon-the-story-of-robert-kennedy.

18   *"badly informed"*   David Margolick, *The Promise and the Dream: The Untold Story of Martin Luther King Jr., and Robert Kennedy* (New York: Rosetta Books, 2018).

18   *Bobby was the Puritan and Jack the Brahmin*   Schlesinger, *Robert Kennedy and His Times*.

18   *Bobby not only loved but protected Jack*   Gross interview of Larry Tye, *Fresh Air*.

18   *"He seemed to look at every aspect"*   Jean Stein, *American Journey: The Times of Robert Kennedy* (New York: Harcourt Brace Jovanovich, 1970).

18   *who knew the Kennedys well*   Mark Perry, *Four Stars: The Inside Story of the Forty-Year Battle Between the Joint Chiefs of Staff and America's Civilian Leaders* (New York: Houghton Mifflin Harcourt, 1989).

19   *no less a source than the brothers' father*   Schlesinger, *Robert Kennedy and His Times*.

19   *with a badly injured Jack*   Thomas Fleming, "The Truth About JFK and His PT Boat's Collision with a Japanese Destroyer in WWII," HistoryNet, Febru-

ary, 22, 2011, accessed October 25, 2022, https://www.historynet.com/john-f
-kennedys-pt-109-disaster/?f.

19   *the whole thing in an enormous cast*   Schlesinger, *Robert Kennedy and His Times*.

19   *Jack needed him in the administration*   Ibid.

19   *"The stage had been set"*   Belafonte, *My Song*.

20   *Bobby didn't trust King*   Gross, *Fresh Air* interview of Larry Tye.

20   *"Burke—This is not getting any better"*   McWhorter, *Carry Me Home*.

3. What It Takes to Begin to Live

21   *they used code words*   Belafonte, *My Song*.

21   *Maybe $500*   Eskew, *But for Birmingham*. The figure at that time was around
      $554.

22   *looked at each other*   Fred Shuttlesworth oral history, Birmingham Public
      Library, Digital Collections, accessed October 25, 2022, https://bplonline
      .contentdm.oclc.org/digital/collection/p15099coll2/search/searchterm
      /shuttlesworth%2C%20fred%20l./field/creato/mode/exact/conn/and.

22   *Black reverend*   Martin Luther King Sr., *Daddy King: An Autobiography* (New
      York: William Morrow, 1980).

22   *and farmer*   Ralph David Abernathy, *And the Walls Came Tumbling Down: An
      Autobiography* (New York: HarperCollins, 1990).

22   *and ne'er-do-well*   Andrew M. Manis, *A Fire You Can't Put Out: The Civil Rights
      Life of Birmingham's Reverend Fred Shuttlesworth* (Tuscaloosa: University of Ala-
      bama Press, 2010).

22   *Belafonte owned the building*   Belafonte, *My Song*.

22   *was stood up for a date one night*   Abernathy, *And the Walls Came Tumbling
      Down*.

22   *"mothered" him*   Sides, *Hellhound on His Trail*.

23   *7,200 square feet*   "Upper West Side Floor Plan of 'The Calypso King,'" NY
      .Curbed.com, May 10, 2006, accessed October 25, 2022, https://ny.curbed
      .com/2006/5/10/10606214/floorplan-porn-upper-west-side-calypso-king.

23   *More than seventy-five people were here*   Branch, *Parting the Waters*. The names
      of everyone who attended the party come from a combination of Branch's book
      and Belafonte, *My Song*; Garrow, *Bearing the Cross*; McWhorter, *Carry Me
      Home*.

23   *gathered the whole crowd in his palatial living room*   Garrow, *Bearing the Cross*.

23   Calypso *outsold Elvis* and *Sinatra*   Henry Louis Gates Jr., "Belafonte's Balanc-
      ing Act," *New Yorker*, August 18, 1996, accessed October 25, 2022, https://
      www.newyorker.com/magazine/1996/08/26/belafontes-balancing-act.

24   *"Harry isn't black* black*"*   Ibid.

24   *Harry's Jamaican grandmother was white*   Belafonte, *My Song*.

24   *"people perceive him as a nice person"*   Gates, "Belafonte's Balancing Act."

24   *more segregated than his forebears'*   Belafonte, *My Song*.

24   *Ed Sullivan thought he was a Communist*   Ibid.

24   *the film's propped-up eunuch*   Gates, "Belafonte's Balancing Act."

25   *"was recruiting me to the movement"*   Belafonte, *My Song*.

25   *was Harry's brainchild*   Ibid.

25   We're going to Birmingham   King, *Why We Can't Wait*.

25   *This privately excited King*   Andrew Young full interview, *Eyes on the Prize* documentary series, Blackside Inc. (*American Experience*, PBS, 1987). The two full Young interviews are now housed in the Washington University at St. Louis Libraries, accessed October 25, 2022, http://repository.wustl.edu/catalog?utf8=%E2%9C%93&search_field=all_fields&q=andrew+young.

26   *"All people are just alike"*   Gladwell, *David and Goliath*.

26   *without running water, without a pair of dress pants*   Manis, *A Fire You Can't Put Out*.

26   *"Shit, do something, goddammit"*   Wyatt Walker oral history, Birmingham Public Library, Digital Collections, accessed October 25, 2022, https://bplonline.contentdm.oclc.org/digital/collection/p15099coll2/id/69/rec/4.

27   *He'd assembled it in 1956*   Alabama Christian Movement for Human Rights papers, Martin Luther King Jr. Research and Education Institute, Stanford University, https://kinginstitute.stanford.edu/encyclopedia/alabama-christian-movement-human-rights-acmhr.

27   *"can't outlaw the movement of a people determined to be free"*   Nichols, "Cities Are What Men Make Them."

27   *Fifteen hundred people came*   Eskew, *But for Birmingham*. The meeting was held at New Hope Baptist Church; Manis, *A Fire You Can't Put Out*.

28   *"I'll do just that thing"*   Eskew, *But for Birmingham*.

28   *mimicking their movements*   Manis, *A Fire You Can't Put Out*.

28   *Charlie Roberson and his wife, Naomi*   Fred Shuttlesworth oral history, interview no. 2, Birmingham Civil Rights Institute (BCRI), accessed October 25, 2022, http://bcriohp.org/items/show/120.

28   *pay a visit to Fred and Ruby*   Ibid.

29   *the haul from the Christmas Day offering*   Fred Shuttlesworth Jr. oral history, Birmingham Public Library, Digital Collections, accessed October 25, 2022, https://bplonline.contentdm.oclc.org/digital/collection/p15099coll2/id/68/rec/31.

29   *leaning against the vanity*   Fred Shuttlesworth oral history, BCRI.

29   *The power from sixteen sticks of dynamite*   Eskew, *But for Birmingham*.

29   *had shattered into a million pieces*   Fred Shuttlesworth oral history, BCRI.

29   *the smell of fire and gunpowder*   Manis, *A Fire You Can't Put Out*. Many of the people there that night said the smells were potent.

30   *shattered windows*   James Roberson oral history, Birmingham Public Library, Digital Collections, accessed October 25, 2022, https://bplonline.contentdm.oclc.org/digital/collection/p15099coll2/id/62/rec/46.

30   *a good mile from the parsonage*   McWhorter, *Carry Me Home*.

30   *a wide gray fedora*   Fred Shuttlesworth oral history, BCRI.

30   *"I am not injured"*   McWhorter, *Carry Me Home*. The following exchange on the lawn is also found in Manis, *A Fire You Can't Put Out*; Eskew, *But for Birmingham*.

31   *to not interview the Klan members suspected of carrying them out*   Raines, *My Soul Is Rested*.

31   *gave him a standing ovation*   Eskew, *But for Birmingham*.

31   *"You couldn't find but pieces of the spring"*   Manis, *A Fire You Can't Put Out*.

32   *He remembered the night before*   Ibid. What he remembered from that night is also found in Fred Shuttlesworth oral history, BPL; Fred Shuttlesworth oral history, BCRI.

32   You can know something in a second   Manis, *A Fire You Can't Put Out*.

32   *"I'm not going to look back to see who's following me"*   McWhorter, *Carry Me Home*.

33   *walked to 12th Street North*   Manis, *A Fire You Can't Put Out*.

33   *"This is all right"*   Ibid.

33   *the back of the bus couldn't believe it*   McWhorter, *Carry Me Home*.

33   *"Would you like my seat?"*   Ibid.

34   *two hundred people had ridden in the front of buses*   Eskew, *But for Birmingham*; Manis, *A Fire You Can't Put Out*.

34   *"I shall be dead before I'll ever be a slave again"*   McWhorter, *Carry Me Home*.

34   *"The fight is on"*   Eskew, *But for Birmingham*. Fred told the press this December 26.

34   *"Fred knows how to do it"*   Manis, *A Fire You Can't Put Out*.

34   *"let the people see what America is"*   McWhorter, *Carry Me Home*.

35   *Bombings of Black residential properties increased*   Ibid.

35   *"unsolved" by the Birmingham PD*   Debbie Elliott, "Remembering Birmingham's 'Dynamite Hill' Neighborhood," *Weekend Edition*, National Public Radio, July 6, 2013, accessed October 25, 2022, https://www.npr.org/sections/codeswitch/2013/07/06/197342590/remembering-birminghams-dynamite-hill-neighborhood.

35   *rifles and shotguns at the ready*   James Roberson oral history, BPL.

35   *segregation remained the de facto law*   McWhorter, *Carry Me Home*.

35   *be named in more cases that reached the Supreme Court*   Matt Schudel, "Fred L. Shuttlesworth, Courageous Civil Rights Fighter, Dies at 89," *Washington Post*, October 5, 2011, https://www.washingtonpost.com/local/obituaries/fred-l-shuttlesworth-courageous-civil-rights-fighter-dies-at-89/2011/10/05/gIQAO73lOL_story.html.

35   *ran through Fred's head so often*   Eugene "Bull" Connor papers, Birmingham Police Department notes of Shuttlesworth's numerous mass meetings, 268.13.2, Birmingham Public Library (BPL).

35   *"You have to be prepared to die"*   King, *Why We Can't Wait*.

35   *That line got to them*   Belafonte, *My Song*.

36   *These New Yorkers accrued their money*   Branch, *Parting the Waters*.

36   *"What can we do to help?"*   King, *Why We Can't Wait*.

36   *In the end they gave $475,000*   Manis, *A Fire You Can't Put Out*.

4. What Was Promising and Impossible

37   *inspecting the line he'd traced on the bottle*   Branch, *Parting the Waters*.

37   *had once attracted Marlon Brando*   Belafonte, *My Song*; Gates, "Belafonte's Balancing Act."

37   *she laughed as Martin inspected the bottle*   Branch, *Parting the Waters*. Julie would laugh anytime Martin inspected it.

37   *previous fundraisers at Harry's Home had lacked*   Belafonte, *My Song*.

37   *"a little razzmatazz"*   Branch, *Parting the Waters.*

38   *What was that about?*   Belafonte, *My Song.*

38   *He was convinced he'd be assassinated*   Sides, *Hellhound on His Trail.*

38   *"He thought in everything he did it meant his death"*   Garrow, *Bearing the Cross,* quoting Andrew Young.

38   *"When I look up at the cross"*   Ibid.

38   *Martin just complained about his "nerves"*   Belafonte, *My Song.*

38   *"It was easy enough to see"*   Ibid.

39   *But Bobby Kennedy, who had not read that speech in advance*   Brauer, *John F. Kennedy and the Second Reconstruction.*

39   *"the Black vote was just a constituency you bought"*   Belafonte, *My Song.*

39   *"You can't afford to endorse him"*   Ibid.

40   *King endorsed no one*   Ibid.

40   *"civil rights demands that can't pass anyway"*   Brauer, *John F. Kennedy and the Second Reconstruction.*

40   *"the limited goal of token integration"*   Margolick, *The Promise and the Dream.*

40   *place a poll tax on its Black voters*   Brauer, *John F. Kennedy and the Second Reconstruction*; Nichols, "Cities Are What Men Make Them."

40   *mailed the White House bottles of ink*   Margolick, *The Promise and the Dream.*

40   *"It does no good to apply Vaseline to a cancer"*   Ibid.

40   *President Eisenhower thought Brown*   Brauer, *John F. Kennedy and the Second Reconstruction.*

41   *Bobby Kennedy had deployed four hundred federal marshals*   "The Kennedys and the Civil Rights Movement," John F. Kennedy National Historic Site, National Park Service, accessed October 25, 2022, https://www.nps.gov/articles/000/the-kennedys-and-civil-rights.htm.

41   *"I am—the Government is—going to be very much upset"*   Schlesinger, *Robert Kennedy and His Times.*

41   *The ICC did Bobby's bidding*   Ibid.

41   *"I find it wholly inexplicable"*   Brauer, *John F. Kennedy and the Second Reconstruction.*

41   *"gratified by directness of your statement"*   Ibid.

41   *Bobby refused*   Ibid.

42   *Bobby called Albany's mayor*   Branch, *Parting the Waters.*

42   *sipped their Harveys Bristol Cream*   Ibid.

42   *Dawn neared*   Ibid.

42   *"Let me be sure this time"*   Ibid.

43   *"the grim business of leading a movement"*   Abernathy, *And the Walls Came Tumbling Down.*

43   *"White folks ain't invented anything in the world"*   Branch, *Parting the Waters.*

5. Departures

47   *to induce labor*   Coretta Scott King, as told to the Rev. Dr. Barbara Reynolds, *My Life, My Love, My Legacy* (New York: Henry Holt, 2017).

48   *his nine-year-old Pontiac*   Branch, *Parting the Waters.* King purchased the car in 1954.

48   *Shouldn't King drive a Cadillac?*   Stephen B. Oates, *Let the Trumpet Sound: The Life of Martin Luther King, Jr.* (New York: New American Library, 1983).

48   *Coretta seldom traveled with Martin*   King, *My Life, My Love, My Legacy.*

49   *"We were both filled with doubt"*   Coretta Scott King, *My Life with Martin Luther King Jr.* (New York: Holt, Rinehart and Winston, 1969).

50   *the largest Black church in the city*   "Ralph David Abernathy," *Encyclopaedia Britannica*, 15th edition (2010).

51   *"Indira and I became friends"*   King, *My Life, My Love, My Legacy.*

51   *their home on Johnson Avenue*   Oates, *Let the Trumpet Sound.*

51   *not as fashionable an area as Coretta would have preferred*   Branch, *Parting the Waters.*

51   *The lease was in Coretta's name*   King, *My Life, My Love, My Legacy.*

51   *Martin asked for a $6,000-a-year salary*   Oates, *Let the Trumpet Sound.*

51   *prosperity-preaching father*   Branch, *Parting the Waters.*

51   *Martin drew only a $1-a-year salary*   Oates, *Let the Trumpet Sound.*

51   *"He felt that much of the corruption in society"*   Scott King, *My Life, My Love, My Legacy.*

52   *"I knew he was searching for a balance"*   Ibid.

52   *"I would not be there to comfort him"*   Scott King, *My Life with Martin Luther King Jr.*

52   *he'd been arrested twelve times in eight years*   Jennifer Gunner, "Martin Luther King Jr. Timeline: His Life & Accomplishments," *Biography.com*, https://biography.yourdictionary.com/answers/timelines/martin-luther-king-jr-timeline.html.

52   *"desperate desire" to be "near my husband"*   Scott King, *My Life with Martin Luther King Jr.*

52   *"I am an activist"*   Jeanne Theoharis, "Coretta Scott King and the Civil-Rights Movement's Hidden Women," *The Atlantic*, February 2018, accessed October 25, 2022, https://www.theatlantic.com/magazine/archive/2018/02/coretta-scott-king/552557/.

52   *"for the longest time"*   Scott King, *My Life, My Love, My Legacy.*

52   *She told herself she was fine*   Scott King, *My Life with Martin Luther King Jr.*

6. Arrival

53   *Flight time to Birmingham*   Any airline flight tracker. Kate Repantis, "Why Hasn't Commercial Air Travel Gotten Any Faster Since the 1960s?" *Slice of MIT*, a Massachusetts Institute of Technology Alumni Association publication, March 19, 2014, accesssed January 9, 2023, https://alum.mit.edu/slice/why-hasnt-commercial-air-travel-gotten-any-faster-1960s.

53   *charts and lists and more blueprints*   Branch, *Parting the Waters*; Nichols, "Cities Are What Men Make Them."

54   *It was seen as the lone spot in the world*   Nichols, "Cities Are What Men Make Them."

54   *northern financiers bribed*   Ibid.

54   *"The Murder Capital of the World"*   George R. Leighton, "Birmingham, Alabama: The City of Perpetual Promise," *Harper's*, August, 1937.

54   *second-highest rate of venereal disease*   Ibid.

54   *lowest spendable income per citizen*   Ibid.

55   *the largest klavern in the nation*   Nichols, "Cities Are What Men Make Them."

55   *and not historical "honor"*   Joe David Brown, "Birmingham, Alabama: A City in Fear," *Saturday Evening Post*, June 12, 1962, accessed October 25, 2022, http://www.saturdayeveningpost.com/wp-content/uploads/satevepost/a-city-in-fear.pdf.

55   *"As the Civil War broke out"*   Scott Horton, "A Heart of Steel," *Harper's*, February 24, 2008, https://harpers.org/2008/02/a-heart-of-steel/.

55   *Politicians sought the local Klan's endorsement*   Nichols, "Cities Are What Men Make Them."

55   *raised in a broken home*   William A. Nunnelley, *Bull Connor* (Tuscaloosa: University Alabama Press, 1990).

55   *be as violent and thieving as any villainous enterprise*   Eskew, *But for Birmingham*.

56   *"They all know me"*   Nunnelley, *Bull Connor*, citing a James Saxon Childers column, *Birmingham News*, May, 19, 1937.

56   *he never worried much*   Eskew, *But for Birmingham*.

56   *Fred Shuttlesworth had told*   Connor papers, BPL, March 12, 1963, meeting.

56   *"was just a dignified Connor"*   King, *Why We Can't Wait*.

56   *the Pupil Placement Act*   Nichols, "Cities Are What Men Make Them"; Albert Boutwell papers, The Martin Luther King Jr. Research and Education Institute, Stanford University, accessed October 25, 2022, https://kinginstitute.stanford.edu/encyclopedia/boutwell-albert.

56   *"there isn't a whole lot of difference"*   Connor papers, BPL, March 12, 1963, meeting.

57   *"I can handle the preachers"*   Branch, *Parting the Waters*.

57   *but not the other reverend*   Abernathy, *And the Walls Came Tumbling Down*.

57   *"Where's Ware?"*   McWhorter, *Carry Me Home*.

57   *represented the city's Black establishment*   Eskew, *But for Birmingham*.

57   *"He's holding a meeting"*   Ibid.

57   *"are probably there, too"*   Abernathy, *And the Walls Came Tumbling Down*.

58   *No one said a word*   Ibid.

59   *number 30, a suite above the lobby*   Carol Jenkins and Elizabeth Gardner Hines, *Black Titan: A. G. Gaston and the Making of a Black American Millionaire* (London: Oneworld, 2005).

59   *Had Fred overpromised whom he could deliver*   Abernathy, *And the Walls Came Tumbling Down*.

7. It Begins

60   *Of Birmingham's 340,000 people*   Birmingham Public Library, government documents, the city's population totals from 1880 to 2000, accessed October 25, 2022, http://www.bplonline.org/resources/government/BirminghamPopulation.aspx.

60   *Bull got 21,648*   Eskew, *But for Birmingham*.

60   *Nearly all of the 10,000 Black people*   McWhorter, *Carry Me Home*.

60   *10 percent of its job force*   Nichols, "Cities Are What Men Make Them." The figures concern the years 1958–1961.

60   *five sticks of dynamite*   Eskew, *But for Birmingham*.

60   *"We are on our way to better things"*   McWhorter, *Carry Me Home*.

61   *he signed off on his civil rights chief*   Ibid.

61   *"pass the message on to Dr. King"*   Ibid.

61   *But there were* 135,000 *Black people* Birmingham Public Library, accessed October 25, 2022, http://www.bplonline.org/resources/government/BirminghamPopulation.aspx.

61   *"showed that he understood nothing"* King, *Why We Can't Wait.*

61   *Privately, though, he wondered* Interview with Wyatt Tee Walker, University of Richmond Libraries, accessed October 25, 2022, https://richmond.access.preservica.com/uncategorized/digitalFile_30fa411f-427f-418f-bad0-07b73ffc9030/.

62   *He had 350 names on his jail list* Branch, *Parting the Waters.* King himself would later say it was perhaps 250 names.

62   *deeply religious adults with ties to Fred's church* Eskew, *But for Birmingham.*

62   *listened to Walker in the basement* Branch, *Parting the Waters.* The Movement-friendly church was A. D. King's.

62   *Walker had the sixty-five sync their wristwatches* McWhorter, *Carry Me Home.*

62   *"This is Birmingham's moment of truth"* Manis, *A Fire You Can't Put Out.*

63   *hot coffee on their heads and laps* Nichols, "Cities Are What Men Make Them."

63   *thirteen people had been arrested* Eskew, *But for Birmingham.*

63   *twenty protesters had been thrown in* Ibid.

64   *Those were terribly low figures* Abernathy, *And the Walls Came Tumbling Down.* Abernathy describes what King felt as well.

64   *around 265 people arrested on the first day* Branch, *Parting the Waters.*

8. Who Will Rise from the Pews?

65   *everyone hoping to get inside* Eskew, *But for Birmingham.* I relied on photos from that day within the book to tell this part of the narrative.

65   *Five hundred people jostled* Manis, *A Fire You Can't Put Out.*

65   *auditorium or balcony* Connor papers, BPL, April 3, 1963, meeting.

65   *"Ain't Gonna Let Nobody Turn Me Round"* Nichols, "Cities Are What Men Make Them"; "Ain't Gonna Let Nobody Turn Me Around," YouTube, posted by Justiciarodante, April 24, 2014, accessed October 25, 2022, https://www.youtube.com/watch?v=WPuBGcng6Tw.

66   *the meeting's master of ceremonies* Eskew, *But for Birmingham.*

66   *"My nonviolent Winchester"* Raines, *My Soul Is Rested.*

66   *"freedom bells will ring in Birmingham"* Connor papers, BPL, April 3 meeting.

66   *never had more than a few thousand members* Manis, *A Fire You Can't Put Out.*

66   *"Follow him to jail!"* Connor papers, BPL, April 3 meeting.

66   *Then King took the pulpit* Ibid. The next three paragraphs are sourced to those meeting notes.

68   *This was the whole of Project X's ambition* King, *Why We Can't Wait.*

68   *a five-hundred-acre farm* "Ralph David Abernathy," *Encyclopaedia Britannica.*

69   *They butchered forty hogs a year* Abernathy, *And the Walls Came Tumbling Down.*

69   *"The eyes of the world are on Birmingham tonight"* Connor papers, BPL, April 3 meeting.

69   *"If you are afraid"* Ibid.

69   *perhaps eighty people* Ibid.

70   *"Not encouraging"* Abernathy, *And the Walls Came Tumbling Down.*

9. Explanations and Accusations

71   *"Weeping may endure for a night"*   Psalm 30:5 (NIV).

71   *"I can do all things through Christ who strengthens me"*   Philippians 4:13 (KJV).

71   *"or sharpness of the tongue"*   Penn Walker interview with Wyatt Walker, "Who Speaks for the Negro?"

71   *"ride the Bull"*   Gladwell, *David and Goliath.*

72   *"when I kissed my wife and children goodbye"*   Wyatt Walker oral history, BPL.

72   *Lane-Liggett drugstore downtown*   Foster Hailey, "4 Negroes Jailed in Birmingham as the Integration Drive Slows," *New York Times*, April 5, 1963, accessed October 25, 2022, https://timesmachine.nytimes.com/timesmachine/1963/04 /05/90568484.pdf.

72   *Four*   Ibid.

72   *That night at the mass meeting*   Connor papers, BPL, April 4, 1963, meeting.

72   *he saw a lot of fear*   Walker oral history, BPL.

72   *The city was "quiet"*   Hailey, "4 Negroes Jailed in Birmingham as the Integration Drive Slows."

72   *"seems to be both wasteful and worthless"*   Eskew, *But for Birmingham.*

73   *"argued against the demonstrations"*   Manis, *A Fire You Can't Put Out.*

73   *the city's only biracial committee*   Eskew, *But for Birmingham.*

73   *"does not appear to materially affect"*   Ibid.

73   *a "one-man show"*   Ibid.

74   *"headstrong and wild for publicity"*   Garrow, *Bearing the Cross.*

74   *he'd said he would integrate Phillips High*   Manis, *A Fire You Can't Put Out.*

75   *"No other man would dare to take Fred's place"*   Ibid.

76   *Was Phillips integrated in 1963?*   Phillips High School website, "The History," accessed October 25, 2022, http://phillips-high-school.com/02_History /Phillips%20High%20School%20NRHP.pdf.

76   *"I might get it desegregated"*   Manis, *A Fire You Can't Put Out.*

76   *"Fred essentially announced to the girls that they were going"*   Ibid.

76   *a "life and death" environment*   Shuttlesworth Jr. oral history, BPL.

76   *Fred's actions may have been comparable*   Ibid.

76   *"I am sure that is the reason we're alive today"*   Ibid.

77   *never had more than a few thousand members*   Manis, *A Fire You Can't Put Out.*

77   *"Your old man ought to leave"*   Shuttlesworth Jr. oral history, BPL.

77   *Walker should have known*   Walker oral history, BPL.

77   *"we owe it to Fred"*   Ibid.

77   *"[Fred] made Black people ashamed"*   Ibid.

78   *with a portrait of Frederick Douglass*   Walker interview, *Eyes on the Prize.*

78   *"It is not light that is needed, but fire"*   Frederick Douglass, "What to the Slave Is the Fourth of July?," *Lapham's Quarterly*, July 5, 1852, accessed October 25, 2022, https://housedivided.dickinson.edu/sites/teagle/texts/frederick-douglass -fifth-of-july-speech-1852/.

78   *"wash the stain off,"* Walker oral history, BPL.

78   *They* would *succeed then*   Halberstam, *The Children.* Halberstam emphasizes in that text on how Walker and Bevel didn't get along.

78   *four the second, ten the third*   Eskew, *But for Birmingham.*

79   *Bevel left Birmingham that first week*   Halberstam, *The Children*.
79   *heated debates about what was going wrong*   Abernathy, *And the Walls Came Tumbling Down*.
79   *Albany's police chief, Laurie Pritchett, was clever enough*   Garrow, *Bearing the Cross*.
79   *"We must have unity"*   McWhorter, *Carry Me Home*.
80   *"broader scope of activities than lunch counters"*   Garrow, *Bearing the Cross*; Shuttlesworth's March 15, 1963, letter to King and Walker, found within Fred Shuttlesworth's papers, MLK Jr. Research and Education Center, Stanford.

10. Optics, Optics, Optics

81   *"Let's get this over with"*   Eskew, *But for Birmingham*.
81   *hauled twenty-nine protesters to jail*   Ibid.; Foster Hailey, "Police Break Up Alabama March," *New York Times*, April 8, 1963, puts those arrested at forty-two that day, but Eskew later showed why that figure was twenty-nine.
82   *King said to Walker Saturday night*   Garrow, *Bearing the Cross*.
82   *"You have got to find a way"*   Gladwell, *David and Goliath*.
82   *"I'm going to find it"*   Ibid.
82   *Every choice the SCLC had made in Birmingham*   Abernathy, *And the Walls Came Tumbling Down*.
82   *prove the press's suspicion*   Ibid.
82   *"were the work of the Devil"*   Ibid.
83   *Even Martin Luther King was distancing himself*   Foster Hailey, "10 More Negroes Seized in Birmingham Sit-Ins," *New York Times*, April 6, 1963, accessed October 25, 2022, https://timesmachine.nytimes.com/timesmachine/1963/04/06/90576315.pdf. Hailey emphasizes that King might "temporarily abandon" the campaign because of its poor public showing.

11. "I've Got It!"

84   *Rougher than Martin, angrier than Martin*   King, *Daddy King*.
84   *little more than a janitor there*   McWhorter, *Carry Me Home*.
84   *Stories of how much he drank*   Ibid.
84   *and with his father's temper*   King, *Daddy King*.
84   *staged sit-ins with Martin, got arrested with Martin*   Ibid.
84   *A "detail man"*   Thomas A. Johnson, "A Rights Activist," *New York Times*, July 22, 1969, accessed October 25, 2022, https://timesmachine.nytimes.com/timesmachine/1969/07/22/90116026.pdf.
85   *Even in the city where he pastored*   McWhorter, *Carry Me Home*. It should be noted that in 1963 A.D. had only been pastoring in Birmingham for a year or so.
85   *"might be temporarily abandoned"*   Hailey, "10 More Negroes Seized in Birmingham Sit-Ins."
85   *supporters might seem more numerous than they were*   Halberstam, *The Children*.
85   *last night's mass meeting had attracted just two hundred people*   Ibid.
85   *"Bull Connor had something in his mind"*   Gladwell, *David and Goliath*.
86   *he'd used cardboard to cover the gaping holes*   Fernanda Santos, "Wyatt Tee Walker, Dr. King's Strategist and a Harlem Leader, Dies at 88," *New York Times*,

January 23, 2018, accessed October 25, 2022, https://www.nytimes.com/2018 /01/23/obituaries/wyatt-tee-walker-dead.html.

86   *"had absolutely no power"*   Nunnelley, *Bull Connor.*

86   *"my niggers"*   Ibid.

87   *"Well, that's your problem"*   Ibid.

87   *Bull banned "unwholesome" films*   "Birmingham's Morals Are Being Watched," editorial, *Birmingham News,* September 24, 1948.

87   *were the "thought police next?"*   "Is The Thought Police Next?," editorial, *Birmingham Post-Herald,* January 20, 1941; Eskew, *But for Birmingham.*

87   *armored riot car*   Ian Philbrick, "Bull Connor's Tank Returns to Birmingham," *Birmingham News,* October 8, 2008.

87   *Bull referred to as his "tank"*   Robert Houston, director, *Mighty Times: The Children's March,* documentary, produced by HBO and the Southern Poverty Law Center, 2004. The film won an Oscar in 2005 for Best Documentary Short Subject.

87   *"A boycott can work both ways"*   Eskew, *But for Birmingham.*

87   *the way to incite Bull, Walker realized*   Gladwell, *David and Goliath;* Penn Warren, "Who Speaks for the Negro?"; Walker oral history, University of Richmond Libraries.

88   *The protesters congregated in St. Paul Methodist Church*   Eskew, *But for Birmingham.*

88   *"We were supposed to march"*   Gladwell, *David and Goliath.*

88   *only twenty-two people*   Ibid.

88   *A. D. King, in his black ministerial robes*   McWhorter, *Carry Me Home;* Eskew, *But for Birmingham.*

89   *beyond this point to City Hall,* King, *Why We Can't Wait.*

89   *"Do something!"*   McWhorter, *Carry Me Home.*

89   *pulled a large knife on the German shepherd*   Eskew, *But for Birmingham.*

90   *"Look at them dogs go"*   McWhorter, *Carry Me Home.*

90   *"I don't know whether I cut him"*   Ibid.

90   *The press had witnessed everything*   Ibid.

90   *reported that the Palm Sunday march numbered in the thousands*   Gladwell, *David and Goliath.*

91   *"I've got it!"*   Ibid.

91   *"We've got a movement"*   Forman and Bond, *The Making of Black Revolutionaries.*

91   *Project X became Project C*   Eskew, *But for Birmingham.*

12. ". . . the Righteous Are Bold as a Lion"

95   *one who loved church and Grandma Williams*   Branch, *Parting the Waters.* King loved his grandmother so much as a boy that he blamed his own sins of pride for her death.

95   *"The great little negotiator"*   King, *Daddy King.*

96   *135 foreign correspondents*   Nichols, "Cities Are What Men Make Them."

96   *King walked into a meeting of two hundred Black pastors*   McWhorter, *Carry Me Home.*

96   *"you are not fit to be a leader"*   Eskew, *But for Birmingham.*

96   *since 1638*   "Winthrop S. Hudson," *Encyclopaedia Britannica*, 2014, accessed October 25, 2022, https://www.britannica.com/topic/Baptist.

96   *The church touched the border of Smithfield*   Nichols, "Cities Are What Men Make Them."

96   *"the most exclusive Black congregation"*   Eskew, *But for Birmingham.*

97   *opposing not only labor unions but Fred Shuttlesworth*   Ibid.

97   *"The Lord wants you to call it off"*   Manis, *A Fire You Can't Put Out.*

97   *"Pray for me"*   McWhorter, *Carry Me Home.*

97   *"tremendous resistance"*   King, *Why We Can't Wait.*

97   *did not have a protesting bone in his body*   Wil Haygood, "The Four Girls," *Boston Globe*, February 3, 1991.

97   *"Don't drive coloreds"*   Ibid.

97   *He had joined the army in 1944*   "The Reverend John H. Cross," obituary, *Atlanta Journal-Constitution*, November 17, 2007.

98   *"more of a chance"*   Eskew, *But for Birmingham.*

98   *"Have all y'all lost your minds"*   McWhorter, *Carry Me Home.*

98   *"We have to stick together"*   Eskew, *But for Birmingham.*

98   *"heart broke"*   King, *Daddy King.*

99   *"Don't you be impressed"*   Ibid.

99   *"skillfully brainwashed"*   King, *Why We Can't Wait.*

99   *"Man cannot ride your back"*   McWhorter, *Carry Me Home.*

99   *Martin walked into a standing ovation*   Connor papers, BPL, April 8, 1963, meeting.

99   *ninety-four in total*   Eskew, *But for Birmingham.*

99   *jostled for seats*   "Bull Connor's Terror Tactics Unit Negroes," *Cleveland Call and Post* (Columbus edition), April 13, 1963, found in Box 29, Shuttlesworth Papers, BCRI.

99   *"We are going to fill all the jails"*   Connor papers, BPL, April 8, meeting.

99   *"Get rid of the Uncle Toms!"*   Ibid.

100   *more Sunday schools than any other place in America*   Nichols, "Cities Are What Men Make Them."

100   *cheered the protesters*   Foster Hailey, "Negroes Uniting in Birmingham," *New York Times*, April 11, 1963, accessed October 25, 2022, https://timesmachine.nytimes.com/timesmachine/1963/04/11/90559485.pdf.

100   *"We want freedom and justice"*   Eskew, *But for Birmingham.*

100   *"Negroes Uniting in Birmingham"*   Hailey, "Negroes Uniting in Birmingham," *New York Times.*

100   whether they liked it or not   Ibid.

13. When Bull Said No to All That

101   *had blinded him in one eye*   Nunnelley, *Bull Connor.*

102   *"If a camera catches you beating anyone"*   McWhorter, *Carry Me Home.*

102   *kept knives and sawed-off shotguns*   Nichols, "Cities Are What Men Make Them."

102   *"Stay out of town"*   Ibid.

102   *"We want to keep our friendship with the Klan"*   McWhorter, *Carry Me Home.*

102   *raping Black women*   Shuttlesworth Papers, Box 30, 35–3, BCRI.

102   *extra days off for a job well done*   McWhorter, *Carry Me Home.*

102   *Just eight Tuesday*   Eskew, *But for Birmingham.*

103   *Dimmed lights, wood-paneled walls*   John Randolph, "'Nother One Bites the Dust—Historic Restaurant La Paree Closing," *Birmingham News*, December 7, 2003.

103   *"would peter out on their own"*   McWhorter, *Carry Me Home.*

103   *"Southern Policemen Adopting"*   Ibid.

14. The Counter to the Countermove

104   *He huddled with Ralph Abernathy and Wyatt Walker*   Nichols, "Cities Are What Men Make Them." Nichols emphasizes how Walker talked with King to ensure escalation of the campaign.

104   *"Bring that nigger over here"*   Ely Landau, director, *King: A Filmed Record, Montgomery to Memphis*, 1970, Library of Congress, accessed October 25, 2022, https://www.youtube.com/watch?v=JlQhST8vMgM.

104   *"you can call him all the names you want"*   McWhorter, *Carry Me Home.*

105   *What was the lesson of the Hibbler story?*   Connor papers, BPL, April 10, 1963, meeting.

105   *"We are not here to do something for you"*   Connor papers, BPL, April 8, 1963, meeting.

15. Upping the Stakes

106   *The order was drafted*   *Walker vs. City of Birmingham*, no. 249, 1967, United States Supreme Court, accessed October 25, 2022, https://caselaw.findlaw.com/us-supreme-court/388/307.html.

106   *at 9:00 p.m.*   Garrow, *Bearing the Cross.*

106   *"The leading instrument of the South"*   King, *Why We Can't Wait.*

106   *King and 138 others*   *Walker vs. City of Birmingham.*

107   *"in violation of numerous ordinances"*   Ibid.

107   *King summoned his top deputies*   Branch, *Parting the Waters.* Branch suggests King knew this injunction was coming.

107   *Walker had called every contact*   McWhorter, *Carry Me Home.*

108   *"as if they were not sitting"*   Ibid.

108   *"electric"*   Ibid.

16. The Garden of Gethsemane

109   *King thought again about the Albany campaign*   Eskew, *But for Birmingham.*

109   *"it was the angriest I'd ever seen Martin"*   Garrow, *Bearing the Cross.* Andrew Young made the statement.

109   *"the symbol of spiritual integrity"*   Ibid. Clarence B. Jones was the activist in question.

110   *His actions haunted him one year later*   Ibid.

110   *"I am prepared to go to jail"*   Foster Hailey, "Negroes Defying Birmingham Writ," *New York Times*, April 12, 1963.

110   *"Almost 2,000 years ago Christ died on the cross for us"*   Ibid.

111   *Bull phoned the bondsman*   McWhorter, *Carry Me Home*.

111   *$50*   *Walker vs. City of Birmingham*.

111   *$100*   Foster Hailey, "Dr. King Arrested at Birmingham," *New York Times*, April 13, 1963, accessed October 25, 2022, https://timesmachine.nytimes.com/timesmachine/1963/04/13/90566313.pdf.

111   *"There were our people in jail"*   King, *Why We Can't Wait*.

111   *do an emergency fundraiser*   Eskew, *But for Birmingham*.

112   *"whatever you do, try your best to be a Christian"*   Connor papers, BPL, April 11, 1963, meeting.

112   *"We ain't afraid of white folks anymore"*   Ibid.

112   *Martin stayed behind the door of room 30*   Eskew, *But for Birmingham*; Branch, *Parting the Waters*.

17. The Good Friday Test

113   *He hadn't slept*   Eskew, *But for Birmingham*.

113   *8:30 a.m. at the Gaston*   Garrow, *Bearing the Cross*.

113   *the hardest test in his decade of activism*   King, *Why We Can't Wait*. See, in particular, Dorothy Cotton's introduction to the edition published in 2011.

113   *come to room 30*   Eskew, *But for Birmingham*.

113   *dragged on a cigarette*   McWhorter, *Carry Me Home*.

114   *"This means you can't go to jail"*   Ibid.

114   *"If you go to jail we are lost"*   King, *Why We Can't Wait*.

114   *"unwise and untimely"*   "Statement by Alabama Clergymen," 1963, Martin Luther King Jr. Research and Education Institute, Stanford University, accessed October 25, 2022, https://kinginstitute.stanford.edu/sites/mlk/files/lesson-activities/clergybirmingham1963.pdf.

114   *To delay the Good Friday march*   McWhorter, *Carry Me Home*.

114   *"you should have gone to jail earlier"*   Ibid.

114   *not the only executive in the SCLC who had gone without sleep*   Ibid.; in fact, Walker said he hadn't slept the previous three nights.

114   *the advisory committee said*   Abernathy, *And the Walls Came Tumbling Down*.

114   *"damage[d] our morale"*   Ibid.

115   *volunteered to march alongside King*   Branch, *Parting the Waters*.

115   *"I was alone in that crowded room"*   King, *Why We Can't Wait*.

115   *he'd wanted someone else to lead the marches*   Garrow, *Bearing the Cross*.

115   *"I neither started the protest nor suggested it"*   Martin Luther King Jr., "My Pilgrimage to Nonviolence," *Fellowship*, September 1958, accessed October 25, 2022, and reprinted here: https://kinginstitute.stanford.edu/king-papers/documents/my-pilgrimage-nonviolence.

115   *"The work of a few hotheads"*   Martin Luther King Jr., "Our God Is Able," sermon, July 1, 1962–March 31, 1963, accessed October 25, 2022, and reprinted

here: https://kinginstitute.stanford.edu/king-papers/documents/draft-chapter
-xiii-our-god-able.

115   *"Before next week you'll be sorry"*   Ibid.

116   *"It seemed that all of my fears"*   Ibid.

116   *"I am afraid"*   Ibid.

116   *his home was bombed two days later*   Ibid.

116   *The noise of his inner monologue*   King, *Why We Can't Wait.*

117   *"I think I was standing also at the center"*   Ibid.

117   *"I have decided to go to jail"*   Ibid.

117   *never seen Martin in anything but a suit and tie*   Ibid., Dorothy Cotton's introduction.

118   *Some in the room smiled*   Andrew Young full interview, *Eyes on the Prize*
documentary series, Blackside Inc. (*American Experience*, PBS, 1987). The
Young interviews are now housed in the Washington University at St. Louis
Libraries, accessed October 25, 2022, http://repository.wustl.edu/catalog?utf8
=%E2%9C%93&search_field=all_fields&q=andrew+young. Young said it was
the moment King became a leader.

118   *"I think at this time my advice would be"*   Garrow, *Bearing the Cross*; Raines, *My
Soul Is Rested.*

118   *Morehouse despite failing its entrance tests*   Branch, *Parting the Waters.*

118   *proclaiming he would marry Alberta*   King, *Daddy King.*

118   *if he could ever "earn" it*   Branch, *Parting the Waters.*

118   *his dream in college to become a professor*   Ibid.

119   *"he was right, segregation was wrong*   Ibid. Branch is that observer.

119   *"My advice would be to you"*   The rest of this section is a confluence of ibid.;
King, *Why We Can't Wait*; King, *Daddy King*; Abernathy, *When the Walls Came
Tumbling Down*; McWhorter, *Carry Me Home.*

119   *"Let me see if I can get in touch"*   Branch, *Parting the Waters.*

120   *Martin led them all, even his father*   King, *Why We Can't Wait.*

120   *Some sang with tears in their eyes*   Ibid., Dorothy Cotton's introduction.

120   *"true leadership"*   Eskew, *But for Birmingham.* Andrew Young is the aide.

18. "Why Have You Forsaken Me?"

121   *telling the press to be at Zion Hill Baptist*   Foster Hailey, "Dr. King Arrested in
Birmingham," *New York Times*, April 13, 1963, accessed October 25, 2022,
https://timesmachine.nytimes.com/timesmachine/1963/04/13/90566313
.pdf.

121   *Footage later emerged*   Smithsonian Channel, "The March That Led to MLK's
Arrest and Famous Letter," from the *America in Color: The 1960s* docuseries,
2018, accessed October 25, 2022, the relevant clip found here: https://www
.youtube.com/watch?v=__2GqomCXLU.

121   *At last, after three hours*   Branch, *Parting the Waters.*

121   *"There he goes! Just like Jesus!"*   Nichols, "Cities Are What Men Make Them."

121   *Walker had told the police where the march would head*   McWhorter, *Carry Me
Home.*

122   *snapping photos*   Branch, *Parting the Waters.*

122   *were joyous, singing, shouting*   Hailey, "Dr. King Arrested in Birmingham."

122   *as King walked by them*   Smithsonian, *America in Color: The 1960s.*

122   *The cop got off the bike, scowled*   Landau, dir., *King: A Filmed Record.*

123   *His eyes showed everything*   Ibid.

19. The Hole

127   *The record sold more than two hundred thousand copies*   Charles K. Wolfe, *Classic Country: Legends of Country Music* (Nashville: Taylor and Francis, 2002).

127   *had always loved as a kid*   Ibid.

128   *"incommunicado for months at a time"*   Eskew, *But for Birmingham.*

128   *"since he seems to be so interested"*   Ibid.

128   *Bull's "favorite technique"*   Harrison E. Salisbury, "Fear and Hatred Grip Birmingham," *New York Times,* April 12, 1960, accessed October 25, 2022, https://credo.library.umass.edu/view/pageturn/mums312-b152-i335/#page/1/mode/1up.

128   *sometimes "tortured" there*   Eskew, *But for Birmingham.*

128   *Guards beat them with rubber hoses*   Ibid.

128   *sliced them open with razors*   Salisbury, "Fear and Hatred Grip Birmingham."

128   *"We kept them"*   Eskew, *But for Birmingham.*

128   *"small-time Gestapo"*   Ibid.

128   *anything he'd seen in fascist Germany*   McWhorter, *Carry Me Home.*

129   *three-story concrete mass*   Kyle Whitmire, "Alabama Tourism Department, Leadership Birmingham to Place Marker at Birmingham Jail, Where King Wrote Famous Letter," *Birmingham News,* February 8, 2013, accessed October 25, 2022, https://www.al.com/spotnews/2013/02/putting_a_mark_on_history_tour.html.

129   *this brought King some comfort*   King, *Why We Can't Wait.*

129   *"For their safety"*   Eskew, *But for Birmingham.*

129   *Just eight paces across*   These details are based on the exhibit I saw on the cell at the Birmingham Civil Rights Institute, June 2021.

129   *The bed had no linen or pillow*   Garrow, *Bearing the Cross*; Eskew, *But for Birmingham.*

129   *rust fell from the cell bars*   These details are based on the exhibit I saw on the cell at the Birmingham Civil Rights Institute, June 2021.

129   *"You will never know the meaning of utter darkness"*   King, *Why We Can't Wait.*

130   *"I was besieged with worry"*   Ibid.

130   *"Those were the longest, most frustrating"*   Ibid.

20. Who Cares About Prison Reform Now?

131   *He phoned Harry Belafonte in New York:*   Branch, *Parting the Waters.*

131   *"I called Bobby Kennedy"*   Belafonte, *My Song.*

132   *"Tell Reverend King we're doing all we can"*   Ibid.; Branch, *Parting the Waters.*

132   *wry paternalism*   Belafonte, *My Song.*

132   *"In these times"*   Foster Hailey, "Birmingham Jails Six More Negroes," *New York Times,* April 14, 1963, accessed October 25, 2022, https://timesmachine.nytimes.com/timesmachine/1963/04/14/89917108.pdf.

132   *Easter weekend vacation spot*   John F. Kennedy Presidential Library (JFK Library), Easter weekend photos, April 14, 1963, accessed October 25, 2022, https://www.jfklibrary.org/search?items_per_page=25&sort_by=search_api_relevance&sort_order=DESC&field_start_date=1963–4–11%2019:0:0&field_end_date=1963–4–14%2018:0:0&f%5B0%5D=source%3A46.

132   Looks like the Kennedys *are* concerned   Belafonte, *My Song.*

21. "This Will Be One of the Most Historic Documents. . . ."

133   *ready to hurl epithets*   King, *A Gift of Love.*

133   *the scion of the W. W. Norton publishing fortune*   Douglas Brinkley, "The Man Who Kept King's Secrets," *Vanity Fair*, April 2006, https://www.vanityfair.com/news/politics/2014/01/clarence-jones-martin-luther-king-jr-secrets.

134   *"I vividly recall being in school"*   Ibid.

134   *"Just because some Negro preacher"*   Ibid.

134   *a "young man who lives in a home"*   Ibid.

135   *He bawled in that pew*   Clarence B. Jones, *Behind the Dream: The Making of a Speech That Transformed a Nation* (New York: St. Martin's Press, 2011).

135   *"Soon," King said*   Brinkley, "The Man Who Kept King's Secrets."

135   *"During my time in the military"*   Jones, *Behind the Dream.*

135   *to an apartment in Harlem*   Ibid.

135   *snuck out from under his dress shirt*   Branch, *Parting the Waters.*

136   *The piece was a reprint*   Eskew, *But for Birmingham.*

136   *They'd praised King and condemned*   Branch, *Parting the Waters.*

136   *"Just as we formerly pointed out"*   Martin Luther King Jr. Papers, "Letter from Alabama Clergymen," Martin Luther King Jr. Research and Education Institute, Stanford University, accessed October 25, 2022, https://kinginstitute.stanford.edu/sites/mlk/files/lesson-activities/clergybirmingham1963.pdf.

136   *"I have to respond to this"*   Jones, *Behind the Dream.*

136   *scraps of newspaper*   Eskew, *But for Birmingham.*

137   *King had once assumed this, too*   Martin Luther King Jr., *Strive Toward Freedom: The Montgomery Story* (New York: Beacon Press, 2010).

137   *"A religion that ends with the individual"*   Ibid.

137   *the social justice reforms of that movement*   "Social Gospel Movement," *Encyclopaedia Britannica*, 15th edition (2010), https://www.britannica.com/event/Social-Gospel.

138   *two-hundred-member congregation with a padlock*   Branch, *Parting the Waters.*

138   *piano in the living room*   Celine Wright, "Moved to Music by Martin Luther King Jr.," *Los Angeles Times*, August 13, 2013, accessed October 25, 2022, https://www.latimes.com/entertainment/arts/la-xpm-2013-aug-13-la-et-cm-mlk-concert-20130814-story.html.

138   *"I could never get out of my mind"*   King, *Strive Toward Freedom.*

138   *ate lunch with students from all over the world*   Branch, *Parting the Waters.*

138   *and over the Christmas break no less*   King, *Strive Toward Freedom.*

138   *He sometimes played until three in the morning*   Branch, *Parting the Waters*; that friend was nicknamed Mac.

138   *Aghast*   Ibid.

138   *"If the soul is left in darkness"*   Victor Hugo, *Les Miserables*, translated by Isabel F. Hapgood (New York: Simon and Brown, 2016).

139   *"a serious intellectual quest"*   King, *Strive Toward Freedom*.

139   *when the city was the fourth-largest in the country*   Kenneth T. Jackson, *The Ku Klux Klan in the City: 1915–1930* (Chicago: Ivan R. Dee, 1992).

139   *from sixty-six members to nearly seven hundred*   Richard Wightman Fox, *Reinhold Niebuhr: A Biography* (New York: Harper and Row, 1987).

139   *"The foundry interested me"*   Reinhold Niebuhr, *Leaves from the Notebook of a Tamed Cynic* (Louisville, KY: Westminster/John Knox Press, 1990).

140   *"Insofar as this treatise has a polemic interest"*   Reinhold Niebuhr, *Moral Man and Immoral Society* (Louisville, KY: Westminster/John Knox Press, 2013).

141   *That seemed true to King*   King, *Strive Toward Freedom*.

141   *"Will not even its most minimum demands"*   Niebuhr, *Moral Man and Immoral Society*.

141   *"The prophetic and realistic elements"*   King, *Strive Toward Freedom*.

141   *Niebuhr argued what King Sr. did*   Branch, *Parting the Waters*.

142   *King read about Gandhi's Salt March in 1930*   King, *Strive Toward Freedom*.

142   *some sixty thousand people marched behind Gandhi*   Dennis Dalton, *Mahatma Gandhi: Nonviolent Power in Action* (New York: Columbia University Press, 1995).

142   *"the sickening whacks of the clubs"*   Brian Martin, *Justice Ignited: The Dynamics of Backfire* (Lanham, MD: Rowman and Littlefield, 2006), with an emphasis on United Press International's Webb Miller's account of the beatings.

143   *"Christ's teachings . . . can only be diffused"*   Leo Tolstoy, *The Kingdom of God Is Within You* (Lincoln: University of Nebraska Press, 1984). Tolstoy describes here what the Quakers taught him.

143   *"refuse to serve"*   Ibid.

143   *had said at the end of his life*   King, *A Gift of Love*.

143   *"Jesus built an empire that depended on love"*   Martin Luther King Jr., "Loving Your Enemies," a sermon delivered for the Dexter Avenue Baptist Church, Martin Luther King Jr's papers, Martin Luther King Jr. Research and Education Institute, Stanford University, accessed October 25, 2022, https://kinginstitute .stanford.edu/king-papers/documents/loving-your-enemies-sermon-delivered -dexter-avenue-baptist-church.

143   *"If someone gives us pain through ignorance"*   Priyanka Kumar, "What King Learned from Gandhi," *Los Angeles Review of Books*, January 16, 2017, accessed October 25, 2022, https://lareviewofbooks.org/article/what-king-learned-from-gandhi/.

144   *Tolstoy Farm*   "Tolstoy Farm," accessed October 25, 2022, http://www.tolstoyfarm .com/the_past.htm.

144   *got nauseated*   Richard L. Johnson, ed., *Gandhi's Experiments with Truth: Essential Writings by and About Mahatma Gandhi* (Lanham, MD: Lexington Books, 2005).

144   *terrorism was easier to defeat than nonviolence*   Ibid.

144   *"True pacifism"*   King, *Strive Toward Freedom*.

144   *"You may well ask: 'Why direct action?'"*   Martin Luther King Jr., "Letter from Birmingham Jail," accessed October 25, 2022, http://www.nlnrac.org/american /american-civil-rights-movements/primary-source-documents/letter-from-a -birmingham-jail.

146   *"I need more paper"*   Branch, *Parting the Waters.*
146   *"I thought it was crazy"*   Jones, *Behind the Dream.*
146   *turn King to more pressing matters*   Branch, *Parting the Waters.*
146   *"Have Dora type it up, okay?"*   Jones, *Behind the Dream.*
146   *"the eight white clergymen had truly upset him"*   Ibid.
146   *"Take this out of here"*   Ibid.
147   *falling down his pants*   Ibid.
147   *he would serve as King's chief speechwriter*   Jones, *Behind the Dream.*
148   *The first draft wasn't flawless*   Branch, *Parting the Waters.*
148   *King also had St. Augustine's penchant*   Ibid.; I didn't see the connection until Branch pointed it out.
148   *"There comes a time"*   King, "Letter from Birmingham Jail."
149   *when a secretary fell asleep at the typewriter*   Branch, *Parting the Waters.*
149   *"Abused and scorned"*   King, "Letter from Birmingham Jail."
149   *"I had never been truly in solitary confinement"*   King, *Why We Can't Wait.*
149   *"Call it," Walker said*   McWhorter, *Carry Me Home.*

22. The Prophet Returns with His Wife

153   *gunning for Alabama in his '59 Rambler*   Ibid.
153   *they'd married*   Halberstam, *The Children.*
154   *"more precious than all the money"*   Ibid.
154   *She'd grown up without the overt promotion*   Bruce Dierenfield, *The Civil Rights Movement* (London: Routledge, 2008).
154   *The fingerprinting at the station*   Ibid.
154   *The cops joked*   Ibid.
154   *even other Black students had mistaken her*   Ibid.
155   *"white people have better things"*   Ibid.
155   *That amazed her*   Halberstam, *The Children.*
155   *the desegregation of Nashville lunch counters*   Samuel Momodu, "Nashville Sit-Ins (1960)," August 3, 2016, Black Past, https://www.blackpast.org/african-american-history/nashville-sit-ins-1960/.
156   *the guard mistook Bevel for a radio*   Halberstam, *The Children.*
156   *She signed her own will and testament*   Heidi Hall, "Years After Change, Activist Lives Her Convictions," *The Tennessean*, March 26, 2013, accessed October 25, 2022, https://www.usatoday.com/story/news/nation/2013/03/26/nashville-civil-rights-diane-nash/2023301/.
156   *"This will be a Black child born in Mississippi"*   "Nash, Diane," *Mississippi Encyclopedia*, University Press of Mississippi, accessed October 25, 2022, https://mississippiencyclopedia.org/entries/diane-nash/.
156   *"Who the hell is Diane Nash?"*   *American Experience: Freedom Riders*, PBS, 2010, accessed October 25, 2022, https://www.youtube.com/watch?v=GIffL6KplzQ.
157   *"doubtful utility"*   "What's Wrong in Birmingham," editorial, *Washington Post*, April 13, 1963.
157   *"To many Birmingham Negroes"*   Quoted in Eskew, *But for Birmingham.*
157   *"The federal government has no authority"*   James Free, "U.S. Plans No Intervention in Situation Here," *Birmingham News*, April 14, 1963.

157   *"We shall not submit to the intimidations of pressure"*   Foster Hailey, "New Bir-
       mingham Regime Sworn In, Raising Hopes for Racial Peace," *New York Times*,
       April 16, 1963, accessed October 25, 2022, https://timesmachine.nytimes.com
       /timesmachine/1963/04/16/82056272.pdf.
157   *"like a picnic"*   Ibid.
157   *They consituted one-fourth of the inaugural crowd*   James Bennett, "Boutwell,
       Council Sworn into Office," *Birmingham Post-Herald*, April 16, 1963.
157   *"more Negroes going to jail for getting drunk"*   McWhorter, *Carry Me Home*.
157   *to rat out Black downtown shoppers*   Ibid.
157   *"This is the only way we can get"*   Eskew, *But for Birmingham*.
158   *"Birmingham is sick"*   Connor papers, BPL, April 12, 1963, meeting.
158   *"You guys are running a scam movement"*   McWhorter, *Carry Me Home*.
158   *an idea almost too radical to be voiced*   Ibid.; the Bevels said they had this idea
       almost as soon as they got to town but took a while to actually propose it.

23. Emergence

159   *"lifted one thousand pounds from my heart"*   King, *Why We Can't Wait*.
159   *"some of it raised"*   Belafonte, *My Song*.
159   *"What quieted me"*   King, *Why We Can't Wait*.
159   *"The life of the movement could not"*   Ibid.
159   *argued that their terms ended in October 1965*   Foster Hailey, "3 in Birmingham
       Face Ouster Suit," *New York Times*, April 17, 1963, accessed October 25, 2022,
       https://timesmachine.nytimes.com/timesmachine/1963/04/17/90892320.pdf.
160   *"Castro brigade"*   Eskew, *But for Birmingham*.
160   *"the strategy for future actions"*   Ibid.
160   *heard by the judge who* issued *the injunction*   *Walker vs City of Birmingham*,
       accessed October 25, 2022, https://caselaw.findlaw.com/us-supreme-court/388
       /307.html.
161   *could be right back in jail*   Ibid.; Eskew, *But for Birmingham*; Branch, *Parting
       the Waters*.
161   *"the absence of justice in Birmingham"*   Eskew, *But for Birmingham*; the protest
       in question happened in Hartford, Connecticut.
161   *started nationwide protests of the department stores*   "Four Chains Target of Racial
       Protests," *New York Times*, April 18, 1963, accessed October 25, 2022, https:
       //timesmachine.nytimes.com/timesmachine/1963/04/18/82057341.pdf.
161   *before an appellate court outside Alabama*   Foster Hailey, "King Leaves Birming-
       ham Jail," *New York Times*, April 21, 1963, accessed October 25, 2022, https:
       //timesmachine.nytimes.com/timesmachine/1963/04/21/120984380.pdf.
161   *Listening to it all, Martin nodded*   King, *Why We Can't Wait*.
161   *He could allude to Scripture*   2 Timothy 1–7 (NIV).
162   *"I will die there if necessary"*   Connor papers, BPL, April 24, 1963, meeting;
       Garrow, *Bearing the Cross*.
162   *Almost no one stepped forward, either*   Connor papers, BPL, April 24, 1963,
       meeting.
162   *slowed to such a "trickle"*   Eskew, *But for Birmingham*.
162   *Coretta flew to him*   McWhorter, *Carry Me Home*.

162   *"lonely and worried"*   King, *My Life, My Love, My Legacy.*

162   *"Good friend that he is"*   King, *My Life with Martin Luther King Jr.*

162   *He had an idea*   McWhorter, *Carry Me Home;* Houston, dir., *Mighty Times.*

24. The Indecent Proposal

163   *fifty or sixty of them got arrested* every day   Nichols, "Cities Are What Men Make Them."

163   *Half the Blacks in Birmingham were laborers*   Eskew, *But for Birmingham.*

163   *white people didn't want Blacks protesting*   Numerous BCRI interviews with child protesters.

164   *A lot of times they still couldn't*   Nichols, "Cities Are What Men Make Them."

164   *had to walk past the front door*   Ibid.

164   *"appealed to something that was already there"*   Carolyn McKinstry oral history, BCRI.

164   *"Hard times make hard people"*   Washington Booker III oral history, BCRI; he did not officially join the protests until May.

165   *The SCLC should switch its emphasis*   Houston, dir., *Mighty Times.*

165   Children? *King stared*   Ibid.; McWhorter, *Carry Me Home.*

165   *Was the man crazy?*   Halberstam, *The Children.*

165   *"Whatever"*   McWhorter, *Carry Me Home.*

165   *Why would the SCLC "use" children*   Jenkins and Gardner Hines, *Black Titan.*

166   *"is a radical of the worst kind"*   McWhorter, *Carry Me Home.*

166   *He'd hold these meetings at 16th Street Baptist*   Ibid.

166   *or New Pilgrim Baptist*   Janice Kelsey oral history, BCRI.

166   Do what you want   Halberstam, *The Children.*

166   *"Your grandmama went along with disenfranchisement"*   McWhorter, *Carry Me Home.*

166   *"how many electronic typewriters do you have"*   Janice Kelsey oral history, BCRI.

166   *an honor-roll student at Ullman*   Janice Kelsey, *I Woke Up with My Mind on Freedom* (Birmingham: Urban Press, 2017).

167   *they have three* rooms *of electronic typewriters*   Kelsey interview, BCRI.

167   *cute boys might be there*   Kelsey, *I Woke Up with My Mind on Freedom.*

167   *Kelsey's brother Alvin's among them*   Ibid.

167   *"Have you ever wondered why your helmets"*   Kelsey interview, BCRI.

167   *"We always paint them"*   Ibid.

167   *"It's because you get Ramsay's discards"*   Ibid.

167   *all-white high school six blocks from Ullman*   Kelsey, *I Woke Up with My Mind on Freedom.*

167   *"Check the copyright"*   Kelsey interview, BCRI.

167   *he looked so different from King*   Kelsey, *I Woke Up with My Mind on Freedom.*

168   *"if you want to do something"*   Kelsey interview, BCRI.

168   *"wake-up call"*   Kelsey, *I Woke Up with My Mind on Freedom.*

168   *"In 40 years"*   McWhorter, *Carry Me Home.*

168   *White kids might attack them*   Halberstam, *The Children.*

169   *walk among the students with a trash can*   Carolyn McKinstry, *While the World Watched: A Birmingham Bombing Survivor Comes of Age During the Civil Rights Movement* (Carol Stream, IL: Tyndale House, 2013).

169   *"the most dynamic person for the young"*   Horace Huntley and John W. McKerley, eds., *Foot Soldiers for Democracy* (Champaign: University of Illinois Press, 2009). James Stewart is the boy quoted.

169   *He mixed street slang with Old Testament Scripture*   Halberstam, *The Children*.

169   *"we're so glad you're here"*   Huntley and McKerley, *Foot Soldiers for Democracy*.

169   *"almost mystical way"*   Halberstam, *The Children*.

169   *He was the thirteenth of seventeen children*   Ibid.

170   *Piney Woods, an early Black boarding school*   School website, accessed October 25, 2022, https://www.pineywoods.org/.

170   *the FBI approached him*   Halberstam, *The Children*.

170   *"The worst thing a man can do"*   Ibid.

170   *nothing less than the acquisition of God's conscience*   Ibid. Halberstam does a great job distilling Dennis's faith.

172   *He began to recruit them at school*   Dorothy Cotton oral history, BCRI.

172   *basketball stars, Miss Parker High School*   Branch, *Parting the Waters*.

172   *"whisper campaign"*   McWhorter, *Carry Me Home*.

172   *"like they were doing something half-sneaky"*   Ibid.

173   *Punches, maulings*   Houston, dir., *Mighty Times*.

173   But look!   Ibid.

173   *King repeatedly told the young people*   Connor papers, BPL, April 24, 1963, meeting; McWhorter, *Carry Me Home*.

173   *getting expelled for going*   Connor papers, BPL, April 24, 1963, meeting.

173   *Martin stayed with the Drews*   John Drew Oral History, Birmingham Public Library.

174   *sent their eleven-year-old to a prep school*   Branch, *Parting the Waters*.

174   *shouldn't have any person younger than eighteen*   Ibid.

174   *Wyatt Walker wanted Bevel fired*   Halberstam, *The Children*.

174   *freely admitted his distaste for child protesters*   Branch, *Parting the Waters*.

174   *contributing to the delinquency of minors*   Ibid.

174   *"The press is leaving"*   Garrow, *Bearing the Cross*.

175   *"A continual series of blows"*   Stein, *American Journey*; Stanley Levison is the advisor.

175   *A story that had always troubled King*   King, *Why We Can't Wait*; King, *A Gift of Love*.

175   *The story described the fear*   Harrison Salisbury, "Fear and Hatred Grip Birmingham," *New York Times*, April 12, 1960, accessed October 25, 2022, https://timesmachine.nytimes.com/timesmachine/1960/04/12/105426614.pdf.

175   *even the church bells chimed "Dixie"*   Nichols, "Cities Are What Men Make Them."

25. The Prophet and the Playboy

176   *He spun records*   McWhorter, *Carry Me Home*.

176   *emblazoned across the side*   Houston, director, *Mighty Times*.

176   *"Good googly moogly"*   Pat Duggins, "Civil Rights Radio," Alabama Public Radio, April 14, 2017, accessed October 25, 2022, https://www.apr.org/arts-life/2017–04–14/alabama-public-radio-civil-rights-radio.

176   *he watched his father kill his mother*   Shelley Stewart, "Lessons Learned over My 80 Years," TEDx Birmingham, April 27, 2015, accessed October 25, 2022, https://www.youtube.com/watch?v=aFpFNWhzoDA.

177   *caught rats and fried them for dinner*   McWhorter, *Carry Me Home*.

177   *Shelley ran away from home*   Stewart, *Ted X Birmingham*.

177   *"Being on the air you had music as the bait"*   Houston, dir., *Mighty Times*.

177   *"Get some education"*   McWhorter, *Carry Me Home*.

177   *"you talk about freedom"*   Houston, director, *Carry Me Home*.

177   *"I am a man"*   Shelley Stewart, *The Road South: A Memoir* (New York: Grand Central, 2002).

178   *"Well, let's check the time"*   Ibid.

178   *who'd hitched a ride in*   Houston, dir., *Mighty Times*.

178   *started recruiting SCLC staffers*   Ibid.; Jesse Jackson, Andrew Young, and Fred Shuttlesworth were among the staffers.

178   *to scoff at any resistance to it*   Ibid.; Halberstam, *The Children*.

178   *did not throw their children to the lions*   Branch, *Parting the Waters*.

179   *He spoke from personal knowledge*   Halberstam, *The Children*.

179   *was old enough to march for freedom*   Branch, *Parting the Waters*.

26. The End of the "Endless" Deliberation

180   *pulled its reporter Foster Hailey*   Foster Hailey, "Alabama Holds 2 in Hiker's Slaying," *New York Times*, April 26, 1963, accessed October 25, 2022, https://timesmachine.nytimes.com/timesmachine/1963/04/26/81801491.pdf.

180   *One piece ran at three paragraphs*   UPI, "9 Churches in Birmingham Accept Negro Worshipers," *New York Times*, April 29, 1963, accessed October 25, 2022, https://timesmachine.nytimes.com/timesmachine/1963/04/29/89922083.pdf.

180   *"For the agitators"*   *Birmingham Post-Herald*, April 18, 1963, p. 14, as found in the archives of the Birmingham Public Library.

180   *and had wanted him fired*   Halberstam, *The Children*.

181   *"we need something new"*   Garrow, *Bearing the Cross*.

181   *"one of the best tactical minds in our movement"*   Wyatt Tee Walker interview, *Eyes on the Prize*.

181   Everything must escalate, *Walker reiterated*   Gladwell, *David and Goliath*.

181   *"Six days in the . . . jail"*   Walker interview, *Eyes on the Prize*.

181   *"Without being immodest"*   Ibid.

181   *"D-Day"*   Houston, dir., *Mighty Times*.

182   *"We've got to use what we got"*   McWhorter, *Carry Me Home*.

182   *"built to withstand storms and tornadoes"*   Connor papers, BPL, April 27, 1963, meeting notes.

182   *twenty-ninth for an opera*   Connor papers, BPL, April 29, 1963, meeting.

182   *and then on to Memphis*   Connor papers, BPL, April 30, 1963, meeting.

182   *An "endless" deliberation*   Alex Haley, "Martin Luther King—The *Playboy* Interview," *Playboy*, January 1965, as found in the archives of the Birmingham Public Library.

27. D-Day

185   *"Kids, there's gonna be a party"*   McWhorter, *Carry Me Home*; Houston, dir., *Mighty Times*.

185   *Fred Shuttlesworth had requested a parade permit*   McWhorter, *Carry Me Home*.

185   *"summarily and permanently expelled"*   Ibid.

186   *"my heart was pounding"*   McKinstry, *While the World Watched*.

186   *Other children remembered*   Numerous BCRI and BPL oral histories.

186   *"It wasn't the fear that kept us"*   Houston, director, *Mighty Times*.

186   *"It's Time"*   Ibid.; McKinstry, *While the World Watched*.

186   *some kids hopped out the first-floor windows*   Houston, director, *Mighty Times*.

186   *They climbed over the gate*   Ibid.; McWhorter, *Carry Me Home*.

186   *it had been the country's largest years prior*   Todd Gerelds, as told to Mark Schlabach, *Woodlawn: One Dream, One Hope, One Way* (Brentwood, TN: Howard Books, 2015).

186   *A school with 2,200 students*   Foster Hailey, "Dogs and Hoses Repulse Negroes in Birmingham," *New York Times*, May 4, 1963, accessed October 25, 2022, https://timesmachine.nytimes.com/timesmachine/1963/05/04/81808290.pdf.

187   *"The job is to get this file [of kids] out"*   Houston, dir., *Mighty Times*; the organizer is James Orange.

187   *"I didn't want to lose my job"*   Ibid.; Cleo George is the teacher.

187   *Just turned her eyes to the chalkboard*   Ibid.

187   *Bevel pacing in a tight circle*   Ibid.

187   *opening all doors*   Ibid.

187   *"The whole campus was outside"*   Ibid.; James Orange is telling this anecdote.

188   *walked up to eighteen miles that day*   Ibid.

188   *shotguns and rifles in hand*   Ibid.

188   *prowling the park on loose leashes*   Foster Hailey, "500 Are Arrested in Negro Protest at Birmingham," *New York Times*, May 3, 1963, accessed October 25, 2022, https://timesmachine.nytimes.com/timesmachine/1963/05/03/81807492.pdf.

188   *"army tanks"*   McKinstry, *While the World Watched*.

188   *cameras from the networks capturing it all*   Houston, director, *Mighty Times*.

188   *"Goose bumps of terror rose on my arms"*   McKinstry, *While the World Watched*.

188   *did Black civic leaders or pressmen learn*   Hailey, "500 Arrested in Negro Protest in Birmingham"; Eskew, *But for Birmingham;* McWhorter, *Carry Me Home*.

189   *"Let those kids stay in school"*   Jenkins and Gardner Hines, *Black Titan*.

189   *"The children understood the stakes"*   King, *Why We Can't Wait*.

189   *"Brother Gaston"*   Jenkins and Gardner Hines, *Black Titan*.

189   *"wrestling with his conscience"*   Houston, dir., *Mighty Times*.

189   *"Martin was about the most indecisive man"*   Eskew, *But for Birmingham;* the quote comes from a footnote citing Garrow, *Bearing the Cross*.

190   *"one big pep rally"*   Houston, dir., *Mighty Times.*

190   *a fast-paced, jaunty pop number*   Ibid.

190   *the kids swayed and clapped*   Ibid.

190   *"They gave me the courage I needed"*   McKinstry, *While the World Watched.*

190   *"we were going to get hurt if we* didn't *do something*   Houston, dir., *Mighty Times.*

190   *Charts and timetables emerged*   Aldridge Willis oral history, Birmingham Civil Rights Institute.

190   At all times do not fight back   Ibid.

191   *kids ranging in age from six to twenty*   McWhorter, *Carry Me Home*; Eskew, *But for Birmingham.*

191   Be nonviolent no matter what   Willis oral history, BCRI.

191   *as a "battle"*   Abernathy, *And the Walls Came Tumbling Down.*

191   *Fred Shuttlesworth saw it as a "miracle"*   Shuttlesworth oral history, part IV, BCRI.

191   *He grabbed a walkie-talkie*   Garrow, *Bearing the Cross.*

191   *He opened the doors to the glare of the afternoon*   Houston, dir., *Mighty Times.*

191   *They sang "We Shall Overcome"*   Ibid.

191   *The children dropped to their knees and prayed*   McWhorter, *Carry Me Home.*

191   *In the filmed footage*   Houston, dir., *Mighty Times.*

192   *"Segregation Is a Sin"*   Branch, *Parting the Waters.*

192   *"I'll Die to Make This Land My Home"*   McWhorter, *Carry Me Home.*

192   *"Bull had something in his mind"*   Gladwell, *David and Goliath.*

192   *"Will You 'Tom' for the Big Bad Bull?"*   McWhorter, *Carry Me Home.*

192   *It became a two- or three-cop job*   Houston, dir., *Mighty Times.*

192   *"Hey, Fred. How many more have you got?"*   Connor papers, BPL, May 2, 1963, meeting; McWhorter, *Carry Me Home.*

192   *Bull Connor brought buses in*   Houston, dir., *Mighty Times.*

192   *"Sing, children, sing"*   McWhorter, *Carry Me Home.*

192   *Maybe five hundred kids had been hauled off*   Houston, dir., *Mighty Times.*

193   *hands on his hips and exasperation on his face*   Ibid.; Eskew, *But for Birmingham.* Officer Jack Warren recalled: "You could see Bull moving, looking, concerned, fidgety. He was just desperate. 'What the hell do I do?'"

193   Your men have to take a break   Houston, dir., *Mighty Times.*

193   *973 children had been arrested*   Ibid.

193   *The mugshots that day showed*   Ibid.

194   *"'Well, I know you gonna kill me'"*   Ibid.

194   *It was a fevered situation*   Ibid.; numerous oral histories with the children in the BCRI's archives.

194   *"They asked us who our parents were"*   Margaret Givener Brown oral history, BCRI.

194   *Janice Kelsey sure did*   Kelsey, *I Woke Up with My Mind on Freedom.*

195   *The units had been designed for eight*   Branch, *Parting the Waters.*

195   *Kelsey's holding area*   Kelsey, *I Woke Up with My Mind on Freedom.*

195   *"The whole world is watching Birmingham!"*   Connor papers, BPL, May 2, 1963, meeting.

195   *"Freedom fighters"*   Manis, *A Fire You Can't Put Out.*

195   *Fred knew these kids*   Ibid.

196   *"one thousand kids"*   Connor papers, BPL, May 2, 1963, meeting.

196   *"There ain't gonna be no meeting"*   Ibid.

196   *Diane, was incarcerated now*   Ibid.

196   *The adults left the pews*   McWhorter, *Carry Me Home.*

196   *King spoke as well*   Connor papers, BPL, May 2, 1963, meeting.

196   *For every child arrested*   Houston, director, *Mighty Times.*

196   *"Some of us might have to spend"*   Connor papers, BPL, May 2, 1963, meeting.

28. Double D-Day

197   *1,500 kids not even bothering*   McWhorter, *Carry Me Home.*

197   *or, judging from subsequent accounts*   Houston, dir., *Mighty Times*; numerous BCRI oral histories.

197   *for aiding a child's truancy*   Houston, dir., *Mighty Times*; McWhorter, *Carry Me Home*; Gladwell, *David and Goliath.*

197   *only 887 of the city's 7,386 Black high school students*   Manis, *A Fire You Can't Put Out.*

197   *half full with knives*   McWhorter, *Carry Me Home.*

198   Not so much as a *peach pit*   Ibid.

198   *"We intend to negotiate from strength"*   Eskew, *But for Birmingham.*

198   *European camera crews*   Dan Rather, "Breakthrough in Birmingham," *Eyewitness*, CBS News, May 10, 1963, accessed October 25, 2022, https://youtu.be/JdX09TmhR2A.

198   *"We want promises, plus action"*   Eskew, *But for Birmingham*; Hailey, "Dogs and Hoses Repulse Negroes at Birmingham."

198   *"crowd control"*   McWhorter, *Carry Me Home.*

199   *One estimate later put it at three thousand people*   Houston, dir., *Mighty Times.*

199   *some of them parents of the kids*   Numerous BCRI oral histories.

199   *"Bull Connor had ordered the white army tanks"*   McKinstry, *While the World Watched.*

199   *who'd been at the church yesterday*   Houston, dir., *Mighty Times.*

199   *when she begged her parents to take her*   McKinstry, *While the World Watched.*

200   *"If you take part in the marches"*   Eskew, *But for Birmingham.*

200   *These children saw how police barricaded certain streets*   Ibid.; McWhorter, *Carry Me Home.*

200   *"We're going to walk, walk, walk"*   Eskew, *But for Birmingham.*

200   *Bull Connor stood in a suit and tie*   Houston, director, *Mighty Times.*

200   *Captain G. V. Evans*   Birmingham Police Department Badge List, Police Department Personnel Miscellaneous, found in the Birmingham Public Library, accessed October 25, 2022, https://bplonline.contentdm.oclc.org/digital/collection/p16044coll1/id/20071/.

200   *"Disperse!"*   McWhorter, *Carry Me Home.*

200   *"Or you're gonna get wet"*   Branch, *Parting the Waters.*

200   *Other firemen quickly mounted their hoses on massive metal tripods*   Ibid.; Houston, dir., *Mighty Times.*

200   *"fogging"*   Branch, *Parting the Waters*; McWhorter, *Carry Me Home.*

201   *"That water stung"*   Houston, dir., *Mighty Times.*

201   *They grabbed each other's hands for balance*   Ibid.

201   *"Blast them with that water!"*   McKinstry, *While the World Watched*.

201   *"Good Lord, I was scared to death"*   Houston, dir., *Mighty Times*; Richard Custer is the firefighter in question.

201   *turned the nozzles to full power*   McWhorter, *Carry Me Home*.

202   *"from automatic machine-gun fire"*   Ibid.

202   *back-flipped him*   Houston, dir., *Mighty Times*.

202   *knock bricks loose from mortar*   Branch, *Parting the Waters*.

202   *struck down some children at perhaps thirty feet*   Houston, dir., *Mighty Times*.

202   *it cartwheeled her through the park*   McWhorter, *Carry Me Home*.

202   *The water slid her perhaps fifty feet*   Houston, dir., *Mighty Times*.

202   *"We could hear the firemen yelling"*   Ibid.

202   *They threw whatever was near*   Ibid.; Branch, *Parting the Waters*; Michael S. Durham, *Powerful Days: The Civil Rights Photography of Charles Moore* (New York: Stewart, Tabori and Chang, 1991).

202   *footage showed victims bleeding from their temples*   Houston, dir., *Mighty Times*.

203   *Carolyn McKinstry being in this group*   McKinstry, *While the World Watched*.

203   *six German shepherds*   McWhorter, *Carry Me Home*.

203   *lunged at a small boy*   Houston, dir., *Mighty Times*. The next few passages come from the documentary as well.

203   *driving his car into the crowd*   Eskew, *But for Birmingham*; Branch, *Parting the Waters*.

204   *like the dog was* feasting *on the boy*   Gadsden image, *New York Times*, May 4, 1963, page A1.

204   *"I've never seen anything like this in my life"*   McWhorter, *Carry Me Home*.

204   *three years as a photographer in the* Marines   Durham, *Powerful Days*.

204   *"revolting"*   Ibid.

204   *blow dog whistles*   McWhorter, *Carry Me Home*.

204   *Equality*   Penn Warren interview of Walker, "Who Speaks for the Negro?"

204   *move back into the church*   McWhorter, *Carry Me Home*.

204   *Around this time a police inspector, William Haley*   Hailey, "Dogs and Hoses Repulse Negroes at Birmingham."

205   *"only too happy to accept the truce"*   Branch, *Parting the Waters*.

205   *sent a telegram demanding that the federal government intervene*   Ibid.

205   *lengthen the format of the nightly news itself*   Nichols, "Cities Are What Men Make Them."

205   *"No one had seen anything quite like it"*   McWhorter, *Carry Me Home*.

205   *"television's greatest hour"*   Ibid. Bayard Rustin said this.

205   *a "dark day" for the police force*   Connor papers, BPL, May 3, 1963, meeting.

205   *"one of the hardest things to accept"*   Barnett Wright and the *Birmingham News* Editorial Staff, *1963: How the Birmingham Civil Rights Movement Changed America and the World* (Birmingham: Birmingham News, 2012).

205   *"Don't worry about your children"*   Houston, dir., *Mighty Times*.

206   *at least three kids had been rushed to the hospital*   Hailey, "Dogs and Hoses Repulse Negroes at Birmingham."

206   *There had been two hundred more arrests*   Ibid.; Houston, dir., *Mighty Times*.

206   *"Your daughters and sons are in jail"*   Branch, *Parting the Waters*.

206   *"And dogs?"*   McWhorter, *Carry Me Home.*

206   *"Nonviolent direct action seeks to create"*   King, "Letter from Birmingham Jail."

29. The View from Washington

207   *"An injured, maimed, or dead child"*   UPI, "Robert Kennedy Warns of 'Increasing Turmoil,'" *New York Times,* May 4, 1963, accessed October 25, 2022, https://timesmachine.nytimes.com/timesmachine/1963/05/04/81808380.pdf.

207   *Bill Hudson had taken the photo*   AP, "Bill Hudson, a Photojournalist During the Civil Rights Era, Dies at 77," *New York Times,* June 26, 2010, accessed October 25, 2022, https://www.nytimes.com/2010/06/27/us/27hudson.html.

208   *The image made President Kennedy "sick"*   McWhorter, *Carry Me Home.*

208   *"embarrass our friends abroad"*   Martin Berger, *Seeing Through Race: A Reinterpretation of Civil Rights Photography* (Berkeley: University of California Press, 2012).

208   *"In this family we want winners"*   Schlesinger, *Robert Kennedy and His Times.*

208   *a rough field of play*   Ibid.

208   *"Neither Jack nor Bobby was accustomed to setbacks"*   Stein, *American Journey.*

208   *Jack had not given "much thought"*   Brauer, *John F. Kennedy and the Second Reconstruction.* Ted Sorensen is the aide.

209   *"punitive"*   Ibid. Kennedy said this in a 1956 paper.

209   *"no hell raiser or barnburner"*   Ibid.

209   *Bobby—the "Puritan":*   Schlesinger, *Robert Kennedy and His Times.*

209   *"high moral standards"*   Ibid.

209   *"I won't say I stayed awake nights"*   Ibid.

209   *"Robert Kennedy was not learned"*   Ibid.

209   *sent a voting rights bill to Congress*   Evan Thomas, *Robert Kennedy: His Life* (New York: Simon and Schuster, 2002).

209   *"I don't think we ever discussed [the legislation]"*   Ibid.

209   *the administration couldn't demand that the South desegregate*   Burke Marshall, *Federalism and Civil Rights* (New York: Columbia University Press, 1964).

209   *they'd get too many challenges*   Schlesinger, *Robert Kennedy and His Times.*

210   *Liberal Supreme Court justice Robert H. Jackson*   "Robert H. Jackson," *Encyclopaedia Britannica,* accessed October 25, 2022, https://www.britannica.com/biography/Robert-H-Jackson, the online entry last updated October 5, 2022.

210   *prosecuted cases at the Nuremberg trials*   "Nuremberg Trial, International Military Tribunal, 1945–1946," Robert H. Jackson Center, accessed October 25, 2022, https://www.roberthjackson.org/nuremberg-timeline/.

210   *and later warned Congress*   U.S. Congress Reports and Documents, 90th Congress, 2nd sess. (1968), nos. 1097–1177, page 222.

210   *where Marshall had worked antitrust cases*   Brauer, *John F. Kennedy and the Second Reconstruction.*

210   *almost every day of the last three years*   Burke Marshall oral history, interview by Anthony Lewis, JFK Library, June 20, 1964, accessed October 25, 2022, https://www.jfklibrary.org/sites/default/files/archives/JFKOH/Marshall%2C%20Burke/JFKOH-BM-05/JFKOH-BM-05-TR.pdf.

210   *how beleaguered he was*   Ibid.

210   We've got to do *something* here   Victor S. Navasky, *Kennedy Justice* (New York: Open Road Integrated Media, 1971).

210   *Formality wasn't his way*   Schlesinger   *Robert Kennedy and His Times.*

211   *they could send in the U.S. Army*   Stein, *American Journey.*

211   *He had thought about it not long after King's campaign*   Arthur M. Schlesinger Jr., *A Thousand Days: John F. Kennedy in the White House* (New York: Houghton Mifflin, 1965).

211   *Eisenhower sent one thousand troops*   Civil Rights Digital Library, "Little Rock Central High School Integration," University of Georgia Libraries, accessed October 25, 2022, http://crdl.usg.edu/events/little_rock_integration/?Welcome &Welcome.

211   *Marshall was on a plane to Birmingham*   Stein, *American Journey*; Burke Marshall oral history, JFK Library.

30. Burke Goes to Birmingham

212   *He was only vaguely familiar with King's demands*   Burke Marshall oral history, JFK Library; McWhorter, *Carry Me Home.*

212   *and yet no more than a dozen of those pages*   I reviewed Marshall's correspondence with RFK during the spring of 1963, JFK Library.

212   *"further training in the tenets of civil disobedience"*   Marshall's letter to Harris Wofford, May 1, 1963, JFK Library.

212   *the best path to a more equitable future*   Navasky, *Kennedy Justice.*

212   *An "enigmatic" hiring*   Brauer, *John F. Kennedy and the Second Reconstruction.*

213   *"You've got to treat people in accordance"*   "In Memoriam: Burke Marshall," *Yale Law Review*, June 2003, accessed October 25, 2022, https://ylr.law.yale.edu /pdfs/v51–1/Marshall.pdf.

213   *"so terribly nervous"*   Schlesinger, *Robert Kennedy and His Times.*

213   *Bobby Kennedy himself nearly rejected Marshall*   Brauer, *John F. Kennedy and the Second Reconstruction.*

213   *"I was reluctant to appoint [Wofford]"*   Schlesinger, *Robert Kennedy and His Times.*

213   *He settled in a motel*   Stein, *American Journey.*

213   *who would work with Marshall*   Foster Hailey, "U.S. Seeking a Truce in Birmingham," *New York Times*, May 5, 1963, accessed October 25, 2022, https: //timesmachine.nytimes.com/timesmachine/1963/05/05/103000214.pdf.

213   *"I said that we thought"*   Stein, *American Journey.*

213   *Marshall was in Birmingham*   Hailey, "U.S. Seeking a Truce in Birmingham."

214   *running from Kelly Ingram Park in their white slips*   McWhorter, *Carry Me Home.*

214   *King was not interested*   Branch, *Parting the Waters.*

214   *He then cuffed any Black person*   Ibid.

214   *the children laughing at what they'd pulled off*   McWhorter, *Carry Me Home.*

215   *"You don't like us but you like our Black pussy!"*   Ibid.

215   *saw at least two dozen bystanders*   Ibid.

215   *began to contact all parties*   Hailey, "U.S. Seeking a Truce in Birmingham."

215   *"Bobby Sox"*   Debbie Elliot, "Reverend Fred Shuttlesworth, Civil Rights Pioneer, Dies," *All Things Considered*, NPR, October 5, 2011, accessed October 25,

2022, https://www.npr.org/2011/10/05/141083711/rev-fred-shuttlesworth
-civil-rights-pioneer-dies.

216   *"Kennedy was . . . the source of trouble"*   Stein, *American Journey*.

31. How Not to Negotiate with the King

217   *"What are you after?"*   Burke Marshall oral history, JFK Library.
217   *"Martin was constantly amazed"*   Stein, *American Journey*, quoting Vincent Harding.
217   *They had paraphrased last night's mass meeting*   McWhorter, *Carry Me Home*.
217   *"I thought it was a bad sign"*   Ibid.
218   *"saved the day"* Ibid.
218   *"I believe that everyone understands"*   UPI, "Robert Kennedy Warns of 'Increasing Turmoil,'" *New York Times*, May 4, 1963, accessed October 25, 2022, https://timesmachine.nytimes.com/timesmachine/1963/05/04/81808380.pdf.
218   *"when our segregated social system"*   King, *Why We Can't Wait*.
218   *"I cannot condone"*   Hailey, "Dogs and Hoses Repulse Negroes at Birmingham."
218   *"Real men don't put their children"*   Gladwell, *David and Goliath*.
218   *"with their protective words"*   King, *Why We Can't Wait*.

32. And Lo, the Pharaoh Shall Weep

219   *"In a few days we will have everything"*   UPI, "Dr. King Confident," *New York Times*, May 6, 1963, accessed October 25, 2022, https://timesmachine.nytimes.com/timesmachine/1963/05/06/86705834.pdf.
219   *Baez said she'd give a free concert*   Foster Hailey, "Birmingham Talks Pushed; Negroes March Peacefully," *New York Times*, May 6, 1963, accessed October 25, 2022, https://timesmachine.nytimes.com/timesmachine/1963/05/06/86705834.pdf.
219   *turn their freedom songs into an album*   Branch, *Parting the Waters*, McWhorter, *Carry Me Home*.
219   *He had introduced "We Shall Overcome"*   McWhorter, *Carry Me Home*. Carawan introduced the song at a SNCC meeting.
220   *"taught us many of the songs"*   Connor papers, BPL, May 5, 1963, meeting.
220   *"Let's just walk"*   Ibid.
220   *the choir and backing band soared*   Branch, *Parting the Waters*.
220   *Walker "fumed"*   Ibid. Much of this exchange between Walker and Bevel comes from Branch, *Parting the Waters*, and McWhorter, *Carry Me Home*.
221   *"practically Walker's ward"*   Branch, *Parting the Waters*.
221   *New Pilgrim's co-pastor*   Barnett Wright, "KKK Savagely Beat Her Father Who Then Taught Her Lessons in Forgiveness," *Birmingham News*, April 26, 2013, https://www.al.com/spotnews/2013/04/kkk_savagely_beat_her_father_w.html.
221   *the Christmas Day bombing in 1956*   Manis, *A Fire You Can't Put Out*.
221   *almost all of tonight's marchers were adults*   McWhorter, *Carry Me Home*.
221   *He soon walked alongside Charles Billups*   Ibid.
221   *Billups, a diminutive movement man*   Wright, "KKK Savagely Beat Her Father Who Then Taught Her Lessons in Forgiveness." See, in particular, the photos of Billups from that piece.

222   *hoses on metal tripods*   McWhorter, *Carry Me Home*; Branch, *Parting the Waters*. The next two pages are primarily drawn from those books.

223   *Helene would be too traumatized*   Wright, "KKK Savagely Beat Her Father Who Then Taught Her Lessons in Forgiveness."

223   *"I felt sorry for them"*   McWhorter, *Carry Me Home*.

224   *"Turn on your water!"*   Ibid.

224   *"Let us proceed!"*   Branch, *Parting the Waters*.

224   *He walked around the line of resistance*   Hailey, "Birmingham Talks Pushed; Negroes March Peacefully."

224   *walking past and sometimes through*   McWhorter, *Carry Me Home*.

225   *Walker broke from the crowd*   Branch, *Parting the Waters*.

225   *an emergency request*   Ibid.

225   *"We're here to put out fires!"*   McWhorter, *Carry Me Home*.

225   *"spiritual intoxication"*   Ibid.

226   *The firemen had "frozen"*   Forman and Bond, *The Making of Black Revolutionaries*.

226   *"hand of God"*   McWhorter, *Carry Me Home*.

226   *"the pride and the* power *of nonviolence"*   Ibid.

226   *"one of the most fantastic events"*   Branch, *Parting the Waters*.

33. Marshall's Interpretation

227   *the phones were tapped*   Marshall oral history, JFK Library.

227   *"We had a series of meetings"*   Stein, *American Journey*.

228   *"I have a constant recollection"*   Ibid.

34. Unintended Outcomes

229   *even the sheriff's department said it looked like one*   McWhorter, *Carry Me Home*.

229   *Monday, May 6*   Claude Sitton, "Birmingham Jails 1,000 More Negroes," *New York Times*, May 7, 1963, accessed October 25, 2022, https://timesmachine.nytimes.com/timesmachine/1963/05/07/80710470.pdf.

229   *with over 4,000 arrests*   Houston, dir., *Mighty Times*.

229   *2,500 of them children*   McWhorter, *Carry Me Home*; Connor papers, BPL, May 6, 1963, meeting.

229   *a single bologna sandwich*   Houston, director, *Mighty Times*.

229   *"something that looked like grits"*   Oral history of Mary Street Parker, Birmingham Civil Rights Institute.

229   *those cattle yards that still stank of cattle*   Houston, dir., *Mighty Times*.

229   *Camera crews arrived*   Ibid.

230   *CBS later showed her*   Rather, "Breakthrough in Birmingham."

230   *tossing blankets or candy bars to their children*   Branch, *Parting the Waters*.

230   *quickened the pace of mediation*   Ibid.

35. "Martin, This Is It!"

231   *Now it was like a dream*   Manis, *A Fire You Can't Put Out.*
231   *the largest single-day total yet*   Sitton, "Birmingham Jails 1,000 More Negroes."
231   *At the front of the procession: Dick Gregory*   Branch, *Parting the Waters.*
231   *Barbara Deming*   Sitton, "Birmingham Jails 1,000 More Negroes."
231   *around 60 percent of the protesters jailed*   Ibid.
231   *It began at St. James*   Connor papers, BPL, May 6, 1963, meeting.
232   *A mass meeting held simultaneously at four churches*   Branch, *Parting the Waters.*
232   *some three hours after the meeting began*   Connor papers, May 6, 1963, meeting.
232   *"There are those who make history"*   Branch, *Parting the Waters.*
232   *Just a few more days*   Manis, *A Fire You Can't Put Out.*
232   *today's protest would be different*   Branch, *Parting the Waters.*
232   *Operation Confusion*   Manis, *A Fire You Can't Put Out.*
232   *Fifteen groups lined up*   Ibid.
233   *"A movement has a way of crescendoing"*   Fred Shuttlesworth oral history, BCRI.
233   *a little before noon*   Manis, *A Fire You Can't Put Out.*
233   *Fourteen children streamed out*   Branch, *Parting the Waters.*
233   *Shuttlesworth hurried outside just to witness*   Manis, *A Fire You Can't Put Out.*
234   *"square blocks of Negroes"*   King, *Why We Can't Wait.*
234   *saw a cop on a motorcycle overturn his bike*   Manis, *A Fire You Can't Put Out.*
234   Martin has to see this   Ibid.
234   *"Martin! This is it!"*   Ibid.
234   *"All we got to do"*   Ibid.

36. "Put Some Water on the Reverend"

235   *"a hero's introduction"*   Ibid.
235   *"You are as good a soldier"*   Ibid.
235   *Shuttlesworth and Bevel sent out two thousand more*   Ibid.
236   Striking them only sets us all back   McWhorter, *Carry Me Home.*
236   *flooring any Black people*   Branch, *Parting the Waters.*
236   *"Put some water on the Reverend"*   Manis, *A Fire You Can't Put Out.*
236   I'm going to die   Ibid.
236   *"Not here; not yet"*   Ibid.
236   *"I'm ready to march!"*   Ibid.

37. This Time, Something New

237   *"I wish they'd carried him away in a hearse"*   Claude Sitton, "Rioting Negroes Routed by Police in Birmingham," *New York Times*, May 8, 1963, accessed October 25, 2022, https://timesmachine.nytimes.com/timesmachine/1963/05/08/82061176.pdf.
237   *sending 250 Alabama state troopers*   Ibid.
237   *sometimes rocked side to side by onlookers*   McWhorter, *Carry Me Home.*
237   *This time the Blacks fought back*   Ibid.

237   *marauding with sawed-off shotguns*   Nichols, "Cities Are What Men Make Them."

238   *"Rioting Negroes"*   Sitton, "Rioting Negroes Routed by Police in Birmingham."

38. Wishful Thinking?

239   *"appeared to have little control"*   Ibid.

239   *and looked uneasy*   McWhorter, *Carry Me Home.*

239   *held once again at multiple locations*   Connor papers, BPL, May 7, 1963, meeting.

239   *"your president"*   McWhorter, *Carry Me Home.*

239   *"foot injury"*   Ibid.

239   *worried about Shuttlesworth's ribs and chest*   Shuttlesworth oral history, BCRI; Manis, *A Fire You Can't Put Out.*

239   *"Our movement is a nonviolent movement"*   Connor papers, May 7, 1963, meeting.

240   *"We don't need to throw rocks"*   Ibid.

39. The Seats at the Table

241   *twenty-eight people had been arrested*   Sitton, "Rioting Negroes Routed by Police in Birmingham."

241   *to incarcerate people at Legion Fields*   Eskew, *But for Birmingham.*

241   *the fifty-four-thousand-seat football stadium*   Wayne Drehs, "History Fades Away at Legion Field," ESPN, November 4, 2004, accessed October 25, 2022, https://www.espn.com/college-football/footballinamerica/news/story?id=1915891.

241   We cannot counter the protests anymore   Eskew, *But for Birmingham.*

241   *"act honorably in the situation"*   Ibid.

241   *Burke Marshall, watching it all*   Diane McWhorter, "Marshall's Law," *Legal Affairs,* September/October 2003, accessed October 25, 2022, https://www.legalaffairs.org/issues/September-October-2003/story_mcwhorter_sepoct03.msp.

242   *"not a damn fool"*   McWhorter, *Carry Me Home.*

242   *"ghost town"*   Branch, *Parting the Waters.*

242   *In the words of* Business Week   Burke Marshall papers, Box 1, file 11, June 1963 clip, JFK Library.

242   *he alone would sign it*   Eskew, *But for Birmingham*; David Vann oral history, BCRI Oral History Project, Birmingham Civil Rights Institute, accessed October 25, 2022, http://bcriohp.org/items/show/35.

242   *Educated at Morehouse, living in the tony*   John Drew oral history, Digital Collections, Birmingham Public Library, accessed October 25, 2022, https://bplonline.contentdm.oclc.org/digital/collection/p15099coll2/id/76/rec/50.

242   *only man in Alabama willing to insure*   McWhorter, *Carry Me Home.*

243   *Black Birminghamians A. G. Gaston*   Branch, *Parting the Waters.*

243   *Lucius Pitts, the president of Miles College*   "Lucius Pitts, Educator, Is Dead," *New York Times,* February 27, 1974, accessed October 25, 2022, https://www.nytimes.com/1974/02/27/archives/lucius-pitts-educator-is-dead-president-of-paine-college-59.html.

243   *"We're over the hump!"*   Branch, *Parting the Waters.*

243   *They'd written them out*   Garrow, *Bearing the Cross*; Eskew, *But for Birmingham.*

244   *the white negotiators agreed to upgrade*   Garrow, *Bearing the Cross.*

244   *would need to include Martin Luther King Jr.*   Branch, *Parting the Waters.*

244   *called Martin by his birth name, Mike*   McWhorter, *Carry Me Home.*

244   *Deenie Drew would even make cocktails and sandwiches*   Ibid.

244   *The remaining whites*   Ibid.

244   *approached it through an alley*   John Drew oral history, BPL.

244   *Fred Shuttlesworth's friends and local activists*   McWhorter, *Carry Me Home.* Many present that night were members of Shuttlesworth's ACMHR.

244   *"sweeping the porch clean of groupies"*   McWhorter, *Carry Me Home.*

244   *the white contingent wouldn't budge*   Garrow, *Bearing the Cross.*

245   *the whites wanted it to occur after sixty days*   Branch, *Parting the Waters.*

245   *"How could a settlement be announced"*   David Vann full interview, *Eyes on the Prize* documentary series, Blackside Inc. (*American Experience*, PBS, 1987). The full Vann interview is now housed in the Washington University at St. Louis Libraries, accessed October 25, 2022, http://digital.wustl.edu/eyesontheprize /browse.html#a1.

245   *he fell to the floor that night and cried*   James T. Montgomery oral history, Digital Collections, Birmingham Public Library, accessed October 25, 2022, https://bplonline.contentdm.oclc.org/digital/collection/p15099coll2/id/58 /rec/47.

245   *whichever came first*   Branch, *Parting the Waters.*

245   *"That's all they want?"*   McWhorter, *Carry Me Home.*

245   *"In part he was just trying to accomplish something"*   Burke Marshall Oral History, JFK Library.

246   *"But I do not think that [King] wanted"*   Ibid.

246   *"He wanted it for himself"*   Ibid.

246   *"lies on its deathbed"*   King, *Why We Can't Wait.*

247   *At 4:00 a.m.*   Branch, *Parting the Waters.*

40. The Betrayal

248   *It was trepidation*   Manis, *A Fire You Can't Put Out.*

248   *"mild delirium"*   Ibid.

248   *three hypos of sedatives*   Branch, *Parting the Waters.*

248   *recommended Fred return to the Gaston*   Manis, *A Fire You Can't Put Out.*

249   *"Fred wanted to be sure that you recognized Fred Shuttlesworth"*   John J. Drew oral history, BPL.

249   *"His quest for the limelight . . . annoyed me"*   Ibid.

249   *John and Deenie were Methodists*   Ibid.

249   *raised outside Philadelphia*   "Obituary of Addine D. Drew," Digital Collections, Birmingham Public Library, accessed October 25, 2022, https://bplonline .contentdm.oclc.org/digital/collection/p15099coll5/id/84.

249   *so light-skinned she'd gone on a spying mission*   McWhorter, *Carry Me Home.*

249   *Deenie had her voter registration drives*   "Obituary of Addine D. Drew," BPL.

249   *John's porch light was always on*   John J. Drew oral history, BPL.

249   *"He had no patience with the wealthy segments"*   Nichols, "Cities Are What Men Make Them."

249   *"They thought Fred was a country preacher"*   Walker oral history, BPL.

250   *King did not walk out to greet them*   Manis, *A Fire You Can't Put Out.*

250   *Ruby helped Fred out of his seat*   Ibid.

250   *"Martin, why did I have to"*   Ibid.

250   *Fred wondered if the morning's sedatives*   McWhorter, *Carry Me Home.*

250   *"Who's we?"*   Garrow, *Bearing the Cross*; Eskew, *But for Birmingham.*

250   *"The merchants say they can't negotiate"*   Manis, *A Fire You Can't Put Out.*

251   *"Well, Martin, it's hard for me"*   McWhorter, *Carry Me Home.*

251   *"The merchants have been negotiating [for weeks]"*   Manis, *A Fire You Can't Put Out.*

251   *"We're not callin' anything off"*   Garrow, *Bearing the Cross.*

251   *"I've been here"*   Manis, *A Fire You Can't Put Out.* The rest of the dialogue in this sequence is drawn from Manis's book.

41. The Unraveling

253   *"They're gonna agree to your demands"*   Ibid.

253   *what King did not*   Branch, *Parting the Waters.* The Kennedys' negotiating efforts remained private.

253   *"very conservative men"*   Burke Marshall oral history, JFK Library.

253   *"And the president also saw to it"*   Ibid.

253   *Norton not only agreed to settle*   McWhorter, *Carry Me Home.*

253   *who had said in a CBS documentary*   CBS News, "Who Speaks for Birmingham?," *CBS Reports*, May 18, 1961. I found this transcript in the Birmingham Public Library.

254   *Kennedy cabinet members wooed and pressured him*   McWhorter, *Carry Me Home.*

254   *"that if we could get the substantial white citizens"*   Kennedy White House tape No. 88–6, as recorded on May 21, 1963, JFK Library.

254   *They even refused to acknowledge phoning*   Branch, *Parting the Waters.*

254   *Bobby was phoning King all the time*   McWhorter, *Carry Me Home.*

254   *created a curious side effect*   Burke Marshall oral history, JFK Library.

254   *"You have no way out"*   McWhorter, *Carry Me Home.*

254   *"Don't worry, Fred"*   Manis, *A Fire You Can't Put Out.*

255   *a one-day moratorium*   Ibid.

255   *"I'm gratified to note the progress"*   Branch, *Parting the Waters.*

255   *Shuttlesworth needed to be placated*   Burke Marshall oral history, JFK Library.

255   *"Don't give me none of that 'Reverend' shit"*   McWhorter, *Carry Me Home.*

255   *Fred worried about truce talks*   Manis, *A Fire You Can't Put Out.*

255   *Bull Connor ordered the signs back up*   Eskew, *But for Birmingham.*

255   *White people couldn't be trusted*   McWhorter, *Carry Me Home.* Shuttlesworth said, "We can't end this movement until Birmingham is freed."

255   *There Brown not only found the SCLC's protesters*   Manis, *A Fire You Can't Put Out*; Claude Sitton, "Hurdles Remain," *New York Times*, May 9, 1963, accessed October 25, 2022, https://timesmachine.nytimes.com/timesmachine/1963/05/09/82064652.pdf.

256   *"They haven't talked to Bull Connor"*   Sitton, "Hurdles Remain."

256   *He wanted to march that afternoon*   Fred Shuttlesworth oral history, BCRI.

256   *"pull out all the stops"*   Manis, *A Fire You Can't Put Out.*

42. The Younger Brother's Complex

257   *deeper into room 30*   McWhorter, *Carry Me Home.*

257   *his "marching shoes"*   Manis, *A Fire You Can't Put Out.*

257   *Young had to restrain him from leaving*   McWhorter, *Carry Me Home.*

257   *"Fred's sort of gone off the deep end"*   Ibid.

257   *"The attorney general would like to speak with you"*   Manis, *A Fire You Can't Put Out.*

258   *Neither Bobby nor Fred would talk about it afterward*   McWhorter, *Carry Me Home.*

258   *"I have a long distance call from Bob"*   Eskew, *But for Birmingham.*

258   *Both men were overachievers*   Schlesinger, *Robert Kennedy and His Times.* Schlesinger writes that Bobby was the family's "over-achiever"; Matt Schudel, "Fred L. Shuttlesworth, Courageous Civil Rights Fighter, Dies at 89," *Washington Post*, October 5, 2011, accessed October 25, 2022, https://www .washingtonpost.com/local/obituaries/fred-l-shuttlesworth-courageous-civil -rights-fighter-dies-at-89/2011/10/05/gIQAO73lOL_story.html. Note, in particular, the idea that Shuttlesworth filed more suits that reached the Supreme Court than any other person in American history.

259   *"Plans are being made"*   McWhorter, *Carry Me Home.*

259   *"does not destroy our faith"*   Ibid.

43. "What I'm About to Tell You Will Not Be Repeated"

260   *From jail King had leverage*   Belafonte, *My Song.* Belafonte went so far as to say that if he raised the money for King's release, King wouldn't go.

260   *Immediately rumors started*   Ibid.

260   *"More militant splinter groups of the Movement"*   Jenkins and Gardner Hines, *Black Titan.*

261   *"The President said that there were no federal statutes"*   Branch, *Parting the Waters.*

261   *bail out the eight hundred kids*   Hedrick Smith, "A Dozen Men Hammered Out Birmingham Agreement in Home of Negro Executive," *New York Times*, May 11, 1963, accessed October 25, 2022, https://timesmachine.nytimes.com /timesmachine/1963/05/11/139951692.pdf.

261   *"I'm in an extremely vulnerable position"*   Belafonte, *My Song.*

261   *"I told him this"*   Ibid.

261   *new negotiations started at the Drews' house*   McWhorter, *Carry Me Home.*

262   *$60 million in ransom*   Branch, *Parting the Waters.*

262   *"What I'm about to tell you will not be repeated"*   Belafonte, *My Song.*

262   *Quill served as the head of the Transit Workers Union*   Brian Hanley, "'A Man the Ages Will Remember,' Mike Quill, the TWU, and Civil Rights," *History Ireland*, Winter 2004, accessed October 25, 2022, https://www.historyireland .com/a-man-the-ages-will-remember-mike-quill-the-twu-and-civil-rights/;

"Michael J. Quill: Fearless Father of the TWU," YouTube, posted by Transit Workers Union Local 100, March 18, 2010, https://www.youtube.com/watch?v=yNVPSIm7vR0.

262   *to pony up $160,000*   McWhorter, *Carry Me Home.*

262   *"hoodlums"*   Alexander M. Bickel, "Robert F Kennedy: The Case Against Him for Attorney General," *New Republic*, January 9, 1961, accessed October 25, 2022, https://newrepublic.com/article/142063/robert-f-kennedy-case-attorney-general. RFK was going after such "hoodlum" union members as far back as 1958.

262   *and sometimes prosecuted*   Anthony Lewis, "Kennedy's Role as Attorney General," *New York Times*, September 4, 1964, accessed October 25, 2022, https://timesmachine.nytimes.com/timesmachine/1964/09/04/118536485.pdf.

262   *and learned Bobby was calling*   Belafonte, *My Song.*

262   *"I did check with Martin"*   Ibid.

263   *Inside was $50,000 in cash*   Branch, *Parting the Waters.*

263   *"to secure the protesters' liberation"*   Jenkins and Gardner Hines, *Black Titan.*

263   *would ultimately write at length*   King, *Why We Can't Wait.*

44. Wrestling with Its Conscience

264   *Andy Young, who sat at the negotiating table*   Branch, *Parting the Waters.*

264   *still "bitterly angry"*   Abernathy, *And the Walls Came Tumbling Down.*

264   *nineteen Jewish leaders*   Eskew, *But for Birmingham*. The *New York Times* had the figure at twenty.

264   *from New Jersey walked in*   Irving Spiegel, "20 Rabbis Head for Birmingham," *New York Times*, May 8, 1963, accessed October 25, 2022, https://timesmachine.nytimes.com/timesmachine/1963/05/08/82061680.pdf.

264   *comparing Bull Connor to the Stasi in East Berlin*   Connor papers, BPL, May 9, 1963, meeting.

264   *a hymn in Hebrew*   Eskew, *But for Birmingham.*

264   *King got at most two hours a night now*   Garrow, *Bearing the Cross*. King ultimately told his congregation at Ebenezer Baptist how little sleep he was getting.

264   *"the time of our greatest stress"*   Nunnelley, *Bull Connor.*

265   *they looked exhausted*   Rather, "Breakthrough in Birmingham."

265   *It was Shuttlesworth, not King, whom Walker praised*   McWhorter, *Carry Me Home.*

265   *who cleared his throat to speak first*   Rather, "Breakthrough in Birmingham."

265   *"The city of Birmingham has reached an accord with its conscience"*   "Negro Leaders' Statements of Birmingham Accord," *New York Times*, May 11, 1963, accessed October 25, 2022, https://timesmachine.nytimes.com/timesmachine/1963/05/11/139951632.pdf.

265   *thick glasses perched on his nose*   Rather, "Breakthrough in Birmingham."

265   *"Birmingham may well offer"*   "Negro Leaders' Statements of Birmingham Accord."

265   *He then discussed the truce's terms*   Ibid.

265   *"We have come today to the climax"*   Ibid.

266   *"They are dealing in good faith"*   Manis, *A Fire You Can't Put Out.*

266   *"Gentlemen, I hope you'll excuse me"*   Ibid.

266   *"complete physical and mental exhaustion"*   Ibid.

267   *even after today's truce, remained segregated*   Ibid.

267   *It was not the total win*   Claude Sitton, "Birmingham Talks Reach an Accord on Ending Crisis," *New York Times*, May 10, 1963, accessed October 25, 2022, https://timesmachine.nytimes.com/timesmachine/1963/05/10/82066657.pdf.

267   *it'd taken another call from Bobby Kennedy*   McWhorter, *Carry Me Home.*

267   *"The alternative to discussion"*   Anthony Lewis, "Accord Pleases Robert Kennedy," *New York Times*, May 11, 1963, accessed October 25, 2022, https://timesmachine.nytimes.com/timesmachine/1963/05/11/139950692.pdf.

267   *"For a city like Birmingham"*   Ibid.

267   *refused Ralph Abernathy entry*   Manis, *A Fire You Can't Put Out.*

267   *One of them was Rev. Herb Oliver*   "Rev. C. Herbert Oliver, Civil Rights Activist, Dies at 96," Associated Press, December 11, 2021, accessed October 25, 2022, https://www.al.com/news/2021/12/rev-c-herbert-oliver-civil-rights-activist-dies-at-96.html.

267   *"I tried to do a good job"*   McWhorter, *Carry Me Home.*

268   *"Tonight is victory night!"*   Connor papers, BPL, May 11, 1963, meeting.

268   *The crowd chanted "yes" over and over*   Branch, *Parting the Waters.*

268   *"deafening"*   Ibid.

269   *"It should make us all feel very happy!"*   Ibid.; Connor papers, BPL, May 11, 1963, meeting.

45. "This Whole Town Has Gone Berserk"

273   *"I'm unwilling to make decisions virtually at gunpoint"*   Sitton, "Birmingham Talks Reach an Accord on Ending Crisis."

273   *avoided a "holocaust"*   McWhorter, *Carry Me Home.*

273   *"I call them a bunch of quisling, gutless traitors!"*   Eskew, *But for Birmingham*; Art Hanes, the outgoing mayor, is the one being quoted.

274   *"non-official" white businessmen*   "What Truce?," editorial, *Birmingham News*, May 11, 1963.

274   *"If this self-appointed committee"*   "Blacks and Whites Together," *Birmingham: Testament of Nonviolence*, Radio Riverside, WRVR, June 18, 1963, a six-part radio docuseries housed today in the American Archive of Public Broadcasting, accessed October 25, 2022, https://americanarchive.org/catalog/cpb-aacip-500-pc2t8j5v.

274   *"didn't gain a thing"*   McWhorter, *Carry Me Home.*

274   *"The Klan is meeting today"*   Ibid.

274   *an open field that Saturday night in Bessemer*   Ibid.

274   *fifteen miles southwest of Birmingham*   Google Maps.

274   *thousands of racist*   "The Klan, Two Bombs, and a Riot," *Birmingham: Testament of Nonviolence*, Radio Riverside, WRVR, June 4, 1963, accessed October 25, 2022, https://americanarchive.org/catalog/cpb-aacip-528-7s7hq3t16s.

274   *flatbed truck atop which the night's speakers paced*   McWhorter, *Carry Me Home.*

274   *they thanked Bull Connor, Governor Wallace*   "The Klan, Two Bombs, and a Riot," *Birmingham: Testament of Nonviolence.*

274   *They later wrote notes of the meeting*   McWhorter, *Carry Me Home.*

274   *an "integrated" future that would produce "mongrel" children*   "The Klan, Two Bombs, and a Riot," *Birmingham: Testament of Nonviolence.*

274   *"We are facing the greatest darkness"*   Ibid.

275   *Around 10:45 that Saturday night*   Ibid. The sourcing here is A. D. King's own testimony, which begins around the twelve-minute mark of the episode.

275   *car 49*   McWhorter, *Carry Me Home.*

275   *"son of a bitch"*   Ibid.

275   *One blew an opening three feet deep and five feet in diameter*   Birmingham Fire Department Report, May 11, 1963, as found in the Birmingham Public Library, file 1125.6.46.

275   *though the blasts destroyed 80 percent of their home*   "The Klan, Two Bombs, and a Riot," *Birmingham: Testament of Nonviolence.*

275   *He kept thinking there were more bombs*   Birmingham Fire Department Report, May 11, 1963.

275   *Roughly an hour later*   Ibid.

275   *A.D. and the authorities heard a thunderous crack*   Branch, *Parting the Waters.*

275   *A.D. thought his own church had been bombed*   Birmingham Fire Department Report, May 11, 1963.

275   *had placed a bomb in the Gaston's reception area*   Branch, *Parting the Waters.*

275   *knocked down the water and electrical lines*   Birmingham Fire Department Report, May 11, 1963.

275   *damaged cars and homes some three blocks away*   Ibid.

276   *It injured four people*   Branch, *Parting the Waters.*

276   *one fatally*   McWhorter, *Carry Me Home.*

276   *Martin had flown back to Atlanta hours earlier*   Ibid.

276   *perhaps two thousand people*   Ibid.; Branch, *Parting the Waters*; Birmingham Fire and Police Department Report, May 11, 1963.

276   *"You'd better get those dogs out of here!"*   Claude Sitton, "50 Hurt in Negro Rioting After Birmingham Blast," *New York Times*, May 13, 1963, accessed October 25, 2022, https://timesmachine.nytimes.com/timesmachine/1963/05/13/90552582.pdf.

276   *Wyatt Walker arrived from A. D. King's house*   McWhorter, *Carry Me Home.*

276   *"Please do not throw any of the bricks"*   Sitton, "50 Hurt in Negro Rioting After Birmingham Blast."

276   *and tried to break up fights*   Branch, *Parting the Waters.*

276   *and set it on fire*   Sitton, "50 Hurt in Negro Rioting After Birmingham Blast."

277   *"Let's go get Bull Connor's house!"*   The quotes here and in the immediately following paragraphs, as well as the action of this sequence, can be found ibid.; McWhorter, *Carry Me Home*; "The Klan, Two Bombs, and a Riot," *Birmingham: Testament of Nonviolence.*

277   *"Let the whole fucking city burn!"*   Thomas, *Robert Kennedy: His Life.*

277   *"Our home was just bombed"*   "The Klan, Two Bombs, and a Riot," *Birmingham: Testament of Nonviolence.*

277   *remained "righteous" and "nonviolent"*   Hedrick Smith, "Bombs Touch Off Widespread Riot at Birmingham," *New York Times*, May 12, 1963, accessed Oc-

tober 25, 2022, https://timesmachine.nytimes.com/timesmachine/1963/05/12/132914892.pdf.

277   *"This whole town has gone berserk"*   McWhorter, *Carry Me Home.*

46. Shaping the Postscript

278   *That Sunday morning he talked*   Garrow, *Bearing the Cross.*

278   *The headlines from there*   Smith, "Bombs Touch Off Widespread Riot at Birmingham."

278   *Black people were to blame for the riot*   White House recorded meeting, JFKPOF-MTG-086–002, May 12, 1963, JFK Library. What's obvious from this recording is that Burke Marshall had been in touch with King throughout the day.

278   *"The people who've gotten out of hand"*   Ibid. I use the words "between calls" because Marshall reports what King has told him so far, then Bobby issues that quote, then Marshall calls King again and reports back what he's hearing.

278   *with a sawed-off shotgun*   Raines, *My Soul Is Rested.*

278   *rifle-butted Wyatt Walker's wife in the face*   Branch, *Parting the Waters.*

279   *"You're damn right it'll kill somebody"*   Eskew, *But for Birmingham.*

279   *The beatings continued*   Branch, *Parting the Waters*; McWhorter, *Carry Me Home.*

279   *the heavy* thonk   Sitton, "50 Hurt in Negro Rioting After Birmingham Blast."

279   *"My brother described the terror"*   Haley, "Martin Luther King—The *Playboy* Interview."

279   *"Tears came to my eyes"*   Ibid.

279   *when he landed in Birmingham Sunday afternoon*   White House recorded meeting, JFKPOF-MTG-086–002, May 12, 1963. We know it's Sunday afternoon because it's late afternoon when the meeting takes place and Burke says King has just gotten to Birmingham when he calls him during the meeting.

279   *Street after charred street*   Branch, *Parting the Waters.*

279   *sealed off a twenty-eight-block area*   Sitton, "50 Hurt in Negro Rioting After Birmingham Blast."

279   *"The nigger King ought to be investigated"*   Ibid.

279   *quarantined overnight without food or water*   McWhorter, *Carry Me Home.*

280   *"We must not use second-class methods"*   Connor papers, BPL, May 12, 1963, meeting.

280   *"You know when the Lord is with you"*   "The Klan, Two Bombs, and a Riot," *Birmingham: Testament of Nonviolence.* The rest of this section comes from the audio of that radio docuseries.

280   *King stopped in bars and pool halls*   The sentiment and facts from this sequence come from Garrow, *Bearing the Cross*; Branch, *Parting the Waters*; McWhorter, *Carry Me Home.*

281   *"were trying to sabotage all that we"*   Philip Benjamin, "Dr. King Visits Pool Halls in Campaign to Restrain Negros from Resuming Riots," *New York Times*, May 14, 1963, accessed October 25, 2022, https://timesmachine.nytimes.com/timesmachine/1963/05/14/90556714.pdf.

281   *"Bull Connor is happy when we use force"*   Garrow, *Bearing the Cross.*

281   *"we must not stab anybody"*   Benjamin, "Dr. King Visits Pool Halls in Campaign to Restrain Negros from Resuming Riots."

281   *"We are not going to have no band"*   Ibid.

282   *The press captured all of this, too*   Ibid.

282   *"We are not going to allow this conflict"*   McWhorter, *Carry Me Home*.

282   *"they may try to bomb a little more"*   "The Klan, Two Bombs, and a Riot," *Birmingham: Testament of Nonviolence*.

282   *with Walker present tonight*   McWhorter, *Carry Me Home*.

282   *"I will never teach any of you"*   "The Klan, Two Bombs, and a Riot," *Birmingham: Testament of Nonviolence*.

282   *under pressure from President Kennedy*   Brauer, *John F. Kennedy and the Second Reconstruction*; White House recorded meeting, JFKPOF-MTG-086–002, May 12, 1963.

282   *would agree to release the names*   Claude Sitton, "Birmingham Pact Picks Up Support," *New York Times*, May 16, 1963, accessed October 25, 2022, https://timesmachine.nytimes.com/timesmachine/1963/05/16/84796076.pdf.

47. Considering the Impossible

284   *Suddenly there were sit-ins in Greensboro*   McWhorter, *Carry Me Home*.

284   *Black people would not listen to the cops*   Thomas, *Robert Kennedy: His Life*.

284   *"I don't think you realize down here"*   McWhorter, *Carry Me Home*.

285   *Massive protests were planned for Robinson's New York*   Ibid.

285   *"Events in Birmingham in the last few days"*   Louis Martin to the Attorney General, WHSF, 365a, JFK Library.

285   *the deputy chairman of the Democratic National Committee*   Neil A. Lewis, "Louis E. Martin, 84, Aide to 3 Democratic Presidents," *New York Times*, January 30, 1997, accessed October 25, 2022, https://www.nytimes.com/1997/01/30/us/louis-e-martin-84-aide-to-3-democratic-presidents.html.

285   *"My own judgment, the judgment of the Attorney General"*   Marshall oral history, JFK Library.

285   *Many advisors in the White House still opposed*   Ibid.

285   *"intellectual blood bank"*   Susan Donaldson James, "Passing the Torch: Kennedy's Touch on Obama's Words," ABC News, February 8, 2008, accessed October 25, 2022, https://abcnews.go.com/Politics/Vote2008/story?id=4259093&page=1.

285   *A civil rights bill would tie up Congress*   Marshall oral history, JFK Library.

286   *4.5 million white voters*   Schlesinger, *A Thousand Days*.

286   *758 civil rights demonstrations in 186 cities*   Thomas, *Robert Kennedy*.

286   *to fly to North Carolina with him*   Marshall oral history, JFK Library.

286   *Once the Air Force plane took off*   McWhorter, *Carry Me Home*.

286   *"the heart of the matter"*   Thomas, *Robert Kennedy*.

286   *"Something that didn't deal with pieces of the problem"*   Marshall oral history, JFK Library.

286   *"The most difficult question"*   Ibid.

286   *"I want our Bill of Rights implemented in fact"*   "Harry S. Truman and Civil Rights," Harry S. Truman National Historic Site, accessed October 25, 2022, https://www.nps.gov/articles/000/harry-s-truman-and-civil-rights.htm.

286   *He had to sign an executive order*   Ibid.

286   *Jacob Javits*   Jacob K. Javits papers, Martin Luther King Jr. Research and Education Institute, Stanford University, accessed October 25, 2022, https://kinginstitute.stanford.edu/king-papers/documents/jacob-k-javits.

286   *Hubert Humphrey*   "Hubert Humphrey: A Featured Biography," United States Senate, accessed October 25, 2022, https://www.senate.gov/senators/FeaturedBios/Featured_Bio_HumphreyHubert.htm.

286   *Javits's in 1960 lost*   Jacob K. Javits papers, Martin Luther King Jr. Research and Education Institute, Stanford University.

287   *Paul Douglas*   "Senator Paul Douglas," biography, United States Senate, accessed October 25, 2022, https://www.senate.gov/artandhistory/history/common/image/DouglasPaul.htm.

287   *Lyndon Johnson's parliamentary maneuvering*   Robert Caro, *Master of the Senate: The Years of Lyndon Johnson* (New York: Vintage, 2003).

287   *"stirred the feelings of every Negro in the country"*   Marshall oral history, JFK Library.

287   *an outline of the legislation on his desk*   McWhorter, *Carry Me Home.*

287   *What it promised was*   Kent B. Germany, "Inside the Kennedy White House 1963," Miller Center, University of Virginia, accessed October 25, 2022, https://prde.upress.virginia.edu/content/JFK_CivilRights1963.

287   *"Get them out of here"*   Thomas, *Robert Kennedy.*

288   *by the latter half of May, it seemed necessary*   Marshall oral history, JFK Library.

288   *Many newspapers in Europe and Asia*   Eskew, *But for Birmingham.*

288   *"If the United States wishes to maintain the respect"*   Ibid.

288   *"Monstrous Crimes Among Racists in the United States"*   Branch, *Parting the Waters.*

288   *who'd served Brooklyn for forty years*   "Celler, Emanuel," biography, United States House of Representatives, accessed October 25, 2022, https://history.house.gov/People/Detail/10788.

288   *"There is ample basis for federal intervention"*   Eskew, *But for Birmingham.*

288   *making civil rights the focal point of his agenda*   Brauer, *John F. Kennedy and the Second Reconstruction.*

48. The Gathering at 24 Central Park South

289   *had just published a searing book*   James Baldwin, *The Fire Next Time* (New York: Dial Press, 1963).

289   *"He'd like to meet with a group of us"*   Belafonte, *My Song.*

290   *"Perhaps the Kennedys were trying to ease us"*   Ibid.

290   *the apartment in New York that Bobby's father, Joe, owned*   McWhorter, *Carry Me Home.*

290   *24 Central Park South*   Schlesinger, *Robert Kennedy and His Times.* This book carried the address of the apartment.

290   *served hors d'oeuvres and a light buffet*   Belafonte, *My Song.*

290   *a Kennedy press aide, Ed Guthman*   Branch, *Parting the Waters.*

290   *"nauseous"*   Stein, *American Journey.*

290   *Bobby snickered, insulted*   McWhorter, *Carry Me Home.*

290   *Bobby turned away from Smith*   Stein, *American Journey*; James Baldwin is describing the action here.

291   *Smith had been on the Freedom Rides in 1961*   Branch, *Parting the Waters*.

291   *Smith was in New York for medical treatment*   McWhorter, *Carry Me Home*.

291   *after the Birmingham campaign*   Stein, *American Journey*; Baldwin said Smith had been in Project C.

291   *"You've got a great many very accomplished people"*   Ibid.

291   *"For [Bobby] it was a political matter"*   Ibid.

291   *"Never! Never! Never!"*   Ibid.

291   *"How can you say that?"*   Belafonte, *My Song*.

291   *Such beliefs were treasonous*   Schlesinger, *Robert Kennedy and His Times*.

292   *"communicated the plain, basic suffering"*   Ibid.

292   *"If you can't understand what this young man"*   Ibid.

292   *"My family has been here"*   Ibid.

292   *"very ugly"*   Stein, *American Journey*.

292   *"one of the most violent, emotional verbal assaults"*   Ibid.; Schlesinger, *Robert Kennedy and His Times*. Kenneth Clark is the one being quoted.

292   *He just sat there, the tension building*   Schlesinger, *Robert Kennedy and His Times*.

292   *"I had never seen him so shaken"*   Belafonte, *My Song*.

293   *She walked out of the meeting*   Stein, *American Journey*.

293   *"the laughter of desperation"*   McWhorter, *Carry Me Home*. Kenneth Clark is again the one being quoted.

293   *He thought he might calm Bobby down*   Branch, *Parting the Waters*.

293   *"You may think you're doing enough"*   Belafonte, *My Song*.

293   They don't know what the laws are   Schlesinger, *Robert Kennedy and His Times*.

293   *"They seemed possessed"*   Ibid.

49. God's Beneficence

294   *Harry Belafonte's phone rang*   Belafonte, *My Song*.

294   *on page one under the headline*   Layhmond Robinson, "Robert Kennedy Fails to Sway Negroes at Secret Talks Here," *New York Times*, May 26, 1963, accessed October 25, 2022, https://timesmachine.nytimes.com/timesmachine/1963/05/26/356801012.pdf.

294   *"sick feeling"*   Belafonte, *My Song*.

294   *Belafonte's phone rang again*   Ibid.

295   *"Maybe it's just what Bobby needed to hear"*   Ibid.

295   *"if the President keeps dawdling"*   Ibid.

295   *dethroned on the same day*   Claude Sitton, "Boutwell Seated in Birmingham; Peace Hopes Rise," *New York Times*, May 24, 1963, accessed October 25, 2022, https://timesmachine.nytimes.com/timesmachine/1963/05/24/90537112.pdf.

295   *been mobbed at the airport*   Branch, *Parting the Waters*.

295   *It had taken bodyguards*   McWhorter, *Carry Me Home*.

295   *as many white people in attendance as Blacks*   Branch, *Parting the Waters*.

296   *"I've never seen such an aroused response!"*   Ibid.

296   *"shrieking like a wolf whistle"*   Ibid.

296   *one hundred arrested in Albany*   Ibid.

296   *"The president must be ready to take a stand"*   Garrow, *Bearing the Cross*. This quote appears in n. 38 of the Birmingham chapter of Garrow's book.

50. The Brother's Message

297   *ultimately stretching to 1,884 pages*   Gene Seymour, "The Evidence of Things Not Seen," *Book Forum*, June/July/August 2017, accessed October 25, 2022, https://www.bookforum.com/print/2402/a-new-book-digs-into-the-fbi-s-extensive-investigation-of-james-baldwin-17976.

297   *"He is a nice fellow"*   Thomas, *Robert Kennedy*.

297   *"worried" about Bobby's "rage"*   Ibid.

297   *"Bobby expected to be made an honorary black"*   Ibid.

297   *questioned any situation by questioning his own actions*   Schlesinger, *Robert Kennedy and His Times*.

298   *"there wasn't a problem that the kids had"*   Ibid.

298   *he actually sympathized with Baldwin*   Thomas, *Robert Kennedy*.

298   *"I guess if I were in [Smith's] shoes"*   Edwin O. Guthman, *We Band of Brothers* (New York: Harper and Row, 1971).

298   *"talk about how he'd feel"*   Thomas, *Robert Kennedy*.

298   *"The United States is dominated by white people"*   Schlesinger, *Robert Kennedy and His Times*. Bobby's remarks were to the Senate Commerce committee on July 1, 1963.

298   *"warpath"*   Schlesinger, *Robert Kennedy and His Times*. Schlesinger himself said this.

298   *educators, lawyers, businesspeople, church people*   Stein, *American Journey*. Burke Marshall is recounting this.

299   *He appeared on May 29*   Schlesinger, *Robert Kennedy and His Times*.

299   *"He was furious"*   Ibid.

299   *Bobby had felt invisible*   Ibid.

299   *"The more he saw"*   Ibid.

300   Everyone *in Jack's cabinet was still against a bill*   Ibid.

300   *"He had a way of saying it"*   Thomas, *Robert Kennedy*.

300   *a White House recording from May 20*   Audio recording, JFKPOF-MTG-088, May 20, 1963, JFK Library, accessed October 25, 2022, https://www.jfklibrary.org/asset-viewer/archives/JFKPOF/MTG/JFKPOF-MTG-088/JFKPOF-MTG-088; Thomas, *Robert Kennedy*.

300   *He staged meetings at the White House*   Stein, *American Journey*.

300   *"I don't think there was anyone in the Cabinet"*   Schlesinger, *Robert Kennedy and His Times*.

300   *"He has not furnished the expected leadership"*   Garrow, *Bearing the Cross*; Russell Baker, "Behind Washington's Postcard Façade: Change, Trouble, and Danger Afflict Capital," *New York Times*, June 10, 1963, accessed October 25, 2022, https://timesmachine.nytimes.com/timesmachine/1963/06/10/81813711.pdf.

300   *King wanted an executive order*   Garrow, *Bearing the Cross*.

300   *"The greatest weapon is the mass demonstration"*   Ibid.

301   *"We suspected all our phones were tapped"* Belafonte, *My Song*.

301   *Burke Marshall had warned King* Garrow, *Bearing the Cross*, citing the memo, Special Agent in Charge New York to Director, 100–106670–33, FBI files, March 30, 1962.

301   *"that the FBI furnish an account"* Garrow, *Bearing the Cross*.

301   *"within hours"* Ibid.

301   *"I think you could make a good strong argument on this"* Peter Lang, *Birmingham, JFK, and the Civil Rights Act of 1963: Implications for Elite Theory* (Bern, Switzerland: International Academic Publishers, 1988). The book is mostly transcripts of White House recordings.

302   *Those first days in June* Ibid. JFK went to the West Coast June 5–9; Dwight A. Weingarten, "'To Thine Own Self Be True': Robert F. Kennedy, the Inner Cities, and the American Civil Rights Movement, 1963–1968," honors thesis, College of William and Mary, May 2014, accessed October 25, 2022, https://scholarworks.wm.edu/cgi/viewcontent.cgi?article=1004&context =honorstheses.

302   *Meeting with senators and numerous representatives* Stein, *American Journey*.

302   *"We haven't accomplished what we should have accomplished"* Weingarten, "'To Thine Own Self Be True,'" Voice of America, press conference, June 4, 1963, Series 10, Speeches 1961–1964, Box #254, JFK Library.

302   *"I need you in this government"* Schlesinger, *Robert Kennedy and His Times*.

303   *"It was politics"* Ibid.

303   *high-ranking senators said a civil rights bill wouldn't pass* Ibid.; Brauer, *John F. Kennedy and the Second Reconstruction*. Senate majority leader Mike Mansfield said the bill wouldn't get the requisite fifty-one votes in his chamber.

303   *"There comes a time"* Brauer, *John F. Kennedy and the Second Reconstruction*.

51. The Speech

304   *Jack Kennedy called Bobby* Schlesinger, *Robert Kennedy and His Times*.

304   *Began to draft a speech* McWhorter, *Carry Me Home*.

304   *"stand in the schoolhouse door"* Debbie Elliott, "Wallace in the Schoolhouse Door," NPR, June 11, 2003, accessed October 25, 2022, https://www.npr.org /2003/06/11/1294680/wallace-in-the-schoolhouse-door.

304   *"the occupation of Tuscaloosa or the arrest of the governor"* Schlesinger, *Robert Kennedy and His Times*.

304   *with Bobby convinced in Washington* Stein, *American Journey*. Burke Marshall is the source for this.

305   *Bobby Kennedy was the lone voice of dissent* Schlesinger, *Robert Kennedy and His Times*.

305   *Jack didn't like it* McWhorter, *Carry Me Home*.

305   *"on the back of an envelope or something"* Schlesinger, *Robert Kennedy and His Times*; Robert Kennedy oral history, interview by Anthony Lewis, December 6, 1964, JFK Library; Robert Kennedy oral history, interview by John Bartlow Martin, April 30, 1964, JFK Library.

305   *wish his brother had a prepared speech* Marshall oral history, JFK Library.

305   *"extemporaneously"*   Robert Kennedy oral history, December 6, 1964, JFK Library.

305   *"I remember him sitting there"*   Schlesinger, *Robert Kennedy and His Times.*

305   *They were comfortable with what Jack would say*   Robert Kennedy oral history, December 6, 1964, JFK Library.

305   *began to tinker*   Branch, *Parting the Waters.*

306   *"Come on now, Burke"*   Ibid.

306   We are confronted primarily by a moral issue   "Televised Address to the Nation on Civil Rights," JFK Library, accessed October 25, 2022, https://www.jfklibrary.org/learn/about-jfk/historic-speeches/televised-address-to-the-nation-on-civil-rights.

307   *send a telegram to the White House*   Weingarten, "'To Thine Own Self Be True.'"

307   *"I have just listened to your speech"*   Branch, *Parting the Waters.*

52. "But for Birmingham . . ."

308   *he had sent the bill to Congress*   Schlesinger, *Robert Kennedy and His Times.*

308   *"now we are in a new phase"*   Schlesinger, *A Thousand Days.*

308   *"Frankly, I have never engaged"*   McWhorter, *Carry Me Home.*

308   *"Including the Attorney General"*   Ibid.; Schlesinger, *A Thousand Days.*

308   *Jack had nicknamed "Bull Connor's Bill"*   Thomas, *Robert Kennedy.*

309   *moved to the South Lawn to pose for pictures*   "Meeting with Robert F. Kennedy (RFK), Martin Luther King, Jr. (MLK), and Burke Marshall," AR7993-B, June 22, 1963, JFK Library, accessed October 25, 2022, https://www.jfklibrary.org/asset-viewer/archives/JFKWHP/1963/Month%2006/Day%2022/JFKWHP-1963–06–22-A?image_identifier=JFKWHP-AR7993-B.

309   *"But for Birmingham"*   Raines, *My Soul Is Rested*; Eskew, *But for Birmingham.*

INDEX

About the Author

Paul Kix is an author and writer whose last book was *The Saboteur*, a bestselling and critically acclaimed true story of the most daring man in World War II. His writing has also appeared in *The New Yorker*, *The Atlantic*, *GQ*, and *ESPN The Magazine*, among other publications. He lives in Connecticut with his family.

CELADON
BOOKS

Founded in 2017, Celadon Books, a division of
Macmillan Publishers, publishes a highly curated list
of twenty to twenty-five new titles a year. The list of
both fiction and nonfiction is eclectic and focuses
on publishing commercial and literary books and
discovering and nurturing talent.